Operations Management for MBAs

Operations Management for MBAs

Jack R. Meredith
Scott M. Shafer

Wake Forest University

John Wiley & Sons, Inc.

New York • Chichester • Weinheim • Brisbane • Singapore • Toronto

Acquisitions Editor: Beth Lang Golub
Marketing Manager: Carlise Paulson
Senior Production Editor: Kelly Tavares
Senior Designer: Laura Boucher
Illustration Editor: Anna Melhorn

This book was set in Garamond by UG Division of GGS Information Services
and printed and bound by Hamilton Printing. The cover was printed by Lehigh Press.

This book is printed on acid-free paper.

Library of Congress Cataloging-in-Publication Data
Meredith, Jack R.
    Operations management for MBAs / Jack R. Meredith, Scott M.
      Shafer.
      p.   cm.
    Includes index.
    ISBN 0-471-29828-X (alk. paper)
     1. Production management. I. Shafer, Scott M. II. Title.
TS155.M393 1999   98-40650
658.5—dc21   CIP

Printed in the United States of America

10 9 8 7 6 5 4 3 2 1

This book is dedicated to our MBA students!

Preface

This book was written because of the express need we felt in our MBA-only program at Wake Forest University for an operations management textbook directed specifically to MBA students, and especially to those who had some real-world experience. We tried all of the current texts but found them either tomes that left no time for the cases and other materials we wanted to spend time on in class, shorter but simplistic quantitative books, or a combination of these two approaches. Moreover, even the short and less colorful books were so expensive they did not allow us to order all the cases, readings, and other supplements (such as E. Goldratt's *The Goal*) that we wanted to include in our course.

What we were looking for was a short, inexpensive book that would cover just the introductory, basic, and primarily conceptual material. This would allow us, as the professors, to tailor the course through supplementary Harvard-level cases and other materials for the unique class we would be teaching: executive, evening, full-time, short-course, etc. Although we wanted a brief, supplementary-type book so we could add other material, we have colleagues who need a short book because they only have a half-semester module for the topic. Or they may have to include another course (e.g., management science, statistics, information systems) in the rest of the quarter or semester. In addition, we didn't need the depth of most texts that have two chapters on inventory management, two chapters on scheduling, two chapters on quality, and so on; one integrated chapter on each topic would be sufficient for our needs.

We also wanted a book that was very contemporary and included topics our MBAs were currently facing such as supply chain management, the balanced scorecard, and yield management, even if these topics didn't fit very well with the standard presentation of topics in operations textbooks. Moreover, we wanted a book that was written with the marketing or finance major in mind—what did these students need to know about operations to help them in their careers? Certainly not shop floor control and many of the other details we traditionally taught in our undergraduate classes! And we wanted a book that took a more strategic point of view since our MBAs were working at the managerial rather than entry level. Finally, we needed a text that had a balance of service examples instead of only manufacturing, even if the topics (e.g., materials management) were product-based since the great majority of our students would be employed in a service firm.

Quantitative aspects were especially challenging. Initially we wanted only realistic problems that real managers would encounter; no toy problems here! However, as our reviewers pointed out, finance and marketing managers would not be solving these "realistic" operations problems (we didn't think about that). Moreover, even operations managers probably wouldn't themselves be solving those problems; more likely, they would assign them to an analyst (we didn't think about that either), or use a spreadsheet to address them. Hence, we tossed much of the heavier quantitative material, keeping only discussions and examples that would help illustrate a particular concept to a non-operations manager.

Our approach to supplementary MBA-level material here is to reference and annotate in the Instructor's Manual good cases, books, video "ticklers," and readings for each of the ten textbook chapters. The annotation is intended to help the instructors select the most appropriate materials for their unique course. Although there are brief caselettes at the end of each chapter in the text that we have personally class-tested and found can form the basis of an interesting class discussion, we primarily rely on our favorite Harvard cases and *Harvard Business Review* readings to fully communicate the nature of the chapter topic we are covering. Although we didn't think that test bank questions, full videos, PowerPoint slides, or virtual tours would be used by most MBA instructors, these materials are available from the publisher also. (The virtual tours on our web site *www.mba.wfu.edu/books/omformbas* with accompanying questions might, however, be of interest to MBAs who lack experience in some of the industries discussed in the text or desire more in-depth information about individual firms.) For that matter, the publisher can also custom bind a book for the MBA class that selects parts from this text as well as our larger or any other Wiley text, should this approach be of interest to the professor.

The result of our thinking just described is ten chapters organized in what we believe to be the most common order of teaching the topics. Yet, the chapters are deliberately constructed and written as standalone entities so they can be selected independently from the others, used in a different order if desired, or even selectively used or not used as needed in a course. We start with the normal overview of operations in Chapter 1: The Nature of Operations where we talk about the systems view, the transformation process, typical operations activities, and the process versus functional approach to management. To illustrate the topics and their organization in each chapter, we include an organization chart of the topics at the beginning of each chapter so the instructor and students can quickly and easily see what is coming and how it is organized.

Chapter 2: Business Strategy and Global Competitiveness starts our discussion of the role of operations in the organization from a strategic point of view. Here we talk about core competencies, the balanced scorecard, mass customization, and so on. Following this, we move into another strategic aspect of operations with Chapter 3: Quality Management where we discuss quality management, process capability, and quality control. Chapter 4: Product/Service Design, Chapter 5: Transformation System Design, and Chapter 6: Capacity and Location Planning cover the up-front planning aspects of operations such as process-flow analysis, theory of constraints, the psychology of waiting, business process design, and even commercialization. Following these, Chapter 7: Scheduling Management, Chapter 8: Materials Management, and Chapter 9: Supply Chain Management and Just-in-Time Systems cover the on-going operational aspects such as revenue management and enterprise resource planning. Chapter 10: Project Management completes the text with coverage of a topic that continues to explode in popularity and need.

We intentionally changed the textual flow of material in the chapters away from the current undergraduate trend. Instead of fracturing the material flow by adding sidebars, examples, applications, solved problems, etc. in an attempt to keep the students' interest and attention, given the maturity of MBA students we instead worked these directly into the discussions to attain a smoother, clearer flow. We also altered the end-of-chapter materials by cutting down the questions to just a few that would intrigue and engage more experienced and mature students. We similarly reduced the bibliography to what would be of interest to current or soon-to-be mid-level managers. We also considered the caselettes to be of interest for this level of student. And as noted earlier, if any exercises are included, they are intended only to help illustrate the concept we are trying to convey rather than make experts out of the students. As noted earlier, the Instructor's Manual includes suggestions for readings, cases, videos, and other course supplements that we have found to be particularly helpful for MBA classes since this book is intended to be only a small part of the MBA class.

We would like to encourage users of this book to send us their comments about how they like this concept of an MBA-oriented text. Tell us if there is something we missed that you would like to see in the next edition (or the Instructor's Manual or Website) or if there is perhaps material that is unneeded for this audience. Also, please tell us about any errors you uncover, or if there are other elements of the book you like or don't like. We would like to keep this a living, dynamic project that evolves to meet the needs of our MBA audience, an audience whose needs are also evolving as our economy and society twists and changes.

We wish to thank our editor, Beth Golub, who listened to our pleas for a book aimed solely at MBA students and approved this project. We also want to thank the many reviewers of our proposal who agreed with the need, and those who reviewed the initial draft of the chapters and pointed out where we missed the mark, what needed further cutting, and what needed to be added: Lawrence D. Fredendall, Clemson University; James A. Fitzsimmons, University of Texas; Robert Handfield, Michigan State University; Janelle Heineke, Boston University; Mehdi Kaighobadi, Florida Atlantic University; Suresh Kumar Goyal, Concordia University, Canada; Manoj Malhorta, University of South Carolina; Gus Manoochehri, California State University, Fullerton; Robert F. Marsh, University of Wisconsin, Milwaukee; Ivor P. Morgan, Babson College; Seungwook Park, Bowling Green State University; Sue Perrott Siferd, Arizona State University; Jaime S. Ribera, IESE-Universidad de Navarra, Spain; Gary D. Scudder, Vanderbilt University; Asoo J. Vakharia, University of Florida; Jerry C. Wei, University of Notre Dame. Last, we want to thank our MBA students, to whom this book is dedicated.

Jack Meredith
Babcock Graduate School
   of Management
Wake Forest University, P.O. Box 7659
Winston-Salem, NC 27109
jack.meredith@mba.wfu.edu
www.mba.wfu.edu/faculty/meredith
336.758.4467

Scott Shafer
Babcock Graduate School
   of Management
Wake Forest University, P.O. Box 7659
Winston-Salem, NC 27109
scott.shafer@mba.wfu.edu
www.mba.wfu.edu/faculty/shafer
336.758.3687

Table of Contents

CHAPTER 1

The Nature of Operations

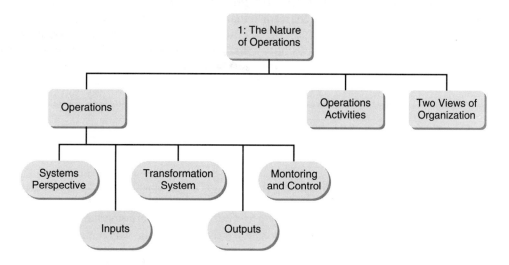

This first chapter serves as an introduction to the field of operations management. At the beginning of the chapter, *operations* is defined as the activities associated with transforming inputs into useful outputs in order to create a result of value. It is also shown that the actual production system is defined in terms of environment, inputs, transformation system, outputs, and the mechanism used for monitoring and control. The four primary ways that value can be added to an entity and the major subject areas within operations are also discussed.

The chapter overviews two alternative ways for organizing work activities. In the traditional functional approach, companies organize activities on the basis of the type of work performed. With this approach, operations, marketing, and finance are defined as the three core functions. Recently, however, many companies have found that they can significantly improve organizational efficiency and effectiveness by organizing activities on the basis of specific value-creating processes.

$\mathcal{I}$NTRODUCTION

- Facing increased competition and customers who are smarter, more demanding, and less brand-loyal, McDonald's is reevaluating the way it makes some of the items on its menu. For example, it is considering a switch to a hamburger bun that does not require toasting. In trial tests, customers seemed to prefer the new bun's taste and texture. Furthermore, not toasting buns should translate into substantial cost savings due to reduced preparation time and the elimination of commercial toasting equipment. At first, such savings may seem trivial; however, consider that McDonald's processes several billion buns for its hamburgers, chicken, and fish sandwiches (Gibson 1995).

- Getting the Olympic flame to Atlanta for the summer Olympics of 1996 was a major undertaking. Ten thousand runners carried the flame 15,000 miles, passing through 42 states in 84 days. More than two years of planning went into this operation. For example, plans had to be coordinated with 2970 local police jurisdictions. Additionally, plans had to be made to deal with rush-hour traffic, no-show runners, or runners who were not able to complete their leg of the relay. In all, it was estimated that the Olympic flame relay cost in the neighborhood of $20 million, not including transportation, computers, and communication equipment used to support the project (Ruffenach 1996).

- It is not well known that the Kmart and Wal-Mart chains both date back to 1962. By 1987 Kmart was clearly dominating the discount chain race, with almost twice as many stores and sales of $25.63 billion to Wal-Mart's $15.96 billion. However, for the retail year that ended in January 1991, Wal-Mart had overtaken Kmart, with sales of $32.6 billion to Kmart's sales of $29.7 billion. Interestingly, although

Wal-Mart had taken the lead in sales in 1991, it still had fewer stores—1721 to Kmart's 2330. By the 1997 retail year, Wal-Mart had clearly established itself as the dominant discount chain, with sales of $106.1 billion to Kmart's $31.4 billion. Perhaps equally telling is the shift in market share experienced by these two companies. For the period from 1987 to 1995 Kmart's market share declined from 34.5 percent to 22.7 percent, while Wal-Mart's increased from 20.1 percent to 41.6 percent.

What accounts for this reversal in fortunes? Kmart's response to the competition from Wal-Mart was to build on its marketing and merchandising strengths and invest heavily in national television campaigns using high-profile spokespeople such as Jaclyn Smith (a former Charlie's Angel). Wal-Mart took an entirely different approach and invested millions of dollars in operations in an effort to lower costs. For example, Wal-Mart developed a companywide computer system to link cash registers to headquarters, thereby greatly facilitating inventory control at the stores. Also, Wal-Mart developed a sophisticated distribution system. The integration of the computer system and the distribution system meant that customers would rarely encounter out-of-stock items. Further, the use of scanners at the checkout stations eliminated the need for price checks. By Kmart's own admission, its employees were seriously lacking the skills needed to plan and control inventory effectively (Duff and Ortega 1995).

These brief examples highlight the diversity and importance of operations. Take the description of McDonald's. This example provides a glimpse of two themes that are central to operations: *customer satisfaction* and *competitiveness*. This example also illustrates a more subtle point—that improvements made in operations can simultaneously increase customer satisfaction and lower costs. The Wal-Mart example demonstrates how a company obtained a substantial competitive advantage by improving basic operational activities such as controlling its inventory. Finally, all three examples illustrate that the field of operations is as applicable to service organizations as it is to manufacturing.

In an international marketplace consumers purchase their products from the provider that offers them the most value for their money. To illustrate, you may be doing your course assignments on a Japanese notebook computer, driving in a German automobile, and watching a sitcom on a television made in Taiwan while cooking your food in a Korean microwave. However, most of your services—banking, insurance, personal care—are probably domestic, although some of these may also be owned by foreign corporations. There is a reason why most services are produced by domestic firms while products may be produced in part, or wholly, by foreign firms, and it concerns an area of business known as operations.

A great many societal changes that are occurring today intimately involve activities associated with operations. For example, there is great pressure among competing nations to increase national productivity, and many politicians and national leaders decry America's poor progress in improving productivity growth in comparison with that of other nations. Similarly, businesses are conducting a national crusade to improve the quality of their offerings in both products and services (though sometimes we consumers wonder if this isn't just another marketing gimmick). As we will see, increasing productivity and improving quality are primary objectives of operations management.

Another characteristic of our modern society is the explosion of new technology. Technologies such as fax machines, e-mail, notebook computers, personal digital assistants, and the Web, to name a few, are profoundly affecting business and are fundamentally changing the nature of work. For example, many banks are shifting their focus from building new branch locations to using the Web as a way to establish and develop new customer relationships. Banks rely on technology to carry out more routine activities as well, such as transferring funds instantly across cities, states, and oceans. Our industries also rely increasingly on technology: robots carry and weld parts and workerless, dark "factories of the future" turn out a continuing stream of products.

This exciting, competitive world of operations is at the heart of every organization and, more than anything else, determines whether the organization survives in the international marketplace or disappears into bankruptcy or a takeover. It is this world that we will be covering in the following chapters.

 OPERATIONS

Why do we argue that operations be considered the heart of every organization? Fundamentally, organizations exist to create value, and operations involves tasks that create value. Regardless of whether the organization is for-profit or not-for-profit, primarily service or manufacturer, public or private, it exists to create value. Thus, even nonprofit organizations like the Red Cross strive to create value for the recipients of their services in excess of their costs. Moreover, this has always been true, from the earliest days of bartering to the modern-day corporations.

Consider McDonald's again. This firm uses a number of inputs, including ingredients, labor, equipment, and facilities; transforms them in a way that adds value to them (e.g., by frying); and obtains an output, such as a chicken sandwich, that can be sold at a profit. This conversion process, termed a *production system*, is illustrated in Figure 1.1. The elements of the figure represent what is known as a **system**[1]: *a purposeful collection of people, objects, and procedures for operating within an environment*. Note the word *purposeful*; systems are not merely arbitrary groupings but goal-directed or purposeful collections. Managing and running a production system efficiently and effectively is at the heart of the operations activities that will be discussed in this text. Since we will be using this term throughout the text, let us formally define it. **Operations** is concerned with transforming inputs into useful outputs and thereby adding value to some entity; this constitutes the primary activity of virtually every organization.

Not only is operations central to organizations; it is also central to people's personal and professional activities, regardless of their position. People too must operate productively, adding value to inputs and producing quality outputs, whether those outputs are information, reports, services, products, or even personal accom-

---

[1]Note that the word *system* is being used here in a broad sense and should not be confused with more narrow usages such as information systems, planning and control systems, or performance evaluation systems.

plishments. Thus, operations should be of major interest to every reader, not just professionally but also personally.

Systems Perspective

As Figure 1.1 illustrates, a ~~production system~~ is defined in terms of environment, inputs, transformation system, outputs, and the mechanism used for monitoring and control. The environment includes those things that are outside the actual production system but that influence it in some way. Because of its influence, we need to consider the environment, even though it is beyond the control of decision makers within the system.

For example, a large portion of the inputs to a production system are acquired from the environment. Also, government regulations related to pollution control and workplace safety affect the transformation system. Think about how changes in customers' needs, a competitor's new product, or a new advance in technology can influence the level of satisfaction with a production system's current outputs. As these examples show, the environment exerts a great deal of influence on the production system.

Because the world around us is constantly changing, it is necessary to monitor the production system and take action when the system is not meeting its goals. Of course, it may be that the current goals are no longer appropriate, indicating a

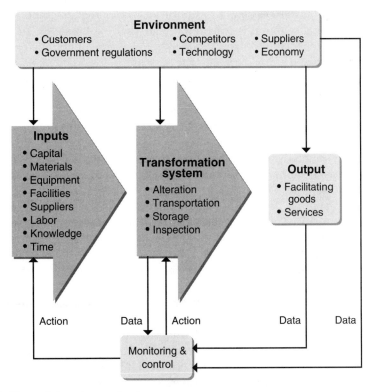

Figure 1.1   The production system.

need to revise the goals. On the other hand, it may be determined that the goals are fine but that the inputs or transformation system or both should be acted upon in some way. In either case, it is important to continuously collect data from the environment, the transformation system, and the outputs. Then, on the basis of an analysis of these data, appropriate actions can be devised to enhance the system's overall performance.

Thinking in terms of systems provides decision makers with numerous advantages. To begin, the systems perspective focuses on how the individual components that make up a system interact. Thus, the systems perspective provides decision makers with a broad and complete picture of an entire situation. Furthermore, the systems perspective emphasizes the relationships between the various system components. Without considering these relationships, decision makers are prone to a problem called *suboptimization*. Suboptimization occurs when one part of the system is improved to the detriment of other parts of the system, and perhaps the organization as a whole. As an example of suboptimization, suppose that a retailer decides to broaden its product line in an effort to increase sales. Such a decision could actually end up hurting the retailer as a whole if it does not have sufficient shelf space available to accommodate the broader product line, sales and service personnel that are knowledgeable about the new products, or if the broader product line increases inventory-related costs more than profits from the increased sales. The point of this example is that decisions need to be evaluated in terms of their effect on the entire system, not simply in terms of how they will affect one component of the system.

It is interesting to note that the components of systems are often themselves systems, called *subsystems*. For example, a factory that assembles personal computers is a system. Within this system there are many subsystems, such as the system that reports financial information, the system for assembling the computers, the system for ordering the raw materials, the system for designing new products, and the system for recruiting and hiring workers. And many of these subsystems could be further divided into sub-subsystems. To illustrate, the system that reports financial information may be composed of a system that reports information to sources outside the organization and another system that provides financial information to employees within the organization.

It also stands to reason that since systems can be divided into component subsystems, it should also be possible to combine them into larger systems. This is indeed the case. Consider the example of the personal computer assembly plant. This plant may be just one of a number of plants making up a particular division of the company. Thus, combining these plants would form a system corresponding to the division of this company. Furthermore, combining the divisions of the company would create a system for the whole company. This logic could be extended to creating systems for the entire industry, and all the way up to creating a system for the entire economy.

This discussion highlights the importance of defining a system's boundary appropriately. Specifically, defining a boundary determines what a decision maker will and will not consider, since things outside the system boundary are considered to be part of the environment and beyond the decision maker's control. Defining a system boundary is important, because if it is defined too narrowly, important relationships among system components may be omitted. On the other hand, extending the boundary increases the complexity and costs associated with developing and using the model. Unfortunately, determining the system boundary is more of an art than a science and is based on the experience, skill, and judgment of the analyst.

Regardless of where the system boundary is defined, all production systems receive inputs from their environments, transform these inputs, and create value in the form of outputs. In the remainder of this section we elaborate on inputs, the transformation system and outputs.

Inputs

The set of inputs used in a production system is more complex than might be supposed and typically involves many other areas such as marketing, finance, engineering, and human resource management. Obvious inputs include facilities, labor, capital, equipment, raw materials, and supplies. Supplies are distinguished from raw materials by the fact that they are not usually a part of the final output. Oil, paper clips, pens, tape, and other such items are commonly classified as supplies because they only aid in producing the output.

Another very important but perhaps less obvious input is knowledge of how to transform the inputs into outputs. The employees of the organization hold this knowledge. Finally, having sufficient time to accomplish the operations is always critical. Indeed, the operations function quite frequently fails in its task because it cannot complete the ***transformation activities*** within the required time limit.

Transformation System

The transformation system is the part of the system that adds value to the inputs. Value can be added to an entity in a number of ways. Four major ways are described here.

1. *Alter.* Something can be changed structurally. That would be a *physical* change, and this approach is basic to our manufacturing industries where goods are cut, stamped, formed, assembled, and so on. We then go out and buy the shirt, or computer, or whatever the good is. But it need not be a separate object or entity; for example, what is altered may be *us*. We might get our hair cut, or we might have our appendix removed.

    Other, more subtle, alterations may also have value. *Sensual* alterations, such as heat when we are cold, or music, or beauty may be highly valued on certain occasions. Beyond this, even *psychological* alterations can have value, such as the feeling of worth from obtaining a college degree or the feeling of friendship from a long-distance phone call.

2. *Transport.* An entity, again including ourselves, may have more value if it is located somewhere other than where it currently is. We may appreciate having things brought to us, such as flowers, or removed from us, such as garbage.

3. *Store.* The value of an entity may be enhanced for us if it is kept in a protected environment for some period of time. Some examples are stock certificates kept in a safe-deposit box, our pet boarded at a kennel while we go on vacation, or ourselves staying in a motel.

4. *Inspect*. Last, an entity may be more valued because we better understand its properties. This may apply to something we own, plan to use, or are considering purchasing, or, again, even to ourselves. Medical exams, elevator certifications, and jewelry appraisals fall into this category.

Thus, we see that value may be added to an entity in a number of different ways. The entity may be changed directly, in space, in time, or even just in our mind. Additionally, value may be added using a combination of these methods. To illustrate, an appliance store may create value by both storing merchandise and transporting (delivering) it. There are other, less frequent, ways of adding value as well, such as by "guaranteeing" something. These many varieties of transformations, and how they are managed, constitute some of the major issues to be discussed in this text.

Outputs

Two types of outputs commonly result from a production system: services and products. Generally, products are physical goods, such as a personal computer, and services are abstract or nonphysical. More specifically, we can consider the characteristics in Table 1.1 to help us distinguish between the two.

However, this classification may be more confusing than helpful. For example, consider a pizza delivery chain. Does this organization produce a product or provide a service? If you answered "a service," suppose that instead of delivering its pizzas to the actual consumer, it made the pizzas in a factory and sold them in the frozen-food section of grocery stores. Clearly the actual process of making pizzas for immediate consumption or to be frozen involves basically the same tasks, although one may be done on a larger scale and use more automated equipment. The point is, however, that both organizations produce a pizza, and defining one organization as a service and the other as a manufacturer seems to be a little arbitrary.

We avoid this ambiguity by adopting the point of view that *any physical entity accompanying a transformation that adds value is a **facilitating good*** (e.g., the pizza). In many cases, of course, there may be no facilitating good; we refer to these cases as *pure services*.

The advantage of this interpretation is that every transformation that adds value is simply a service, either with or without facilitating goods! If you buy a piece of lumber, you have not purchased a product. Rather, you have purchased a bundle of services, many of them embodied in a facilitating good: a tree-cutting service, a saw mill service, a transportation service, a storage service, and perhaps even an advertising service that told you where lumber was on sale. We refer to these services as a bundle of "benefits," of which some are tangible (the sawed length of lumber, the type of tree) and others are intangible (courteous salesclerks, a convenient location, payment by charge card). Some services may, of course, even be negative, such as an audit of your tax return. In summary, ***services are bundles of benefits, some of which may be tangible and others intangible, and they may be accompanied by a facilitating good or goods.***

Firms often run into major difficulties when they ignore this aspect of their operations. They may think of and even market themselves as a "lumberyard" and not as providing a bundle of services. They may recognize that they have to include certain tangible services (such as cutting lumber to the length desired by the cus-

$\mathscr{T}$ABLE 1.1 • Characteristics of Products and Services

Products	Services
Tangible	Intangible
Minimal contact with customer	Extensive contact with customer
Minimal participation by customer in the delivery	Extensive participation by customer in the delivery
Delayed consumption	Immediate consumption
Equipment-intense production	Labor-intense production
Quality easily measured	Quality difficult to measure

tomer) but ignore the intangible services (charge sales, having a sufficient number of clerks).

While the broader perspective of the facilitating good concept helps clarify the ambiguity associated with whether an organization produces a product or service, it also blurs the distinction between operations and marketing. To illustrate, earlier we defined operations as including the tasks that add value. However, when outputs are viewed broadly as a bundle of benefits, it becomes clear that marketing, as well as other areas of an organization, contribute to the value outputs provide.

Another reason for not making a distinction between manufacturing and services is that making such a distinction can be harmful. Specifically, when a company thinks of itself as a manufacturer it tends to focus on measures of internal performance such as efficiency and utilization; and when companies classify themselves as services they tend to focus externally and ask questions such as, "How can we serve our customers better?" This is not to imply that improving internal performance measures is not desirable. Rather, it suggests that improved customer service should be the primary impetus for all improvement efforts. It is generally not advisable to seek internal improvements if these improvements do not ultimately lead to corresponding improvements in customer service and customer satisfaction.

In this text we will adopt the point of view that all value-adding transformations (i.e., operations) are services, and there may or may not be a set of accompanying facilitating goods. Figure 1.2 illustrates how the tangible product (or facilitating good) portion and the intangible service portion for a variety of outputs contribute to the total value provided by each output. The outputs shown range from virtually pure services to what would be known as products. Although we work with "products" as extensively as with services throughout the chapters in this book, bear in mind that in these cases we are working with only a *portion* of the total service, the facilitating good. In general, we will use the nonspecific term *outputs* to mean either products or services.

Monitoring and Control

Suppose that in our production system we make a mistake. We must be able to observe this through, for example, accounting records (monitor), and we must change our system to correct for it (control). The activities of monitoring and control, as illustrated in Figure 1.1, are used extensively in systems, including management systems, and will be encountered throughout this text. In essence, the monitoring process

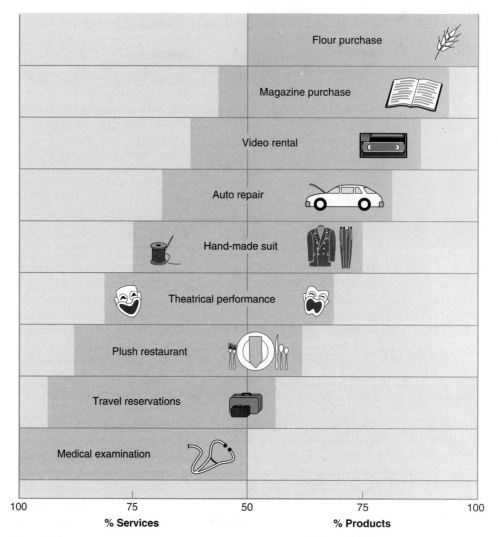

Figure 1.2   The range from services to products.

must tell the manager when significant changes are occurring in any part of the production system. If the changes are not significantly affecting the outputs, then no control actions need be taken. But if they are, management must intercede and *apply corrective control* to alter the inputs or the transformation system and, thereby, the outputs.

Table 1.2 lists some components of the five elements of the production system for a variety of common organizations.

OPERATIONS ACTIVITIES

Operations include not only those activities associated specifically with the production system but also a variety of other activities. For example, purchasing or procurement activities are concerned with obtaining many of the inputs needed in the

*T*ABLE 1.2 • Examples of Organizations and Their Components

Organization	Inputs	Transformation System	Outputs	Monitor/Control	Environment
Post office	Labor Equipment Trucks	Transportation Printing	Mail deliveries Stamps	Weather Mail volumes Sorting/loss errors	Transportation network Weather Civil service
Bank	Checks Deposits Vault ATMs	Safekeeping Investment Statement preparations	Interest Electronic transfer Loans Statements	Interest rates Wage rates Loan default rates	Federal Reserve Economy
Cinema	Films Food People Theater	Film projection Food preparation	Entertainment Snacks	Film popularity Disposable incomes	Economy Entertainment industry
Manufacturer	Materials Equipment Labor Technology	Cutting Forming Joining Mixing	Machines Chemicals Consumer goods Scrap	Material flows Production volumes	Economy Commodity prices Consumer market
School	Books Teachers Facility Students	Learning Counseling Motivating	Educated students Skills Research	Demographics Grievances	State and county boards Tax system

production system. Similarly, shipping and distribution are sometimes considered marketing activities and sometimes considered operations activities. Because of the important interdependencies of these activities, many organizations are attempting to manage these activities as one process commonly referred to as *supply chain management.*

As organizations begin to adopt new organizational structures based on business processes and abandon the traditional functional organization, it is becoming less important to classify activities as operations or nonoperations. However, to understand the tasks more easily, we divide the field of operations into a series of subject areas as shown in Table 1.3. These areas are quite interdependent, but to make their workings more understandable we discuss them as though they were easily separable from each other. In some areas, a full-fledged department may be responsible for the activities, such as quality control or scheduling, but in other areas the activities (such as facility location) may be infrequent and simply assigned to a particular group or project team. Moreover, some of the subareas such as supply chain management or maintenance are critically important because they are a part of a larger business process or because other areas depend on them. Finally, since we consider all operations to be services, these subject areas are equally applicable to organizations that have traditionally been classified as manufacturers and services.

*T*ABLE 1.3 • Major Subject Areas in Operations

- *Strategy*: Determining the critical operations tasks to support the organization's overall mission.
- *Output planning*: Selecting and designing the services and products the organization will offer to customers, patrons, or recipients.
- *Capacity planning*: Determining when to have facilities, equipment, and labor available and in what amounts.
- *Facility location*: Deciding where to locate production, storage, and other major facilities.
- *Transformation system design*: Determining the physical transformation aspects of the production activities.
- *Facility layout*: Devising an appropriate material flow and equipment layout within the facility to efficiently and effectively accommodate the transformation activities.
- *Aggregate planning*: Anticipating the yearly needs for labor, materials, and facilities by month or week within the year.
- *Inventory management*: Deciding what amounts of raw materials, work-in-process, and finished goods to hold.
- *Project management*: Learning how to plan and control project activities to meet specifications for performance, schedule, and cost.
- *Material requirements planning*: Determining when to order or produce materials, and in what amounts, to meet a master delivery schedule.
- *Supply chain management*: Organizing the activities from the customer's order through final delivery for speed, efficiency, and quality.
- *Quality control*: Determining how quality standards are to be developed and maintained.
- *Reliability and maintenance*: Determining how the proper performance of both the output and the transformation system itself is to be maintained.

*T*WO VIEWS OF ORGANIZATIONS

Traditionally, companies have been organized on the basis of the type of work performed. Thus, organizations were divided into marketing, finance, accounting, engineering, operations, and other departments. This type of organization is referred to as a *functional organization* because work is organized on the basis of the function performed.

In the functional view, all organizations must perform three core functions: operations, finance, and marketing. Clearly, if they are to continue to exist all organizations must create value (operations), get the output to the customer (marketing), and raise capital to support their operations (finance). Additionally, organizations perform a number of other important functional activities such as reporting financial information (accounting) and designing new products (engineering)—to name just two.

As a result of recent advances in technology and increased international competition, many organizations have recognized a need for better methods of grouping and integrating organizational activities. Figure 1.3 illustrates how organizational structures are currently evolving to meet this need. Figure 1.3*a* depicts the traditional functional organization. In the functional organization, employees at any level are coordinated by having a common supervisor, who controls the information that is shared across the groups and resolves problems that arise between groups.

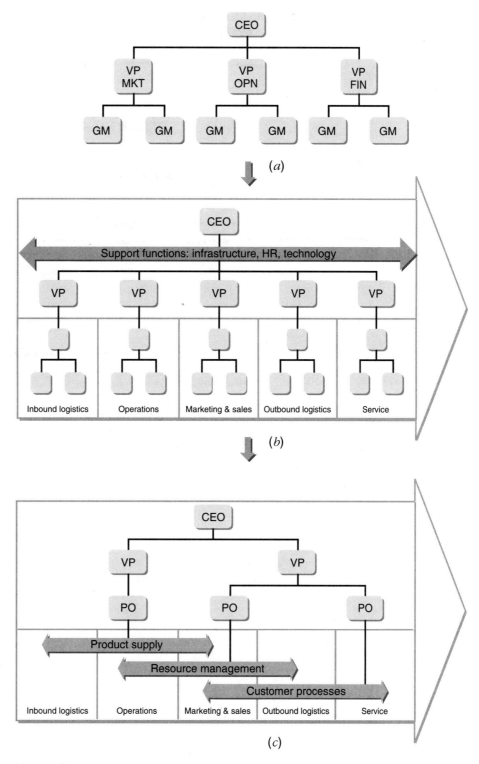

Figure 1.3 Evolution of organizational structures: (*a*) traditional functional organization; (*b*) value-chain approach; (*c*) process-centered structure.

In the 1980s Michael Porter, a professor at the Harvard Business School, developed the concept of a *value chain* as a way to improve the coordination among various functional groups. The value-chain approach (Figure 1.3b) emphasized the organization as a system of interdependent activities that create value for the customer. Superimposing the value chain over the functional hierarchy provides a coordinating mechanism for linking sequentially related organizational activities. In effect, this is accomplished by organizational groups viewing subsequent organizational groups along the value chain as their "internal" customers. Thus, Porter's value chain presented a new view of management, depicting the organization as a system of value-creating vertical processes rather than a collection of independent activities.

As business became increasingly globalized and competition grew fiercer, organizations were forced to become even more efficient and effective. The current phase of the evolution is shown in Figure 1.3c: organizations are now adopting organizational structures based on specific value-creating processes rather than simply using the value chain to coordinate separated functional groups. Thus, the traditional vertical structure based on functional specialists is being abandoned in favor of a horizontal structure based on process generalists. Furthermore, in comparing Figures 1.3b and c, we observe that the traditional management positions are also changing. For example, vice president (VP) and general management (GM) positions that were responsible for specific functional activities such as operations, marketing, and finance, are evolving into process management positions. Managers of processes, often referred to as process owners (PO), have responsibility for entire value-creating processes, such as supplying a product from the receipt of raw materials to the distribution of the final product.

The evolution to process organizational structures makes the topics in this course all the more relevant. Specifically, in the old functional organizational structure, only people in the operations area thought in terms of value-creating processes. However, in the new process-centered organization, all employees are organized on the basis of specific value-creating process. Thus, all employees must now think in terms of how their efforts fit into and support a particular value-creating process.

EXPAND YOUR UNDERSTANDING

1. Since value is always in the mind of the beholder, how does altering a product differ from advertising or guarantees in terms of added value?

2. Why is it so hard to increase productivity in the service sector?

3. Identify some other major differences between services and products besides those listed in Table 1.1.

4. The U.S. government has strict laws regarding pollution, antitrust activities, and bribery by U.S. firms. Yet many other countries have no such laws. Indeed, firms and individuals in those countries may well expect to receive a kickback (return of cash) for orders placed or delivered. How ethical is it for a firm based in the United States to meet foreigners' expectations? How ethical is it for the U.S. government to restrict the activities of domestic firms but not those of foreign firms operating in the United States?

5. Many foreign firms have been successful in the following areas: steel, autos, cameras, radios, and televisions. Are services more protected from foreign competition? How?

6. It is commonly said that Japanese firms employ 10 times as many engineers per operations worker as U.S. firms and 10 times fewer accountants. What effect would you expect this to have on their competitiveness? Why?

APPLY YOUR UNDERSTANDING _____
Taracare, Inc.

Taracare, Inc., operates a single factory in Miami, where it fabricates and assembles a wide range of outdoor furniture including chairs, tables, and matching accessories. Taracare's primary production activities include extruding the aluminum furniture parts, bending and shaping the extruded parts, finishing and painting the parts, and then assembling the parts into completed furniture. Upholstery, glass tabletops, and all hardware are purchased from outside suppliers.

Craig Johnson purchased Taracare in 1993. Before that, Craig had distinguished himself as a top sales rep of outdoor furniture for one of the leading national manufacturers. However, after spending 10 years on the road, Craig decided to pursue other opportunities. After searching for a couple of months, he came across what he believed to be an ideal opportunity. Not only was it in an industry that he had a great deal of knowledge about, but he would be his own boss. Unfortunately, the asking price was well beyond Craig's means. However, after a month of negotiation, Craig convinced Jeff Lewis, Taracare's founder, to maintain a 25 percent stake in the business. Although Jeff had originally intended to sell out completely, he was impressed with Craig's knowledge of the business, his extensive contacts, and his enthusiasm. He therefore agreed to sell Craig 75 percent of Taracare and retain 25 percent as an investment.

Craig's ambition for Taracare was to expand it from a small regional manufacturer to one that sold to major national retailers. To accomplish this objective, Craig's first initiative was to triple Taracare's sales force in 1994. As sales began to increase, Craig increased the support staff by hiring an accountant, a comptroller, two new designers, and a purchasing agent.

By the middle of 1997, Taracare's line was carried by several national retailers on a trial basis. However, Taracare was having difficulty meeting the deliveries its sales reps were promising and had difficulty satisfying the national retailers' standards for quality. To respond to this problem, Craig hired Sam Davis as the new manufacturing manager. Before accepting Craig's offer, Sam was the plant manager of a factory that manufactured replacement windows sold by large regional and national retailers.

After several months on the job—and after making little progress toward improving on-time delivery and quality—Sam scheduled a meeting with Craig to discuss his major concerns. Sam began:

> I requested this meeting with you, Craig, because I am not satisfied with the progress we are making toward improving our delivery performance and quality. The bottom line is that I feel I'm getting very little cooperation from the other department heads. For example, last month purchasing switched to a new supplier for paint; and although it is true that the new paint costs less per gallon, we have to apply a thicker coat to give the furniture the same protection. I haven't actually run the numbers, but I know it is actually costing us more, in both materials and labor. Another problem is that we typically run a special promotion to coincide with launching new product lines. I understand that the sales guys want to get the product into the stores as quickly as possible, but they are making promises about delivery that we can't meet. It takes time to work out the bugs and get things running smoothly. Then there is the problem with the designers. They are constantly adding features to the product that make it almost impossible for us to produce. At the very least, they make it much more expensive for us to produce. For example, on the new "Destiny" line, they designed table legs that required a new die at a cost of $25,000. Why couldn't they have left the legs alone so that we could have used one of our existing dies? On top of this, we have the accounting department telling us that our equipment utilization is too low. Then, when we increase our equipment utilization and make more product, the finance guys tell us we have too much capital tied up in inventory. To be honest, I really don't feel that I'm getting very much support.

Rising from his chair, Craig commented

> You have raised some important issues. Unfortunately, I have to run to another meeting. Why don't you send me a memo outlining these issues and your recommendations? Then perhaps I will call a meeting and we can discuss these issues with the other department heads. At any rate, our

production problems are really no worse than that of our competitors, and we don't expect you to solve all of our problems overnight. Keep up the good work and send me that memo at your earliest convenience.

Questions

1. Does Sam's previous experience running a plant that made replacement windows qualify him to run a plant that makes outdoor furniture?

2. What recommendations would you make if you were in Sam's shoes?

3. Given Craig's background and apparent priorities, how is he likely to respond to your recommendations? On the basis of this likely response, is it possible to rephrase your recommendations so that they may be more appealing to Craig?

BIBLIOGRAPHY

Albrecht, K., and R. Zemke. *Service America: Doing Business in the New Economy.* Homewood, Ill.: Dow Jones–Irwin, 1985.

Cohen, S. S., and J. Zysman. *Manufacturing Matters: The Myth of the Post–Industrial Economy.* New York: Basic, 1987.

Collier, D. A. *Service Management: The Automation of Services.* Reston, Va.: Reston, 1985.

Duff, C., and B. Ortega. "How Wal-Mart Outdid a Once-Touted K-Mart in Discount-Store Race." *Wall Street Journal* (March 24, 1995): A1, A4.

Gibson, R. "At McDonald's, New Recipes for Buns, Eggs." *Wall Street Journal* (June 13, 1995): B1, B6.

Porter, M. E. *Competitive Advantage.* New York: Free Press, 1985.

Ruffenach, G. "Getting the Olympic Flame to Atlanta Won't Be a Simple Cross-Country Run." *Wall Street Journal* (February 29, 1996): B1.

Schoenberger, R. J. *World Class Manufacturing: The Lessons of Simplicity Applied.* New York: Free Press, 1986.

Shafer, S. M., and S.L. Oswald. "Product Focused Manufacturing for Strategic Advantage." *Business Horizons* (November–December 1996): 24–29.

CHAPTER 2

Business Strategy and Global Competitiveness

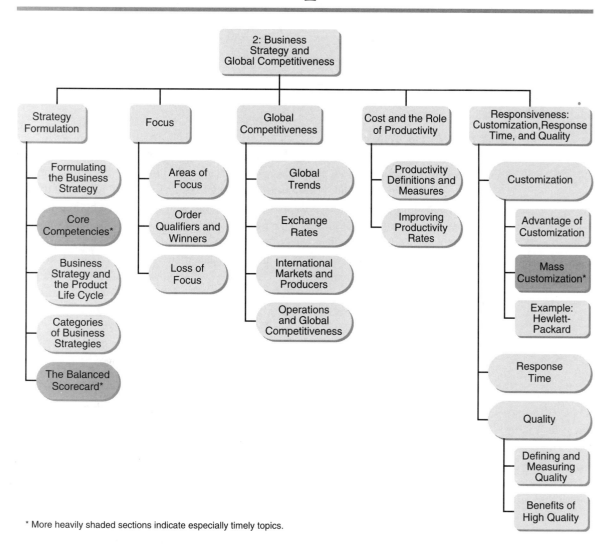

* More heavily shaded sections indicate especially timely topics.

CHAPTER IN PERSPECTIVE

This chapter continues our introduction to operations management. In the first part of the chapter, business strategy is defined and the process of formulating a business strategy based on core competencies is overviewed. Next, we describe four major business strategies and the use of the balanced scorecard. Following this, the concept of focus is discussed, including areas of focus, the distinction between order qualifiers and order winners, and how organizations often lose their focus.

The second part of the chapter is concerned with issues related to global competitiveness. Here the discussion centers on international competitiveness, the impact of exchange rates, and six primary characteristics of the transformation system. Next, productivity is defined and the productivity (and growth in productivity) of several industrialized nations is discussed. Finally, the chapter concludes with a discussion of how customization, response time, and quality each affect an organization's responsiveness.

INTRODUCTION

- Concerned about a shortage of labor, Manor Care is designing its Sleep Inns the way an industrial engineer designs an assembly line. To minimize the size of the housekeeping staff, nightstands are attached to the wall so there are no legs to be vacuumed around. The closets have no doors to open and close. Rounded shower stalls are used to eliminate corners, which collect dirt and are difficult to clean. An advanced security system logs the time a maid inserts her card and enters a room and is used to track the maid's time. The same system permits guests to use their credit cards to enter the room, thus eliminating the need for the hotel to handle keys. Asphalt and shrubbery are used to limit the amount of lawn mowing required. The result of these efforts is that cleaning a room takes 20 minutes versus the industry standard of 30 minutes. Furthermore, an entire 92-room hotel is operated with the equivalent of 11 full-time workers (Wessel 1989).

- In the early 1980s, the biggest threat to the largest U.S. steelmakers was foreign competition. However, after closing inefficient plants, modernizing others, and reducing payrolls during the 1980s, large U.S. steelmakers can now go toe to toe with these foreign competitors. As an example, in 1982 in the United States it took 10.59 labor hours to produce and ship 1 metric ton of steel; in Japan it took 10.01 hours. By the early 1990s, U.S. producers reversed this advantage. As a result of improving their productivity faster than their foreign counterparts, by the middle of 1991 U.S. steelmakers were able to produce 1 metric ton with 5.4 labor hours, compared with 5.6 hours for Japanese steelmakers. Furthermore, in addition to improving their productivity, large U.S. steelmakers have simultaneously improved their quality. To illustrate, in the early 1980s Ford rejected about 8 percent of its domestic steel shipments, and 20 percent of its steel shipments were late. By the early 1990s, its steel rejects had been reduced to less than 1 percent and 99 percent of its shipments were delivered on time (Pare 1991).

- In early 1995, Kansas City Power and Light began installing automatic meter readers in its 420,000 meters. An automatic meter reader is a small electronic device that broadcasts data on electricity usage every few minutes and eliminates the need for $15-an-hour human meter readers. Coca-Cola is testing a similar technology to be used in the millions of vending machines that stock its product. Using such a device, Coca-Cola will be able to reduce costs by scheduling deliveries for only those vending machines that are out of stock. Without the devices, delivery schedules and quantities are based primarily on hunches. Also, Coca-Cola anticipates that the use of these devices will lead to increased sales through more timely restocking of the machines. Finally, the data collected will be used to help Coca-Cola evaluate the effectiveness of various advertising campaigns (Zachary 1995).

For a wide variety of reasons, numerous companies are investing substantial amounts of time and other resources in improving organizational efficiency or productivity. In the case of Manor Care, a shortage of labor required it to find ways to operate its hotels with fewer employees. In the case of domestic steel producers, the impetus for improving productivity was a desire to remain competitive in a global marketplace. The opportunities that new technologies often provide to improve organizational efficiency and effectiveness are illustrated by Kansas City Power and Light and Coca-Cola. Regardless of the specific reasons a particular organization cites for improving productivity, such programs are almost always undertaken with the intent of sustaining or improving the organization's competitive position in the marketplace.

Making and keeping an organization competitive is top management's job, and this is accomplished partly through the business strategy that top management adopts. This strategy gives the firm its direction and vision for the future and guides its decisions in both the short term and the long term. A common strategy in the recent past, particularly for small firms, was to be a local supplier who could react quickly to the immediate needs of its customers.

But global producers are now competing in virtually all markets, whether local, domestic, or foreign. Thus, even if a firm sees itself as only a small, local business, it must be globally competitive to survive. For example, small regional foundries have been driven out of business by the thousands and replaced by international competitors. Thus, it is incumbent on every firm's top management to consider international competition in its business strategy.

Our description of the production system in Chapter 1 assumed that the organization had some specific, well-defined goal—such a goal might be making gourmet cookies for an upscale market, for example. This goal implies awareness of marketing: What services and facilitating goods do customers want? But any independent financial goal (to make the company rich) or marketing goal (to increase sales 10 percent) is only wishful thinking unless the operations of the organization can deliver what is needed with the available resources. What transformation activities are needed? What level of quality is required? Is transportation necessary?

The organization's business strategy provides the information needed to design business processes for the firm to achieve its goals. The business strategy also provides the information for all activities carried out in the organization to support the production system in its task. In the functional organization, this specification of how each function is going to support the overall business strategy was known as a functional strategy. Thus, there was a marketing strategy, a finance strategy, an operations strategy, and so on. In organizations structured on the basis of business processes, separate functional strategies specifying how each functional area will support the overall business strategy are not needed. Rather, a strategy for how each business process supports the overall business strategy is developed.

STRATEGY FORMULATION

The organization's business strategy is a set of objectives, plans, and policies for the organization to compete successfully in its markets. In effect, the business strategy specifies what an organization's competitive advantage will be and how this advantage will be achieved and sustained. As we will see, a key aspect of the business strategy is defining the organization's core competencies and focus. The actual strategic plan that details the business strategy is typically formulated at the executive committee level (CEO, president, vice presidents). It is usually long-range, in the neighborhood of 3 to 5 years.

In fact, however, the decisions that are made over time are the long-range strategy. In too many firms, these decisions show no pattern at all, reflecting the truth that they have no active business strategy, even if they have gone through a process of strategic planning. In other cases these decisions bear little or no relationship to the organization's stated or official business strategy. The point is that an organization's actions often tell more about its true business strategy than its public statements.

Formulating the Business Strategy

The general process of formulating a business strategy is illustrated in Figure 2.1. Relevant inputs to the strategic planning process are the products and services needed by customers; the strengths and weaknesses of the competition; the environment in general; and the organization's own strengths, weaknesses, culture, and resources.

After collectively considering these inputs, strategic planning is often initiated by developing a vision statement, a mission statement, or both. **Vision statements** are used to express the organization's values and aspirations. **Mission statements** express the organization's purpose or reason for existence. In some cases, organizations may choose to combine the vision and mission statements into a single statement. Regardless of whether separate statements or combined statements are developed, the intent is to communicate the organization's values, aspirations, and purpose so that employees can make decisions that are consistent with and support these objectives.

Effective vision and mission statements tend to be written using language that inspires employees to high levels of performance. Further, to foster employees'

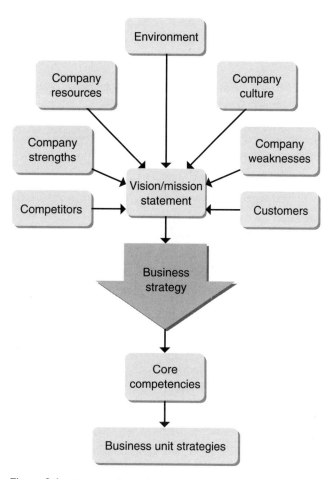

Figure 2.1   Strategy formulation.

commitment, it is advisable to include a wide variety of employees in the development of the vision or mission statement, rather than enforcing top management's view by edict. Once the vision and mission statements are developed for the organization as a whole, divisions, departments, process teams, project teams, work groups, and so on can develop individual vision-mission statements that support the organization's overall statement. For example, after a university develops its overall vision-mission statement, each college could develop its own unique statements specifying the role that it will play in supporting the overall mission of the university. Likewise, once each school develops its own vision-mission statement, the departments within the school can develop unique statements. Having each organizational unit develop its own unique statements promotes wider participation in the process, helps employees think in terms of how their work supports the overall mission, and results in statements that are more meaningful to a select group of employees. Some examples of actual vision-mission statements are provided in Figure 2.2.

Once the vision-mission statement is drafted, a business strategy is formulated specifying how the vision and mission will be accomplished. One important result

COCA-COLA COMPANY'S MISSION STATEMENT

Our Mission

We exist to create value for our share owners on a long-term basis by building a business that enhances the Coca-Cola Company's trademarks. This also is our ultimate commitment.

As the world's largest beverage company, we refresh the world. We do this by developing superior soft drinks, both carbonated and noncarbonated, and profitable nonalcoholic beverage systems that create value for our Company, our bottling partners and our customers.

In creating value, we succeed or fail based on our ability to perform as stewards of several key assets:

1. Coca-Cola, the world's most powerful trademark, and other highly valuable trademarks.
2. The world's most effective and pervasive distribution system.
3. Satisfied customers, who make a good profit selling our products.
4. Our people, who are ultimately responsible for building this enterprise.
5. Our abundant resources, which must be intelligently allocated.
6. Our strong global leadership in the beverage industry in particular and in the business world in general.

THE CENTRAL INTELLIGENCE AGENCY

Our Vision

To be the keystone of a U.S. Intelligence Community that is pre-eminent in the world, known for both the high quality of our work and the excellence of our people.

Our Mission

We support the President, the National Security Council, and all who make and execute U.S. national security policy by:

- Providing accurate, evidence-based, comprehensive, and timely foreign intelligence related to national security; and
- Conducting counterintelligence activities, special activities, and other functions related to foreign intelligence and national security as directed by the President.

APICS—THE EDUCATIONAL SOCIETY FOR RESOURCE MANAGEMENT

Vision

To inspire individuals and organizations toward lifelong learning and to enhance individual and organizational success.

Mission

To be the premier provider and global leader in individual and organizational education, standards of excellence, and information in integrated resource management.

Sources: http://www.cocacola.com/co/mission.html, http://www.odci.gov/cia/information/mission.html, http://www.industry.net/c/orgunpro/apics/plan (February 12, 1997).

Figure 2.2   Examples of vision and mission statements.

DILBERT ©United Feature Syndicate. Reprinted with permission.

of developing a business strategy is identifying the organization's core competencies. **Core competencies** are the collective knowledge and skills an organization has that distinguish it from the competition. Typically, core competencies center on an organization's ability to integrate a variety of specific technologies and skills in the development of new products and services. Clearly, one of top management's most important activities is to identify and develop the core competencies the organization will need to successfully execute the business strategy. Given this importance, we discuss core competencies in more detail in the next section.

Once a business strategy is formulated, and the core competencies are specified, each business unit develops its own strategy to guide its activities so that they are consistent and support the organization's overall business strategy. Although formulating the business strategy is displayed as rather straightforward in Figure 2.1, in reality it is very iterative.

Core Competencies[1]

As previously mentioned, core competencies are the collective knowledge and skills that distinguish an organization from the competition. In effect, core competencies provide the basis for developing new products and services, and they are a primary factor in determining an organization's long-term competitiveness. Therefore, an important part of strategic planning is identifying and predicting the core competencies that are critical to sustaining and enhancing the organization's competitive position. On this basis, an organization can assess suppliers' and competitors' capabilities. If the organization finds that it is not the leader, it must determine the cost and risks of catching up with the best versus the cost and risks of losing the core competency.

---

[1]Shaded section headings indicate especially timely topics.

Often, it is more useful to think of an organization in terms of its portfolio of core competencies, rather than its portfolio of businesses or products. For instance, Sony is known for its expertise in miniaturization; 3M for its knowledge of substrates, coatings, and adhesives; Black and Decker for small electrical motors and industrial design; Boeing for its ability to integrate large-scale complex systems; and Honda for engines and power trains. Had Sony initially viewed itself as primarily a manufacturer of Walkmans, rather than as a company with expertise in miniaturization, it might have overlooked several profitable opportunities, such as entering the camcorder business. As another example, Boeing has successfully leveraged its core competency related to integrating large-scale systems in its production of commercial jetliners, space stations, fighter-bombers, and missiles.

As these examples illustrate, core competencies are often used to gain access to a wide variety of markets. Cannon used its core competencies in optics, imaging, and electronic controls to enter the markets for copiers, laser printers, cameras, and image scanners. In a similar fashion, Honda's core competencies in engines and power trains are the basis for its entry into other businesses: automobiles, motorcycles, lawn mowers, and generators.

In addition to providing access to a variety of markets, a core competence should be strongly related to the key benefits provided by the product or service. In Sony's case, its expertise in miniaturization translates directly into important product features such as portability and aesthetic designs. Alternatively, suppose that Sony developed a core competence in writing understandable user manuals. Since people who purchase a Walkman or camcorder rarely base their decision on the quality of the user manual (when was the last time you read a user manual?), this competence would provide little if any competitive advantage.

Another characteristic of a core competence is that it should be difficult to imitate. Clearly, no sustainable competitive advantage is provided by a core competence that is easily imitated. For example, Sony's expertise in miniaturization would mean little if other electronics manufacturers could match it simply by purchasing and taking apart Sony's products (this is called *reverse engineering*).

The topic of core competence is also strongly related to outsourcing. ***Outsourcing***—an approach that is being increasingly used—involves subcontracting out certain activities or services. For example, a manufacturer might outsource the production of certain components, the management and maintenance of its computer resources, employee recruitment, or the processing of its payroll.

When we consider the concept of core competence, it is important to recognize that not all parts or activities are equal. Rather, activities and parts can be thought of as falling on a continuum ranging from strategically unimportant to strategically important. Parts and activities are considered strategically important when

- They are strongly related to what customers perceive to be the key characteristics of the product or service.
- They require highly specialized knowledge and skill.
- They require highly specialized physical assets, and few other suppliers possess these assets.
- The organization has a technological lead or is likely to obtain one.

Activities that are not strategic are candidates for outsourcing. These parts or activities are not strongly linked to key product characteristics, do not require highly specialized knowledge, do not need special physical assets, and the organization does not have the technological lead in this area. Thus, if it is beneficial to outsource these parts or activities—perhaps because of lower cost or higher quality—no loss in competitiveness should result.

On the other hand, when most of a firm's complex parts and production are outsourced, particularly to a foreign supplier, the firm is called hollow. As we have discussed, the wise firm will outsource only nonstrategic, simple, relatively standard parts such as nuts and bolts that are not worth the firm's time to produce itself; the complex, proprietary parts that give their products an edge in the marketplace are produced internally. If the firm outsources these parts as well, it soon finds that the engineering design talent follows the production of the part outside the firm, too. Then, the firm has been *hollowed out,* becoming merely a distributor of its supplier's products.

So what is the problem? If a supplier can deliver the parts at lower cost and better quality when they are needed, why not use them? The problem is that the supplier gains the expertise to produce the critical parts your firm needs. After a while, when the supplier has improved on the process and you have forgotten how to make the parts, it is likely to start producing the products you have been selling in competition with you and drop you as a customer. This is even more dangerous if, as already noted, the product and transformation system has also been hollowed out, following the production activities to the supplier. This happened extensively in the television industry, where the Japanese learned first how to produce, and then how to engineer black-and-white and later color television sets. They then started tentatively introducing their own brands, to see if U.S. customers would buy them. Their products were inexpensive, were of high quality, and caught on quickly in the free-enterprise American markets. The Japanese now virtually control this industry.

An example of a company recently pondering this issue is Sara Lee Corporation (Miller 1997, and Rose and Quintanilla 1997). In September 1997, Sara Lee announced a "fundamental reshaping" of its business away from in-house production of its brand-name products which include L'eggs hosiery, frozen deserts, Wonderbras, Coach leather goods, and Kiwi shoe polish. Referring to the plan as to "de-verticalize," Sara Lee's chairman and CEO, John Bryan, stated, "the business of Sara Lee Corporation has been and will continue to be the building of branded leadership positions," not manufacturing. Mr. Bryan mentioned Nike and Coca-Cola as model companies that have chosen to avoid manufacturing. Indeed, company officials estimate the program will reduce costs up to $125 million annually.

Sara Lee exemplifies a growing trend among U.S. manufactures. The Big Three automakers are well-known examples of manufacturers that extensively outsource. As other examples, Deere & Co. puts its name on midrange utility tractors produced by a Japanese company, and Agco Corp. outsources the production of almost all of the transmissions and engines used in its farm equipment. Of course, not all manufacturers are jumping on the outsourcing bandwagon. New Balance Athletic Shoes, for example, is investing $25 million in its manufacturing facilities as part of an overall strategy to do more assembly in-house.

Some critics argue that the use of outsourcing is aimed at simply reducing labor costs. Others are concerned that the trend could ultimately weaken the industrial base in the United States. However, Gordon Richards, an economist with the National Association of Manufacturers, notes that "this doesn't mean the amount of manufacturing activity is going to decrease."

Business Strategy and the Product Life Cycle

A wide variety of common business strategies are described in this section and the following section. A number of them are tied to the stages in the standard *life cycle* of products and services, shown in Figure 2.3. Studies of the introduction of new products indicate that the life cycle (or *stretched-S growth curve*, as it is also known) provides a good pattern for the growth of demand for a new output. The curve can be divided into three major segments: introduction and early adoption, acceptance and growth of the market, and maturity with market saturation. After market saturation, demand may remain high or decline; or the output may be improved and possibly start on a new growth curve.

The length of product and service life cycles has been shrinking significantly in the last decade or so. In the past, a life cycle might have been five years, but it is now six months. This places a tremendous burden on the firm to constantly monitor its strategy and quickly change a strategy that becomes inappropriate to the market.

The life cycle begins with an *innovation*—a new output or process for the market. The innovation may be a patented product or process, a new combination of existing elements that has created a unique product or process, or some service that was previously unavailable. Initial versions of the product or service may change relatively frequently; production volumes are small, since the output has not caught on yet; and margins are high. As volume increases, the design of the output stabilizes and more competitors enter the market, frequently with more capital-intensive equipment. In the mature phase, the now high-volume output is a virtual commodity, and the firm that can produce an acceptable version at the lowest cost usually controls the market.

Clearly, a firm's business strategy should match the life-cycle stages of its products and services. If a firm is good at innovation—as, for example, Hewlett-Packard is—it may choose to focus only on the introduction and acceptance phases of the product's life cycle and then sell or license production to others as the product moves beyond the introduction stage. If its strength is in high-volume, low-cost

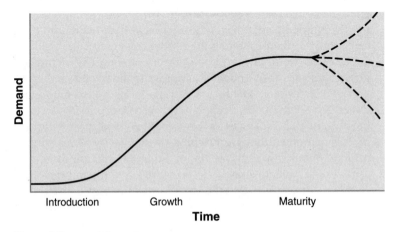

Figure 2.3   The life-cycle curve.

production, the company should stick with proven products that are in the maturity stage. Most common, perhaps, are firms that attempt to stick with products throughout their life cycle, changing their strategy with each stage.

Categories of Business Strategies

One approach to categorizing an organization's business strategy is based on its timing of introductions of new outputs. Two researchers, Maidique and Patch, suggest the following four product development strategies:

- *First-to-market.* Organizations that use this strategy attempt to have their products available before the competition. To achieve this, strong applied research is needed. If a company is first to market, it has to decide if it wants to price its products high and thus skim the market to achieve large short-term profits or set a lower initial price to obtain a higher market share and perhaps larger long-term profits.

- *Second-to-market.* Organizations that use this strategy try to quickly imitate successful outputs offered by first-to-market organizations. This strategy requires less emphasis on applied research and more emphasis on fast development. Often, firms that use the second-to-market strategy attempt to learn from the mistakes of the first-to-market firm and offer improved or enhanced versions of the original products.

- *Cost minimization or late-to-market.* Organizations that use this strategy wait until a product becomes fairly standardized and is demanded in large volumes. They then attempt to compete on the basis of costs as opposed to features of the product. These organizations focus most of their research and development on improving the production system, as opposed to focusing on product development.

- *Market segmentation.* This strategy focuses on serving niche markets with specific needs. Applied engineering skills and flexible manufacturing systems are often needed for the market-segmentation strategy.

Be aware that a number of implicit trade-offs are involved in developing a strategy. Let us use the first-to-market strategy to demonstrate. A first-to-market strategy requires large investments in product development in an effort to stay ahead of the competition. Typically, organizations that pursue this strategy expect to achieve relatively higher profit margins, larger market shares, or both as a result of initially having the market to themselves. The strategy is somewhat risky because a competitor may end up beating them to the market. Also, even if a company succeeds in getting to the market first, it may end up simply creating an opportunity for the competition to learn from its mistakes and overtake it in the market. To illustrate, although Sony introduced its Betamax format for VCRs in 1975, JVC's VHS format—introduced the following year—is the standard that ultimately gained widespread market acceptance.

Such trade-offs are basic to the concept of selecting a business strategy. Although specific tasks must be done well to execute the selected strategy, not everything needs to be particularly outstanding—only a few things. And of course, strategies based on anything else—acquisitions, mergers, tax loss carry-forwards, even streams of high-technology products—will not be successful if the customer is ignored in the process.

The Balanced Scorecard

Once the strategy has been formulated, the next step is to implement it. The ***balanced scorecard*** approach is becoming increasingly recognized for helping organizations translate their mission and strategy into appropriate performance measures.

In the past, it was not uncommon for managers to rely primarily on financial performance measures. However, when inadequacies of these measures were discovered, managers often responded by either trying to improve them or by abandoning them in favor of operational performance measures such as cycle time and defect rates. Many organizations now realize that no single type of measure can provide insight into all the critical areas of the business. Thus, the purpose of the balanced scorecard is to develop a set of measures that provides a comprehensive view of the organization.

Organizations that have developed a balanced scorecard report numerous benefits, including:

- An effective way to clarify and gain consensus of the strategy
- A mechanism for communicating the strategy throughout the entire organization
- A mechanism for aligning departmental and personal goals to the strategy
- A way to ensure that strategic objectives are linked to annual budgets
- Timely feedback related to improving the strategy

One problem with traditional performance measurement systems based primarily on financial measures is that they often encourage short-sighted decisions such as reducing investments in product development, employee training, and information technology. The balanced scorecard approach corrects this problem by measuring performance in four major areas: financial performance, customer performance, internal business process performance, and organizational learning and growth. The financial performance measures included in the balanced scorecard are typically related to profitability, such as return on equity, return on capital, and economic value added. Customer performance measures focus on customer satisfaction, customer retention, customer profitability, market share, and customer acquisition. The internal business process dimension addresses the issue of what the organization must excel at to achieve its financial and customer objectives. Examples of performance measures for internal business processes include quality, response time, cost, new-product launch time, and the ratio of processing time to total throughput time. Finally, the learning and growth dimension focuses on the infrastructure the organization must build to sustain its competitive advantage. Learning and growth performance measures include employee satisfaction, employee retention, worker productivity, and the availability of timely and accurate information.

The process of developing a balanced scorecard begins with top management translating the mission and strategy into specific customer and financial objectives. Based on the customer and financial objectives, related measures for the internal business processes are identified. Finally, investments in employee training and information technology are linked to the customer, financial, and internal business process objectives. Note that a properly constructed balanced scorecard contains an appropriate mix of outcome measures related to the actual results achieved and measures that drive future performance.

The balanced scorecard is based on the premise that a strategy is a set of hypotheses about cause-and-effect relationships that can be stated as if-then statements. For example, management of a department store might hypothesize that increasing the training that sales associates receive will lead to improved selling skills. These managers might further hypothesize that better selling skills will translate into higher commissions for the sales associates and will therefore result in less turnover. Happier and more experienced sales associates would likely lead to increased sales per store, which ultimately translates into an increase in return on investment. Since a properly developed balanced scorecard tells a story about the cause-and-effect relationships underlying the strategy, all measures included in the scorecard should be an element in the chain of cause-and-effect relationships.

OCUS

In the previous section, we discussed the issue of core competence. Now we look in more depth at the basic aim of the strategy. The goal of each strategy is to utilize an organization's core competencies to establish and maintain a unique strength, or **focus**, for the firm that leads to a sustainable competitive advantage. A number of industry studies have found that, over time, the successful companies are the ones that have demonstrated a continuous, single-minded determination to achieve one or both of the following competitive positions within their respective industries:

1. Have the *lowest cost* compared with the competition. If the quality of the output is acceptable, then the firm can adopt a very competitive pricing policy that will gain profitable volume and increase market share.
2. Have an *outstanding strength* (short lead time, advanced technology, high quality, and so on) that differentiates a firm from the competition and is valued in the marketplace. Then, if the firm has an acceptable cost structure, it can adopt a pricing policy to gain large margins and fund reinvestment in its differentiated strength.

In addition to the advantages of being focused, there are also some dangers. A narrowly focused firm can easily become uncompetitive in the market if the customers' requirements change. In addition to being focused, a firm must also be flexible enough to alter its focus when the need changes and to spot the change in time. Frequently, a focus in one area can be used to advantage in another way, if there is enough time to adapt—for example, to move into a new product line or alter the application of the focus.

Areas of Focus

McKinsey & Company, a top management consulting firm, studied 27 outstanding successful firms to find their common attributes. Two of the major attributes reported in *Business Week* are directly related to the formulation of the business strategy:

1. *Stressing one key business value.* At Hewlett-Packard, the key value is developing new products; at Dana Corporation, it is improving productivity.
2. *Sticking to what they know best.* All the outstanding firms define their core competencies (or strengths) and then build on them. They resist the temptation to move into new areas or diversify.

When an organization chooses to stress one or two key areas of strength, it is referred to as a *focused organization.* For example, IBM is known for its customer service, General Electric for its technology, and Procter & Gamble for its consumer marketing. In general, most but not all areas of focus relate to operations. Some firms, such as those in the insurance industry, focus on financial strength and others focus on marketing strengths. Kenner Toys, for example, considers its strength to be a legal one: the ability to win contracts for exclusive production of popular children's toys. As a final example, many health care organizations are achieving significant operational efficiencies by focusing on a narrow range of ailments. For example, by treating only long-term acute cases, Intensiva HealthCare has been able to reduce its costs to 50 percent of those of a traditional intensive-care ward.

Table 2.1 identifies several areas of focus that organizations commonly choose when forming their competitive strategy; all are various forms of differentiation. In a later section on global competitiveness, we discuss these areas in more detail. Note that the concept of focus applies to pure service organizations as well as product firms.

*T*ABLE 2.1 • Common Areas of Organizational Focus

- *Innovation:* Bringing a range of new products and services to market quickly
- *Customization:* Being able to quickly redesign and produce a product or service to meet customers' unique needs
- *Flexibility of products and services:* Switching between different models or variants quickly to satisfy a customer or market
- *Flexibility of volume:* Changing quickly and economically from low-volume production to high volumes and vice versa
- *Performance:* Offering products and services with unique, valuable features
- *Quality:* Having better craftsmanship or consistency
- *Reliability of the product or service:* Always working acceptably, enabling customers to count on the performance
- *Reliability of delivery:* Always fulfilling promises with a product or service that is never late
- *Response:* Offering very short lead times to obtain products and services
- *After-sale service:* Making available extensive, continuing help
- *Price:* Having the lowest price

Order Qualifiers and Winners

Recent competitive behavior among firms seems to be dividing most of the factors in Table 2.1 into two sets that Terry Hill, an operations strategist and researcher in England, calls *order qualifiers* and *order winners*. An **order qualifier** is a characteristic of the product or service that is required if the product is even to be considered or in the running. In other words, it is a prerequisite for entering the market. An **order winner** is a characteristic that will win the bid or the purchase. These qualifiers and winners vary with the market, of course, but some general commonalties exist across markets. For example, response time, performance, customization, innovation, quality, and price seem to be frequent order winners, and the other factors (e.g., reliability and flexibility) tend to be order qualifiers. Working with marketing and sales to properly identify which factors are which is clearly of major strategic importance.

Loss of Focus

An organization can sometimes lose its focus. For example, in the traditional functional organization purchasing may buy the cheapest materials it can. This requires buying large quantities with advance notice. Scheduling, however, is trying to reduce inventories so it orders materials on short notice and in small quantities. Quality control is trying to improve the output, so it carefully inspects every item, creating delays and extensive rework. In this example, each functional department is pursuing its own objectives but is not focusing on how it can support the organization's overall business strategy. In an effort to eliminate these types of problems, many organizations are adopting organizational structures based on specific value-creating processes, as opposed to organizing work on the basis of the type of activity performed. Organizing work on the basis of value-creating processes enables each employee to focus on the desired end result.

There may even be a loss of focus at the top management level. For example, one firm decided to consolidate its production of made-to-order products in a remodeled central plant. Previously, the products were made in three separate plants that were obsolete and inefficient. One plant produced high volumes of cheap fasteners (screws, nails) on demand for the construction industry. It used large, dirty equipment to stamp out the fasteners in short lead times with minimal quality control. The second plant produced expensive, high-quality microwave ovens. Engineering design was the critical function, with long lead times, extensive testing, and purchases in small lots. The third plant produced custom integrated circuits in clean rooms with expensive computerized equipment. The consolidation proved to be a disaster. Although this is an extreme example, many firms do exactly the same thing with a variety of product lines that have grown up in the same plant. Clearly, these firms once had some competitive advantage, or they never would have survived.

How do organizations lose their focus and get into trouble? There are a number of ways this can happen.

- *New outputs*: This is the situation in the previous example. Managers, in an attempt to reap what they feel will be economies of scale, add products or services to the organization's offerings that require expertise in a wide variety of areas. Unable to control the variety of expertise required of each line, the organization becomes unfocused.

- *New attributes*: This occurs when management adds a new twist to the output that conflicts with the existing focus, or the market demands a new twist that the firm cannot meet. For example, the firm may have been producing a high-quality custom product, and a competitor develops a new process to produce a standard item at a cheap price. Management might decree that a low-cost version of the item is now needed in the marketplace, but operations cannot meet this requirement and also stay focused on high-quality custom products.

- *New tasks*: Management may add new tasks to operations, such as reducing costs, raising quality, or improving product safety. Such requirements may come about because of new laws or regulations, union contracts, or other such reasons. But the requirement will compromise the firm's existing focus and may make it uncompetitive in the marketplace.

- *Life-cycle changes*: As products go through their life cycle, the task of operations often changes, as shown in Figure 2.4. Initially, the task is to get an adequate-quality item into a market that has just discovered this new output. The form of the output often changes at this early, experimental stage, so the organization must be flexible enough to accept changes in design. As the market accepts the item, the task becomes dual: meeting the growing demand in the marketplace while remaining somewhat flexible in terms of minor design modifications. Finally, as the design solidifies and more and more competitors enter the market, the pressure to cut cost becomes paramount. At this stage the output may be fairly classified as a commodity. Throughout this life cycle, the focus of the organization has to change, if it stays with the same output. Many firms, however, choose to compete at only one stage of the life cycle and abandon other stages, so that they can keep the strength of their original focus.

- *Departmental professionalism*: Sometimes an organization loses its focus when particular specialties (e.g., finance and marketing) are allowed to follow the guidelines of their profession rather than the needs of the organization. Although the professional guidelines are always admirable, they may not apply at a particular time in a particular firm. For example, finance may pressure production to reduce inventory levels in an effort to lower inventory-related costs, while marketing may simultaneously pressure production to increase inventory levels so that delivery dates can be shortened and sales increased. Clearly, allowing each functional area to pursue its own professional guidelines independently can severely compromise the organization's overall focus.

- *Ignorance and noncommunication*: The most common reason a firm loses its focus is simply that the focus was never clearly identified in the first place. Never having been well defined, it could not be communicated to the employees, could therefore not gain their support, and thus was lost. Sometimes a focus is identified but not communicated throughout the organization, because management thinks that lower-level employees don't need to know the strategic focus of the firm in order to do their jobs. This point is illustrated by Rolm Telecommunications.

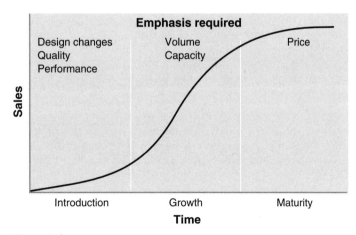

Figure 2.4 Product life-cycle: stages and emphasis.

A major building block in Rolm Telecommunications' business strategy is "vision." Rolm has found that the critical factor in companies' performance is largely the employees' image of what the business is, where it is going, and how each of the parts fits into the whole. As Wayne Mehl, Rolm's general manager, says, "That image determines the outcome." In working with their people to better understand the whole of what Rolm is, managers found it necessary to break down the walls between functions, to let people see the entire organization and what it was about. They involved their people more closely with management, with other functions, and even with suppliers and customers. Rolm considers its primary unit of value to be its people. The people make things happen—people have the vision and carry out the plans. Without people, nothing happens.

One example of this interplay between vision and people is in the area of quality. In too many firms, poor quality is expected and accepted. Only 1 percent defective goods is considered excellent in many manufacturing firms.

But Mehl asks us to consider some examples where poor quality is unacceptable, such as banking and music. What would you think about a bank that had 99 percent accurate statements? Of every 100 entries on your statement, one would be wrong, on average. For many people that would mean an average of one error on every statement. What would you think about a bank that sent you a statement that was wrong every month and was proud of its quality? Or suppose you went to a concert with a date and the orchestra played 99 percent of the notes correctly. Some of the results of this attention to Rolm's employees and their vision of the firm are clearly evident. For example, inventories have been cut in half, defective products in process have been reduced by a factor of six, and rework has almost been eliminated. Mehl quotes a production supervisor as saying, "I used to have seven people doing rework, and now I have one. My goal is none."

GLOBAL COMPETITIVENESS

The previous sections have overviewed the formulation of a business strategy and areas of focus. In this section we build on that foundation as we investigate global competitiveness. **Competitiveness** can be defined in a number of ways. We may think of it as the long-term viability of a firm or organization; or we may define it in a short-term context such as the current success of a firm in the marketplace as measured by its market share or its profitability. We can also talk about the competitiveness of a nation, in the sense of its aggregate competitive success in all markets. The President's Council on Industrial Competitiveness gave this definition in 1985:

> Competitiveness for a nation is the degree to which it can, under free and fair market conditions, produce goods and services that meet the test of international markets while simultaneously maintaining and expanding the real incomes of its citizens.

Global Trends

The trend in merchandise trade for the United States is illustrated in Figure 2.5. Although some might think that foreign competition has been taking markets away from U.S. producers only in the past decade, this figure indicates that the nation's merchandise imports have grown considerably in the last 30 years. Although *exports* have increased over this period as well, they have not increased as fast as imports; the result is a growing trade deficit with foreign countries as shown by the cumulative net exports curve in Figure 2.5. Partly as a result of this deficit, the United States is now the biggest debtor nation in the world. Although the trade deficit has received major attention only since it burgeoned in the early 1980s, Figure 2.5 indicates that it is actually part of a long-term trend.

Newspapers and network news programs often report on the bilateral trade deficit of the United States with various foreign countries. These stories frequently focus on the bilateral trade gap between the United States and Japan. There are a number of problems, however, with bilateral trade statistics. For instance, when Japan shifts some of its production to other countries such as China or Thailand, it appears that the trade gap between the United States and Japan has decreased. Similarly, Japanese-owned companies operating in the United States are partly responsible for the increase in exports to Japan. Both of these occurrences tend to distort the true nature of the balance of trade between the United States and Japan.

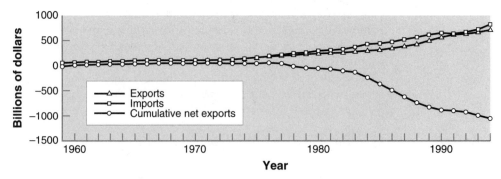

Figure 2.5   The United States' merchandise trade. *Source:* Economic Report of the President, February 1996.

Exchange Rates

When the United States buys more imports from overseas with dollars, and foreigners buy fewer American exports, a surplus of dollars accumulates abroad that tends to reduce the desirability of holding dollars, so the value of the dollar falls. This is illustrated in the trade-weighted dollar exchange rate plotted in Figure 2.6. The trade-weighted dollar exchange rate is the weighted-average price of the U.S. dollar to the foreign currencies of the G-10[2] countries. A large value of the trade-weighted dollar exchange rate indicates a strong dollar, making it easier for Americans to afford imports but also making it more difficult for people in other countries to afford U.S. exports. Although other factors, such as intervention by a central bank and changes in national interest rates, can alter the exchange rate in the short term, the basic economic factors of competitiveness tend to show through over the long term. Although the value of the dollar often fluctuates widely relative to the value of a particular country's currency, Figure 2.6 indicates that the exchange rate of the dollar to the weighted average currency of the G-10 countries has been relatively stable since the late 1980s.

On the other hand, consider what it means to Americans and to the average foreign consumer when the dollar declines in value relative to a foreign currency. A weaker dollar means that Americans will have to pay more for products imported from the foreign country in question. Meanwhile, however, the prices for products produced in the United States and exported to the foreign country will decline. Thus, a decline in the value of the dollar is a double-edged sword. Such a decline makes imported goods more expensive for Americans to purchase but at the same time makes exports less expensive for foreign consumers, increasing the demand for domestic products.

According to economic theory, a weaker dollar should make American products more desirable (or competitive) in foreign markets, and imports less desirable in American markets. However, some market actions that governments and businesses often take to keep from losing customers can alter this perfect economic relationship. For instance, when the price of Japanese products in the United States

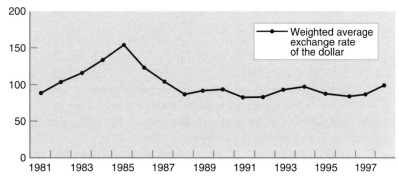

Figure 2.6   Purchasing power of the dollar. *Source:* Federal Reserve Board, *www.bog.frb.fed.us/releases/H10/hist/* June 15, 1998.

---

[2]The G-10 countries are Belgium, Canada, France, Germany, Italy, Japan, the Netherlands, Sweden, Switzerland, and the United Kingdom.

started increasing in terms of dollars, Japanese firms initiated huge cost-cutting drives to reduce the cost (and thereby the dollar price) of their products, to keep from losing American customers. This strategy has largely been successful.

Instead of American products becoming significantly cheaper in Japan, some claim that many of these products have been politically blocked from access to Japanese markets by the Japanese government, which tries to protect domestic firms from foreign competition. When a government does this to protect a developing domestic industry while it is struggling to become competitive in world markets, the short-run strategy may be wise. But in Europe, a result of protectionism has been that consumers buy only half as many electronic components (TV sets, etc.) as Americans and yet pay two to three times as much for them.

In Southeast Asia, already troubled by the collapse of real-estate markets, bad lending practices, nervous consumers, and increasing unemployment, the difficulties were compounded in the spring of 1997. In what is commonly referred to as the Asian Crisis, the economies of several Asian countries continued to weaken through 1998, resulting in declining currencies and stock markets. With Japan in recession, it was less able to import from other countries in the region or make loans to them. Accounting for approximately 70 percent of the region's output, Japan's yen is often used as a barometer of the region's health. From the beginning of 1995 to beginning of 1998, the value of the yen weakened significantly, from 100.5 to 132.4 yen to the U.S. dollar. The cheap yen allowed Japan to undercut other countries in the region that were hoping to use exports to ease their own difficulties. For example, the weakening yen put pressure on China to devalue its currency, which many speculated would lead to a new round of currency devaluations.

Further compounding the problem, many analysts expressed concern that a falling yen would increase tensions between the United States and Japan as it would provide Japan with a competitive advantage in the form of lower costs and increase its imports to the United States. One option for the United States is to lower its interest rates in an effort to make the dollar less attractive and other currencies relatively more appealing. Furthermore, such a reduction in interest rates would help numerous domestic industries, including construction, automobiles, and heavy equipment. On the other hand, the risk of lowering interest rates is that it could overstimulate the domestic economy and increase inflation (of course, cheap imports tend to keep inflation low).

Another negative factor associated with a rising dollar is that domestic companies that do business overseas must translate foreign sales and profits into relatively fewer U.S. dollars. For example, Hewlett-Packard estimated that the stronger dollar reduced its revenue growth in the second quarter of 1998 by five percentage points as its foreign sales translated into fewer U.S. dollars.

Not all foreign currencies have improved, relative to the dollar, as steeply as Japan. For example, the currency of South Korea has weakened relative to the dollar and Hong Kong's currency has maintained its relative proportion to the dollar. As a result, these countries are now "low-wage" producers and are replacing Japan in the production of basic commodities such as clothing, steel, toys, and even electronics. Given their low domestic wages in combination with the easy availability of machinery for high-volume production, we even see Brazil, the Philippines, Malaysia, and Mexico (particularly with its free-trade "Maquiladora" zone near the United States border) moving into the production of major durable goods such as automobiles and television sets. Meanwhile, Japan, Germany, and other traditionally export-oriented nations are moving upscale and producing technically advanced, higher-priced goods for sale around the world.

International Markets and Producers

The way current trends are developing, it now seems that there will soon be three major trading regions in the world: Europe, North America, and the Pacific rim, as illustrated in Figure 2.7. Note that Africa, middle Asia, and Latin America are not included. It was thought that by 1992 "fortress Europe" would emerge, under the sponsorship of the European Union (EU), as one of the largest unified markets in the world; all existing labor, paperwork, and trade barriers would fall as the giant free-trade region emerged. This region is even larger than the North American region, which consists primarily of the United States and Canada. However, there are still several issues being resolved, such as currency and sovereignty, before the goal of a unified European market is realized. The Pacific rim is composed of the Asian countries, including Japan, Korea, Taiwan, Hong Kong, and Singapore. These countries currently are major exporters of goods, but not importers.

International competition has grown very complex in the last few years. Previously, firms were either domestic, exporters, or international. A domestic firm produced and sold in the same country. An exporter sold goods, often someone else's, abroad. An international firm sold domestically produced as well as foreign-produced goods both domestically and in foreign countries. However, domestic sales were usually produced domestically, and foreign sales were made either in the

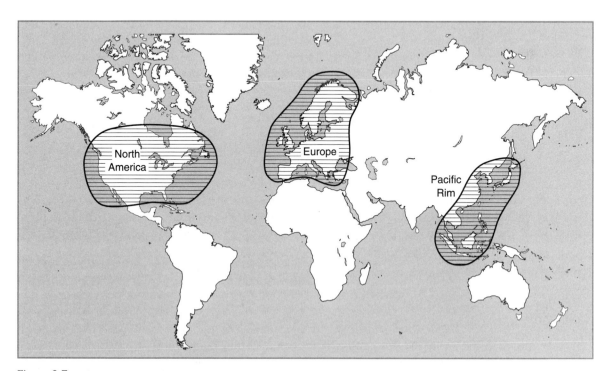

Figure 2.7　Three major trading regions.

home country or in a plant in the foreign country, typically altered to suit national regulations, needs, and tastes.

Now, however, there are global firms, joint ventures, partial ownerships, foreign subsidiaries, and other types of international producers. For example, Canon is a global producer that sells a standard "world-class" camera with options and add-ons available through the local dealer. And the "big three" American automobile producers—Ford, Chrysler, and General Motors—all own stock in foreign automobile companies. Mazak, a fast-growing machine tool company, is the U.S. subsidiary of Yamazaki Machinery Company of Japan. Part of the reason for cross-ownerships and cross-endeavors is the spiraling cost of bringing out new products. A new drug can cost $200 million to develop and bring to market. Even more expensive are new computers, at $1 billion, or new memory chips, at $4 billion for those introduced in the early 1990s. By using joint ventures and other such approaches to share costs (and thereby lower risks), firms can remain competitive.

Whether to build offshore, assemble offshore, use foreign parts, employ a joint venture, and so on is a complex decision for any firm and depends on a multitude of factors. For example, the Japanese are expanding many of their automobile manufacturing plants in the United States. The reasons are many: to circumvent U.S. governmental regulation of importers, to avoid the high yen cost of Japanese-produced products, to avoid import fees and quotas, to placate U.S. consumers, and so on. Of course, other considerations are involved in producing in foreign countries: culture (e.g., if women are part of the labor force), political stability, laws, taxes, regulations, and image.

Other complex arrangements of suppliers can result in hidden international competition. For example, many products that bear an American nameplate have been totally produced and assembled in a foreign country and are simply shipped in under the U.S. manufacturer's or retailer's nameplate, such as IBM's original Epson printers or Nike shoes. Even more confusing, many products contain a significant proportion of foreign parts, or may be composed entirely of foreign parts and only assembled in the United States (e.g., toasters, mixers, hand tools).

Operations and Global Competitiveness

Operations commonly plays a critical role in international competitiveness. Its activities are concerned with such factors as the efficiency and effectiveness of domestic production compared with outsourcing, the appropriate locations for international facilities, the output capacities needed for various plants, and the labor–machinery trade-offs in each facility. For example, in some countries there may be an excess of low-cost labor and a high cost of capital to buy equipment, so the transformation system should be designed to be labor-intensive.

In general, six primary characteristics of the transformation system are critical. Each of these can also be an area of organizational focus, as noted in an earlier section and in Table 2.1.

1. *Efficiency*: This is usually measured as output per unit of input. The problem in trying to compare different transformation systems, of course, is choosing good measures for outputs and inputs. In a store, it might be dollars of sales per square foot. In a maternity suite, it might be deliveries per day.

2. *Effectiveness*: Whereas efficiency is known as "doing the thing right," effectiveness is known as "doing the right thing." That is, is the right set of outputs being produced? Are we focused on the right task?

3. *Capacity*: Capacity, too, is different from efficiency in that it specifies the maximum rate of production that is attainable. Equipment and tools tend to significantly increase capacity, though if their cost is too high, they may reduce overall efficiency.

4. *Quality*: The output may not work well or last long, in which case we say it is of poor quality.

5. *Response time*: How quickly can the output be produced? If a custom output or a totally new output is desired, response time refers to the time needed to produce the first unit of this different output.

6. *Flexibility*: Can the transformation system be used to produce other, different outputs? How easily? How fast? What variety or level of customization can be achieved?

Operations must provide, through the transformation system, products and services that embody the factors critical to success in the market. In general, customers seek to maximize the value of their transactions; they desire the most performance for the lowest possible price. In the vast majority of global markets today, only a few factors can differentiate between producers because the other factors are relatively standard for a given product or service. For example, on-time delivery, multiple product functions, friendly service, and credit are all expected and are commonly offered by the competing suppliers; those without these order qualifiers are not even in the running.

The critical order-winning factors that are emphasized by the competing organizations are price and what we refer to as **responsiveness**: customization, quality, and response time. These factors vary in importance for each market, and the most successful organization will be closest to striking the proper balance between them.

In the next two sections we discuss these factors in detail. We start with the basic driver of the price to the customer—cost—and the role of productivity in determining the cost of a product or service. The following section moves into a discussion of responsiveness.

COST AND THE ROLE OF PRODUCTIVITY _____

Operational activities play a major role in determining the cost of a product or service, particularly during the up-front design for the output. It is commonly said that approximately 70 percent of the cost is built in at the design-engineering stage. That is, anything happening after this point can affect the cost by only about 30 percent. Thus, in the traditional functional organization, it is important for all interested parties—research and development, marketing, engineering, and especially operations—to be represented on the design team. Such integration is the foundation upon which activities are grouped together in process-centered organizations.

It is worth noting that cost to the producer and price to the customer are two very different factors. You might expect that the price would always be set greater than the cost, but in many situations it is not. For example, in a recession or an oversupply situation, a producer may dump its product on the market to salvage any revenue it can. Or a firm may try to break into a market by offering a product at a low price as a "come-on" to encourage consumers to become familiar with its brand. Or a producer may even try to capture an entire market by driving competitors out with its low prices, planning to raise prices after the competition has left the market.

Yet it is not always clear when a firm is dumping, because costs are never a clear-cut issue. First, on many occasions American firms have claimed that foreign firms were dumping when, in fact, the foreign firms were simply more efficient and were able to offer the same goods at much lower prices while still making a profit. Second, if a firm is producing one product successfully but has excess capacity on some of its resources (e.g., machines), it may be able to produce another product for simply the additional cost of the raw materials and then make a nice profit at a much lower price to the consumer. That is, the "marginal contribution" becomes the full profit, since the normally fixed expenses were available free.

Nevertheless, it is always to the producers' advantage to keep their absolute costs as low as possible. This allows them the flexibility of reducing price and still making a profit if competition moves into the market, or of making an excellent profit on a reasonable price if competition is minimal. The primary method of keeping costs low entails a concept called *productivity*, which we discuss in the remainder of this section.

Productivity Definitions and Measures

Productivity is a special measure of efficiency and is normally defined as output per worker-hour. Note that there are two major ways to increase a firm's productivity: increase the numerator (output) or decrease the denominator (worker-hours). Also, of course, productivity would increase slightly if both increased but output increased faster than worker-hours, or if both decreased but worker-hours decreased faster than output.

This definition of productivity is actually what is known as a *partial factor* measure of productivity, in the sense that it considers only worker-hours as the productive factor. Productivity could easily be increased by substituting machinery for labor, but that doesn't mean that this is a wise decision. We can also define a variety of other partial productivity measures such as capital productivity (using machine-hours or dollars invested), energy productivity (using kilowatt-hours), and materials productivity (using inventory dollars).

A *multifactor* productivity measure uses more than a single factor, such as both labor and capital. Obviously, the different factors must be measured in the same units, such as dollars. An even broader gauge of productivity, called *total factor* productivity, is measured by including *all* the factors of production—labor, capital, materials, and energy—in the denominator. This measure is to be preferred in making any comparisons of productivity.

Perhaps the best use of a productivity measure is to track changes over time. Investigating how productivity changes over time usually provides more useful managerial information than simply comparing the same measure at a specific point in time for different organizational units within the same company, or comparing the productivity of the entire organization with other organizations. Ideally, productivity should exhibit a general upward trend over time. A drop in productivity should be investigated so that corrective action can be taken if necessary.

Improving Productivity Rates

Improving productivity is important because for a society to increase its standard of living, it must first increase its productivity. Figure 2.8 shows overall productivity for several countries and Hong Kong. In Figure 2.8 productivity is calculated by dividing output (as measured by GDP or GNP) by the country's total population. Thus, productivity is measured as the dollar value (in 1990 U.S. dollars) of per capita outputs. For example, the United States produced a little more than $21,500 worth of goods and services per capita. An increase in this measure of productivity means that on average, each person in the country produced more goods and services. Figure 2.9 shows annual rates of growth in productivity. Note that although the United States currently enjoys the highest productivity, productivity has been growing almost three times as fast in Japan and Hong Kong.

How can the United States improve its productivity growth? It has been estimated that technology has been responsible for at least half of the growth in productivity in the United States between 1948 and 1966. It would appear, then, that this one approach holds the most promise for continuing increases in productivity. Technology in the past resulted in the substitution of mechanical power for human physical labor (*mechanization*). This trend is continuing even faster today, where electronic equipment is replacing human sensing skills (*automation*). We often read in magazines and newspapers about new "factories of the future" that are improving productivity and, frequently, replacing factory workers. It is not hard to imagine complex equipment doing much of the work that occupies humans in today's jobs.

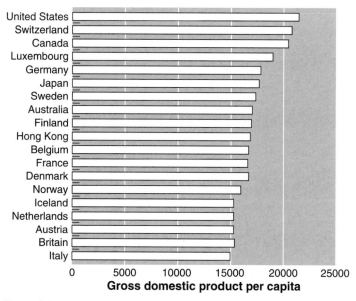

Figure 2.8 International comparisons of productivity. *Source:* "The World Economy in Charts," *Fortune*, 128(2), 1993, p. 96.

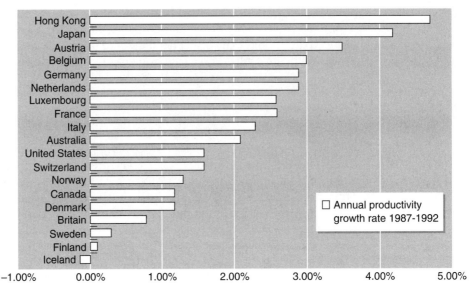

Figure 2.9   International comparisons of growth in productivity. *Source:* "The World Economy in Charts," *Fortune*, 128(2), 1993, p. 96.

We must be careful, however, not to focus solely on productivity as the problem, but rather, to consider overall competitive ability. Any solution must include quality, lead time, innovation, and a host of other such factors aimed at improving customers' satisfaction. Furthermore, since 50 to 60 percent of a typical manufacturer's cost is for materials, improved supply-chain management (covered in Chapter 9) is also critical to long-term competitiveness.

In the next section, we will look at this bigger picture of competitiveness and the various components that go into it. Productivity's major competitive impact is through cost, but this is not the only factor in a firm's competitiveness.

$\mathcal{R}$ESPONSIVENESS: CUSTOMIZATION, RESPONSE TIME, AND QUALITY

In addition to *price*, attained through productive cost reductions, the other primary factor in competitiveness is responsiveness to the needs of the customer. This concept of responsiveness goes beyond the usual order qualifiers such as meeting promised delivery dates, offering the features that are normally expected, and providing the expected after-sales service. Firms these days are winning markets by being particularly responsive to customers in terms of higher levels of customization to fit a customer's particular needs, extremely fast response to a customer's requests, and outstanding quality. We discuss each of these aspects of responsiveness next.

Customization

Customization, in the sense that we are using it, refers to offering a product or service exactly suited to a customer's desires or needs. However, many needs are relatively nonspecific, such as a toaster or an oil change for your car, and total customization is not particularly necessary or desirable. In these cases, "variety" to meet the need may be completely adequate, as long as customers get about the right kind of oil (10W–30 or 5W–40) put into the proper hole in the engine.

Thus, there is a range of accommodation to the customer's needs, as illustrated in Figure 2.10. At the left, there is the completely standard, world-class (suitable for all markets) product or service. Moving to the right is the standard with options, continuing on to variants and alternative models, and ending at the right with made-to-order customization. In general, the more customization the better, if it can be provided quickly, with acceptable quality and economy.

Advantages of Customization

To offer different levels of variety or customization requires flexibility on the part of the producer, commonly obtained through advanced technologies or particularly skilled workers. There are more than a dozen different types of flexibility that we will not pursue here—design, volume, routing through the production system, product mix, and many others. But having the right types of flexibility can offer a producer the following major competitive advantages:

- Faster matches to customers' needs because changeover time from one product or service to another is quicker
- Closer matches to customers' needs
- Ability to supply the needed items in the volumes required for the markets as they develop
- Faster design-to-market time to meet new customer needs
- Lower cost of changing production to meet needs
- Ability to offer a full line of products or services without the attendant cost of stocking large inventories
- Ability to meet market demands even if delays develop in the production or distribution process

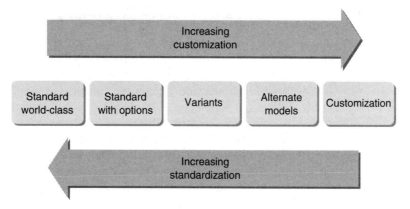

Figure 2.10   Continuum of customization.

Mass Customization

Until recently, it was widely believed that producing low-cost standard products (at the far left in Figure 2.10) required one type of transformation system and producing higher-cost customized products (far right) required another type of system. However, in addition to vast improvements in operating efficiency, an unexpected byproduct of continuous improvement programs of the 1980s was substantial improvement in flexibility. Indeed, prior to this, efficiency and flexibility were thought to be trade-offs. Increasing efficiency meant that flexibility had to be sacrificed, and vice versa.

Thus, with the emphasis on continuous improvement came the realization that increasing operating efficiency could also enhance flexibility. For example, many manufacturers initiated efforts to reduce the amount of time required to set up (or change over) equipment from the production of one product to another. Obviously, all time spent setting up equipment is wasteful, since the equipment is not being used during this time to produce outputs that ultimately create revenues for the organization. Consequently, improving the amount of time a resource is used productively directly translates into improved efficiency. Interestingly, these same reductions in equipment setup times also resulted in improved flexibility. Specifically, with shorter equipment setup times, manufacturers could produce economically in smaller-size batches, making it easier to switch from the production of one product to another.

In response to the discovery that efficiency and flexibility can be improved simultaneously and may not have to be traded off, the strategy of mass customization emerged. Organizations pursuing ***mass customization*** seek to produce low-cost, high-quality outputs in high variety. Of course, as was mentioned earlier, not all products and services lend themselves to being customized. This is particularly true of commodities such as sugar, gas, electricity, and flour. On the other hand, mass customization is often quite applicable to products characterized by short life cycles, rapidly advancing technology, or changing customer requirements. However, recent research suggests that successfully employing mass customization requires an organization to first develop a transformation system that can consistently deliver high-quality outputs at a low cost. With this foundation in place, the organization can then seek ways to increase the variety of its offerings while at the same time ensuring that quality and cost are not compromised.

In an article published in *Harvard Business Review*, James Gilmore and Joseph Pine II identified four categories of mass customization:

1. *Collaborative customizers.* These organizations establish a dialogue to help customers articulate their needs and then develop customized outputs to meet these needs. For example, purchasing eyewear is often a difficult task for the typical customer. Because these customers often have little knowledge about what type of frame will best fit their face, they are forced to try on an endless number of frames. To address this problem one Japanese eyewear retailer developed a computerized system to help customers select eyewear. The system combines a digital image of the customer's face and customers' statements about their desires and then develops a recommended lens size and shape. The recommended lens is displayed on the digital image of the customer's face. This allows the

optician and the customer to collaborate and modify the lens. The system contains similar features for selecting the nose bridge, hinges, and arms. Once the customer is satisfied, the customized glasses are produced at the retail store within an hour.

2. *Adaptive customizers*. These organizations offer a standard product that customers can modify themselves. For example, many home-improvement stores sell closet organizers. Each closet-organizer package is the same, but includes instructions and tools to cut the shelving and clothes rods so that the unit can fit a wide variety of closet sizes. Also, each customer can specify the dimensions of the various components of the closet organizer on the basis of his or her needs: some customers may want more shelf space; others may need more rod space.

3. *Cosmetic customizers*. These organizations produce a standard product but present it differently to different customers. For example, Planters packages its peanuts and mixed nuts in a variety of containers on the basis of specific needs of its retailing customers such as Wal-Mart, 7-Eleven, and Safeway.

4. *Transparent customizers*. These organizations provide custom products without the customers' knowing that a product has been customized for them. For example, an on-line computer service might track how each customer uses its service and then suggest additional features that the customer may find useful.

Example: Hewlett-Packard

Faced with increasing pressure from its customers for quicker order fulfillment and for more highly customized products, Hewlett-Packard (HP) wondered whether it was really possible to deliver mass-customized products rapidly, while at the same time continuing to reduce costs (Feitzinger and Lee 1997). On the basis of recent experiences in several of its key businesses, including computers, printers, and medical products, HP has concluded that this is indeed possible. HP's approach to mass customization can be summarized as effectively delaying tasks that customize a product as long as possible in the product supply process.

More specifically, HP's mass customization program is based on three principles:

- Products should be designed around a number of independent modules that can be easily combined in a variety of ways.

- Manufacturing tasks should also be designed and performed as independent modules that can be relocated or rearranged to support new production requirements.

- The product supply process must perform two functions. First, it must cost-effectively supply the basic product to the locations that complete the customization activities. Second, it must have the requisite flexibility to process individual customers' orders.

HP has discovered that modular design provides three primary benefits. First, components that differentiate the product can be added during the later stages of production. For example, the company designed its DeskJet printers so that country-specific power supplies are combined with the printers at local distribution centers and actually plugged in by the customer when the printer is set up. Second, production time can be significantly reduced by simultaneously producing the required modules. Third, producing in modules facilitates the identification of production and quality problems.

A primary benefit of this modular production system is that it allows HP to change the sequence in which production activities are performed. For example, HP's disk-drive division was having difficulty matching supply and demand. The problem was that customers would often change their orders at the last minute. These changes required inserting different printed circuit boards into the drive. Inserting these circuit boards into the drives did not itself create much of a problem, but the time-consuming test procedures that followed did. After adopting its modular production system, HP addressed this problem by dividing test procedures into two subprocesses. One subprocess was concerned with performing the standard tests that all disk drives undergo. The second subprocess performed all the tests required for a particular printed circuit board. By dividing the testing activities in this fashion, HP could perform all the standard tests before inserting the circuit boards and then needed to conduct unique tests only after the customers' requirements were known.

Response Time

The competitive advantages of faster response to new markets or to the individual customer's needs have only recently been noted in the business media. For example, in a recent study of the U.S. and Japanese robotics industry, the National Science Foundation found that the Japanese tend to be about 25 percent faster than Americans, and to spend 10 percent less, in developing and marketing new robots. The major difference is that the Americans spend more time and money on marketing, whereas the Japanese spend five times more than the Americans on developing more efficient production methods.

Table 2.2 identifies a number of prerequisites for, and advantages of, fast response. These include higher quality, faster revenue generation, and lower costs through elimination of overhead, reduction of inventories, greater efficiency, and fewer errors and scrap. One of the most important but least recognized advantages for managers is that by responding faster, they can allow a customer to delay an order until the exact need is known. Thus, the customer does not have to change the order—a perennial headache for most operations managers.

Faster response to a customer also can, up to a point, reduce the unit costs of the product or service, sometimes significantly. On the basis of empirical studies reported by Meredith (1994) and illustrated in Figure 2.11, it seems that there is about a 2:1 relationship between response time and unit cost. That is, starting from typical values, a 50 percent reduction in response time results in a corresponding 25 percent reduction in unit cost. The actual empirical data indicated a range between about 5:3 and 5:1, so for a 50 percent reduction in response time there could be a cost reduction from a high of 30 percent to a low of 10 percent. This is an overwhelming benefit because if corresponding price reductions are made, it improves the value delivered to the customer through both higher responsiveness and lower price. The result for the producer is a much higher market share. If the producer chooses not to reduce the price, then the result is both higher margins and higher sales, for significantly increased profitability.

$\mathcal{T}$ABLE 2.2 • Prerequisites for and Advantages of Rapid Response

1. *Sharper focus on the customer.* Faster response for both standard and custom-designed items places the customer at the center of attention.

2. *Better management.* Attention shifts to management's real job, improving the firm's infrastructure and systems.

3. *Efficient processing.* Efficient processing reduces inventories, eliminates non–value-added processing steps, smoothes flows, and eliminates bottlenecks.

4. *Higher quality.* Since there is no time for rework, the production system must be sufficiently improved to make parts accurately, reliably, consistently, and correctly.

5. *Elimination of overhead.* More efficient, faster flows through fewer steps eliminate the overhead needed to support the eliminated steps, processes, and systems.

6. *Improved focus.* A customer-based focus is provided for strategy, investment, and general attention (instead of an internal focus on surrogate measures such as utilization).

7. *Reduced changes.* With less time to delivery, there is less time for changes in product mix, engineering changes, and especially changes to the order by the customer who just wanted to get in the queue in the first place.

8. *Faster revenue generation.* With faster deliveries, orders can be billed faster, thereby improving cash flows and reducing the need for working capital.

9. *Better communication.* More direct communication lines result in fewer mistakes, oversights, and lost orders.

10. *Improved morale.* The reduced processing steps and overhead allow workers to see the results of their efforts, giving a feeling of working for a smaller firm, with its greater visibility and responsibility.

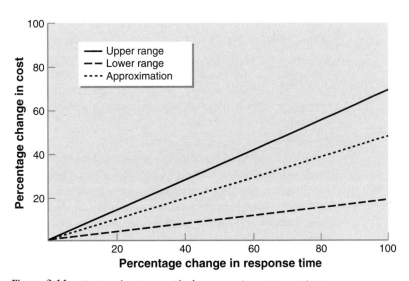

Figure 2.11   Cost reductions with decreases in response time.

Quality

In the long run, the most important single factor affecting a business unit's competitive ability is the quality of its products and services, relative to those of competitors. In the days of the craftspeople and guilds, the quality of an individual's output was *advertising*, a declaration of *skill*, and a source of *personal pride*. With the coming of the Industrial Revolution and its infinite degree of specialization and interchangeability of parts (and workers), pride in one's work became secondary to effective functioning of the individual as simply one cog in an enormous organizational system. Quite naturally, quality deteriorated and therefore had to be specifically identified and controlled as a functional aspect of the output.

This recognition of the need to specifically consider the quality of an output was given impetus during World War II, when the military adopted statistical sampling procedures through Military Standard 105. The result was a significant increase in interest in quality control in firms supplying arms and materials to the armed forces, which then spread to firms in the general economy.

In addition, this interest spread to Japan, which by the middle 1950s was producing cheap imitations of American and other foreign goods and exporting them around the world. As described in greater detail in the next chapter, this interest culminated in an invitation from Japan to W. Edwards Deming, an American expert in quality control, to come to Japan and speak on his ideas about using teams of workers to improve quality.

Defining and Measuring Quality

Quality is a relative term, meaning different things to different people at different times. Richard J. Schonberger has compiled a list of 12 dimensions that customers perceive as associated with products and services:

1. *Conformance to specifications.* Conformance to specifications is the extent to which the actual product matches the design specifications. An example of nonconformance would be a pizza delivery operation that consistently required 35 minutes or more to make and deliver pizzas when the company advertised that pizzas would be delivered in 30 minutes or less.

2. *Performance.* Surveys suggest that customers most frequently equate the quality of products and services with their performance.[3] Examples of performance include how quickly a sports car accelerates from 0 to 60 miles per hour, how good a steak tastes at a restaurant, and the range and clarity of a wireless phone.

3. *Quick response.* Quick response is associated with the amount of time required to react to customers' demands. Examples of quick response include travel agencies that can produce boarding passes at the time airline reservations are made, mail-order catalogs that ship from inventory overnight, automobile manufacturers that can design a new model in less than three years, and fire and rescue services that are on the scene within minutes of a 911 call.

---

[3]Spencer Hutches, Jr., "What Customers Want: Results of ASQC/Gallop Survey," *Quality Progress* (February 1989), pp. 33–35.

4. *Quick-change expertise.* Examples of quick-change expertise include a 10-minute oil change, a motorcycle assembly line that can switch over and make any model with little or no delay, and costume and set changes in the theater.

5. *Features.* Features are the attributes that a product or service offers. Examples of features include a videocassette recorder with on-screen programming, side impact airbags in automobiles, and a salad bar with more than 50 ingredients.

6. *Reliability.* Reliability is the probability that a product or service will perform as intended on any given trial or the probability that a product will continue to perform for some period of time. Examples of reliability are the probability that a car will start on any given morning, and the probability that a car will not break down in less than four years.

7. *Durability.* Durability refers to how tough a product is. Examples of durability include a notebook computer that still functions after being dropped, watches that are waterproof 100 meters underwater, and a knife that can cut through steel and not need sharpening.

8. *Serviceability.* Serviceability refers to the ease with which maintenance or a repair can be performed. A product for which serviceability is important is a copier machine. (Have you ever been in an office when the copier was down?)

9. *Aesthetics.* Aesthetics are factors that appeal to human senses. Aesthetic factors associated with an automobile, for instance, include its shape, its color, and the sound of its engine.

10. *Perceived quality.* Quality is not an absolute but, rather, is based on customers' perceptions. Customers' impressions can be influenced by a number of factors, including brand loyalty and an organization's reputation.

11. *Humanity.* Humanity has to do with how the customer is treated. An example of humanity is a private university that maintains small classes so students are not treated like numbers by the professors.

12. *Value.* The value of a product or service relates to how much of the preceding 11 dimensions of quality customers get relative to what they pay. The value dimension of quality suggests that enhancing one or more of the dimensions of quality does not automatically lead to perceived higher quality. Rather, enhancements of quality are evaluated by customers relative to their effect on cost.

It is worth noting that not all the dimensions of quality are relevant to all products and services. Thus, organizations need to identify the dimensions of quality that are relevant to the products and services they offer. Market research about customers' needs is the primary input for determining which dimensions are important. Once the important dimensions have been determined, how the organization and its competitors rate on these dimensions should be assessed. If an organization rates lower on a given dimension than the competition, it can either try to improve on that dimension or attempt to shift customers' attitudes so that the customers will place more emphasis on the dimensions the organization rates highest on. Of course, measuring the quality of a service can often be more difficult than measuring the quality of a product or facilitating good. However, the dimensions of quality apply to both.

Benefits of High Quality

Many benefits are associated with providing products and services that have high quality. Obviously, customers are more pleased with a high-quality product or service. They are more apt to encourage their friends to patronize the firm, as well as giving the firm their own repeat business. Top quality also establishes a reputation for the firm that is very difficult to obtain in any other manner, and it allows the firm to charge a premium price. This was verified in the Profit Impact of Market Strategy (PIMS) study conducted by the Strategic Planning Institute: it was found that high-quality products and services were not only the most profitable but also garnered the largest market shares.

High quality also tends to protect the firm from competition, which may have to offer competing outputs at an especially low price (with correspondingly low margins) in order to stay in business. It enhances the attractiveness of follow-up products or services so that their chances of success are much improved. And, of course, high quality minimizes risks to safety and health and reduces liability.

High quality has implications for production as well. If quality is built into the production system, it improves workers' morale, reduces scrap and waste, smooths work flows, improves control, and reduces a variety of costs. As a result, Philip Crosby, a well-known quality consultant, and others state that "quality is free." Crosby estimates that firms are losing up to 25 percent of the amount of their sales because of poor quality. Similarly, the American Society for Quality Control estimates that for U.S. products and services, poor quality consumes between 15 and 35 cents of every sales dollar. By comparison, the corresponding figure for Japanese products is between 5 and 10 cents. A study conducted by Ken Matson of Litton's Industrial Automation Systems Division verified these estimates, finding that the annual cost of nonconformance in quality, by itself, was about 14 cents for every dollar of equipment assets.

Clearly, the link between quality and productivity can be mutually beneficial. The traditional view was that improvements in quality come at the expense of lower productivity. However, Japanese companies have demonstrated that improvements in quality usually lead to improvements in productivity. To draw an analogy, if you try to work faster on a mathematics test, you are likely to make more errors. This is the case in production too, but it depends on what has been invested up front to improve overall quality. For instance, if processes have been simplified and improved, workers and machines can work both faster and with fewer errors. Analogously, a student with a solid understanding of both math principles and the operation of a calculator can work faster on a math test than one with limited knowledge of the functioning of a calculator. Further, a calculator solves much more complicated problems than can be done by hand.

EXPAND YOUR UNDERSTANDING _____

1. It is said that a firm's strategic plan is the one locked in the safe. Contrast this concept with that of the strategic plan as a series of decisions made by the firm over time.

2. Is there any commonality in the three generic strategies of low cost, differentiated product or service, and niche position?

3. Is it wise for a firm to stick to what it knows best, or should it expand its market by moving into adjoining products or services? How can it avoid losing its focus?

4. With regard to the Rolm Telecommunications example, do you think that perfect quality, or at least a significantly higher level of quality, is expected more in services than in products?

5. Can you think of any other areas of possible focus for a firm besides those identified in Table 2.1?

6. How might the addition of equipment to a production system *lower* efficiency? What does this say about replacing labor with equipment to increase productivity?

7. What types of outputs do *not* require high quality?

8. According to K. Blanchard and N. V. Peale (*The Power of Ethical Management,* New York: Morrow, 1988), the following three ethical tests may be useful: (1) Is it legal or within company policy? (2) Is it balanced and fair in the short and long term? (3) Would you be proud if the public or your family knew about it? Apply these tests to the following situations:

   a. A foreign firm subsidizes its sales in another country.

   b. A foreign firm dumps its products (sells them for less than cost) in another country.

   c. A country imports products that, had they been made domestically, would have violated domestic laws (e.g., laws against pollution).

9. Why do Americans invest more in marketing new products while the Japanese invest more in engineering? What advantages accrue to each investment?

10. Where might the cost savings in faster response to a customer's need come from?

11. Which of the 12 dimensions of quality typifies a meal in a gourmet restaurant? A CD player? A surgical operation?

12. What is your reaction to Sara Lee's "de-verticalize" strategy? What is Sara Lee implying about its core competency?

APPLY YOUR UNDERSTANDING
Kateland Metropolitan University

Kateland Metropolitan University (KMU) was chartered as a state university in 1990. The university opened its doors in 1994 and grew rapidly during its first three years. By 1997, the enrollment reached just over 9300 students. However, with this rapid growth came a number of problems. For example, because the faculty had to be hired so quickly, there was no real organization. Curriculum seemed to be decided on the basis of which adviser a student happened to consult. The administrative offices resembled "organizational musical chairs," with vague responsibilities and short tenures.

The faculty of the Business School was typical of the confusion that gripped the entire university. The 26 faculty members were mostly recent graduates of Ph.D. programs at major universities. There were 21 assistant professors and instructors, 3 associate professors, and 2 full professors. In addition, funds were available to hire 3 additional faculty members, either assistant or associate professors. The newly recruited dean of the Business School was recently promoted to associate professor after five years of teaching at a large northeastern university.

Upon arriving at the Business School, the dean asked the faculty to e-mail their concerns to her so that she could begin to get a handle on the major issues confronting the school. Her office assistant selected the following comments as representative of the sentiments expressed.

"Our student–teacher ratio is much higher than what it was at my former university. We need to fill those open slots as quickly as possible and get the provost to fund at least two more faculty positions."

"If we don't get the quality of enrollments up in the MBA program, the Graduate School will never approve our application for a Ph.D. program. We need the Ph.D. program to attract the best faculty, and we need the Ph.D. students to cover our courses."

"Given that research is our primary mission, we need to fund more graduate research assistants."

"The travel budget isn't sufficient to allow me to attend the meetings I'm interested in. How can we improve and maintain our visibility if we get funding for only one to two meetings per year?"

"We need better secretarial support. Faculty members are required to submit their exams for copying five days before they are needed. However, doing this makes it difficult to test the students on the material covered in class right before the exam, since it's difficult to know ahead of time exactly how far we will get."

"I think far too much emphasis is placed on research. We are here to teach."

"Being limited to consulting one day a week is far too restrictive. How are we supposed to stay current without consulting on a more frequent basis?"

"We need a voice mail system. I never get my important messages."

Questions

1. What do the comments by the faculty tell you about KMU's strategy?

2. What would you recommend the dean do regarding the Business School's strategic planning process? What role would you recommend the dean play in this process?

3. Productivity is defined as the ratio of output (including both goods and services) to the input used to produce it. How could the productivity of the Business School be measured? What would the effect be on productivity if the professors all received a 10 percent raise but continued to teach the same number of classes and students?

BIBLIOGRAPHY

Crosby, P. B. *Quality Is Free: The Art of Making Quality Certain.* New York: McGraw-Hill, 1979.

Feitzinger, E., and H. L. Lee. "Mass Customization at Hewlett-Packard: The Power of Postponement." *Harvard Business Review* (January–February 1997): 116–121.

Ferdows, K., ed. *Managing International Manufacturing.* New York: North-Holland, 1989.

Gilmore, J. H., and B. J. Pine II. "The Four Faces of Mass Customization." *Harvard Business Review* (January–February 1997): 91–101.

Hammonds, K. H., N. Harris, and B. Koenig. "Medical Lessons from the Big Mac." *Business Week* (February 19, 1997): 94.

Hayes, R. H., and G. P. Pisano. "Beyond World-Class: The New Manufacturing Strategy." *Harvard Business Review* (January–February 1994): 77–86.

Hill, T. *Manufacturing Strategy: Text and Cases.* Homewood, Ill.: Irwin, 1989.

Jonas, N. "The Hollow Corporation." *Business Week* (March 3, 1986): 57–85.

Kaplan, R. S., and D. P. Norton. *The Balanced Scorecard.* Boston: Harvard Business School Press, 1996.

Mehl, W. "Strategic Management of Operations: A Top Management Perspective." *Operations Management Review* (Fall 1983): 29–40.

Meredith, J. R., D. M. McCutcheon, and J. Hartley. "Enhancing Competitiveness Through the New Market Value Equation." *International Journal of Operations and Production Management*, vol. 14, no. 11: 7–21.

Miller, J. P., "Sara Lee Plans 'Fundamental Reshaping.'" *The Wall Street Journal* (September 16, 1997): A3, A10.

Pare, T. "The Big Threat to Big Steel's Future." *Fortune* (July 15, 1991): 104–108.

Philllips, M. M. "Surging American Economy May Mean the Dollar Will Continue Rising." *The Wall Street Journal* (June 15, 1998): A2, A8.

Pine, B. J., II, B. Victor, and A. C. Boynton. "Making Mass Customization Work." *Harvard Business Review* (September–October 1993): 108–119.

Porter, M. E. ed. *Competition in Global Industries.* Boston: Harvard Business School Press, 1986.

Prahalad, C. K., and G. Hamel. "The Core Competence of the Corporation." *Harvard Business Review* (May–June 1990): 79–91.

Rose, R. L., and C. Quintanilla. "Sare Lee's Plan to Contract Out Work Underscores Trend among U.S. Firms." *The Wall Street Journal* (September 17, 1997): A3.

Schoeberger, R. J. *Building a Chain of Customers.* New York: Free Press, 1990.

Skinner, W. *Manufacturing: The Formidable Competitive Weapon.* New York: Wiley, 1985.

Skinner, W. "The Productivity Paradox." *Harvard Business Review* (July–August 1986): 55–59.

Wessel, D. "With Labor Scarce, Service Firms Strive to Raise Productivity." *The Wall Street Journal* (June 1, 1989): A1, A16.

Zachary, G. P. "Service Productivity Is Rising Fast—and So Is the Fear of Lost Jobs." *The Wall Street Journal* (July 8, 1995): A1, A10.

Quality Management

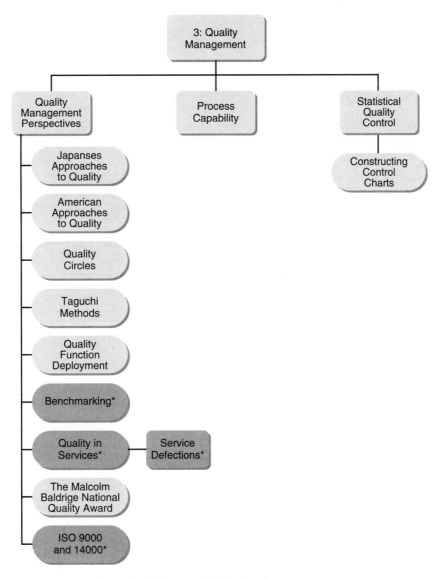

* More heavily shaded sections indicate especially timely topics.

This chapter discusses one of the most important ways operational activities support the business strategy and enhance competitiveness: through quality management. The chapter begins with a discussion of quality costs and trade-offs. Next, the philosophies of the leading quality experts are presented, with an overview of the most widely used quality programs, awards, and certifications. Last, we describe how to use statistical quality control techniques to control the quality of outputs. We include brief discussions of inspection, sampling, process control, and control charts for both variables and attributes.

$\mathcal{I}$NTRODUCTION

- In 1991, the West Babylon school district of Long Island, New York, began applying continuous improvement and quality to its administrative and education processes. The objectives of these initiatives were to affirm the district's commitment to providing high-quality education, to emphasize the importance of lifelong learning, and to provide students with opportunities to take pride in their work. Given these objectives, the district adopted the term *total quality education* (TQE) to describe the initiatives. Initially, the district's superintendent and board of education agreed to apply W. Edwards Deming's "14 Points for Management" to the administration process. To facilitate this, the superintendent attended quality training programs taught by two of the leading experts in quality management, Joseph Juran and Deming himself. Numerous improvements were made throughout the district, ranging from creating more appealing lunch menus to placing less emphasis on exams to changing students' report cards in order to better evaluate actual learning (Manley and Manley 1996).

- National Semiconductor was an early proponent of total quality. Its first quality circles were created in 1981; it began a preventive maintenance program in 1982; it began using statistical process control in 1983; it used design of experiment techniques in 1984; and in 1986 it implemented design for manufacturing techniques. In the 1990s, National Semiconductor initiated a second stage of total quality by submitting an application to be considered for the Malcolm Baldrige National Quality Award. During its second stage, National Semiconductor focused its attention on customer–supplier relationships, customers' satisfaction, developing scorecards for customers, analyzing its processes, empowering its employees, and developing team strategies, problem-solving techniques, and "visioning." Also, National Semiconductor worked on becoming ISO 9000–certified during this period. In its third and current stage, National Semiconductor is focusing on becoming a learning organization. In this phase the company is concerned with concepts such as personal mastery, shared vision, systems thinking, and team learning (Rau 1995).

- NCR's plant in West Columbia, South Carolina, produces business information processing systems. With competition increasing, NCR recognized the necessity of continuously improving its products through the use of statistical techniques. The NCR plant began using statistical process control techniques in 1985 to monitor its autoinsertion operation on its assembly line for printed circuit boards, which was producing an unacceptable number of defective boards. As part of the quality assurance program, the quality engineering department established process averages, control limits, and guidelines for action for "out-of-control" conditions where production would stop until the cause was identified. Random samples of 1000 insertions were collected each hour, and the results of the sample were plotted on a c chart. NCR learned a great deal about the autoinsertion operation from using the control charts. For example, the problem of broken parts was traced to a specific supplier. Because this experiment was a success, statistical process control was implemented across the entire assembly line. NCR has since changed its approach from "inspect and repair" to "prevent and design for quality" (Dobbins and Padgett 1993).

- As a result of environmental restrictions and reduced quantities of high-quality large-diameter trees, timber companies have used a number of statistical quality control techniques to maximize the quality and quantity of finished lumber produced from each tree. The cut lumber stacking and drying operation provides a good illustration of how sawmills are using statistical quality control. This operation is particularly important because the way the boards are stacked determines the straightness of the finished lumber. Separators are placed between the layers of stacked wood to form an air channel that carries heat to the wood and allows moisture to move away from it.

  Because automated equipment is used to stack the lumber, it is important to monitor the alignment of the separators. To illustrate, it is estimated that each misplaced separator increases costs $31.50, owing to board warping. Because an average sawmill handles upward of 30,000 separators each day, the annual cost of misplacing just 1 percent of the separators would exceed $2.3 million. To monitor separator alignment, the total number of misplaced separators is divided by the total number of separators in the stack of lumber. Plotting this result on a p chart, workers can monitor the stacking equipment and identify problems before an out-of-control situation arises so that corrective action can be initiated (Maki and Milota 1993).

Chapter 2 ended with a brief discussion of quality as a factor in international competitiveness. Because of its direct link to competitiveness, quality management is clearly one of the most timely topics in business today, as the introduction illustrates. Furthermore, quality management is applicable to all organizations, whether they exist to make a profit (National Semiconductor), or are nonprofit organizations (West Babylon school district), and whether or not a tangible output is produced.

In this chapter we build on the material in Chapter 2 related to the important role of quality in competitiveness and discuss quality management in greater detail. We first note the costs and trade-offs involved with quality and trying to improve quality. We then describe a number of Japanese and American quality philosophies, programs, and awards. Following this, we turn our attention to the capabilities of the production process and some classic techniques for controlling the quality of the outputs, known as *quality control* or sometimes statistical process control (SPC).

QUALITY MANAGEMENT PERSPECTIVES

An often neglected point of significant importance in marketing is that customers are frequently willing to pay for excellent quality. In the traditional view it was thought that products and services of excellent quality would translate into higher costs. Of course this view neglects the negative consequences of gaining a reputation for producing shoddy outputs. Also, the Japanese have demonstrated across numerous industries that it is often possible to improve quality and lower costs at the same time. One explanation for this phenomenon is that it is simply cheaper to do a job right the first time than to try to fix it or rework it later. Philip B. Crosby, an author and expert on quality, expressed this view in the title of a book, *Quality Is Free*, which sold approximately 1 million copies.

Two primary sets of costs are involved in quality: control costs and failure costs. The aggregate of these costs runs between 15 and 35 percent of sales for many U.S. firms. Traditionally, these costs are broken down into four categories, as shown in Table 3.1: prevention costs, appraisal costs, internal costs of defects, and external costs of defects. The first two costs are incurred in attempting to control quality, and the last two are the costs of failing to control quality. Costs of defects (or nonconformance) can run from 50 to 90 percent of the total cost of quality.

We will overview some of the more common quality programs here and describe their benefits. Before doing so, however, let us first look more closely at the difference between traditional attitudes toward quality in American and Japanese management.

Japanese Approaches to Quality

Although you might think that "made in Japan" signifies a product of superior quality, it may surprise you to learn that many of the techniques and philosophies Japanese companies employ today were actually developed in the United States, usually around the end of World War II. Unfortunately, the sentiment among domestic manufacturers at the end of World War II was that they already produced the highest-quality products in the world at the lowest cost. Thus, they were not particularly interested in or concerned with improving quality.

Japan was an entirely different story. Its products had a reputation for poor quality, and after it lost the war its economy was a shambles. As a result, Japanese manufacturers were eager for help related to quality improvement. In 1950 the Japanese government invited W. Edwards Deming (then a professor at New York University) to give a series of lectures on quality control to help Japanese engineers reindustrialize the country. But Deming insisted that the heads of the

$\mathcal{T}$ABLE 3.1 • Four Categories of Quality Costs

Category 1: Prevention costs. These costs are incurred in the process of trying to prevent defects and errors from occurring. They consist of such elements as
- Planning the quality control process
- Training for quality
- Educating the firm's suppliers
- Designing the product for quality
- Designing the production system for quality
- Preventive maintenance

Category 2: Appraisal costs. These are the costs of determining the current quality of the production system. They consist of factors such as
- Measuring and testing parts and materials
- Running special test laboratories
- Acquiring special testing equipment
- Conducting statistical process control programs
- Receiving inspection
- Reporting on quality

Category 3: Internal costs of defects. These costs are incurred when defects and errors are found before shipment or delivery to the customer. They consist of elements such as
- Labor and materials that go into scrap
- Engineering change notices
- Reworking and retesting to correct defects
- Lost profits on downgraded products and services
- Lost yield from malfunctioning equipment or improperly trained workers
- Downtime of equipment and labor sitting idle while waiting for repairs
- Expediting to get orders of appropriate quality delivered on time

Category 4: External costs of defects. These are the costs of trying to correct defects and errors after receipt by the customer. They include items such as
- Quick response to complaints
- Adjustments to correct the problem
- Lost goodwill
- Recalls to correct the problem for other customers
- Warranties, insurance, and settlements of lawsuits

companies attend the talks too. As a result, the top Japanese managers were also invited, and they all showed up.

According to Deming, the major cause of poor quality is *variation*. Thus, a key tenet of Deming's approach is to reduce variability in the manufacturing process. Deming stressed that improving quality was the responsibility of top management. However, he also believed that all employees should be trained in the use of problem-solving tools and especially statistical techniques. Perhaps the contribution that Deming is most associated with is his *14 Points*, summarized and illustrated in Table 3.2.

Deming believed that improvements in quality created a chain reaction. Accordingly, improved quality leads to lower costs, which then translate into higher productivity. The resulting better quality and lower prices lead to increased market

$\mathcal{T}$ABLE 3.2 • Application of Deming's 14 Points to Services

The table illustrates how the West Babylon school district and a law firm applied Deming's 14 Points to their operations. West Babylon was discussed at the beginning of the chapter. The law firm—Turner, Padget, Graham, and Laney—operates a general trial practice and employs 41 lawyers. Its offices are located in three cities in South Carolina. Not only do these examples illustrate the applicability of Deming's 14 Points to service-oriented organizations, but they also illustrate the applicability of the points to nonprofit organizations.

Deming's 14 Points	School District	Law Firm
1. Create a constancy of purpose toward improvement of product and service, with a plan to become competitive, stay in business, and provide jobs.	Developed a mission statement for the school district.	Committed to quality for long term.
2. Adopt the new philosophy. We can no longer live with commonly accepted levels of delays, mistakes, defective materials, and defective workmanship.	Cross-functional teams set up as quality circles.	Recognized a need for better management.
3. Cease dependence on mass inspection. Require, instead, statistical evidence that quality is built in to eliminate the need for inspection on a mass basis.	Less emphasis on exams.	Emphasized quality of inputs (e.g., staff) and improved processes (e.g., research, filing, billing).
4. End the practice of awarding business on the basis of price tags. Instead, depend on meaningful measures of quality, along with price.	Suppliers who delivered poor quality were taken off list of bidders.	Applied this to purchases of computer systems and office supplies.
5. Improve constantly and forever the system of production and service, to improve quality and productivity, and thus constantly decrease costs.	Quality circles continued to work toward improving the delivery of services.	Improved all processes, measured them by maintaining records, and reduced variation.
6. Institute modern methods of training.	Quality circle used to help select training materials. Teachers trained in use of new classroom technologies.	Improved training material and facilities. Reduced amount of job training by coworkers.
7. Institute modern methods of supervision.	All supervisors received training five times a year on advanced techniques in cooperative supervision. Emphasis was that leading means helping others do their jobs better.	Managed more by coaching and mentoring.
8. Drive out fear so that everyone may work effectively for the company.	Developed new solutions and encouraged experimentation.	Made staff feel secure. Didn't manage by fear.
9. Break down organization barriers—everyone must work as a team to foresee and solve problems.	Superintendent's quality council created with representatives from personnel, student services, testing, finance, transportation, and lunch programs.	Created teams of partners, associates, secretaries, and support staff.
10. Eliminate arbitrary numerical goals, posters and slogans for the work force, which seek new levels of productivity without providing the methods.	Transportation staff was given responsibility for reducing waste and accidents.	Provided employees with the means, including training and equipment, to do the job.
11. Eliminate work standards and numerical quotas.	Bell-shaped curve was not used to force grade distribution.	Placed less emphasis on billable hours. Rewarded employees for client services.

$\mathscr{T}$ABLE 3.2 • (continued)

Deming's 14 Points	School District	Law Firm
12. Remove barriers that rob employees of pride of workmanship.	Focused on how to prevent defects, not fix them after the fact.	Improved communications. Recognized that staff wanted to do a good job.
13. Institute a vigorous program of education and training.	Teachers received regular training in computer technology and multimedia technology.	Emphasized education and training. Trained staff on teamwork and problem solving.
14. Create a structure that will push 13 prior points every day.	Each semester, employees developed one to three goals and a plan to accomplish these goals.	Management pushed plans and vision.

Sources: Deming, W. Edwards. *Quality, Productivity, and Competitive Position* (Cambridge, Mass.: MIT, Center for Advanced Engineering Study, 1982), pp. 16–17. Manley, R. and J. Manley. "Sharing the Wealth: TQM Spreads from Business to Education." *Quality Progress* (June 1996), pp. 51–55. Blodget, N. "Law Firm Pioneers Explore New Territory." *Quality Progress* (August 1996), pp. 90–94.

share. Higher market share means that the company can stay in business and create more jobs.

Deming promised the Japanese that if they followed his advice, they would be able to compete with the West within just a few years. They did! Now the most prestigious industrial quality award given in Japan each year is named the Deming Prize.

The Deming Prize was established in 1950 and is still administered by the Japanese Union of Scientists and Engineers (JUSE). The prize is actually a medal and is used to recognize organizations that have excelled in total quality management (TQM). It is open to all organizations regardless of their national origin.

The Deming Prize is based on the following 10 criteria:

1. *Policies and objectives:* the methods used to develop policies and objectives, the use of statistical methods, and the implementation and assessment of objectives

2. *Operation of the organization:* whether lines of responsibility are clearly defined, how well activities are delegated, the extent to which divisions cooperate with one another, and the use of quality circles

3. *Education:* the educational plans, the education of workers and suppliers in statistical methods, the activities of quality circles, and how well a suggestion system is used

4. *Information management:* information-gathering activities, the dissemination of information throughout the organization, and the speed with which information is collected and used

5. *Analysis:* the methods that are used to select problems, the analytical tools used to solve these problems, and the organization's openness to suggestions for improvement

6. *Standardization:* the methods used to adopt and update standards, the actual content of the standards, the use of the standards, and the record keeping associated with maintaining standards

7. *Control:* the organization's quality control systems, the use of statistical methods, the location of control points in the process, the items that are controlled, and activities of quality circles related to control

8. *Quality assurance:* the procedures for developing new products, ensuring product safety, process design, use of statistical methods, and issues related to measurement and inspection

9. *Results:* the visible and the invisible results obtained; also, the gap between predicted and actual results is assessed

10. *Future plans:* the organization's plans for promoting quality in the future and the relationship between short-range and long-range planning

But the Japanese did not stop there. They tied the concept of quality control directly into their production system—and now they have even tied it into their entire economy through inspections to guarantee the quality of exports. The natural inclinations of Japanese culture and traditions were exploited in this quality crusade:

- Quality circles (described shortly), were based on natural teamwork procedures and individual workers' responsibility for results. Behavioral and attitudinal factors were considered of primary importance in improving quality levels.

- Extensive training for all levels of workers, as well as suppliers, helped instruct them in the use of quality control procedures.

- Cross-training and job rotation were used to demonstrate the importance of quality.

- Lifetime employment made clear the necessity of living with the product's reputation.

- The disinclination to store unneeded materials fostered the development of just-in-time operations, which furthered the quality concept through immediate inspection, processing, and use. If a product was defective, that was immediately clear.

- Patience was exercised in testing and checking components extensively before installing them in products—and then in taking the time to check the products again before shipping them to customers.

After nearly two decades of a national emphasis on quality, Japan's reputation for producing shoddy goods was totally reversed. And, when high quality is combined with competitive pricing—another strength of the Japanese system—the result is extremely strong competition for existing producers.

American Approaches to Quality

A number of programs and awards, some successful and some unsuccessful, have been instituted in the United States over the years to help improve quality. Typical of such programs is "zero defects," a program developed in the aerospace industry in 1962. This program attempted to prevent errors by eliminating their cause, rather than remedying them after they had been made.

However, Philip Crosby, another quality advocate, suggested that zero defects was the only meaningful performance standard and the cost of quality (including the cost of nonconformance) the only performance measure. To Crosby, quality meant not elegance but conformance to requirements. He believed that a problem with quality did not exist per se, but, rather, that the organization had functional problems. Crosby also argued that it was always more cost-effective to perform an activity right the first time. In contrast to Deming, Crosby focused more on management, organizational processes, and changing corporate culture than on the use of statistical techniques.

A more recent concept, similar to zero defects that the Japanese and some American firms have embraced, is called *total quality management* (TQM) or *total quality control* (TQC). The basic idea of TQM is that it is extremely expensive to "inspect" quality into a company's outputs and much more efficient and effective to produce them right in the first place. As a result, responsibility for quality has been taken away from the quality control department and placed where it belongs— with the workers who produce the parts or provide the service in the first place. This is called *quality at the source*. It is the heart of *statistical quality control* (SQC), sometimes called *statistical process control* (SPC)—programs being implemented in many firms in the United States today—and described more fully in a later section of this chapter.

The beginning of TQM dates back to the 1930s, when Dr. W. A. Shewart began using statistical control at the Bell Institute. In fact, both Juran and Deming were students of Shewart's. In 1951 Juran wrote the *Quality Control Handbook*, which was considered by many to be the "bible" of quality and continues to be a useful reference to this day. In 1954 Juran made his first trip to Japan. In 1956 Japan adopted quality as its national slogan.

In contrast to Deming, Juran tended to work more within the existing system rather than trying to effect major cultural changes. Also, at the top management level, Juran focused more on quality cost accounting and Pareto analysis than on statistical techniques of process control. Finally, Juran's definition of quality was "fitness for use," whereas Deming never offered a specific definition.

Just as Deming is probably best remembered for his 14 points, Juran is probably best remembered for his *quality trilogy*:

1. *Quality planning.* This is the process of preparing to meet quality goals. During this process customers are identified and products that meet their needs are developed.

2. *Quality control.* This is the process of meeting quality goals during operations. Quality control involves five steps: (1) deciding what should be controlled, (2) deciding on the units of measure, (3) developing performance standards, (4) measuring performance, and (5) taking appropriate actions based on an analysis of the gap between actual and standard performance.

3. *Quality improvement.* This encompasses the activities directed toward achieving higher levels of performance.

Juran suggested that organizations typically progress through four quality phases. In the first phase, organizations seek to minimize their prevention and appraisal costs. However, because a large number of defects are produced, these organizations incur large external failure costs. To alleviate this problem, the organization increases its appraisal costs in the second phase. This effectively lowers the shipment of defects but increases internal failure costs because defects are discovered earlier. Typically, however, overall total quality costs decrease. In the third phase the organization introduces process control, thereby increasing its appraisal costs but lowering internal and external failure costs even more. Finally, in the fourth phase, the organization increases prevention costs in an effort to decrease total quality costs once again.

In the early 1950s, military standards were developed for quality and applied to the aerospace industry and at nuclear facilities. The objective of these military standards was to make sure that prescribed manufacturing procedures were followed and to establish procedures for inspecting parts. In 1952 the concept of *quality assurance* was proposed. Its proponents argued that in contrast to quality control, which relies on inspection, quality assurance is better because it develops a system that can produce high-quality products in the first place. Quality control and TQM are further contrasted in Table 3.3.

Although each organization may have its own definition of TQM, most definitions include the notion that all employees are responsible for *continuously* improving the quality of the organization's products and services. Thus, the word *total* is meant to signify that the quality of the organization's outputs is the concern of all employees. Furthermore, because competition is a moving target, continuous improvement programs that provide a steady stream of incremental improvements to the current business processes are an important component of TQM. In general, TQM typically includes the following five steps:

1. Determining what the customers want
2. Developing products and services that meet or exceed what the customers want (and even "delight" the customers)
3. Developing a production system that permits doing the job right the first time
4. Monitoring the system and using the accumulated data to improve the system
5. Including customers and suppliers in this process

$\mathcal{T}$ABLE 3.3 • Quality Control versus TQM

Quality Control	Total Quality Management
Inspection after the fact	Design quality into the product and production system
Focus on consequences of poor quality	Focus on identifying and eliminating causes of poor quality
Customer is purchaser	Customer is user
Some number of defects is normal	Goal is zero defects
Responsibility for quality control assigned to individuals or departments	Quality is the responsibility of everyone
Improving quality increases cost	Improving quality typically pays for itself

Quality Circles

Traditionally, the Japanese tend to work together in teams for production, so team analysis was a natural way to attack production problems. These teams, known as quality circles, focus not solely on quality but on all problems facing the workers and are often a key component of an organization's continuous improvement program. The first *quality circles* were created in Japan in 1957 and in the United States in 1974. Circles are composed of natural work groups and range from a few employees to more than a dozen. In some firms, the concept is not limited to shop workers but includes the clerical staff and even the managers. A trained facilitator usually leads the circle, perhaps the supervisor or even a coworker or team leader. The circle spends a couple of hours a week, usually on company time, analyzing and discussing its problems and brainstorming solutions. It then works on implementing the solutions on the job. An important element of the problem analysis is a set of continuous improvement tools and skills that are taught to the employees. Some of these are illustrated in Figure 3.1 and described as follows.

- *Process analysis*: This is basically a flow chart of how a system or process works, showing inputs, operations, and outputs. By depicting the process visually, the workers can often spot the source of a problem they are facing, or identify where more information is needed to solve a problem.

- *Run chart*: This graph shows how a variable has changed over time. By analyzing the data points, an operator can determine if the operation is doing what it is supposed to do. There may be excessive variation in the data, a disturbing trend, or random unacceptable points.

- *Control chart*: By putting control limits on a chart of sample data, the operator can determine if the operation or activity is out of control or experiencing natural variation. However, the natural variation may still not be acceptable, so that a better or improved operation may be needed to reduce variation to acceptable limits.

- *Pareto chart*: This chart, a type of bar chart, is based on a natural tendency for the *majority* of problems to be due to a *minority* of causes. Typically, 80 percent of the symptoms (problems) are due to 20 percent of the causes. By concentrating on the primary problems, most of the difficulties can be resolved.

- *Histogram*: This type of bar chart shows the statistical frequency distribution of a variable of interest. From this chart it can be determined how often some variable is "too low" or "too high" and whether further action is required.

- *Scatter diagram*: These charts show the correlation between two variables and can be used for problem investigation. If defects occur primarily on days when the temperature is over 50° C, for instance, the temperature-sensitive aspects of the operation (including the workers) should be looked into.

- *Fishbone chart*: A fishbone chart is also known as a cause–effect diagram. It lays out the process as a convergence of activities that result in the final product, or event. Major activity lines are plotted along the result line, and minor activities that make up the major activities are plotted as short lines

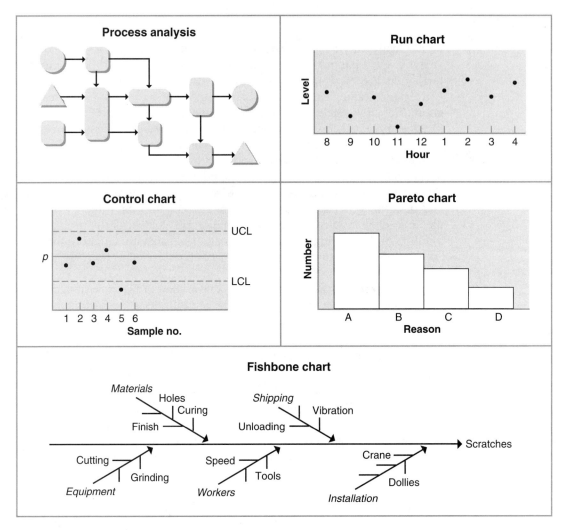

Figure 3.1   Tools for continuous improvement

along the major lines. The result looks like a fishbone. As with the process flow chart, the source of problems can often be identified on the basis of events and inputs in the diagram.

A good example of the use of a fishbone diagram is illustrated by the West Babylon school district, where it was widely perceived by the teachers that insufficient time was being spent covering the curriculum. To help understand and analyze the problem, a quality circle developed a fishbone chart. A simplified version of the fishbone chart developed by the team is shown in Figure 3.2.

- *Presentation skills*: Not all the training for circles involves charts. Attention is also paid to facilitating good communication and presenting analyses clearly, both orally and in writing.

- *Analysis skills*: Time is also spent teaching the workers about the concepts of statistical quality control and the collection and analysis of data. Collecting

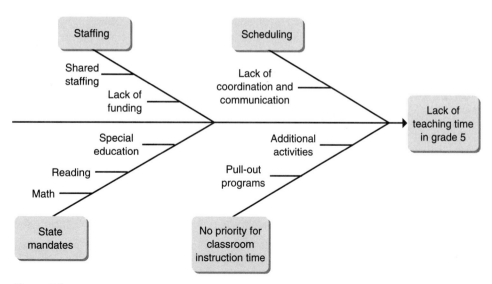

Figure 3.2 Fishbone diagram to analyze problem of insufficient time being spent covering the curriculum.
Source: Adapted from Manley, R. and J. Manley. "Sharing the Wealth: TQM Spreads from Business to Education." *Quality Progress* (June 1966), pp. 51–55.

invalid data, or making inferences on inappropriate information, can be more damaging than helpful.

- *Brainstorming*: Finally, time is spent training the employees how to brainstorm and use other methods of attacking problems.

Taguchi Methods

Most of the quality of products and services is built in at the design stage, and the production system can affect it only slightly. Genichi Taguchi has focused on this fact to develop an approach to designing quality into outputs. Rather than trying to constantly control machinery and workers to stay within specifications—sizes, finishes, times—he has devised a procedure for statistical testing to determine the best combination of product design and transformation system design to make the output relatively independent of normal fluctuations in the production system.

To do this, statistical experimentation is conducted to determine what product and transformation system designs produce outputs with the highest uniformity at lowest cost. Interestingly, the Japanese use the Taguchi method primarily in product design, whereas Americans use the method primarily in design of the production system. Obviously, this is more an engineering procedure than an operations approach, and we will not pursue it in detail here.

Quality Function Deployment

As we noted earlier, the TQM approach involves developing products and production systems to meet customers' specific requirements. *Quality function deployment* (QFD) is a powerful tool for helping to translate customers' desires directly into attributes of products and services. It involves all functions of the firm in translating the customer's needs into specific technical requirements for each stage of output and production system design: from research and development to engineering to operations to marketing to distribution. In this manner, outputs are delivered to the customer faster, with better quality, and at lower cost. We discuss QFD in greater detail in Chapter 4, where we describe the design of the product or service output in more detail.

Benchmarking

In conjunction with their efforts to improve products and key processes, many organizations are engaging in a relatively new activity called **benchmarking**. Essentially, benchmarking involves comparing an organization's performance with the performance of the best.

Benchmarking generally involves three steps. The first step is concerned with preparing for the benchmarking study. In this phase it is important to get the support of senior management and its input on what should be benchmarked. Problem areas, activities related to serving the customer better, and activities related to the mission of the organization are all appropriate candidates for inclusion in the benchmarking study.

The second phase of benchmarking consists of collecting data. There are two general sources of benchmarking data. One source is *published data*. These are often available from universities, financial filings (e.g., 10k reports), consultants, periodicals, trade journals, and books. The other source of data is *original research* conducted by the organization itself. If this approach is employed, a list of organizations to benchmark might include companies that have recently received quality awards or other business awards, are top-rated by industry analysts, have been the subject of recent business articles, or have a track record of superior financial performance. Once the companies have been identified, data can be collected in a variety of ways including interviews, site visits, and surveys.

The third and final phase of benchmarking involves using what has been learned to improve organizational performance. Once the second phase has been completed, identified gaps in performance can be used to set challenging but realistic goals (often called *stretch goals*). Also, the results of the benchmarking study can be used to overcome and eliminate complacency within the organization.

Quality in Services

Measuring the quality of the service portion of an output is often more difficult than measuring the quality of the facilitating good for a variety of reasons—including the service portion being abstract rather than concrete, transient rather than permanent, and psychological rather than physical. One way to cope with these difficulties is to use customer satisfaction surveys. For example, J. D. Power and Associates makes extensive use of customer satisfaction surveys to rate domestic airlines, upscale hotels, and rental car companies[1]. To rate the performance of domestic

---

[1]Source: *http://www.jdpower.com*, June 21, 1998.

airlines, J. D. Power relies on the opinions of seasoned travelers that average 27 round trips per year. According to these travelers, on-time performance is the single most important factor, accounting for 22 percent of overall satisfaction with a domestic flight. Other important factors include flight accommodations (15%), airport check-in (15%), seating comfort (12%), gate location (9%), and aircraft interior (7%). In 1998, TWA received the highest ranking in the long flight category, and America West was ranked highest in the short flight category.

J. D. Power ranks upscale hotels and rental car companies in a similar fashion. For example, in 1998 J. D. Power ranked the overall satisfaction of 11 upscale hotels on the basis of 8,067 individual evaluations of these hotels. According to the results, guests of upscale hotels consider satisfaction with the guest room to be the most important factor, accounting for 28 percent of overall satisfaction. Other important factors include satisfaction with the arrival process (20%), the ratio of price to value (19%), hotel services (13%), departure process (12%), and food and beverages (8%). In 1998, Renaissance was the highest ranked upscale hotel. In terms of rental car companies, in 1998 National, Hertz, and Avis all tied for first place.

A common approach to improving the quality of services is to methodically train the employees in standard procedures and to use equipment that reinforces this training. The ultimate example is McDonald's Hamburger University, where managers, in particular, are intensively trained in McDonald's system of food preparation and delivery. Not only is training intensive, but follow-up checkups are continuous, and incentives and rewards are given for continuing to pay attention to quality. Furthermore, the equipment is designed to reinforce the quality process taught to the employee, and to discourage sloppy habits that lead to lesser quality.

The value of better quality is becoming known in office processes as well (Berstein 1991). For example, University Microfilms Inc. (UMI) of Ann Arbor, Michigan, was facing a growing backlog of requests for theses: 8000. Upon investigation, UMI found that the average thesis waits 150 days for processing but is processed only for a total time of two hours; much of the time is spent waiting for the author to reply to questions. By working on the quality of its editing and processing techniques, UMI cut the time in half within six months; it is now down to 60 days. As a result, customers' complaints were reduced by 17 percent and output increased by almost 50 percent with the same people.

Financial services can also benefit from better quality. Several years ago, First National Bank of Chicago noticed that its requests for letters of credit were handled by nine different employees who conducted dozens of steps, a process that consumed four days. By retraining its employees so that each would be able to process a customer's request through all the steps, First Chicago was able to let each customer deal with only one employee, who could complete the process within a day. Now each time a letter of credit is ordered, the customer is placed back with the same employee. As a result, the department involved has been able to double its output of letters of credit using the services of 49 percent fewer employees.

By paying attention to the quality delivered to customers, American Express was able to cut the processing time for new credit applications from 22 days to 11 days, thereby more than doubling the revenue per employee in its credit card division. It had previously tracked errors and processing time internally but had ignored the impacts on the customer. When it began focusing on the customer, it suddenly found that speed in the credit department was often immaterial in shortening the customer's waiting time for credit approval, because four more departments still had to process every new application.

Service Defections

When a tangible product is produced, quality is often measured in terms of defects. In services, the analogy to a product defect is a defecting customer—that is, a customer who takes his or her business elsewhere. Thus, service defections can be measured in a variety of ways, such as the percent of customers that do not renew their membership (health clubs), percent of sales from new versus repeat customers (office supply store), and the number of customers that cancel their service (long-distance phone companies). Of course, the concept of a defecting customer is equally applicable to organizations that produce tangible outputs.

Organizations should monitor their defecting customers for a number of reasons. First, research suggests that longtime customers offer organizations a number of benefits. For example, the longer a customer has a relationship with an organization, the more likely that customer is to purchase additional products and services and the less price-sensitive they are. In addition, no advertising is necessary to get the business of long-term customers. In fact, long-term customers may actually be a source of free advertising for the company. One study published in *Harvard Business Review* concluded that cutting defections in half more than doubles the average company's rate of growth. Likewise, improving customer retention rates by 5 percent can double profits.

Defections by customers can provide a variety of useful information. First, feedback obtained from defecting customers can be used to identify areas that need improvement. Also, the feedback can be used to determine what can be done to win these customers back. Finally, increases in the defection rate can be used as an early warning signal.

The Malcolm Baldrige National Quality Award

In response to Japan's Deming Prize, in 1987 the United States established the Malcolm Baldrige National Quality Award. The award is given in three categories: manufacturing, service, and small business. Also, up to two organizations may receive the award in each category each year. The 1997 criteria for the award are summarized in Table 3.4.

ISO 9000 and 14000

Unlike the Deming Prize or the Baldrige Award, ISO 9000 is not an award for which companies must compete. Rather, ISO 9000 was developed as a guideline for designing, manufacturing, selling, and servicing products. In fact, in contrast to the Deming Prize and the Baldrige Award, which recognize organizations for excellent performance, ISO 9000 is intended as more of a checklist of good business practices. Thus, the intent of the ISO 9000 standard is that, if an organization selects a supplier that is ISO 9000–certified, it has some assurance that the supplier follows accepted business practices in the areas specified in the standard.

𝒯ABLE 3.4 • Criteria for the Malcolm Baldrige Award of 1997

Category	Items	Point Values	
1	**Leadership**		**110**
1.1		Leadership System	80
1.2		Company Responsibility and Citizenship	30
2	**Strategic Planning**		**80**
2.1		Strategy Development Process	40
2.2		Company Strategy	40
3	**Customer and Market Focus**		**80**
3.1		Customer and Market Knowledge	40
3.2		Customer Satisfaction and Relationship Enhancement	40
4	**Information and Analysis**		**80**
4.1		Selection and Use of Information and Data	25
4.2		Selection and Use of Comparative Information and Data	15
4.3		Analysis and Review of Company Performance	40
5	**Human Resource Development and Management**		**100**
5.1		Work Systems	40
5.2		Employee Education, Training, and Development	30
5.3		Employee Well-Being and Satisfaction	30
6	**Process Management**		**100**
6.1		Management of Product and Service Processes	60
6.2		Management of Support Processes	20
6.3		Management of Supplier and Partnering Processes	20
7	**Business Results**		**450**
7.1		Customer Satisfaction Results	130
7.2		Financial and Market Results	130
7.3		Human Resource Results	35
7.4		Supplier and Partner Results	25
7.5		Company-Specific Results	130
TOTAL POINTS			**1000**

Source: http://www.quality.nist.gov/docs/97_crit/itemlist.htm, December 18, 1996.

However, one criticism of ISO 9000 is that it does not require any specific actions, and therefore each organization determines how it can best meet the requirements of the standard.

ISO 9000 was developed by the International Organization for Standardization and first issued in March 1987. Since that time, it has become the most widely recognized standard in the world. To illustrate its importance, in 1993 the European Community required that companies in several industries become certified as a condition of conducting business in Europe. The ISO 9000 standard consists of 20 elements (standards), which are summarized in Table 3.5.

ISO 14000 is a series of standards covering environmental management systems, environmental auditing, evaluation of environmental performance, environmental labeling, and life-cycle assessment. Like ISO 9000, ISO 14001 (a subset of the ISO

$\mathscr{T}$ABLE 3.5 • Elements of ISO 9000

1. Management responsibility	12. Inspection and test status
2. Quality system	13. Control of nonconforming product
3. Contract review	14. Corrective and preventive action
4. Design control	15. Handling, storage, packaging, preservation, and delivery
5. Document and data control	
6. Purchasing	16. Control of quality audits
7. Control of customer-supplied product	17. Internal quality audits
8. Product identification and traceability	18. Training
9. Process control	19. Servicing
10. Inspection and testing	20. Statistical techniques
11. Control of inspection, measuring, and test equipment	

14000 series) is a standard in which organizations can become certified. The focus of ISO 14001 is on an organization's environmental management system. However, like ISO 9000, ISO 14001 does not prescribe specific standards for performance or levels of improvement. Rather, its intent is to help organizations improve their environmental performance through documentation control, operational control, control of records, training, statistical techniques, and corrective and preventive actions.

DILBERT ©United Feature Syndicate. Reprinted with permission.

$\mathscr{P}$ROCESS CAPABILITY

To maintain the quality of their output, organizations must inspect and test throughout their operations. Both machines and humans can start to deteriorate and begin producing defects. As a machine wears out, for example, its process capability may degrade to the point that it cannot hold the tolerances specified by engineering design. Figure 3.3 illustrates this situation.

With the advent of total quality management programs and their emphasis on "making it right the first time," organizations are becoming increasingly concerned with the ability of a production system to meet design specifications rather than evaluating the quality of products after the fact with acceptance sampling. Process

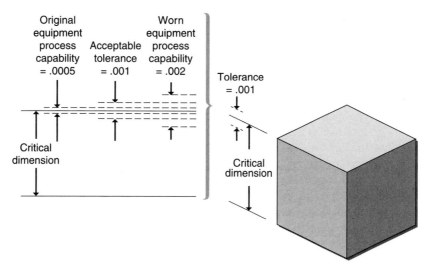

Figure 3.3   Engineering tolerance versus process capability.

capability measures the extent to which an organization's production system can meet design specifications. As shown in Figure 3.4, process capability depends on:

1. Location of the process mean
2. Natural variability inherent in the process
3. Stability of the process
4. Product's design requirements

In Figure 3.4*a* the natural variation inherent in the process and the product's design specifications are well matched, resulting in a production system that is consistently capable of meeting the design requirements. However, in Figure 3.4*b* the natural variation in the production system is greater than the product's design requirements. This will lead to the production of a large amount of product that

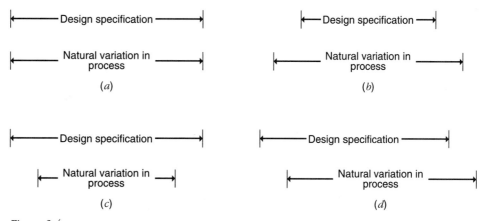

Figure 3.4   Natural variation in a production system versus product design specifications.

does not meet the requirements: the production system simply does not have the necessary ability. Options in this situation include improving the production system, relaxing the design requirements, or producing a large quantity of product that is unfit for use.

In Figure 3.4c the situation is reversed: the product has wider design specifications than the natural variation inherent in the production system. In this case the production system is easily able to meet the design specifications, and the organization may choose to investigate more economical production systems in order to lower costs. Finally, although the widths of design specifications and process variation are equal in Figure 3.4d, their means are out of sync. Thus, this system will produce a fair amount of output above the upper specification limit (USL). In this situation the solution would be to shift the process mean to the left so that it is better aligned with the design specifications.

More formally, the relationship between the natural variation in the production system and the product's design specifications can be quantified using a ***process capability index***. The process capability index C_p is typically defined as the ratio of the width of the product's design specification to 6 standard deviations of the production system. Six standard deviations for the production system is used because 3 standard deviations above and below the production system's process mean will include 99.7 percent of the possible production outcomes, assuming that the output of the production system can be approximated with a normal distribution. Mathematically, the process capability index is calculated as

$$C_p = \frac{\text{product's design specification range}}{6 \text{ standard deviations of the production system}} = \frac{\text{USL-LSL}}{6\sigma}$$

where LSL and USL are a product's lower and upper design specification limits, respectively, and σ is the standard deviation of the production system.

According to this index, a C_p of less than 1 indicates that a particular process is not capable of consistently meeting design specifications; a C_p greater than 1 indicates that the production process is capable of consistently meeting the requirements. As a rule of thumb, many organizations desire a C_p index of at least 1.5 (Evans and Lindsay 1996). However, a recent trend is the pursuit of ***six sigma quality***, providing a C_p index of 2.0 and yielding only 3.4 defective parts per million.

Figure 3.5 illustrates the effect that changes in the natural variation of the production system have on the C_p index for fixed product design specifications. In Figure 3.5a the natural variation in the process is much less than the product's design specification range, yielding a C_p index greater than 1. In contrast, in Figure 3.5b the natural variation in the process is larger than the product's design specifications, yielding a C_p index less than 1. Finally, in Figure 3.5c the natural process variation and the design specifications are equal, yielding a C_p index equal to 1.

One limitation of the process capability index is that it only compares the magnitudes of the product's design specification range and the process's natural variation. It does not consider the degree to which these ranges are actually aligned. For example, the situations shown in Figure 3.4a and Figure 3.4d both yield a C_p index of 1. However, as was pointed out earlier, a considerable

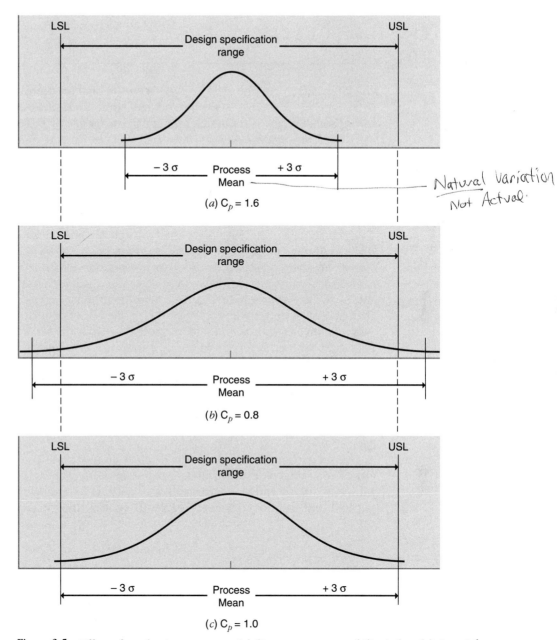

Figure 3.5 Effect of production system variability on process capability index. (*a*) C_p = 1.6; (*b*) C_p = 0.8; (*c*) C_p = 1.0.

amount of defective product would be produced in the situation shown in Figure 3.4*d*, owing to the lack of alignment between the design specifications and the process mean. Although beyond the scope of this book, we note that one way to evaluate the extent to which the process mean is centered within the product's design specification range is to calculate a one-sided process capability index.

STATISTICAL QUALITY CONTROL

One of management's most difficult decisions in quality control centers on whether an activity needs adjustment. This requires some form of inspection, either *measuring* something or simply determining the *existence* of a characteristic. Measuring, called *inspection for variables*, usually relates to weight, length, temperature, diameter, or some other variable that can be *scaled*. Identifying a characteristic, called *inspection of attributes*, can also examine scaled variables but usually considers *dichotomous* variables such as right–wrong, acceptable–defective, black–white, timely–late, and other such characteristics that either cannot be measured or do not *need* to be measured with any more precision than yes–no.

Walter A. Shewhart developed the concept of statistical **control charts** in the 1920s to distinguish between *chance variation* in a system and variation caused by the system's being out of control—*assignable variation*. Should a process go out of control, that must first be detected, then the assignable cause must be identified, and finally the appropriate action or adjustment must be performed. The control chart is used to detect when a process has gone out of control.

A repetitive operation will seldom produce *exactly* the same quality, size, and so on; rather, with each repetition the operation will generate variation around some average. This variation is particularly characteristic of a sampling process where random samples are taken and a sample mean is calculated, as in quality control. Because this variation usually has a large number of small, uncontrollable sources, the pattern of variability is often well described by a standard frequency distribution such as the *normal distribution*, shown plotted against the vertical scale in Figure 3.6.

The succession of measures that result from the continued repetition of some process can thus be thought of as a *population* of numbers, normally distributed, with some mean and standard deviation. As long as the distribution remains the same, the process is considered to be in control and simply exhibiting chance

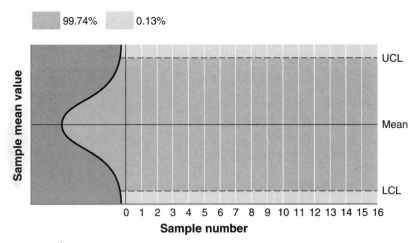

Figure 3.6   Control chart with the limits set at 3 standard deviations.

variation. One way to determine if the distribution is staying the same is to keep checking the mean of the distribution—if it changes to some other value, the operation may be considered to be out of control. The problem, however, is that it is too expensive for organizations to keep constantly checking operations. Therefore, *samples* of the output are checked instead.

In sampling output for inspection, it is imperative that the sample fully *represent* the population being checked; therefore, a *random sample* should be used. But when checks are made only of sample averages, rather than 100 percent of the output, there is always a chance of selecting a sample with an unusually high or low mean. The problem facing the operations manager is thus to decide what is *too high* or *too low* and therefore should be considered out of control. Also, the manager must consider the fact that the more samples eventually taken, the higher the likelihood of accidentally selecting a sample with too high (or too low) a mean *when the process is actually still under control.*

The values of the mean that are too high or low are called the **upper control limit** (UCL) and the **lower control limit** (LCL), respectively. These limits generally allow an approach to control that is known as *management by exception,* since, theoretically, the manager need take no action unless a *sample mean* exceeds the control limits. The control limits most commonly used in organizations are plus and minus *3 standard deviations.* We know from statistics that the chance that a sample mean will exceed 3 standard deviations, in either direction, due simply to chance variation, is less than 0.3 percent (i.e., 3 times per 1000 samples). Thus, the chance that a sample will fall above the UCL or below the LCL because of natural random causes is so small that this occurrence is strong evidence of assignable variation. Figure 3.6 illustrates the use of control limits set at 3 standard deviations. Of course, using the higher limit values (3 or more) increases the risk of not detecting a process that is only slightly out of control.

An even better approach is to use control charts to predict when an out-of-control situation is likely to occur rather than waiting for a process to actually go out of control. If only chance variation is present in the process, the points plotted on a control chart will not typically exhibit any pattern. On the other hand, if the points exhibit some systematic pattern, this is an indication that assignable variation may be present and corrective action should be taken.

The control chart, though originally developed for quality control in manufacturing, is applicable to all sorts of repetitive activities in any kind of organization. Thus, it can be used for services as well as products, for people or machines, for cost or quality, and so on.

For the control of variables—that is, measured characteristics—two control charts are required:

1. Chart of the *sample means* ($\overline{X}$)
2. Chart of the *range* (R) of values in each sample (largest value in sample minus smallest value in sample)

It is important to use two control charts for variables because of the way in which control of process quality can be lost. To illustrate this phenomenon we will use the data supplied in Table 3.6, which correspond to weights of tacos made at a fast-food restaurant. Three samples are taken each day: one during the lunch-hour rush, one during the dinner-hour rush, and one a couple of hours before the

$\mathcal{T}$ABLE 3.6 • Sample Data of Weights
of Tacos (Ounces)

Sample	Scenario 1	Scenario 2
1	$\bar{X} = 5$ ← 4, 5, 6 → $R = 2$	5, 4, 6 $\bar{X} = 5$ $R = 2$
2	$\bar{Y} = 7$ ← 6, 7, 8 → $R = 2$	3, 5, 7 $\bar{X} = 5$ $R = 4$
3	$\bar{X} = 8$ ← 7, 9, 8 → $R = 2$	8, 2, 5 $\bar{X} = 5$ $R = 6$

restaurant is closed. Each sample consists of three tacos randomly selected from a bin that stores completed tacos waiting to be sold to customers.

Referring to scenario 1, we can easily determine that the average of sample 1 is 5 ounces and the range is 2 ounces ($\overline{X}_1 = 5$, $R_1 = 2$). Similarly, $\overline{X}_2 = 7$, $R_2 = 2$, $\overline{X}_3 = 8$, and $R_3 = 2$. If we consider only the ranges of the samples, no problem is indicated, because all three samples have a range of 2 (assuming that a range of 2 ounces is acceptable to management). On the other hand, the behavior of the process means shows evidence of a problem. Specifically, the process means (weights) have increased throughout the day from an average of 5 ounces to an average of 8 ounces. Thus, for the data listed in scenario 1, the sample ranges indicate acceptable process performance while the sample means indicate unacceptable process performance.

The sample statistics can be calculated in the same way for scenario 2: $\overline{X}_1 = 5$, $R_1 = 2$, $\overline{X}_2 = 5$, $R_2 = 4$, $\overline{X}_3 = 5$, and $R_3 = 6$. In contrast to scenario 1, the sample means show acceptable performance while the sample ranges show possibly unacceptable performance. Thus, we see the necessity of monitoring both the mean and the variability of a process.

Figure 3.7 illustrates these two patterns of change in the distribution of process values more formally. These changes might be due to boredom, tool wear, improper training, the weather, fatigue, or any other such influence. In Figure 3.7a the variability in the process remains the same but the mean changes (scenario 1); this effect would be seen in the means ($\overline{X}$) chart but not in the range (R) chart. In Figure 3.7b the mean remains the same, but the variability tends to in-

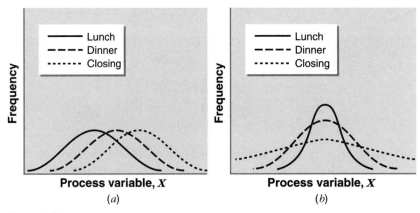

Figure 3.7   Patterns of change in process distributions.

crease (scenario 2 above); this would be seen in the range (R) chart but not the means ($\overline{X}$) chart.

In terms of quality of the output, either type of change could result in lower quality, depending on the situation. Regarding control limits, the lower control limit (LCL) for the means chart may be negative, depending on the variable being measured. For example, variables such as profit and temperature can be negative, but variables such as length, diameter, and weight cannot. Since (by definition) the range can *never* be negative, if calculations indicate a negative LCL for the range chart, it should simply be set to zero.

As indicated earlier, control limits for the means chart are usually set at plus and minus 3 standard deviations. But if a range chart is also being used, these limits for the means chart can be found by using the average range, which is directly related to the standard deviation, in the following equations (where $\overline{\overline{X}}$ is the average of the sample means):

$$\mathrm{UCL}_{\overline{X}} = \overline{\overline{X}} + A_2\,\overline{R}$$
$$\mathrm{LCL}_{\overline{X}} = \overline{\overline{X}} - A_2\overline{R}$$

Similarly, control limits for the range chart are found from:

$$\mathrm{UCL}_R = D_4\overline{R}$$
$$\mathrm{LCL}_R = D_3\overline{R}$$

The factors A_2, D_3, and D_4 vary with the sample size and are tabulated in Table 3.7. To better illustrate the concept of using means and range charts to control quality, consider the following example.

TABLE 3.7 • Control Chart Factors to Determine Control Limits

Sample Size, n	A_2	D_3	D_4
2	1.880	0	3.267
3	1.023	0	2.575
4	0.729	0	2.282
5	0.577	0	2.115
6	0.483	0	2.004
7	0.419	0.076	1.924
8	0.373	0.136	1.864
9	0.337	0.184	1.816
10	0.308	0.223	1.777
12	0.266	0.284	1.716
14	0.235	0.329	1.671
16	0.212	0.364	1.636
18	0.194	0.392	1.608
20	0.180	0.414	1.586
22	0.167	0.434	1.566
24	0.157	0.452	1.548

Constructing Control Charts

Perhaps the best way to illustrate the construction of control charts is by example. For example, assume a chain of 10 ice cream stores is interested in monitoring the age of the ice cream served at its stores. To maintain a continuing check on this quality, one could select stores at random from the chain each day and note the age of the ice cream served. To set up the control charts, initial samples need to be taken. This data will, if considered by management to be representative, be used to set standards (i.e., control limits) for future ice cream inventory. For our example, we assume that a sample of $n = 4$ of the 10 stores each day will give the best control for the trouble involved.

The mean age and range in ages for the initial samples were entered into the spreadsheet shown in Table 3.8. Note that each sample mean and sample range shown in Table 3.8 is based on data collected by randomly visiting four stores. The

$\mathcal{T}$ABLE 3.8 • Mean and Range of Ages of Ice Cream

	A	B	C
1		Sample	Sample
2	Date	Mean	Range
3	June 1	10	18
4	June 2	13	13
5	June 3	11	15
6	June 4	14	14
7	June 5	9	14
8	June 6	11	10
9	June 7	8	15
10	June 8	12	17
11	June 9	13	9
12	June 10	10	16
13	June 11	13	12
14	June 12	12	14
15	June 13	8	13
16	June 14	11	15
17	June 15	11	11
18	June 16	9	14
19	June 17	10	13
20	June 18	9	19
21	June 19	12	14
22	June 20	14	14
23	Average	11	14

$$\overline{\overline{x}}_T \qquad \overline{R}_T$$

grand mean $(\bar{\bar{X}})$, and the average range $(\bar{R})$ were also calculated (cells B23 and C23, respectively). The grand $(\bar{\bar{X}})$ mean is then simply the average of all the daily means:

$$\bar{\bar{X}} = \frac{\Sigma \bar{X}}{N}$$

where N is 20 days of samples and the average range is:

$$\bar{R} = \frac{\Sigma R}{N}$$

The data in Table 3.8 can now be used to construct control charts that will indicate to management any sudden change, for better or worse, in the quality (age) of the ice cream. Both a chart of means, to check the age of the ice cream being served; and a chart of ranges, to check consistency among stores should be used. The grand mean and average range will give the center line on these charts, respectively. The values of A_2, D_3, and D_4 are obtained from Table 3.7 for $n = 4$, resulting in the following control limits:

$$\text{UCL}_{\bar{X}} = 11 + 0.729\,(14) = 21.206$$
$$\text{LCL}_{\bar{X}} = 11 - 0.729\,(14) = 0.794$$
$$\text{UCL}_R = 2.282\,(14) = 31.948$$
$$\text{LCL}_R = 0\,(14) = 0$$

The control charts for this example were developed using a spreadsheet and are shown in Figures 3.8 and 3.9. In addition, the data in Table 3.8 are graphed on the

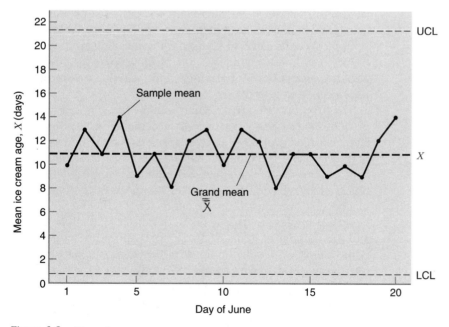

Figure 3.8   Mean ice cream age.

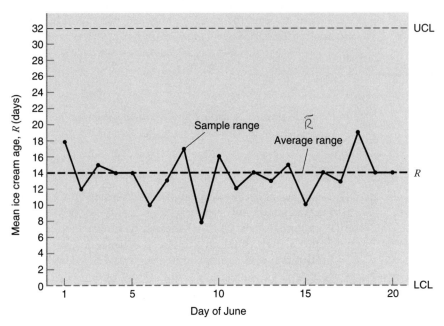

Figure 3.9   Range in ice cream age.

charts. As seen in Figure 3.8, no pattern is apparent from the data; the points appear to fall randomly around the grand mean (centerline) and thus are considered by management to be representative.

The range chart, Figure 3.9, again shows no apparent pattern and is also acceptable to management. Each day, as a new sample is taken, $\overline{X}$ and R will be calculated and plotted on the two charts. If either $\overline{X}$ or R is outside the LCL or UCL, management must then undertake to find the assignable cause for the variation.

Control charts can also be used for controlling attributes of the output. The most common of these charts are the *fraction-defective p chart* and the *number-of-defects c chart.* As with the range chart, the lower control limit for attribute charts can never be negative.

The fraction-defective p chart can be used for any two-state (*dichotomous*) process such as heavy versus light, acceptable versus unacceptable, on-time versus late, or placed properly versus misplaced (see the timber example at the beginning of the chapter). The control chart for p is constructed in much the same way as the control chart for $\overline{X}$. First, a large sample of historical data is gathered, and the fraction (percent) having the characteristic in question (e.g., too light, defective, misplaced), $\overline{p}$, is computed on the entire set of data as a whole.

Large samples are usually taken because the fraction of interest is typically small and the number of items in the samples should be large enough to include some of the defectives. For example, a fraction defective may be 3 percent or less. Therefore, a sample size of 33 would have to be taken (i.e., $1/0.03 = 33$) to expect to include even one defective item. Note that the data used to *derive* the control chart does not have to use the same size sample as is collected to use the chart. *Any* set of data can be used to determine $\overline{p}$.

Since the fraction defective follows a *binomial* distribution (bi means "two": either an item is or it is not) rather than a normal distribution, the standard deviation may be calculated directly from $\bar{p}$ as

$$\sigma_p = \sqrt{\frac{\bar{p}\,(1-\bar{p})}{n}}$$

where n is the uniform sample size to be used for controlling quality. Although the fraction defective follows the binomial distribution, if $\bar{p}$ is near 0.5, or n is "large" (greater than 30 or so), the normal distribution is a good approximation and the control limits of $3\sigma_p$ will again represent 99.7 percent of the sample observations. Again, the LCL cannot be negative.

The number-of-defects c chart is used for a single situation in which any number of incidents may occur, each with a small probability. Typical of such incidents are scratches in tables, fire alarms in a city, typesetting errors in a newspaper, and the number of improper autoinsertions per printed circuit board (see NCR example at the beginning of the chapter). An average number of incidents, $\bar{c}$, is determined from combined past data by dividing the total number of incidents observed by the number of items inspected. The distribution of such incidents is known to follow the *Poisson distribution* with a standard deviation of

$$\sigma_c = \sqrt{\bar{c}}$$

Again, the normal distribution is used as an approximation to derive control limits with a minimum LCL of zero.

EXPAND YOUR UNDERSTANDING

1. How is quality handled differently in service firms and product firms? Does quality mean something different in a service firm?

2. Suppose a firm has identified the most cost-effective level of quality for its product, and any higher quality would make it unprofitable. Yet, it is occasionally unsafe at its current quality level. Discuss the ethical issues facing the firm.

3. If a plastic imitation cannot be distinguished from the real thing, what difference does it make?

4. Under what kinds of circumstances might an organization wish to use control limits of 2 standard deviations or even 1 standard deviation? What should it bear in mind when using these lower limits?

5. Why are two control charts not necessary in controlling for attributes? Might not the variability of the fraction defective or the number of defects also be going out of control?

6. It is generally not appropriate to apply control charts to the same data that were used to derive the mean and limits. Why? What are the two possible outcomes if this is done, how likely is each, and what are the appropriate interpretations?

7. In deriving the p chart, why can the sample size vary? What must be remembered if the p chart is applied to a different sample size each time?

8. Firms regularly employ a taster for drinkable food products. What is the purpose of this taster?

9. What is meant by six sigma quality?

10. Are all quality management programs aimed at improving quality in the same way? How do they differ in their focus?

APPLY YOUR UNDERSTANDING _____

Officetech, Inc.

Officetech, Inc., produces office equipment for small businesses and home offices. Several months ago it launched its PFS 1000, a single unit that functions as a color printer, color scanner, color copier, and fax machine. The PFS 1000 won rave reviews for its functionality, affordable price, and innovative design. This, coupled with Officetech's reputation for producing highly reliable products, quickly led to a severe backlog. Officetech's plant simply could not keep up with demand.

Initially, Officetech's CEO, Nancy Samuelson, was extremely concerned about the backlog and put a great deal of pressure on the plant manager, George Johnson, to increase production. However, Nancy abruptly shifted gears when a new report indicated that returns and complaints for the PFS 1000 were running four times higher than the usual industry rate. Because Officetech's reputation was on the line, Nancy decided that the problem required immediate attention. She also decided that the quickest way to diagnose the problem and to avoid the usual mentality of "blaming it on the other department" would be to bring in an outside consultant with expertise in these matters.

Nancy hired Ken Cathey to investigate the problem. Nancy and Ken agreed that Ken should spend his first week interviewing key personnel in an effort to learn as much about the problem as possible. Because of the urgency of the problem, Nancy promised Ken that he would have complete access to—and the cooperation of—all employees. Nancy would send out a memo immediately informing all employees that they were expected to cooperate and assist Ken in any way they could.

The next morning, Ken decided to begin his investigation by discussing the quality problem with several of the production supervisors. He began with the supervisor of the final assembly area, Todd Allision. Todd commented:

> I received Nancy's memo yesterday, and frankly, the problem with the PFS 1000 does not surprise me. One of the problems we've had in final assembly is with the casing. Basically, the case is composed of a top and a bottom. The problem that we are having is that these pieces rarely fit together, so we typically have to force them together. I'm sure this is adding a lot of extra stress on the cases. I haven't seen a breakdown on what the problems with quality are, but it wouldn't surprise me if one of the problems was cracked cases or cases that are coming apart. I should also mention that we never had this problem with our old supplier. However, when purchasing determined that we could save over $1 per unit, we switched to a new supplier for the cases.

The meeting with Todd lasted for about 1½ hours, and Ken decided that rather than meet with someone else, he would be better off reviewing the notes he had taken and filling in any gaps while the conversation was still fresh in his mind. Then he would break for lunch and meet with one or two additional people in the afternoon.

After returning from lunch, Ken stopped by to talk with Steve Morgan, the production supervisor for the printed circuit boards. Ken found Steve and an equipment operator staring at one of the auto-insertion machines used to place components such as integrated circuits, capacitors, and resistors on the printed circuit board before wave soldering. Arriving, Ken introduced himself to Steve and asked, "What's up?" Steve responded:

> We are having an extremely difficult time making the printed circuit boards for the PFS 1000. The designers placed the components closer together than this generation of equipment was designed to handle. As a result, the leads of the components are constantly being bent. I doubt that more than 25 percent of the boards have all their components installed properly. As a result, we are spending a great deal of time inspecting all the boards and reworking the ones with problems. Also, because of the huge backlog for these boards and the large number that must be reworked, we have been trying to operate the equipment 20 percent faster than its normal operating rate. This has caused the

machine to break down much more frequently. I estimate that on a given eight-hour shift, the machine is down one to two hours.

In terms of your job—to determine the cause of the problems with quality—faulty circuit boards are very likely a key contributor. We are doing our best to find and correct all the defects, but inspecting and reworking the boards is a very tedious process, and the employees are putting in a lot of extra hours. In addition, we are under enormous pressure to get the boards to final assembly. My biggest regret is that I didn't have more input when they were building the prototypes of the PFS 1000. The prototypes are all built by highly trained technicians using primarily a manual process. Unfortunately, the prototypes are built only to give the engineers feedback on their designs. Had they shown some people in production the prototypes, we could have made suggestions on changes that would have made the design easier to produce.

Ken decided to end the day by talking to the plant manager, Harvey Michaels. Harvey was in complete agreement with Todd and Steve and discussed at length the enormous pressure he was under to get product out the door: "The bottom line is that no one cooperates. Purchasing changes suppliers to save a few bucks, and we end up with components that can't be used. Then our own engineers design products that we can't produce. We need to work together."

On his second day, Ken decided to follow up on the information he had gathered the day before. He first visited the director of purchasing, Marilyn Reagan. When asked about the problem of the cases that did not fit together, Marilyn responded:

The fact of the matter is that switching suppliers for the cases saved $1.04 per unit. That may not sound like a lot, but multiply that by the 125,000 units we are expecting to sell this year, and it turns out to be pretty significant. Those guys in production think the world revolves around them. I am, however, sympathetic to their problems, and I plan on discussing the problem with the supplier the next time we meet. That should be some time next month.

After wrapping up the meeting with Marilyn, Ken decided he would next talk to the director of engineering. On the way, he recognized a person at a vending machine as the worker who had been standing next to Steve at the auto-insertion machine. Ken introduced himself and decided to talk with the worker for a few minutes. The worker introduced himself as Jim and discussed how he had been working in the shipping department just two weeks ago. The operator before Jim had quit because of the pressure. Jim hadn't received any formal training in operating the new equipment, but he said that Steve tried to check on him a couple of times a day to see how things were going. Jim appreciated Steve's efforts, but the quality inspectors made him nervous and he felt that they were always looking over his shoulder.

Ken thanked Jim for his input and then headed off to meet with the director of engineering, Jack Carel. After introducing himself, Ken took a seat in front of Jack's desk. Jack began:

So you are here to investigate our little quality snafu. The pressure that we are under here in engineering is the need to shrink things down. Two years ago fax machines, printers, scanners, and copiers were all separate pieces of equipment. Now, with the introduction of the PFS 1000, all this functionality is included in one piece of equipment not much larger than the original printer. That means design tolerances are going to be a lot tighter and the product is going to be more difficult to manufacture. But the fact of the matter is that manufacturing is going to have to get its act together if we are going to survive. The engineering department did its job. We designed a state-of-the-art piece of office equipment, and the prototypes we built proved that the design works. It's now up to the manufacturing guys to figure out how to produce it. We have done all that we can and should be expected to do.

To end his second day, Ken decided to meet with the director of quality assurance, Debbie Lynn. Debbie commented:

My biggest challenge as director of quality assurance is trying to convince the rest of the organization the importance quality plays. Sure everyone gives lip-service to the importance of quality, but as the end of the month approaches, getting the product out the door is always the highest priority. Also, while I am officially held accountable for quality, I have no formal authority over the production workers. The quality inspectors that report to me do little more than inspect product and tag it if it doesn't meet the specifications so that it is sent to the rework area. In all honesty, I am quite optimistic about Nancy's current concern for quality and very much welcome the opportunity to work closely with you to improve Officetech's quality initiatives.

Questions

1. Which departments at Officetech have the most impact on quality? What role should each department play in helping Officetech improve overall quality?

2. Draw a fishbone chart to help explain how the other functional areas are creating problems for manufacturing—which ultimately may be the causes of the excessive complaints and returns.

3. What recommendations would you make to Nancy concerning Officetech's problem with quality? What role should the quality assurance department play?

PAINT TINT

Late last month, Jim Runnels, a sales representative for the Paint Tint Corporation, was called to the plant of Townhouse Paint Company, one of his largest accounts. The purchasing agent for Townhouse Paint was complaining that the tubes of paint tint it had received over the last couple of weeks were not within the specified range of 4.9 to 5.1 ounces.

The off-weight tubes had not been detected by Townhouse's receiving clerks and had not been weighed or otherwise checked by their quality control staff. The problem arose when Townhouse began to use the tubes of tinting agent and found that the paint colors were not matching the specifications. The mixing charts used by the salespeople in Townhouse's retail stores were based on 5-ounce tubes of tinting agent. Overfilled or underfilled tubes would result in improper paint mixes, and therefore in colors that did not meet customers' expectations.

In consequence, Townhouse had to issue special instructions to all its retail people that would allow them to compensate for the off-weight tubes. The Townhouse purchasing agent made it clear that a new supplier would be sought if this problem recurred. Paint Tint's quality control department was immediately summoned to assist in determining the cause of the problem.

Paint Tint's quality manager, Ronald Wilson, speculated that the cause of the problem was with the second shift. To analyze the problem, he entered into a spreadsheet the data from all the previous samples taken over the last two months. As it turned out, 15 random samples had been taken over the two-month period for both the first and the second shifts. Samples always consisted of 10 randomly selected tubes of paint tint. Also, separate sampling schedules were used for the first and second shifts so that the second shift would not automatically assume that it would be subject to a random sample just because the first shift had been earlier in the day.

After entering the sample weight data of the tubes into the spreadsheet below and calculating the sample means, Ronald was quite puzzled. There did not seem to be any noticeable difference in the average weights across the two shifts. Furthermore, although the lines were running at less than full capacity during the first six samples, there still did not seem to be any change in either line after reaching full production.

	A	B	C	D	E	F	G	H	I	J	K	L	M	N	O	P
1	**First Shift**															
2								**Sample Number**								
3	**Observation**	**1**	**2**	**3**	**4**	**5**	**6**	**7**	**8**	**9**	**10**	**11**	**12**	**13**	**14**	**15**
4	**1**	4.90	5.05	4.96	4.92	4.96	5.03	4.99	5.00	5.02	5.03	5.01	4.95	5.02	4.96	5.06
5	**2**	5.03	5.04	4.96	5.00	5.00	4.99	5.03	5.01	5.05	4.90	4.94	4.95	4.95	4.97	4.97
6	**3**	5.00	5.00	4.92	5.05	5.03	4.98	5.01	4.95	5.00	4.95	5.00	5.06	5.00	4.93	5.00
7	**4**	5.03	5.11	5.01	5.03	4.98	4.99	5.02	5.01	5.01	5.01	5.00	5.02	4.98	5.01	5.00
8	**5**	5.02	4.94	4.98	5.01	5.00	4.98	5.01	4.99	5.03	5.01	4.96	4.94	5.04	5.00	5.03
9	**6**	4.92	5.02	5.00	5.02	5.02	5.01	4.99	4.98	5.00	4.94	4.98	4.99	5.02	5.04	5.08
10	**7**	5.04	5.03	4.98	5.02	5.00	4.99	5.06	4.96	5.01	4.98	5.01	4.97	4.99	4.98	4.97
11	**8**	4.92	5.00	5.00	4.96	5.01	5.01	5.05	5.00	4.97	4.98	4.97	4.97	5.05	5.08	4.98
12	**9**	4.95	4.95	4.94	5.02	4.95	4.98	4.97	4.94	5.07	5.00	5.00	4.96	5.02	4.94	5.00
13	**10**	5.02	4.99	5.08	4.94	5.00	4.95	5.04	4.98	5.02	5.01	4.98	5.02	5.06	5.02	4.97
14	**Average**	**4.98**	**5.01**	**4.98**	**5.00**	**5.00**	**4.99**	**5.02**	**4.98**	**5.02**	**4.98**	**4.99**	**4.98**	**5.01**	**4.99**	**5.01**
15																
16																
17	**Second Shift**															
18								**Sample Number**								
19	**Observation**	**1**	**2**	**3**	**4**	**5**	**6**	**7**	**8**	**9**	**10**	**11**	**12**	**13**	**14**	**15**
20	**1**	5.03	5.02	4.99	4.96	5.03	5.02	5.08	5.10	5.16	5.00	4.97	5.11	5.11	4.90	5.02
21	**2**	4.90	4.95	4.97	4.97	4.98	5.03	4.97	4.93	4.92	4.97	4.91	5.05	4.98	4.92	4.98
22	**3**	5.02	4.94	5.04	4.98	5.00	4.98	4.93	4.92	4.99	5.08	5.15	4.93	5.13	4.97	4.86
23	**4**	4.98	5.05	5.02	5.00	4.97	5.06	4.84	4.93	5.00	5.07	4.96	5.15	5.15	4.92	4.94
24	**5**	5.01	4.95	5.02	5.02	4.98	5.04	5.07	5.03	4.98	4.94	4.91	4.98	5.10	5.04	4.93
25	**6**	4.99	4.99	4.99	5.03	5.00	5.04	4.95	4.96	4.99	4.96	5.07	4.88	5.12	5.03	4.97
26	**7**	4.99	4.97	5.00	4.98	4.99	4.99	4.93	4.86	5.01	5.13	5.15	4.74	5.01	4.91	5.05
27	**8**	5.02	5.00	5.00	4.96	4.98	4.98	4.99	5.08	5.07	4.93	4.95	4.90	4.93	4.95	4.97
28	**9**	5.01	5.00	5.05	5.02	5.03	4.97	4.82	4.96	4.93	4.96	4.91	5.03	5.04	4.98	5.03
29	**10**	4.97	4.99	4.95	5.03	5.00	4.99	5.05	5.14	5.03	4.91	5.11	5.04	5.03	5.08	4.92
30	**Average**	**4.99**	**4.99**	**5.00**	**5.00**	**5.00**	**5.01**	**4.96**	**4.99**	**5.01**	**5.00**	**5.01**	**4.98**	**5.06**	**4.97**	**4.97**

Questions

1. Can you identify any difference between the first and second shifts that explains the weight problem? If so, when is this difference first detectable?

2. How would you rate the ability of Paint Tint's production process to meet Townhouse Paint's requirements? What are the implications of your evaluation?

EXERCISES

1. A principal at a high school was concerned about the writing skills of the students. Over a two-week period she took random samples of students' papers and tallied the errors by category. Develop a Pareto chart for the results of the study, summarized in the table below.

Type of Error	Number of Errors
Punctuation	43
Subject-verb agreement	29
Incomplete sentences	87
Capitalization	52
Spelling	195
Tense change	98

2. A gym monitors the number of memberships that are not renewed or are canceled each month. Develop a runs chart for last year's data. Should the manager of the gym be concerned?

Month	Number of Cancellations and Nonrenewals	Month	Number of Cancellations and Nonrenewals
January	5	July	7
February	3	August	8
March	2	September	10
April	7	October	14
May	6	November	10
June	7	December	17

3. Top management of the Security National Bank monitors the volume of activity at 38 branch banks with control charts. If deposit volume (or any of perhaps a dozen other volume indicators) at a branch falls below the LCL, there is apparently some problem with the branch's market share. If, on the other hand, the volume exceeds the UCL, this is an indication that the branch should be considered for expansion or that a new branch might be opened in an adjacent neighborhood.

Given the 10-day samples for each of the six months below, prepare an $\overline{X}$ chart for monthly deposit volume (in hundreds of thousands of dollars) for the Transurban branch. Use control limits of $\pm 3\sigma$. The average range of the six samples was found to be $85,260.

	Average of 10-Day Deposits ($\overline{X}$) ($100,000)
June	0.93
July	1.05
August	1.21
September	0.91
October	0.89
November	1.13

4. Using the following weekly demand data for a new soft drink, determine the upper and lower control limits that can be used in recognizing a change in demand patterns. Use $\pm 3\sigma$ control limits.

Week	Demand (6-packs)
1	3500
2	4100
3	3750
4	4300
5	4000
6	3650

5. A control chart has a mean of 50 and two-sigma control limits of 40 and 60. The following data are plotted on the chart: 38, 55, 58, 42, 64, 49, 51, 58, 61, 46, 44, 50. Should action be taken?

6. Given the following data, construct a 3σ range control chart.

Day of Sample	Sample Values
Saturday	22, 19, 20
Sunday	21, 20, 17
Monday	16, 17, 18
Tuesday	20, 16, 21
Wednesday	23, 20, 20
Thursday	19, 16, 21

a. If Friday's results are 15, 14, and 21, is the process in control?

b. Construct a 3σ means control chart and determine if the process is still in control on Friday.

7. Customers of Dough Boy Inc. have specified that pizza crusts they order should be 28 to 32 centimeters in diameter. Sample data recently collected indicate that Dough Boy's crusts average 30 centimeters in diameter, with a standard deviation of 1.1 centimeters. Is Dough Boy's pizza crust production system capable of meeting its customers' requirements? If not, what options does Dough Boy have to rectify this situation?

8. Design specifications for a bottled product are that it should contain 350 to 363 milliliters. Sample data indicate that the bottles contain an average of 355 milliliters, with a standard deviation of 2 milliliters. Is the filling operation capable of meeting the design specifications? Why or why not?

9. a. Using the following data, prepare a p chart for the control of picking accuracy in a wholesale food warehouse. Sample size is 100 cases.

Day Picks	Number of Cases Picked	Number of Incorrect
1	4700	38
2	5100	49
3	3800	27
4	4100	31
5	4500	42
6	5200	48

b. Determine if days 7, 8, and 9 are under control.

Day Incorrect	Cases Picked	
7	4600	53
8	6100	57
9	3900	48

10. A new machine for making nails produced 25 defective nails on Monday, 36 on Tuesday, 17 on Wednesday, and 47 on Thursday. Construct an $\overline{X}$ chart, p chart, and c chart based on the results for Monday through Wednesday and determine if Thursday's production was in control. The machine produces 1 million or so nails a day. Which is the proper chart to use?

BIBLIOGRAPHY

Berstein, A. "Quality Is Becoming Job One in the Office, Too." *Business Week* (April 29, 1991): 52–54.

Crosby, P. B. *Quality Is Free: The Art of Making Quality Certain.* New York: McGraw-Hill, 1979.

Crosby, P. B. *Quality Without Tears.* New York: McGraw-Hill, 1984.

Deming, W. E. *Out of Crisis.* Cambridge, Mass.: MIT Press, 1986.

DiPrimio, A. *Quality Assurance in Service Organizations.* Radnor, Pa.: Chilton, 1987.

Dobbins, J. G., and W. J. Padgett. "SPC in Printed Circuit Board Assembly." *Quality Progress* (July 1993): 65–67.

Evans, J. R., and W. M. Lindsay. *The Management and Control of Quality,* 3rd ed. St. Paul, Minn.: West, 1996.

Garvin, D. A. "Competing on the Eight Dimensions of Quality." *Harvard Business Review* (November–December 1987): 101–109.

Garvin, D. A. "Quality on the Line." *Harvard Business Review* (September–October 1983): 64–75.

George, S., and A. Weimerskirch. *Total Quality Management.* New York: Wiley, 1994.

Gitlow, H. S., and S. J. Gitlow. *The Deming Guide to Quality and Competitive Position.* Englewood Cliffs, N.J.: Prentice-Hall, 1987.

Greising, D. "Quality: How to Make It Pay." *Business Week* (August 8, 1994): 54–59.

Harrington, H. J., and J. S. Harrington. *High Performance Benchmarking.* New York: McGraw-Hill, 1996.

Juran, J. M., F. M. Gryna, Jr., and R. S. Bingham, Jr., eds. *Quality Control Handbook,* 4th ed. New York: McGraw-Hill, 1988.

Lawler, E. E., III, and S. Mohrman. "Quality Circles After the Fad." *Harvard Business Review* (January–February 1985): 65–71.

Maki, R. G., and M. R. Milota. "Statistical Quality Control Applied to Lumber Drying." *Quality Progress* (December 1993): 75–79.

Manley, R., and J. Manley. "Sharing the Wealth: TQM Spreads from Business to Education." *Quality Progress* (June 1996): 51–55.

Rau, H. "15 Years and Still Going . . ." *Quality Progress* (July 1995): 57–59.

Reichheld, F. F., and W. E. Sasser, Jr. "Zero Defections: Quality Comes to Services." *Harvard Business Review* (September–October 1990): 105–111.

Sager, I. "How IBM Became a Growth Company Again." *Business Week* (December 9, 1996): 154–162.

CHAPTER 4

Product/Service Design

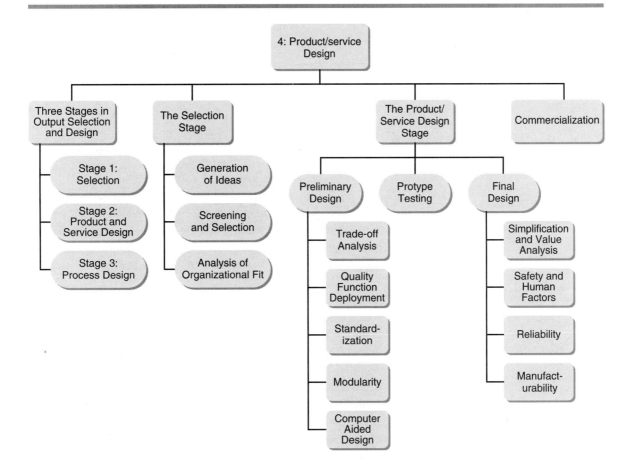

The design of products and services is strongly related to the material covered in Chapter 2 on business strategy and international competitiveness. For instance, the business strategy guides organizational efforts directed at selecting and designing new products and services. Furthermore, the ability to design and commercialize new products and services is a key determinant of an organization's overall competitive success. In this chapter we see that output selection and design consist of three stages: selection, design, and transformation system design. This chapter discusses the importance of developing products and services that simultaneously meet customers' requirements and are producible. Finally, it considers the increasing importance of developing commercialization capabilities.

INTRODUCTION

- In the years before 1988, Progressive carved out a profitable niche in the automobile insurance industry by writing policies for high-risk drivers that its competitors weren't interested in and charging these customers high prices. In 1988 two events occurred that required Progressive to rethink its strategy: Allstate had overtaken it in the high-risk niche, and California, which accounted for 25 percent of Progressive's profits, passed Proposition 103, sharply curtailing insurance rates.

  Progressive's response was the development of its round-the-clock "immediate response" program. With this program, claims adjusters are equipped with special vans complete with air-conditioning, comfortable chairs, a desk, and two cellular phones. Using the vans, the claims adjusters can travel to the scene of an accident and are often able to provide clients with a settlement check before the tow truck clears the scene. Before adopting the immediate response program, claims adjusters spent the majority of their time on the phone and shuffling papers. With the immediate response program, contact is made with 80 percent of accident victims within nine hours of learning of the accidents. Further, 70 percent of the damaged vehicles are inspected within one day, and typically the claim is wrapped up within a week (Henkoff 1994).

- In 1992 Thermos's 25 percent share of the $1-billion barbecue grill market accounted for a significant portion of its sales. However, the product was becoming a commodity, as numerous competitors were offering similar black gas boxes. The CEO of Thermos, Monte Peterson, believed that consumers were too intelligent and demanding to be tricked by clever advertising or slick packaging. According to Peterson, survival in this brutal environment requires that companies constantly innovate and create products that provide their customers with high quality at the right price—in other words, value.

To accomplish this objective, Peterson formed a flexible interdisciplinary team with representatives from marketing, manufacturing, engineering, and finance to develop a new grill that would stand out in the market. The interdisciplinary approach was used to reduce the time required to complete the project. For example, by including the manufacturing people in the design process from the beginning, the team avoided some costly mistakes later on. Initially, for instance, the designers opted for tapered legs on the grill. However, after manufacturing explained at an early meeting that tapered legs would have to be custom-made, the design engineers changed the design to straight legs. Under the previous system, manufacturing would not have known about the problem with the tapered legs until the design was completed. The output of this project was a revolutionary electric grill that uses a new technology to give food a barbecued taste. One major advantage of the electric grill is that it burns cleaner than gas or charcoal grills. Early indications are that the grill will be a huge success: it won four design awards in its first year (Dumaine 1993).

- Designers at Caterpillar are using a virtual-reality system called *cave automatic virtual environment* (CAVE) to take their large earthmoving equipment for a test-drive before it is actually built. CAVE incorporates a surround-screen and surround-sound in a cube with 10-foot sides. A supercomputer is used to project 3D graphics onto the walls. Inside the CAVE, humans can walk around and operate imaginary controls. The system responds to such movements and adjusts the sights and sounds accordingly. The CAVE provides design engineers with a variety of perspectives on the machinery, ranging from sitting in the earthmover and operating its controls to standing outside the cab and looking up and walking around it. The CAVE has provided Caterpillar design engineers with numerous tangible benefits. For example, a backhoe and a wheel loader that were recently introduced incorporate improvements in visibility and performance based on data collected from virtual test drives in the CAVE (Bylinsky 1994).

These examples illustrate a number of important themes related to designing products and services. To begin, note that two of the examples are related to the design of a tangible product (the grill and earthmoving equipment) and one example (processing insurance claims) is related to the design of a service. It might not have occurred to you that design activities are as applicable to services as they are to a tangible product. This could be because many services are designed and developed rather informally, whereas product design is typically the result of a concerted, formalized effort.

A second important theme illustrated by the examples is the central role product and service design activities play in determining how competitive an organization is. In the case of Progressive and Thermos, increased competition was the major impetus for developing a new product or service.

A third theme is the important role technology plays in product and service design. In the case of Thermos, new technology was incorporated into the actual product (i.e., a new technology to give food a barbecued flavor). In the case of Progressive, new technology, such as cellular phones, made the immediate response program possible. In Caterpillar's case, new technology was used to enhance the actual design process.

A final theme illustrated in the examples is the need to include people throughout the organization in design activities. At Thermos, design teams were created with representatives from a variety of functional areas such as engineering, marketing, and manufacturing. In effect, firms that take such an approach are recognizing the advantages of organizing work on the basis of processes as opposed to functions. Such design teams effectively become virtual process organizations. As more firms adopt process-centered organizational structures, there will be less need to form these teams ad hoc.

In Chapter 2 we identified four common business strategies: first-to-market, second-to-market, cost minimization, and market segmentation. To be successful, each of the different strategies involves many decisions about the timing, selection, and design of the firm's intended output and involves managers in finance, marketing, purchasing, engineering, accounting, and human resources, as well as operations. These decisions will have corresponding effects on the resulting quality, response time, cost, and variety of the outputs, and thus, on the firm's success in the marketplace. Some examples of these decisions and their potential impacts are described in Table 4.1.

TABLE 4.1 • Impacts of Selection and Design Decisions

- *Fit:* How this product or service fits with existing offerings. If the new output matches the firm's existing focus and markets, then it may be synergistic with current products and services, thereby increasing their acceptability and exposure. If not, it may "defocus" the firm and impair the firm's existing competitive strengths.

- *Materials:* The types of materials chosen. Materials affect the strength, performance, durability, cost, producibility, and longevity of a product or a facilitating good. If the output is to be long-lasting and of particularly high quality, the materials will probably be different from those chosen if a cost minimization strategy, using cheaper materials, is pursued.

- *Labor:* The labor skills needed. For custom services and products, or highly varying, innovative ones, well-trained or educated labor is probably needed. For low-cost, high-volume production on very specialized, automated machines, the skill levels are significantly less.

- *Equipment:* The equipment that will be required. High-volume, automated equipment is more appropriate for a cost minimization strategy that offers a standard output, whereas more general-purpose, flexible equipment is appropriate when a skilled labor force produces customized outputs in conjunction with a market segmentation strategy.

- *Operations:* The production operations to be employed. The design of the product or service greatly affects the production operations required to produce the output. For example, robots are very unreliable at screwing nuts onto screws and bolts when attaching parts together. However, they are quite adept at snapping plastic parts together. Thus, when IBM redesigned the Proprinter for automated production, it used snap-together parts instead of nuts and screws.

- *Financing:* The capital financing required. If the output is designed for high-volume, low-cost production, then large, up-front capital outlays are normally required for the specialized machines needed. However, variable costs will be minimal, since the labor requirements are low. Profits will come from low margins with high volumes, if the strategy is successful. But if customized outputs are produced with highly skilled workers, then equipment costs can be low but wage and salary costs will be higher. Profit margins on the outputs will also be high, but unit volumes will be small. (As was discussed in Chapter 2, some of the flexible new technologies can alter this trade-off and allow organizations to pursue a mass customization strategy.)

$\mathscr{T}$HREE STAGES IN OUTPUT SELECTION AND DESIGN

Designing products and services is a key business process. This process consists of three primary stages: selection, product/service design, and transformation system design, as illustrated in Figure 4.1. We briefly describe each of these stages and then elaborate on the first two stages, deferring the third stage to Chapter 5. Included within the product/service design stage is the description of a technique called *quality function deployment*, which is used to ensure that newly designed

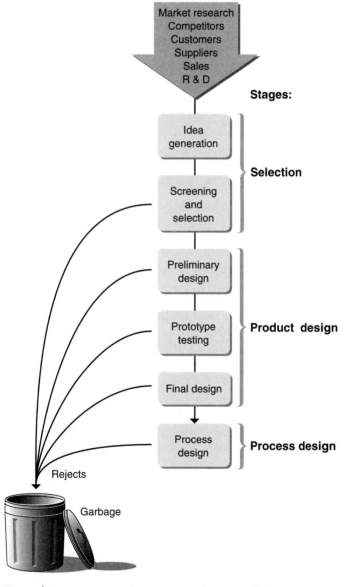

Figure 4.1   Steps in product-service selection and design.

outputs satisfy market requirements and are ultimately producible by the firm. The chapter concludes with a final section that describes how an organization's ability to commercialize its new offerings influences the extent to which newly designed products and services succeed in the market.

Stage 1: Selection

- *Generation of ideas*: Ideas for promising potential products or services can come from a large number of sources: customers, market research, salespersons, internal research and development (R&D) laboratories, suppliers, and even competitors. Those that originate from an identified need, such as a need for high-speed connections to the Internet by people with home computers, are known as **marketing pull**. Those that come from R&D, such as lasers, plastics, and microwaves, are known as **technology push**.

- *Screening and selection*: Ideas must pass a large variety of tests and screens before receiving the final go-ahead for full-scale production, and typically only 1 in 50 or so will pass them all. Screening includes market analysis and forecasts of customers' needs, assessments of the reaction of competitors, analyses of economic viability, studies of technical feasibility, and checklists for organizational fit. On the basis of these analyses and studies, one or a few ideas are selected for further study.

Stage 2: Product and Service Design

- *Preliminary design*: The preliminary design focuses on decisions concerning major aspects of the product or service: Will the product be made out of metal or plastic? Will the service be performed by people or machines? What tasks will be performed by the customers? Will the product be attached with screws or snapped together? And so on. Specific attributes of the product or service, such as cost, are first set as goals; various designs are then considered that may have the potential to achieve them. Basic but critical trade-offs (e.g., reliability versus price) are considered and made at this stage. These provide the information necessary for the construction of a prototype and lay the foundation for the final design that comes later.

- *Prototype testing*: For a *service*, a mock-up of the facility, servers, equipment, and other features may be put together and tested on volunteers typical of the target consumers. The efficiency and effectiveness of operation are also checked. For a *product*, a model or simplified representation of the final design is often built and tested. A clay or wooden model may be adequate to test appearance, or a limited version of operation may be sufficient to test technical performance and customers' reactions and tastes. Alternatively, the example of Caterpillar at the beginning of this chapter illustrates how organizations can use computer models in lieu of physical prototypes. Models based on computer technology can be developed to simulate a new production system or the operation of a product, and virtual-reality systems can be used to actually see and interact with new products and systems before they are created.

- *Final design*: On the basis of reactions to the prototype and any desirable changes or alterations in the preliminary design, a final design is developed, with full drawings, specifications, procedures, policies, and other information needed for the production system. If the changes from the preliminary design are extensive, a new prototype may be constructed and tested again.

Stage 3: Process Design

- *Transformation system design*: Once the final design has been frozen, the production operations for making it must also be specified. As the examples at the beginning of the chapter illustrate, the limitations of producibility should be considered throughout the selection and design stages and may well alter the design substantially. This is exactly what happened at Thermos when its manufacturing people informed the designers that tapered legs were more difficult and more expensive to produce than straight legs. Nevertheless, a full operation plan is needed at this stage. The plan includes not only the product specifications, but also the quality required, capacity rates, technological needs, skill levels, materials required, production methods, and so on. This topic is so extensive that the entire next chapter is devoted to it.

Although these three stages are shown as a linear process in Figure 4.1, the use of product design teams allows many of these issues to be considered simultaneously. And whether or not design teams are used, often it is necessary to recycle back through the selection and design stages as ideas are tested, analyzed, evaluated, and rejected at all stages. For example, more realistic costs and market forecasts obtained late in the process can be reevaluated for continuing viability in the screening phase. Likewise, more realistic prototypes can be test-marketed for continued acceptability.

HE SELECTION STAGE

This section focuses on generation of ideas and on screening. As we will see, several marketing, R&D, and financial activities support the selection of products and services.

Generation of Ideas

Clearly, because of their ties to customers, people who perform marketing activities play a key role in generating new ideas. These people can suggest new products or services for their customers, new regions, new types of customers for existing products and services, and even a change in the organization's focus, if needed.

R&D activities focus on creating and developing (but not producing) the organizational outputs. On occasion, R&D also creates new production methods by which outputs, either new or old, may be produced. *Research* itself is typically divided into two types: pure and applied. Pure research is simply working with basic technology to develop new knowledge. Applied research is attempting to develop new knowledge along particular lines. For example, pure research might focus on developing a material that conducts electricity with zero resistance, whereas applied research could focus on further developing this material to be used in cable products. *Development* is the attempt to utilize the findings of research and expand the possible applications, typically along the sponsor's line of interest (e.g., the development of cable to connect computers together in a local-area network).

The development end of R&D is more on the applications side and often consists of modifications or extensions to existing outputs. Figure 4.2 illustrates the range of applicability of development as the output becomes more clearly defined. In the early years of a new output, development is oriented toward removing "bugs," increasing performance, improving quality, and so on. In the middle years, options and variants of the output are developed. In the later years, development is oriented toward extensions of the output that will prolong its life.

Currently—as compared with 20 or 30 years ago—the development effort in R&D is much, much larger than the research effort. Some scholars of R&D attribute the shift away from research and toward the simple extension of existing outputs to the extensive influence of marketing on organizations. These scholars postulate that the marketing approach, "giving the customers what they want," is basically wrong because neither the customer nor the marketer has the vision to see what new technology can offer. By draining off funds from research and spending them on ever greater development of existing outputs, and on advertising those outputs, the organization leaves itself vulnerable to those competitors who are willing to invest in research to develop entire new generations of outputs.

Unfortunately, the returns from R&D are frequently meager, whereas the costs are great. Figure 4.3 illustrates the ***mortality curve*** (fallout rate) associated with the concurrent design, evaluation, and selection for a hypothetical group of 50 potential chemical products, assuming that the 50 candidate products are available for consideration in year 3. (The first three years, on the average, are required for the

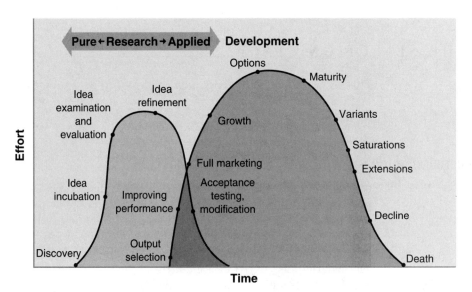

Figure 4.2   The development effort.

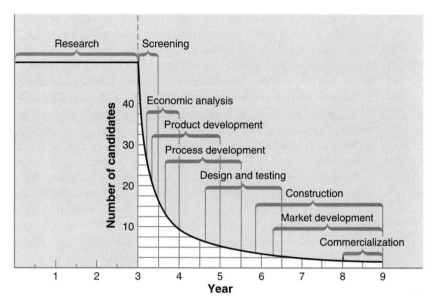

Figure 4.3 Mortality curve of chemical product ideas from research to commercialization. *Source:* Adapted from *This Is DuPont 30.* Wilmington, DE, by permission of DuPont de Nemours and Co.

necessary research preceding each candidate product.) Initial evaluation and screening reduce the 50 to about 22, and economic analysis further reduces the number to about 9. Development reduces this number even more, to about 5, and design and testing reduce it to perhaps 3. By the time construction (for production), market development, and a year's commercialization are completed, there is only one successful product left. (Sometimes there are none!) A recent study found that, beyond this, only 64 percent of the new products brought to market were successful, or about two out of three.

Two alternatives to research frequently used by organizations are *imitation* of a proven new idea (i.e., employing a second-to-market strategy) or outright *purchase* of someone else's invention. The outright purchase strategy is commonly employed in high-technology industries where technology advances so rapidly that there isn't enough time to employ a second-to-market strategy. For example, in March 1998 Cabletron Systems acquired Yago Systems to add wire speed routing and layer-4 switching products and solutions to its existing line of network products. Although imitation does not put the organization first on the market with the new product or service, it does give an opportunity to study any possible defects in the original product or service and rapidly develop a better design, frequently at a better price. The second approach—purchasing an invention or the inventing company itself—eliminates the risks inherent in research, but it still requires the company to develop and market the product or service before knowing whether it will be successful. Either route spares the organization the risk and tremendous cost of conducting the actual research leading up to a new invention or improvement.

In addition to *product research* (as it is generally known), there is also *process research*, which involves the generation of new knowledge concerning *how to produce* outputs. Currently, the production of many familiar products out of plastic (toys, pipe, furniture, etc.) is an outstanding example of successful process research.

Motorola, to take another example, extensively uses project teams that conduct process development at the same time as product development.

In regards to services and service process research, it can be useful to identify the service design and delivery "gaps" between what the customer/client needs and what the service provider offers (Parasuraman et al., 1988). By identifying the possible gaps in the service process, a service provider can better control the quality, productivity, cost, and performance of their service offering, thereby resulting in greater profit and market share. If used by a firm looking for a competitive opening in a service process, it can also help identify any such areas. (Obviously, this concept applies to manufacturers as well but will be presented here in its original service context).

Figure 4.4, modified from Parasuraman et al., illustrates the concept. Essentially, there is commonly a gap between what the customer/client actually needs and what is delivered that involves gaps throughout the selection, design, and delivery process. We start with gap 1, the reasonable difference between the ideal service that the customer actually needs and what the customer expects. This gap is based on common sense, experience, knowledge, and perhaps most importantly, advertising and

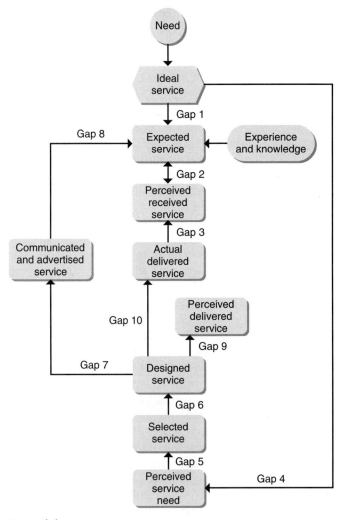

Figure 4.4   Gap identifier.

other communications form the service provider. Gap 2 is the imbalance between what the customer expected and the customer's perception of what was actually received. Gap 3 is the final gap on the customer's side; it represents the difference between what was actually delivered and the customer's perception of that reality.

The six remaining gaps are all on the provider's side. The first gap on this side, gap 4, is the misperception by the service provider of what the customer truly needs. The next gap, 5, is the difference between that misperception and what the provider chooses to offer (the selected service). Gap 6 is the discrepancy between the service that was selected and the service that was designed. Gap 7 concerns marketing and sales and is the disparity between the designed service and what these functions understand it to be. Continuing this path, gap 8 concerns the difference between what the provider is attempting to communicate to the customer and what the customer actually understands. Returning to the service delivery process, the last two gaps concern the contrast between what was designed and what was perceived as delivered (gap 9) and what was actually delivered (gap 10).

Clearly, with nine possible opportunities for the service provider to not meet the customer's expectations, not to mention the customer's needs (gap 1), there are a lot of ways to fail in the service provision process. It behooves every service (and product) provider to carefully examine each of these potential failure points in their own business to see if they can improve their service provision process, especially before someone else discovers the opportunity and moves to close the gaps.

From the previous discussion it is clear that there is a close relationship between the design of a product or service and the design of the production system. Actually, the link is even closer than it seems. Figure 4.5 illustrates the relationship between the changes throughout the life cycle of a product or service and changes throughout the life cycle of its production system. At the left, when the product or service is introduced, innovations and changes in its design are frequent. At this point, the production system is relatively uncoordinated and very general, since the design is still changing (the number of *product* innovations is high). Toward the middle, the product design has largely stabilized, and cost competition is forcing innovations in the production process, particularly the substitution of machinery for labor (the number of *process* innovations is high). At the right, this phenomenon has subsided and innovations in production methods are primarily the result of competitors' actions, government regulations, and other external factors.

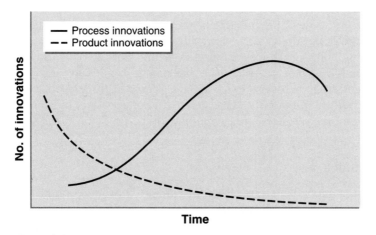

Figure 4.5 Product-process innovations over time.

Although not typically involved on the research side of such innovations in production methods (a laboratory engineering function), the operations manager is intimately involved in *applying* these developments in day-to-day production. The possible trade-offs in such applications are many and complex. The new production system might be more expensive but might produce a higher-quality output (and thus, the repeat volume may be higher or the price can be increased). Or the new production system might be more expensive and might produce a lower-quality output but be simpler and easier to maintain, resulting in a lower total cost and, ultimately, higher profits. Clearly, many considerations—labor, maintenance, quality, materials, capital investment, and so on—are involved in the successful application of research to operations.

Screening and Selection

The mortality curve shown in Figure 4.3 indicates the significant impact of screening and economic analysis, reducing research-derived ideas from 50 down to about 9, and then to just one or so by the end of the other evaluation activities. At this stage it is important to consider the consumer's needs and wants, as well as the typical consumer's reactions to the offerings of the firm's competitors. Considerations along these lines include expectations about promotion, sufficiency of demand, synergy with the current product or service line, current and potential competition, and adequacy of meeting customers' needs as regards price, performance, reliability, availability, and quality. Also, the possibility of segmenting the market by offering specially tailored outputs should be considered.

Operational activities include assessing the technical feasibility of the product or service—that is, the ability to produce it successfully. This would include the compatibility of the production system with existing equipment and methods, labor skills, facilities, and suppliers' abilities. The potential for patenting the product, as well as the possibility of patent infringements, also needs to be determined.

Financial activities at this stage are concerned with the up-front capital needs of the new product or service, as well as the returns. Here the possible risk of the project, the length of the life cycle, the anticipated profit margins, the initial investment required, the return on that investment, and the cash flows from the project are all evaluated.

To aid in this evaluation, payback period, return on investment (ROI), or net present value of the project may be calculated. These results offer a quick estimate of the opportunity the new product or service offers compared with other possible investments or choices the firm is facing. For example, many firms use a rule of thumb that to be acceptable an investment should have a payback (amount of time for profits to recover the investment) of two or three years, or a yearly ROI of 25 or 30 percent. Obviously, these rules are not absolute, but they do give managers a feel for the riskiness and profitability of the potential investment.

Analysis of Organizational Fit

Last, a general analysis of *organizational fit* is often conducted—that is, the fit between the new product or service and the existing organization is evaluated. Any new output should capitalize on an organization's core competencies and competitive advantage, complement the organization's existing outputs, and fit into the organization's structure, goals, and plans for the future.

General areas of strength (or weakness) are:

1. Experience with the particular output
2. Experience with the production system required for the output
3. Experience in providing an output to the same target recipients
4. Experience with the distribution system for the output

The organization must also consider the effect a new output will have on both the demand and the production methods used for existing outputs, a consideration of major importance to the operations manager. For example, introduction of inkjet printers reduced the demand for laser printers. Clearly, a new output may very well change the "best" production methods to be used for existing outputs in terms of labor skills, type of equipment, and possibly even the operations focus of the organization. It will certainly change scheduling, routing, and other aspects of production planning in the operations area.

Sometimes, of course, a new output totally changes the organization and its goals. On occasion, organizations do this on purpose to move into a new product or service area, especially if the old output is near the end of its life cycle.

One simple method for assessing the organizational fit of candidate outputs is to use a checklist, such as the one shown for *products* in Figure 4.6. Although such a list is not a substitute for analysis, it does provide a starting point for analysis. We

Area of fit	Poor	Fair	Good	Excellent
I. General				
1. Fits long-term organizational goals				√
2. Capitalizes on organizational strengths			√	
3. Appeals to management				√
4. Utilizes organizational experience		√		
II. Market				
1. Adequate demand			√	
2. Existing or potential competition		√		
3. In line with market trend				√
4. Enhances existing line	√			
III. Economics				
1. Cost		√		
2. Price				√
IV. Production				
1. Capacity availability			√	
2. Material supply and price	√			
3. Engineering know-how			√	
Totals	2	3	4	4

Figure 4.6 Typical checklist for organizational fit.

can begin by concentrating attention on the areas of "poor" fit and analyzing their impact and the trade-offs available between "poor" and "excellent" areas.

THE PRODUCT/SERVICE DESIGN STAGE

Several recent trends have profoundly affected product design. One such trend is the emphasis being given to reducing the time required for product development. According to a study conducted by *Business Week* of 200 American companies, from 1991 to 1996 the average development time for breakthrough products was reduced by approximately 17 percent. Likewise, over this same period the average development time for new product lines, major product revisions, and minor product revisions was reduced 19 percent, 22 percent, and 25 percent, respectively.

Outsourcing product design is also becoming increasingly popular. By outsourcing the design of key components to suppliers, an organization can lower its cost of product development and tap the expertise of its suppliers. However, as was discussed in Chapter 2, a company must be careful not to outsource parts or activities that are strategically important to maintaining its competitive position.

In the remainder of this section, we divide the product design stage into three chronological steps: preliminary design, prototype testing, and final design. In preliminary design, the design team considers various alternatives and makes early, basic trade-offs. The result is one or two preliminary designs for further consideration. Next, one or more prototypes are constructed to test the design or designs. The team then evaluates the results of various tests on the prototype and alters and improves the original design; this results in the final design.

Preliminary Design

Preliminary design follows from the screening step in which various ideas and concepts were advanced and evaluated. Here, the team identifies the final specifications, describing how the product or service *should perform*, and then makes some basic trade-offs. That is, the team does *not* specify the item or service itself; rather, the team specifies how it should function when the customer uses it: how long it should last, what it should do, and how fast it should execute its functions.

Next, the team has to make some decisions regarding the trade-offs needed to achieve the desired performance. These basic trade-offs will narrow the many avenues for achieving this performance: Will it be made of cheaper plastic or more rugged metal? Will it be battery-driven or will it use household current? And so on. The result of these basic trade-offs is the design concept. Ideally, adequate decisions will be made at this stage so that the prototype based on this design concept will perform acceptably at the next stage. If poor decisions are made about the preliminary design and the prototype fails (as happens often), then the team must return to the preliminary design stage and repeat the entire process. The tasks involved in achieving the design concept are described next.

Trade-Off Analysis

Some of the basic factors to be considered in the initial trade-off analysis are listed in Table 4.2. The design task is to trade off these characteristics to best meet the demands of the marketplace. For example, gasoline stations and fast-food restaurants have become self-service to reduce the cost, as well as the service time, to the recipient. In return for the improvements in these two characteristics of the services, customers have had to give up such conveniences as checks of the battery, oil, and tire pressure; waiters and waitresses; full-line menus; and individual attention. For those people who still desire these features, numerous alternatives for car service or dining are available.

In both product and service design, many alternatives usually exist that will meet the basic function of the output. The key to good design is a recognition of the major characteristics of the demand and a detailed analysis of the trade-offs available between and among the various attributes. Often, several different versions of the same output can be produced so that different market segments will find the output appealing. For example, Procter & Gamble offers a dazzling array of detergents, many of which even compete with each other. In the fast-food business, the major companies experimented with expanding their menus (at the risk

Table 4.2 • Trade-Off Analysis: Factors to Consider

- *Function:* The new design must properly perform the function (meet the recipient's need) for which it is required.
- *Cost:* The total cost (materials, labor, processing, etc.) cannot be excessive for the market under consideration.
- *Size and shape:* These must be compatible with the function and not distasteful or otherwise unacceptable to the market.
- *Appearance:* For some applications the appearance of the product or service is irrelevant; in other instances (e.g., art, sports cars) the appearance is equivalent to the function.
- *Quality:* The quality should be compatible with the purpose. Excessive quality may increase cost unnecessarily; insufficient quality leads to dissatisfied customers and decreased demand.
- *Reliability:* The output should function normally when used and should last the expected duration. Outputs with complex combinations of elements, all of which must work, will tend to have lower reliability unless this is allowed for in the design.
- *Environmental impact:* The output should not degrade the environment or pose a hazard to the recipient.
- *Producibility:* The output should be easily and speedily producible. The examples at the beginning of the chapter illustrate how organizations can use design teams with representatives from manufacturing to help ensure that the products being designed by the team are producible.
- *Timing:* The output should be available when desired. This characteristic is especially relevant to service outputs.
- *Accessibility:* The recipient should be able to obtain the output without difficulty.
- *Recipients' input requirements:* The amount and type of input required of the recipient should be considered in the design. "Do-it-yourself" projects are an example of product outputs, and "self-service" is an example of service outputs.

of loss of focus) to broaden the appeal to new markets. For example, McDonald's has experimented with offering chili and pizzas at test locations.

Quality Function Deployment

The success of the design effort hinges on two criteria: the extent to which the new product or service meets customers' needs, and the extent to which the organization can produce or deliver it. Clearly, no amount of clever advertising and no degree of production efficiency will entice customers to purchase a product or service that does not meet their needs. Likewise, it serves no purpose for an organization to design new products or services when it does not have the capability to produce or deliver them. For instance, it would not make sense for a local phone company to design a new service that offers interactive cable television programming if it currently does not have the bandwidth necessary to deliver this type of service. Even if the phone company was able to work out the bugs for interactive programming in the lab, it would still take years to install the fiber-optic cable infrastructure that is necessary to deliver this type of service to the public. Of course, the development of new products and services can serve as the impetus for acquiring additional production capabilities; however, organizations typically seek to develop new products and services that capitalize on their existing capabilities.

Quality function deployment (QFD) is a useful tool for helping to ensure that designs for new products and services satisfy market requirements and are ultimately producible by the firm. As Figure 4.7 illustrates, QFD uses a series of matrices or tables to maintain the links between customers' attributes, technical requirements, component requirements, and operation requirements.

With QFD, market requirements are specified in terms of customers' attributes. These attributes are often referred to as the "voice of the customer" because they are expressed in the customer's own terms. Examples of attributes for an electric

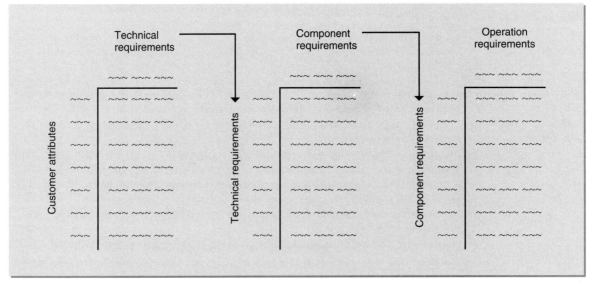

Figure 4.7   Using quality function deployment to link customers' attributes to technical, component, and operation requirements.

guitar might include statements such as "It should have consistent action," "There should be no buzzing at the frets," and "The neck should not be bolted on."

After a comprehensive list of customers' attributes has been developed, the technical requirements for the product are specified and matched to the attributes, using the chart shown in Figure 4.7. Technical requirements are expressed in the specialized language associated with engineering. Thus, technical requirements may be expressed in terms of dimensions, weights, performance, tensile strength, and compression. Two important outcomes result from using this table. First, it helps to ensure that each attribute noted by customers is addressed by the product designers. Second, it ensures that designers do not add technical requirements to the product that do not satisfy a particular requirement of customers. Designers who do not specifically consider customers' requirements run the risk of adding a number of "bells and whistles" that the customer may not be interested in. In these cases the designers are simply adding to the cost of the final product or service without proportionally increasing its value. For example, it might be an interesting challenge for an engineer to design a five-speed motor for garage doors. However, since customers would most likely operate it at only its fastest speed, adding the extra controls for additional speeds would not add value for the typical customer.

In the middle of Figure 4.7, the technical requirements for the product developed at the left are now linked to specific requirements for components or parts. Again, using Figure 4.7 ensures two important outcomes: (1) each technical requirement is addressed by the components used to make the product and (2) component requirements that are not related to specific technical requirements are not added.

In the right side of Figure 4.7, the operation requirements necessary to produce the components are determined. Like the other requirements charts, this table ensures that each component requirement is matched to specific operation requirements, and that each operation requirement is linked to specific component requirements. The former result ensures that the organization has the capability to produce the components; the latter result ensures that the organization does not attempt to develop production system capabilities that are not related to the component requirements.

Thus, we see that QFD provides a simple and straightforward approach for ensuring that product designs meet customers' requirements and are producible. This is accomplished by first translating the voice of the customer into the technical language of engineers. Next, these technical requirements are translated into specific requirements for the components of the new product. Finally, the component requirements are translated into specific requirements for the production system.

A more detailed example of the table on the left is shown in Figure 4.8 for a car door. This table is often called the house of quality. A triangular correlation table between the technical requirements at the top forms the roof of the house. This table identifies which technical requirements are synergistic with each other and which are in conflict.

On the right side of the house, opposite customers' attributes, are two sets of information. First is the importance rating (from 1 to 10) for that attribute. Next is the customers' evaluations (running from better to worse) of a product, based on each of the requirements. Thus, a producer can see how a particular product stacks up against the customer's wants or a competitor's offering. At the bottom of the house, opposite the technical requirements, are the specifications for each characteristic that will meet the customer's requirements and, beneath that, an engineering

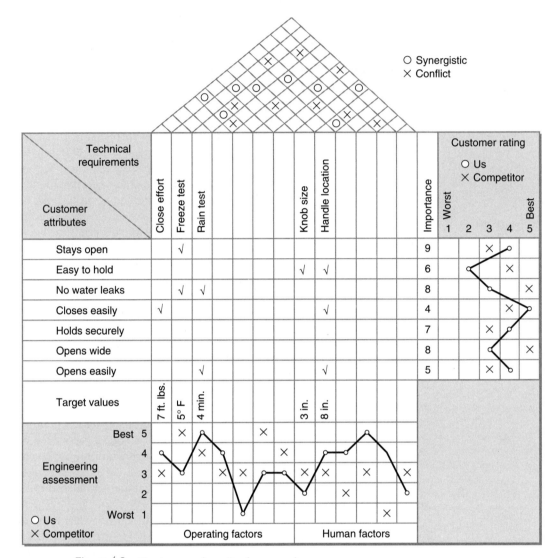

Figure 4.8 The house of quality for a car door.

assessment (again running from better to worse) of the product in terms of its meeting those specifications.

By the use of the visual tool, a firm can analyze its outputs in terms of customers' desires, compare its outputs with competitors' outputs, determine what it takes to better meet the customer's requirements, and figure out how to do it. A number of Japanese and American firms such as Toyota and Hewlett-Packard have taken this approach and found that it cut their product development time by one-third to one-half and their costs by up to 60 percent (while improving quality).

Standardization

Many years ago the primary purpose of output design was to facilitate the production system. Since demand for goods was plentiful as long as the price was low, companies desired to minimize the unit cost of items. One method of reducing unit cost was increasing capacity through *mass production* or assembly-line manufacture. Thus, companies moved toward standardization and thereby interchangeability of parts to minimize both the costs and the difficulty of assembly. Standardization had the following cost-related advantages:

1. It minimized the number of different parts to stock.
2. It minimized the number of changes necessary in production equipment.
3. It simplified operations procedures and thus reduced the need for controls.
4. It allowed larger purchases with quantity discounts.
5. It minimized problems with repair and servicing.

Standardization is still an effective way to hold costs down. Beyond this, it provides many advantages for consumers too. For example, standardization lets us buy common items at the store such as lightbulbs, film, videotapes, and automobile tires without worrying about fit or proper function. In services, we depend on zip codes and area codes to direct our correspondence and phone calls correctly and efficiently. On the other hand, standardization has several drawbacks. For example, using standard parts rather than specially made parts sometimes means lower quality or reduced performance. The major disadvantage of standardization is the inflexibility of production; little variety is possible. For example, what happens when you order a Big Mac at a McDonald's drive-through and ask them to hold the pickles? The classic comment on standardization comes from Henry Ford, who reputedly declared that his customers could have any color Model T they desired, as long as it was black!

A good example of the use of standardization is the current trend among global producers toward common product platforms, such as at Whirlpool. Whirlpool's European plant in Italy has what would appear to be an extremely difficult task (Oster and Rossant 1994). In this one plant a wide variety of ovens are produced, from boxy, expensive Bauknecht ovens to rounder, more modern Whirlpool-branded ovens to no-frills ovens bearing the Ingnis brand name. Interestingly, although each brand seems different on the basis of its outward appearance, the ovens all have a common interior. Building its new products around these common platforms has provided Whirlpool with a number of benefits. For example, operating margins for the first three quarters of 1994 were 6.5 percent, compared with 3.6 percent in 1990. Also, over this same period, Whirlpool was able to increase its market share from 11.5 percent to 13 percent. Using common platforms has provided Whirlpool with a number of operating benefits, as well. For example, it has reduced the number of suppliers of power cords for its refrigerators from 17 to 2. Across the board, similar reductions in its supplier base for other parts has contributed to Whirlpool's reducing its inventory by one-third.

Modularity

One method used to obtain variety, or at least a semblance of variety, and still hold down cost is ***modularity***. This means producing the output in "modules" or interchangeable subassemblies, thus giving the customer some choice. For instance, the purchaser of a new car can specify engine size, type of transmission, upholstery, color, and numerous other aspects of the product. Such variety is achieved not by producing some number of every possible model but, rather, by producing modules (e.g., engines, transmission, bodies with varying colors, upholstery, tires and wheels, etc.) and then joining the appropriate modules together in final assembly according to the customer's order. An example of this was the description of mass customization at Hewlett-Packard in Chapter 2.

One example of modularization is an automobile that has three possible engines, two possible transmissions, five different exterior colors, and three different interiors available to the customer but requires that the operations manager keep track of only 13 modules. However, these 13 modules can be combined to form $3 \times 2 \times 5 \times 3 = 90$ different versions of the same model.

This, of course, is what Whirlpool is striving for with its new common platforms, as described earlier. By using a standard low-cost platform, Whirlpool is able to efficiently produce a wide range of appliances for a variety of different markets.

Computer-Aided Design

Engineers are making increasing use of the computer for product design and production planning. In ***computer-aided design*** (CAD), the engineer forms a drawing on the computer screen with the keyboard, a light pen, or a mouse and pad. Lines can be specified through coordinates, or the points can be "spotted" on the screen or pad and the computer will draw the line between the points.

CAD software provides the engineer with many of the same benefits word-processing programs provide you. For instance, before graduating from college you may wish to send out your résumé and a cover letter to prospective employers. Word-processing programs facilitate this task in that you can create a basic cover letter, retrieve this file as needed, and make minor changes to it for each prospective employer. In a similar fashion, when engineers need to design a new part, they can retrieve a design for a similar part and make changes to the design right on the computer screen. This saves considerable time, since the engineer doesn't have to develop each new design from scratch. In addition, just as word-processing programs can check documents for spelling and grammatical errors, CAD software can often automatically check designs. For example, CAD software can be used to check the fit of parts that will be assembled together.

As the engineer designs the part, the CAD systems can be instructed to enlarge certain portions for a closer examination, rotate the design to show it from different angles, and so on. The capabilities of these systems have been growing tremendously in the last few years, while the prices of the software have fallen just as fast. Many excellent microcomputer CAD packages are now available. Productivity increases on the order of 300 and 400 percent are typical.

When the design is completed, it can be printed out on a graphics plotter or stored electronically to be used or changed later. As was mentioned before, most of the engineer's design work is initiated by retrieving a similar product or part from the system database—a similar wheel for another customer in the past, a recent factory layout—which cuts the design time by better than half. Rarely does the engineer draw a product totally from scratch. In addition, many marketing, R&D, and manufacturing activities are facilitated through the use of the electronic database on the parts. For example, the CAD database of parts can be used to obtain the bill of materials or the dimensions of critical parts.

CAD is being used for more and more purposes as the software becomes more user-friendly and prices drop. In addition to being used for designing products and components of products, CAD is used by architects to design buildings and bridges, designers to create new children's toys, automobile stylists to design futuristic cars, fire analysts to study the historical pattern of fires in a city and design new routes for fire engines and emergency vehicles, jewelers to design rings and other jewelry, and physicians to develop replacements for degenerated or irreparably injured bones.

Once an engineer has the product design on the CAD system, the database can be used for a number of other purposes. For example, computer-aided engineering (CAE) software uses CAD designs but then subjects them to stress, loads, and vibrations to determine their strength and reliability. Advanced engineering techniques such as finite element analysis are incorporated in the software to conduct the engineering analyses and save tremendous amounts of expensive skilled engineering time.

Computer-aided process planning (CAPP) is the technique of turning a part design into a manufacturing production plan, including routings, operations, inspections, times, and so on. Such a system is invaluable in overcoming problems that frequently occur at the interface between engineering and manufacturing.

Computer-aided manufacturing (CAM) was originally the specification by a computer of the machining instructions, based on a computer-aided design conducted beforehand. With CAM, the instructions to control the movement of machines are stored electronically and processed by computers. Before CAM was developed, the movement of machines was often controlled by instructions stored on a roll of paper with holes punched in it. The location of the holes triggered different machine functions. These types of machines are called numerical control machines. A player piano is an example of a numerical control machine: the location of the holes on the paper roll determines which note is struck. With the advent of microprocessor technology, microprocessors were added to machines, and machining instructions were stored magnetically on tapes and disks instead of being punched on paper. Equipping machines with microprocessors is called *computer numerical control.* An alternative to storing machining instructions on tapes and disks is to store these instructions on a central computer and download the instructions to the machines as needed. Using a central computer to control multiple machines in this fashion is called direct numerical control. CAM is applicable to a variety of manufacturing methods including turning, laser cutting, and other methods of fabrication or cutting.

Prototype Testing

The concept developed in the preliminary design step is tested as a ***prototype*** in the next step. The prototype may take the form of a physical model, a computer simulation, or a real product or service. Examples of prototypes include the clay models of new car designs used in the 1960s as well as the computer simulations used in the 1990s. The Air Force uses actual first-off production units as prototypes of new fighters and bombers, such as the B–2 Stealth, to test original concepts such as radar invisibility and in-flight performance. Ray Kroc's original McDonald's restaurant in California was the service prototype for the thousands of franchised facilities that soon followed. Software prototypes (often referred to as alpha and beta versions) for new Web browsers and graphics programs are basic to the software industry. In fact, these prototypes can often be downloaded at no charge and evaluated by potential users to determine how they perform and to ensure they are free of bugs.

On the basis of these tests, the preliminary design may be accepted and extended, modified, or completely rejected. Inadequate prototype testing has frequently resulted in disasters for the firm's stock price—as when well-known software firms released packages that still included bugs or were not user-friendly. Hardware firms have made similar mistakes with computers, such as the widely publicized flaw in the Pentium chip. Most often, however, only minor changes are indicated to fine-tune the performance and achieve even better results on the critical variables. This fine-tuning is then incorporated into the final design.

Final Design

Fine-tuning is based on the preliminary design, customers' reactions to the preliminary design, evaluation of the prototype tests, detailed financial analysis, and other relevant inputs. Although certain aspects are initiated somewhat before this stage, we also discuss them here: simplification and value analysis, safety and human factors, reliability, and manufacturability.

Simplification and Value Analysis

Simplification programs reduce the number of separate parts and operations required to produce an output. Fewer parts generally mean fewer materials, less labor, simplified assembly, easier service, and greater reliability. Often, the design team combines functions into one part so that two or three are not needed. Sometimes a molded plastic part will embody the function of two to six separate metal parts that previously needed to be welded or screwed together. For example, IBM redesigned its Proprinter for ease of robotic assembly, eliminating two-thirds of the former assembly operations.

The design team uses *value analysis* (sometimes called *value engineering*) to achieve the *function* of a product or service at less cost. The team considers cheaper methods, materials, and designs. Every element of the output that adds cost but not value is a candidate for examination. The procedure used in value analysis is a formalized approach that examines first the basic objective, second the basic function required, and then secondary functions. Team members propose ways to improve the secondary functions, such as combining, revising, or eliminating them. Ways to achieve the objective by using other basic functions are also considered.

Safety and Human Factors

During this final design step the team is also concerned with issues related to ease of use and the safety of the product or service. For example, the height or weight of a product and the location of its dials and switches can severely restrict its utility for many people. Buildings and facilities for the disabled (ramps, elevators, parking, lavatories) are a recent requirement that has assumed considerable importance in design.

Product liability is a major concern of firms, since civil lawsuits have severely restricted how firms operate, not to mention their profitability. We need only mention the hazards of asbestos, poisons, caustic chemicals, combustibles, and power tools to see the range of potential problems in the design stage. When hazards do exist, safety devices must be installed to eliminate the potential for an accident. Warning labels are also required in a number of situations.

Federal and state regulations concerning pollution, safety, disclosure of terms and conditions, drug prohibitions, and so forth also affect product design. Sometimes these prohibitions and regulations affect the design of the product or service itself (emission restrictions and mileage mandates on automobiles, for example), and sometimes they affect the production process (particulate discharges, water pollution, requirements for workers' safety).

Reliability

Reliability is one component of quality. There are two perspectives on calculating the reliability of a product or service. One is the likelihood that it will work on any given attempt to use it. The second is the likelihood that it will operate properly for a certain period of time.

One of the most important aspects of quality in the mind of the consumer is reliability. When we consider the reliability of a product, we generally separate items that are used or consumed only once, such as food and supplies (paper, bleach), from items that are reusable (a toaster, an automobile, or a stereo). The latter consist of a number of subcomponents that must all function properly for the product to work reliably.

Manufacturability

A major design consideration of current national interest is that of **manufacturability**, also called *simultaneous engineering, concurrent engineering, design for producibility, design for assembly*, and a variety of other, similar names. As the examples at the beginning of the chapter illustrate, the basic approach here is to form a team that includes the people responsible for *producing* an output, as well as the people responsible for *designing* it.

These teams commonly include representatives of marketing, finance, R&D, suppliers, and other interested parties. Thus, a complete product design is possible that does not hit any snags in the process of moving from concept to commercialization. Moreover, the product or service is generally brought to market much faster.

The major players on this team are the design engineers and manufacturing engineers. In the past, the typical American practice was for design engineers to design something and then "throw it over the wall" to the manufacturing engineers, almost with the challenge: "Let's see you make this one!" As noted earlier, the cost and even the success of a product are essentially *designed in* by the design engineers. There are typically many alternative ways to design a product to perform a particular function; if engineering chooses an unreliable, unsafe, or expensive way, no amount of efficiency in manufacture or advertising will make the product or service a success.

The design team can use a variety of tools and techniques to achieve manufacturability. These include quality approaches, techniques for enhancing productivity, computer integration, and faster responses, as well as the approaches described earlier such as standardization, quality function deployment, simplification, and modularity.

Using design teams also has some disadvantages. For example, the design engineers are no longer unrestricted in how they design parts and products. They may not be allowed to use certain hole sizes, because drills in that size are not standard items for the firm; or certain materials or procedures may not be acceptable to other members on the team for reasons of safety or cost. In the team approach, everyone accepts more constraints on individual creativity in return for fewer hassles and problems in getting the product or service to market. In the process, better products and services are produced at less cost with much shorter lead times.

Global competitors are innovating faster and bringing out new products and services in about half the time that it takes in the United States. For example, U.S. companies require about four to five years to bring new models of automobiles to market, but Japanese companies take only two to three years. In other industries, the Japanese maintain that the consumer research so commonly conducted by firms in the United States is a waste of time because they can bring to market and test actual new products in the same time it takes to do the consumer research.

The result is that U.S. firms in all industries are now trying new methods for speeding the process of designing and introducing a product or service. Some of the new methods being evaluated are described in Table 4.3.

$\mathscr{T}$ABLE 4.3 • Methods of Speeding the Introduction of New Outputs

- *Contract R&D:* Use external R&D laboratories to conduct the research work in your market.

- *Form product and process teams:* Use teamwork to develop the production system at the same time as the product or service.

- *Overlap developmental stages:* Proceed almost simultaneously on the stages described here, with only slight lags between them. That is, start the following stage when early returns from the prior stage start coming in.

- *Combine or eliminate stages:* Combine the design of product and production system. Eliminate final design. Use new technologies such as simulation and computer-aided engineering (CAE) to eliminate the need for testing a prototype.

- *Emphasize incremental changes:* Strive for incremental improvements rather than breakthrough innovations. Breakthroughs are harder to come up with in the first place, they take longer to design and test, and they result in more failures. Batching the incremental improvements will allow significantly improved products and services to be offered on a regular basis.

- *Use more extensive application:* Use the standard approaches and techniques such as standardization, modularization, part commonality, and simplification more extensively.

- *Use new technologies:* Employ CAD, CAE, and other technologies more widely and quickly. Be aggressive technologically.

COMMERCIALIZATION _____

In the previous section we discussed the importance of designing new products and services that meet customers' requirements and can be produced by the firm. The final ingredient in determining whether a new product or service will succeed is the organization's ability to commercialize its new offerings. Though not a stage in the product/service design, the topic of commercialization is so crucial to the success of the firm's business strategy that a brief discussion is warranted here.

Commercialization refers to the process of moving an idea for a new product or service from concept to market. It is frequently noted by top managers and academics alike that although quality and manufacturing excellence were the key to competitive success in the 1980s, commercialization of technology will be the key to competitive success in future decades.

Consider a common product such as the typewriter. The earliest modern typewriter was the mechanical typewriter, which dominated the market for 25 years. After the mechanical typewriter came the electromechanical typewriter, which dominated the market for 15 years. Then came the entirely electric typewriter, which dominated the market for the next 7 years. After the electric typewriter came the first generation of microprocessor-based machines, which dominated the market for another 5 years until the next generation of microprocessor-based machines became the market leader. Notice that the amount of time that each succeeding generation dominated the market decreased. The mechanical typewriter dominated the market for 25 years, but the first generation of microprocessor-based machines dominated the market for only 5 years. Couple significantly shorter product life cycles with a marketplace that is becoming increasingly competitive as a result of globalization, and you begin to get an idea of how important it is for organizations to be able to rapidly move ideas for new products and services from concept to market.

In the late 1980s McKinsey & Company conducted a study of the differences between leading and lagging companies with respect to commercialization (Nevens, Summe, and Uttal 1990). The results of the study indicated that leading companies had the following four characteristics in common:

1. The leading companies commercialized two to three times as many new products and processes as their competitors (given equal sizes of firms).

2. The leading companies incorporated two to three times as many technologies in their products.

3. The leading companies were able to get their products to market in less than half the time of their competitors.

4. The leading companies generally competed in twice as many product and geographic markets.

This study provided a number of other interesting insights related to commercialization. First, it was observed that the leading companies tended to view commercialization as a highly disciplined process. Also, not surprisingly, a strong relationship was observed between an organization's competitiveness and its commercialization capabilities. Further, the researchers observed that those companies first to market with products based on new technologies realized higher margins and increased market shares.

It is not uncommon for managers to dramatically underestimate the benefits of being first to market. For example, assume that you are leading a design team charged with designing a new laser printer. Assume that the market for laser printers is growing 20 percent annually, that prices for laser printers are declining by 12 percent per year, and that the life cycle for these printers is 5 years. As project leader, if you had to choose between incurring a 30 percent cost overrun to finish the project on schedule or miss the deadline by six months but meet the original budget, which would you choose? It turns out that under these circumstances, incurring the 30 percent cost overrun will reduce cumulative profits by only 2.3 percent, whereas launching the printer six months late will reduce cumulative profits by approximately 33 percent!

The first step an organization should take to improve its commercialization capabilities is to begin to measure this capability. The McKinsey study suggested a number of measures of commercialization capability, including the following:

- *Time to market.* It is crucial to get products to the market as quickly as possible.
- *Range of markets.* Since the cost of developing new technologies is increasing, it is important for organizations to spread this development cost across multiple product and geographic markets.
- *Number of markets.* The McKinsey study found that the leading companies tend to serve more market segments than the laggards.
- *Breadth of technologies.* This refers to the number of different technologies a company integrates into its new products and services.

Once appropriate measures for assessing commercialization capability have been established, organizations can begin working toward improving them. The McKinsey researchers recommend the following actions:

- Make commercialization a top priority in the organization.
- Set goals and benchmarks to motivate progress.
- Build cross-functional teams to speed up the handoffs and reduce roadblocks.
- Promote hands-on management to speed actions and decisions.

EXPAND YOUR UNDERSTANDING

1. In what kind of organizations might new ideas have a low mortality rate? A high rate?

2. Has standardization hurt the service industry's image in any way?

3. For years, industry has tended to favor development over research, and product research over process research. How might this tendency be dangerous?

4. Is there any product or service you use that would be improved by greater industry standardization?

5. Consider a new product that comes in two battery sizes, three colors, two levels of performance, four weights, and two shapes. How many different combinations can be offered to customers? How many different modules will operations have to produce?

6. Since services are easier to compete in than products, why didn't foreign firms start with services when they invaded U.S. markets?

7. Which is more profitable, product or process research? Which is likely to provide a more sustainable competitive advantage?

8. How might a service use the house of quality?

APPLY YOUR UNDERSTANDING _____
Microstat, Inc.

After designing a highly innovative notebook computer as part of his senior engineering project at West Coast University, Patrick McKinsey founded Microstat to develop and market the computer. Having completed the initial design, Patrick decided that his first task was to find a company that could produce the computers. He searched a number of directories of the computer industry, discussed the matter with several of his former professors, and attended several industry trade shows in search of an appropriate company. As it turned out, several Korean electronics companies expressed an interest. After extensive follow-up discussions, Patrick decided to form a partnership with Leesung Electronics. As a relatively new company itself, Leesung had been particularly aggressive in trying to get Microstat's business.

With this decision made, Patrick spent his days designing a Web site that he planned to use to promote and sell the computer—and his nights working with Leesung's engineers to finalize the computer's design. Given that the primary selling point of his notebook computer was its highly innovative design, Patrick deemed it extremely important for the computer to incorporate the latest and most advanced technology and features. Leesung agreed to produce the computers as orders came in and to ship them to Microstat. Microstat would install the necessary software, test the computers, and then ship them directly to the customers. Patrick named his notebook computer the "2500 series," since he was 25 years old at the time.

Almost immediately, orders began to trickle in. Within a couple of months the volume of orders for the 2500 series exceeded even Patrick's most optimistic forecasts, despite its premium price. Much of this success was due to the praise the 2500 was receiving in computer magazines. Patrick quickly had to hire a number of employees to install the software, test the computers, and respond to E-mail from customers. During this time, Patrick preferred to spend his own time designing the next computer series (which he originally hoped would be the 2600 series but now seemed more likely to be the 2700). However, as the volume of business continued to grow, Patrick filled in wherever he was most needed, whether it was responding to E-mail inquiries, installing software, or packing up computers for shipment.

By the end of the first year, Microstat reached a landmark, selling 100 computers per day. If sales continued to grow at their current pace, Microstat would easily double its sales volume in the next year. However, even if the sales volume doubled, sales revenue would only show a slight increase and profits might actually decrease because price cuts had recently been forced on Microstat by new competitors. The importance of having a new follow-up product line quickly became apparent to Patrick.

During Microstat's second year, Patrick dedicated himself to the design of the 2700 series. His highest priority was to develop a new product that would enhance Microstat's reputation for highly innovative designs incorporating the latest technology. Because of its solid financial foundation, Patrick determined that Microstat would also produce the new 2700. Overall, Patrick was satisfied with Leesung's performance; however, he felt that the lead times resulting from using an overseas manufacturer were too long and could eventually become a competitive disadvantage.

The design for the 2700 series was becoming finalized midway through the second year, and Patrick found an electronics plant for sale in San Antonio that, with some minor modifications, could assemble it. Within a month, he purchased the plant and persuaded the plant manager and other key employees to stay on. By the end of the second year, the design for the 2700 was final, and it was in production at the plant in San Antonio.

Market acceptance of the 2700 series was extremely positive and all indications were that the 2700 would continue to fuel Microstat's growth. On the basis of this success, Patrick decided that Microstat would continue this strategy of introducing a new highly innovative model line incorporating the latest technology and features every two years. The two-year time frame would give Microstat 1½ years to design the next computer series and six months to ramp-up the plant to produce it.

After the launch of the 2700 series, Patrick immediately formed a design team to begin work on the 2900 series. The design of the 2900 was proceeding on schedule and was to be handed off to production when a new cursor technology called a "touchpad" became available. Given Microstat's strategy of innovation, Patrick was adamant about incorporating a touchpad into the 2900. He argued that if the 2900 did not include a touchpad it would be another two years before Microstat had a computer that incorporated this technology, and that this would hurt Microstat's reputation. On the other hand, changing the design to incorporate the touchpad would require redesigning a significant portion of the computer and would add as much as four months to the design time, giving production only two months to ramp-up. Patrick immediately ruled out delaying the introduction of the 2900 series as inconsistent with Microstat's strategy. Microstat faced additional pressure because—unlike most of the other major notebook computer manufacturers, who changed their designs incrementally every six to nine months—Microstat modified its design only in conjunction with the launch of a new product line.

Ultimately, the 2900 was redesigned to incorporate the touchpad. The redesign delayed the project by 3½ months, giving manufacturing less than half the time usually allocated for ramping-up production. By working numerous 15-hour days, six to seven days a week, the plant staff managed to get the new production line operational within the 2½ months that remained.

Within a couple of months of the launch of the 2900 series, Microstat was experiencing an unusually large amount of returns for repairs. Extremely concerned that Microstat's image would be damaged, Patrick hired Amanda Jordan as Microstat's new director of quality. Amanda's first task was to identify the causes of the problem. She was to submit a report to Patrick detailing how the problem could be rectified and recommend ways to prevent such problems from occurring in the future.

Amanda began her investigation by interviewing the team leader in the rework area, Michael Scott. Michael commented:

> The majority of the computers are returned because of a missing resistor on one of the printed circuit boards or cracked casings where the display attaches to the base, or both. The casings are cracking because the plastic material we used simply cannot withstand the pressure the hinges place on the base when the computer is opened and closed.

On the basis of the information Michael provided, Amanda decided that she would follow up with the production manager, Bill Mitchell. After introducing herself to Bill, she explained that she was interested in determining the cause of the missing resistor and the cracked casings. Bill began:

> In my opinion, the problem of the missing resistor is a result of our not having enough time to ramp-up production. To be perfectly honest, 2½ months is not enough time to set up, test, and debug a new production line for a brand-new product. To me its actually amazing that we did get the line up and running in such a short time. But looking back, there is no way we could have done an adequate job of testing the product and working out the bugs in the process.
>
> The problem with the casing is also related to not having enough time. I don't know how much you know about our product development process. The way it works is that the engineers begin designing a computer. At various times during the design, the engineers and some highly skilled technicians build a prototype to see how the design is progressing and to help them get a feel for the computer. Because only a few prototypes are constructed, different materials, suppliers, and production methods are used to make them. Thus, although the plastic casing material used in the prototypes held up fine, the production-grade material we selected does not. Had we had more time to test the computer, we would have most likely discovered this problem and been in a good position to change the material.

Questions

1. In what ways does Microstat's approach to developing new products contribute to its problems with quality?

2. In hindsight, do you think Patrick made the right decision when he incorporated the touchpad into the 2900, reduced the ramp-up time, and did not delay the 2900's introduction?

3. What would be the advantages of including production earlier in the product development process?

BIBLIOGRAPHY

Albrecht, K., and R. Zemke. *Service America*. Homewood, Ill.: Dow Jones–Irwin, 1985.

Business Week. "Development Time Is Money" (January 27, 1997): 6.

Bylinsky, G. "The Digital Factory." *Fortune* (November 14, 1994): 92–110.

Dean, J. H., Jr., and G. I. Susman. "Organizing for Manufacturable Design." *Harvard Business Review* (January–February 1989): 28–36.

Dumaine, B. "Payoff from the New Management." *Fortune* (December 13, 1993): 103–110.

Henkoff, R. "Service Is Everybody's Business." *Fortune* (June 27, 1994): 48–60.

Meredith, J. R., and S. J. Mantel, Jr. *Project Management: A Managerial Approach*, 3rd ed. New York: Wiley, 1995.

Nevens, T. M., G. L. Summe, and B. Uttal. "Commercializing Technology: What the Best Companies Do." *Harvard Business Review* (May–June 1990): 60–69.

Oster, P., and J. Rossant. "Call It Worldpool." *Business Week* (November 28, 1994): 98–99.

Parasuraman, A., V. A. Zeithaml, and L. L. Berry. "SERVQUAL: A Multiple-Item Scale for Measuring Consumer Perceptions of Service Quality." *Journal of Retailing*, Vol. 64, No. 1 (Spring 1988): 12–40.

Uttal, B. "Speeding New Ideas to Market." *Fortune* (March 2, 1987): 62–66.

Transformation System Design

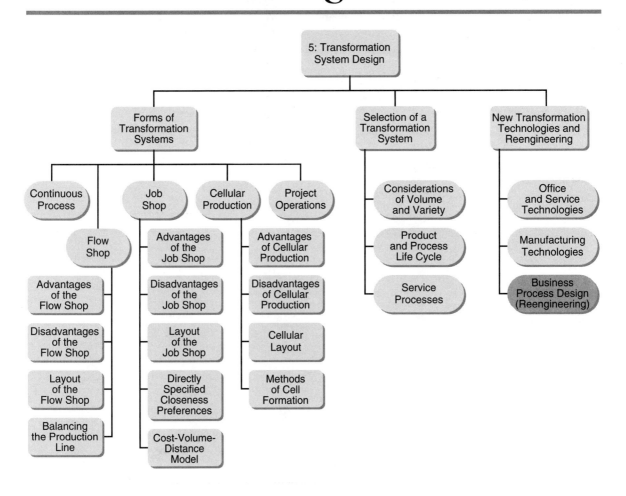

Chapter 4 addressed the highly interdependent nature of product design and the selection and design of the transformation system. This chapter discusses the selection and design of the transformation system in detail. The chapter begins with an overview of the five types of transformation systems and their respective advantages and disadvantages. Next, issues related to the selection and facility layout of an appropriate transformation system—such as considerations of volume, variety, and product life cycles—are discussed. Last, we describe how to reanalyze the transformation system, called Business Process Design (BPD) or reengineering, in order to use new technologies for developing entirely new systems.

INTRODUCTION

- Fender's Custom Shop has produced guitars for many famous and gifted guitarists, including Eric Clapton, John Deacon (Queen), David Gilmour (Pink Floyd), Yngwie Malmsteen, and Stevie Ray Vaughan, to name a few. The Custom Shop uses relatively new equipment and in some cases, prototypical equipment. To produce guitars, computer-controlled routers and lathes are first used to shape the bodies and necks to precise tolerances. Also, Fender has a state-of-the-art machine called a neck duplicator, which can produce a copy of the neck of any existing guitar. After the necks and bodies are fabricated, they are hand- and machine-sanded. Next, detailed inlay work is done with a Hegner precision scroll saw. Following this, paint and finishing operations are done in a special room where air is recirculated 10 times per minute to keep dust and impurities out of the finishes. After paint and finishing, the guitar parts are buffed and then hung up to be seasoned for two weeks. Next, they are moved to the final assembly area, where necks are attached to bodies, and the electronics and hardware are installed. Final assembly of the guitars is done by actual musicians (Bradley 1988).

- The assembly line at IBM's plant in Charlotte, North Carolina, is unlike any other in the world. What makes it unique is that it was designed to produce 27 significantly different products. Indeed, the variety of products produced by the team of 40 workers who operate this line is astounding; these products include hand-held bar-code scanners, portable medical computers, fiber-optic connectors, and satellite communications devices. The assembly line operates by delivering to each worker a "kit" of parts based on the production schedule. Since each product requires different assembly procedures, each worker has a computer screen at his or her station that displays updated assembly instructions for the current product (Bylinsky 1994).

- Rickard Associates is an editorial production company that produces magazines and marketing materials. Interestingly, only two of its employees actually work at its headquarters in New Jersey. The art director works in Arizona; the editors are located in Florida, Georgia, Michigan, and the District of Columbia; and the freelancers are even more scattered. To coordinate work, the Internet and America Online are used. For example, art directors are able to submit electronic copies of finished pages to headquarters in a matter of minutes using these computer networks (Verity 1994).

- Martin Marietta's aerospace electronics manufacturing facility in Denver, Colorado, was initially set up as a job shop with numerous functional departments. As is typical of most job shops, the Marietta plant had high levels of work-in-process and long lead times, and parts had to travel long distances throughout the plant to complete their processing. Also, as is typical of functional organizations, departmental divisions created barriers to communication and often resulted in conflicting goals. To address these problems, Martin Marietta organized its plant into three focused factories. Each focused factory was completely responsible and accountable for building electronic assemblies for a particular application (e.g., flight, space, or ground use). The intent was to make each focused factory a separate business enterprise.

  A factory manager was assigned to each focused factory. The factory managers then engaged in a sort of "NFL draft" to select employees for their teams. Workers not drafted had to find other positions either inside or outside the company. Within the focused factories, product families were identified; these were based on the technology and processing requirements of the products. Next, standardized routings and sequences were identified for each product family. The plant realized a number of improvements as a result of these and other changes, including seven consecutive months of production with no scrap, a 50 percent reduction in work-in-process inventory, a 21 percent average reduction in lead times, and a 90 percent reduction in overtime (Ferras 1994).

- In the early 1990s, Nynex released Robert Thrasher from his duties as chief operating officer and assigned him to lead an effort aiming to reinvent the company. From the very beginning, Thrasher chose not to examine the company in the traditional way in terms of its divisions, departments, and functions. Rather, he opted to analyze the company in terms of four core processes that cut across the entire organization. Thrasher defined these processes as customer operations, customer support, customer contact, and customer provisioning. With the processes defined, Thrasher decided to obtain the services of the Boston Consulting Group (BCG) to help reengineer the projects. Teams were then formed from 80 Nynex employees and 20 BCG consultants with the charge of reducing operating expenses by 35 to 40 percent.

  To stimulate their thinking and to learn from the best, team members visited 152 "best practice" companies, thereby identifying a number of major inefficiencies at Nynex. For example, the teams learned that Nynex purchased 83 different brands of personal computers, that $500 per truck was being spent painting newly purchased trucks a different shade of white, and that $4.5 million was spent to identify and pursue $900,000 in unpaid bills. After identifying these problems, the teams developed a list of 85 "quick wins." For instance, Nynex will save $7 million a year in postage costs by printing on both sides of customers' bills and will save $25 million by standardizing on two personal computer models. Companywide, the teams' suggestions reduced Nynex's $6 billion operating expenses by $1.5 to $1.7 billion in 1997. Doing this was expected to provide Nynex with an internal rate of return of 1025 percent and pay back its investment in two years (*Business Week* 1994).

These examples illustrate several transformation systems. The Fender Custom Shop is a job shop that has specialized departments for routing, lathe operations, inlaying, paint and finishing, and final assembly. Likewise, because work is organized by the task performed, Rickard Associates is also a job shop—even though the work is not performed in one location. Actually, companies like Rickard, which rely on information technology to bring separated workers together, are beginning to be known as *virtual organizations*. Martin Marietta converted into *focused factories*. And assembly lines like the one IBM uses are referred to as flow shops.

This chapter continues the discussion of the design of the transformation system initially presented in Chapter 4. There, our discussion centered on the interdependence of developing a new product or service and developing the transformation system to produce and deliver it. This chapter is devoted to the design of the transformation system for maximum competitiveness including selecting the form of transformation system and how the operations are laid out for each form.

The general procedure in designing a transformation system is to consider all alternative forms and combinations to devise the best strategy for obtaining the desired outputs. The major considerations in designing the transformation system— *efficiency, effectiveness, capacity, lead time, flexibility,* and so on—are so interdependent that changing the system to alter one will change the others, as well.

The main purpose of *layout analysis* is to maximize the efficiency (cost-orientation) or effectiveness (e.g., quality, lead time, flexibility) of operations. In the examples at the beginning of the chapter, benefits realized by the companies after adopting a new layout included reduced work-in-process inventory, shorter lead times, less scrap, shorter travel distances, and less need for manufacturing space. Other purposes also exist, such as reducing safety or health hazards, minimizing interference or noise between different operational areas (e.g., separating painting from sanding), facilitating crucial staff interactions, or maximizing customers' exposure to products or services.

In laying out service operations, the emphasis is often more on accommodating the customer than on operations per se. Moreover, capacity and layout analyses are frequently conducted simultaneously by analyzing service operations and the wait that the customer must endure. Thus, *waiting line* (or *queuing*) *theory* is heavily used in the design of a service delivery system. The layouts of parking lots, entry zones, reception rooms, waiting areas, service facilities, and other areas of customer contact are of top priority in service-oriented firms such as nightclubs, restaurants, and banks.

In a constantly changing environment, the transformation system and its layout may have to be constantly maintained and even redesigned to cope with new demands, new products and services, new government regulations, and new technology. Robots, microcomputers, increasing global competition, and shortages of materials and energy are only a few examples of changes in the past decade that have forced organizations to recognize the necessity of adapting their operations.

The five basic forms of transformation systems are (1) continuous process, (2) flow shop, (3) job shop, (4) cellular, and (5) project. The continuous process industries are in many ways the most advanced, moving fluid material continuously through vats and pipes until a final product is obtained. Flow shops produce discrete, usually standardized outputs on a continuous basis by means of assembly lines or mass production, often using automated equipment. Cellular shops produce "families" of outputs within a variety of flow cells, but numerous cells within the plant can offer a range of families of outputs. Job shops offer a wide range of possible outputs, usually in batches, by individualized processing into and out of a number of functionally specialized departments. These departments typically consist of a set of largely identical equipment, as well as highly skilled workers. (Potentially, job shops could also produce unique—that is, one-of-a-kind—customized outputs, but job shops that do this are commonly called *model shops* or, in Europe, *jobbers*.) Finally, projects are one-of-a-kind endeavors on a massive scale when the labor and equipment are brought to each site rather than to a fixed production facility.

$\mathscr{F}$ORMS OF TRANSFORMATION SYSTEMS _____

Continuous Process

The ***continuous transformation process*** is used to produce highly standardized outputs in extremely large volumes. In some cases these outputs have become so standardized that there are virtually no real differences between the outputs of different firms. Examples of such *commodities* include water, gases, chemicals, electricity, ores, rubber, flour, spirits, cements, petroleum, and milk. The name *continuous process* reflects the typical practice of running these operations 24 hours a day, 7 days a week. One reason for running these systems continuously is to spread their enormous fixed cost over as large a volume as possible, thereby reducing unit costs. This is particularly important in commodity markets, where price can be the single most important factor in competing successfully. Another reason for operating these processes continuously is that stopping and starting them can be prohibitively expensive.

The operations in these industries are highly automated, with very specialized equipment and controls, often electronic and computerized. Such automation and the expense it entails are necessary because of strict processing requirements. Because of the highly specialized and automated nature of the equipment, changing the rate of output can be quite difficult. The facility is typically a maze of pipes, conveyors, tanks, valves, vats, and bins. The layout follows the processing stages of the product, and the output rate is controlled through equipment capacity and flow and mixture rates. Labor requirements are low and are devoted primarily to monitoring and maintaining the equipment.

The major characteristic of processing industries is that there is often one primary, "fluid"-type input material (gas, wood, wheat, milk, etc.). This input is then often converted to multiple outputs, although there may be only one (e.g., water). In contrast, in discrete production many types of materials are made or purchased and combined to form the output.

Although human variation in continuous processing firms does not usually create the problems it creates in discrete manufacturing, the demands of processing are usually more critical. For example, chemical reactions must be accurately timed. The result is that initial setup of equipment and procedures is even more complex and critical than it is for flow shops. Fixed costs are extremely high; the major variable cost is materials. Variable labor (excluding distribution) is usually insignificant.

Flow Shop

The *flow shop* is a transformation system similar to the continuous process, the major difference being that in the flow shop there is a discrete product, whereas in continuous processes the end product is not naturally divisible. Thus, in continuous processes an additional step, such as bottling or canning, might be needed to get the product into discrete units. Like the continuous process, the flow shop treats all the outputs as basically the same, and the flow of work is thus relatively continuous. Organizations that use this form are heavily automated, with large, special-purpose equipment. The characteristics of the flow shop are a fixed set of inputs, constant throughput times, and a fixed set of outputs. Examples of the flow form are pencil manufacturing, steelmaking, automobile assembly, the car wash, and processing insurance claims.

An organization that produces, or plans to produce, a high volume of a small variety of outputs will thus probably organize its operations as a flow shop. In doing so, the organization will take advantage of the simplicity and the savings in variable costs that such an approach offers. Since outputs and operations are standardized, specialized equipment can be used to perform the necessary operations at low per-unit costs, and the relatively large fixed costs of the equipment are distributed over a large volume of outputs.

Continuous types of materials-handling equipment, such as conveyors—again operating at low per-unit costs—can be used because the operations are standardized and, typically, all outputs follow the same path from one operation to the next. This standardization of treatment provides for a known, fixed throughput time, giving managers easier control of the system and more reliable delivery dates. The flow shop is easier to manage for other reasons as well: routing, scheduling, and control are all facilitated because each output does not have to be individually monitored and controlled. Standardization of operations means that less skilled workers can be used and each manager's span of control can increase.

The general form of the flow shop is illustrated in Figure 5.1, which shows a *production line*. (If only assembly operations were being performed, as in many automotive plants, the line would be called an *assembly line*.) This production line could represent new military inductees taking their physical exams, small appliances being assembled, or double-decker hamburgers being prepared.

Note that both services and products can be organized as flow shops and can capitalize on the many advantages of this form of processing.

Advantages of the Flow Shop

The primary advantage of a flow shop is the low per-unit cost that is attainable owing to specialized high-volume equipment, bulk purchasing, lower labor rates,

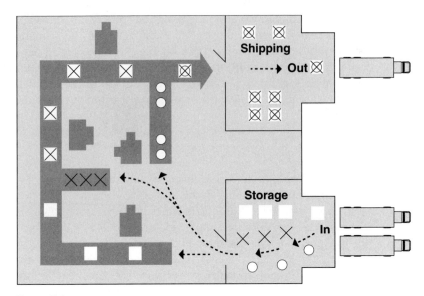

Figure 5.1   A generalized flow shop operation.

efficient utilization of the facility, low in-process inventories, and simplified managerial control. Because of the high rate of output, materials can often be bought in large quantities at a significant savings. Also, because operations are standardized, processing times tend to remain constant so that large in-process inventories are not required to queue up for processing. This minimizes investment in in-process inventory and queue (*buffer*) space. Furthermore, because a standardized product is produced, inventory control and purchasing decisions are routine.

Because the machines are specialized, less-skilled operators are needed, and therefore, lower wages can be paid. In addition, fewer supervisors are needed, further reducing costs. Since the flow shop is generally continuous, with materials handling often built into the system itself, the operations can be designed to perform compactly and efficiently with narrow aisles, thereby making maximum use of space.

The simplification in managerial control of a well-designed flow shop should not be overlooked. Constant operations problems requiring unending managerial attention penalize the organization by distracting managers from their normal duties—planning and decision making.

Disadvantages of the Flow Shop

In spite of the important cost advantage of the flow shop, it can have some serious drawbacks. Not only is a variety of output difficult to obtain; even changes in the rate of output are hard to make. Changing the *rate* of output may require using overtime, laying off workers, adding additional shifts, or temporarily closing the plant. Also, because the equipment is so specialized, minor changes in the design of the product often require substantial changes in the equipment. Thus, important changes in product design are infrequent, and this could weaken the organization's marketing position.

A well-known problem in flow shops is boredom and absenteeism among the labor force. Since the equipment performs the skilled tasks, there is no challenge for the workers. And, of course, the constant, unending, repetitive nature of the manufacturing line can dehumanize the workers. Since the rate of work flow is generally set (*paced*) by the line speed, incentive pay and other output-based incentives are not possible.

The flow production line form has another important drawback. If the line should stop for any reason—a breakdown of a machine or conveyor, a shortage of supplies, and so forth—production may come to an immediate halt unless work-in-process (WIP) is stored at key points in the line. Such occurrences are prohibitively expensive.

Other requirements of the flow shop also add to its cost and its problems. For example, parts must be standardized so that they will fit together easily and quickly on the assembly line. And, since all machines and labor must work at the same repetitive pace in order to coordinate operations, the work loads along the entire line are generally *balanced* to the pace of the slowest element. To keep the line running smoothly, a large support staff is required, as well as large stocks of raw materials, all of which also add to the expense.

Last, in the flow shop, simplicity in *ongoing operation* is achieved at the cost of complexity in the initial *setup*. The planning, design, and installation of the typically complicated, special-purpose, high-volume equipment are mammoth tasks. The equipment is costly not only to set up originally but also to maintain and service. Furthermore, such special-purpose equipment is very susceptible to obsolescence and is difficult to dispose of or to modify for other purposes.

Layout of the Flow Shop

The crux of the problem of realizing the advantages of a flow shop is whether the work flow can be subdivided sufficiently so that labor and equipment are utilized smoothly throughout the processing operations. If, for example, one operation takes longer than all the others, this will become a bottleneck, delaying all the operations following it and restricting the output rate to its low value.

Obtaining smooth utilization of workers and equipment across all operations involves assigning to groups tasks that take about the same amount of time to complete. This balancing applies to production lines where parts or outputs are produced, as well as to assembly lines where parts are assembled into final products.

Final assembly operations usually have more labor input and fewer fixed-equipment cycles and can therefore be subdivided more easily for smooth flow. Either of two types of lines can then be used. A **paced line** uses some sort of conveyor and moves the output along at a continuous rate, and operators do their work as the output passes by them. For longer operations the worker may walk or ride alongside the conveyor and then have to walk back to the starting workstation. The many disadvantages of this arrangement, such as boredom and monotony, are, of course, well known. An automobile assembly line is a common example of a paced line. Workers install doors, engines, hoods, and the like as the conveyor moves past them.

In unpaced lines, the workers build up queues between workstations and can then vary their pace to meet the needs of the job or their personal desires; however, average daily output must remain the same. The advantage of an unpaced line is that a worker can spend longer on the more difficult outputs and balance this with the easier outputs. Similarly, workers can vary their pace to add variety to a boring task. For example, a worker may work fast to get ahead of the pace for a few seconds before returning to the task.

There are some disadvantages to unpaced lines, however. For one thing, they cannot be used with large, bulky products because too much in-process storage space is required. More important, minimum output rates are difficult to maintain because short durations in one operation usually do not dovetail with long durations in the next operation. When long durations coincide, operators downstream from these operations may run out of in-process inventory to work on and may thus be forced to sit idle.

For operations that can be smoothed to obtain the benefits of a production line, there are two main elements in designing the most efficient line. The first is formulating the situation by determining the necessary output rate, the available work time per day, the times for operational tasks, and the order of precedence of the operations. The second element is actually to solve the balancing problem by subdividing and grouping the operations into balanced jobs. To more clearly communicate the concept of a balanced production line, we will give an example that addresses both of these main elements. In reality, of course, one of a variety of computer packages would be employed.

Balancing the Production Line

We illustrate the formulation of the ***line balancing*** situation with an example. Longform Credit receives 1200 credit applications a day, on the average. Longform competes on the basis of its ability to process applications within hours. Daily application processing tasks, average times, and required preceding tasks (tasks that must be completed before the next task) are listed in Table 5.1.

The *precedence graph* for these tasks is shown in Figure 5.2; it is constructed directly from Table 5.1. This graph is simply a picture of the operations (boxed) with

𝒯ABLE 5.1 • Tasks in Credit Application Processing

Task	Average Time (Minutes)	Immediately Preceding Tasks
Open and stack applications	0.20	none
Process enclosed letter; make note of and handle any special requirements	0.37	*a*
Check off form 1 for page 1 of application	0.21	*a*
Check off form 2 for page 2 of application; file original copy of application	0.18	*a*
Calculate credit limit from standardized tables according to forms 1 and 2	0.19	*c, d*
Supervisor checks quotation in light of special processing of letter, notes type of form letter, address, and credit limit to return to applicant	0.39	*b, e*
Secretary types in details on form letter and mails	0.36	*f*
Total	1.90	

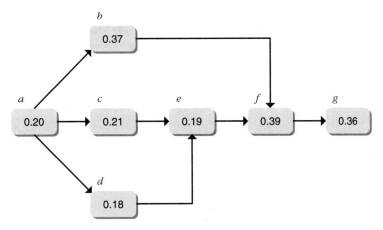

Figure 5.2   Precedence graph for credit applications.

arrows indicating which tasks must precede others. The number or letter of the operation is shown above the box, with its time inside.

In balancing a line, the intent is to find a ***cycle time*** in which each workstation can complete its tasks. A workstation is usually a single person, but it may include any number of people responsible for completing all the tasks associated with the job for that station. Conceptually, at the end of this time every workstation passes its part on to the next station. Task elements are thus grouped for each workstation so as to utilize as much of this cycle time as possible but not to exceed it. Each workstation will have a slightly different *idle time* within the cycle time.

$$\text{Cycle time} = \text{available work time/demand}$$

$$= \frac{8 \text{ hrs. } \times 60 \text{ min./hr.}}{1200 \text{ applications}} = 0.4 \text{ min./application}$$

The cycle time is determined from the required output rate. In this case, the average daily output rate must equal the average daily input rate, 1200. If it is less than this figure, a backlog of applications will accumulate. If it is more than this, unnecessary idle time will result. Assuming an 8-hour day, 1200 applications per 8 hours means completing 150 every hour or 1 every 0.4 minute—this, then, is the cycle time.

Adding up the task times in Table 5.1, we can see that the total is 1.9 minutes. Since every workstation will do no more than 0.4 minute's worth of work during each cycle, it is clear that a minimum of 1.9/0.4 = 4.75 workstations are needed—or, always rounding *up*, 5 workstations.

> Number of theoretical workstations, $N_T = \Sigma$ task times/cycle time
>
> $$= \frac{1.9}{0.4} = 4.75 \text{ (i.e., 5)}$$

It may be, however, that the work cannot be divided and balanced in five stations—that six, or even seven, may be needed. For example, precedence relationships may interfere with assigning two tasks to the same workstation. This is why we referred to N_T as the *theoretical* number of workstations needed. If more workstations are actually needed than the theoretical number, the production line will be less efficient. The *efficiency* of the line with N_A actual stations may be computed from

$$\text{Efficiency} = \frac{\text{output}}{\text{input}} = \frac{\text{total task time}}{(N_A \text{ stations}) \times \text{cycle time}}$$

$$= \frac{1.9}{5 \times 0.4} = 95 \text{ percent if the line can be balanced with 5 stations}$$

$$= \frac{1.9}{6 \times 0.4} = 79 \text{ percent if 6 stations required}$$

In the formula for efficiency, input is represented by the amount of work required to produce one unit, and output is represented by the amount of work that actually goes into producing one unit.

Now that the problem has been formulated, we can attempt to balance the line by assigning tasks to stations. We begin by assuming that all workers can do any of the tasks and check back on this later. There are many heuristic rules for which task to assign to a station next. We will use the LOT rule; select the task with the *longest operation time* next.

The general procedure for line balancing is as follows:

- Construct a list of the tasks whose predecessor tasks have already been completed.
- Consider each of these tasks, one at a time, in LOT order and place them within the station.
- As a task is tentatively placed in a station, new follower tasks can now be added to the list.
- Consider adding to the station any tasks in this list whose time fits within the remaining time for that station.
- Continue in this manner until as little idle time as possible remains for the station.

We will now demonstrate this procedure with reference to Longform, using the information in Table 5.1 and Figure 5.2. The first tasks to consider are those with no preceding tasks. Thus, task *a*, taking 0.2 of the 0.4 minute available, is assigned to station 1. This, then, makes tasks *b* (0.37 minute), *c* (0.21 minute), and *d* (0.18 minute) eligible for assignment. Trying the longest first, *b*, then *c*, and last *d*, we find that only *d* can be assigned to station 1 without exceeding the 0.4-minute cycle time; thus, station 1 will include tasks *a* and *d*. Since only 0.02 minute remains unassigned in station 1 and no task is that short, we then consider assignments to station 2.

Only *b* and *c* are eligible for assignment (since *e* requires that *c* be completed first), and *b* (0.37 minute) will clearly require a station by itself; *b* is, therefore, assigned to station 2. Only *c* is now eligible for assignment, since *f* requires that both *e* and *b* be completed and *e* is not yet completed. But when we assign *c* (0.21 minute) to station 3, task *e* (0.19 minute) becomes available and can also be just accommodated in station 3. Task *f* (0.39 minute), the next eligible task, requires its own station; this leaves *g* (0.36 minute) to station 5. These assignments are illustrated in Figure 5.3 and Table 5.2.

We now check the feasibility of these assignments. In many cases, several aspects

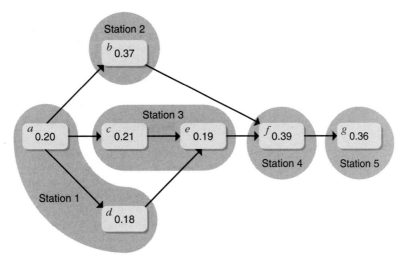

Figure 5.3 Station assignments.

must be considered in this check (as discussed later), but here our only concern is that the clerk or the secretary does not do task *f* and that the supervisor does not do task *g* (or, we hope, much of a through *e*). As it happens, task *f* is a station by itself, so there is no problem.

Job Shop

The ***job shop*** gets its name because unique jobs must be produced. In this form of transformation system each output, or each small batch of outputs, is processed differently. Therefore, the flow of work through the facility tends to be intermittent. The general characteristics of a job shop are *grouping* of staff and equipment according to function; a large *variety* of inputs; a considerable amount of *transport* of staff, materials, or recipients; and large *variations* in system flow times (the time it takes for a complete "job"). In general, each output takes a different route through

𝒯ABLE 5.2 • Station Task Assignments

Station	Time Available	Eligible Tasks	Task Assigned	Idle Time
1	.40	*a*	a	
	.20	*b, c, d*	d	
	.02	*b, c*	none will fit	.02
2	.40	*b, c*	b	
	.03	*c*	c will not fit	.03
3	.40	*c*	c	
	.19	*e*	e	.00
4	.40	*f*	f	
	.01	*g*	g will not fit	.01
5	.40	*g*	g	.04

the organization, requires different operations, uses different inputs, and takes a different amount of time.

This type of transformation system is common when the outputs differ significantly in form, structure, materials, or processing required. For example, an organization that has a wide variety of outputs or does custom work (e.g., custom guitars) would probably be a job shop. Specific examples of product and service organizations of this form are tailor shops, general offices, machine shops, public parks, hospitals, universities, automobile repair shops, criminal justice systems, and department stores. By and large, the job shop is especially appropriate for service organizations because services are often customized, and hence, each service requires different operations.

Clearly, the efficient management of a job shop is a difficult task, since every output must be treated differently. In addition, the resources available for processing are limited. Furthermore, not only is it management's task to ensure the performance of the proper functions of each output, where considerations of quality and deadlines may vary, but management must also be sure that the available resources (staff, equipment, materials, supplies, capital) are being efficiently utilized. Often there is a difficult trade-off between efficiency and flexibility of operations. Job-based processes tend to emphasize flexibility over efficiency.

Figure 5.4 represents the flow through a job shop. This facility might be a library, an auto repair shop, or an office. Each particular "job" travels from one area to another, and so on, according to its unique routing, until it is fully processed. Temporary in-process storage may occur between various operations while jobs are waiting for subsequent processing (standing in line for the coffee machine).

Advantages of the Job Shop

The widespread use of the job shop form is due to its many advantages. The job shop is usually selected to provide the organization with the flexibility needed to

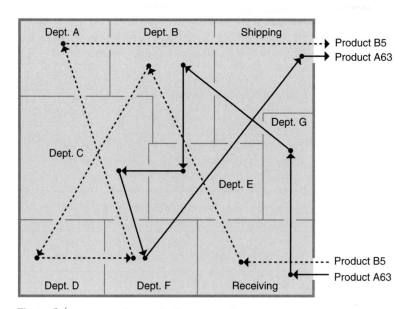

Figure 5.4 A generalized job shop operation.

respond to individual, small-volume demands (or even custom demands). The ability to produce a wide variety of outputs at reasonable cost is thus the primary advantage of this form. General-purpose equipment is used, and this is in greater demand and is usually available from more suppliers at a lower price than special-purpose equipment. In addition, used equipment is more likely to be available, further reducing the necessary investment. There is a larger base of experience with general-purpose equipment; therefore, problems with installation and maintenance are more predictable, and replacement parts are more widely available. Last, since general-purpose equipment is easier to modify or use elsewhere and disposal is much easier, the expense of obsolescence is minimized.

Because of the functional arrangement of the equipment, there are also other advantages. Resources for a function requiring special staff, materials, or facilities (e.g., painting or audiovisual equipment) may be centralized at the location of that function, and the organization can thus save expense through high utilization rates. Distracting or dangerous equipment, supplies, or activities may also be segregated from other operations in facilities that are soundproof, airtight, explosion-proof, and so forth.

One advantage to the staff is that with more highly skilled work involving constantly varying jobs, responsibility and pride in one's work are increased, and boredom is reduced. Other advantages to the staff are that concentrations of experience and expertise are available and morale increases when people with similar skills work together in centralized locations (all music teachers together). Because all workers who perform similar activities are grouped together, each worker has the opportunity to learn from others, and the workers can easily collaborate to solve difficult problems. Furthermore, because the pace of the work is not dictated by a moving "line," incentive arrangements may be set up. Last, because no line exists that must forever keep moving, the entire set of organizational operations does not halt whenever any one part of the operation stops working; other functional areas can continue operating, at least until in-process inventory is depleted. Also, other general-purpose resources can usually substitute for the nonfunctioning resource: one machine for another, one staff member for another, one material for another.

Disadvantages of the Job Shop

The general-purpose equipment of job shops is usually slower than special-purpose equipment, resulting in higher variable (per-unit) costs. In addition, the cost of direct labor for the experienced staff necessary to operate general-purpose equipment further increases unit costs of production above what semi-skilled or unskilled workers would require. The result, in terms of costs of the outputs, is that the variable costs of production are higher for the general-purpose than for the special-purpose equipment, facilities, and staff, but the initial cost of the equipment and facilities is significantly less. For small-output volumes the job shop results in a lower total cost. As volume of output increases, however, the high variable costs begin to outweigh the savings in initial investment. The result is that, for high-production volumes, the job shop is not the most economic approach (although its use may still be dictated by other considerations, as when particular equipment threatens workers' health or safety).

Inventories are also frequently a disadvantage in the job shop, especially in product organizations. Not only do many types of raw materials, parts, and supplies have to be kept for the wide variety of outputs anticipated, but *in-process invento-ries,* that is, jobs waiting for processing, typically become very large and thereby represent a sizable capital investment for the organization. It is not unusual for batches of parts in these environments to spend 90 to 95 percent of the time they are in the shop either waiting to be moved or waiting to be processed. Further-more, because there are so many inventory items that must travel between operat-ing departments in order to be processed, the cost of handling materials is also typically high. Since job routings between operations are not identical, inexpensive fixed materials-handling mechanisms like conveyor belts cannot be used. Instead, larger and more costly equipment is used; therefore, corridors and aisles must be large enough to accommodate it. This necessitates allocating even more space, be-yond the extra space needed to store additional inventories.

Finally, managerial control of the job shop is extremely difficult, as mentioned earlier. Because the output varies in terms of function, processing, quality, and tim-ing, the managerial tasks of routing, scheduling, cost accounting, and such become nearly impossible when demand for the output is high. Expediters must track down lost jobs and reorder priorities. In addition to watching the progress of indi-vidual jobs, management must continually strive to achieve the proper balance of materials, staff, and equipment; otherwise, highly expensive resources will sit idle while bottlenecks occur elsewhere.

Layout of the Job Shop

Because of its relative permanence, the layout of the operations is probably one of the most crucial elements affecting the efficiency of a job shop. In general, the problem of laying out operations in a job shop is quite complex. The difficulty stems from the variety of outputs and the constant changes in outputs that are characteristic of organizations with an intermittent transformation system. The opti-mal layout for the existing set of outputs may be relatively inefficient for the out-puts to be produced six months from now. This is particularly true of job shops where there is no proprietary product and only for-contract work is performed. One week such a shop might produce 1000 ashtrays and the next week it might produce an 8000-gallon vat. Therefore, a job-shop layout is based on the histori-cally stable output pattern of the organization and expected changes in that pat-tern, rather than on current operations or outputs.

A variety of factors can be important in the interrelations among the operations of a job shop. If all the qualitative and quantitative factors can be analyzed and combined, the relative importance of locating each department close to or far from each of the other departments may be used to determine a layout. This approach is particularly useful for service operations where movements of materials are not particularly significant. To illustrate how this concept might be achieved in practice we next present a simplified example. Following this, we illustrate how a purely cost-based layout could be achieved.

Directly Specified Closeness Preferences

As a simplified example, consider Table 5.3, where six departments have been ana-lyzed for the desirability of closeness to each other. Assume we are given the orga-nization's *closeness preferences,* indicated by the letters A, E, I, O, U, and X, with

$\mathcal{T}_{ABLE}$ 5.3 • Directly Specified Closeness Preferences*

Department	Department					
	1	2	3	4	5	6
1		E	A	U	U	U
2			U	I	I	U
3				U	U	A
4					I	U
5						I
6						

*Note:
A = Absolutely necessary   O = Ordinary closeness OK
E = Especially important   U = Unimportant
I = Important   X = Undesirable

the meanings given in the table. In general, the desirability of closeness decreases along the alphabet until U, which is "immaterial," and then jumps to "undesirable" with X; there is no range of undesirability in this case, although there could be, of course.

One way of starting the layout process is simply to draw boxes representing the departments in the order given in the table and show closeness preferences on the arcs (line segments) joining them. Figure 5.5a illustrates this for Table 5.3. The next step is to shift the departments with A on their arcs nearer each other and those with X away from each other. When these have been shifted as much as possible, the E arcs, then the I arcs, and finally the O arcs will be considered for relocation, resulting in an improved layout, such as in Figure 5.5b.

Cost–Volume–Distance Model

In the cost–volume–distance (CVD) approach, the desirability of closeness is based on the total cost of moving materials or people between departments. Clearly, a layout

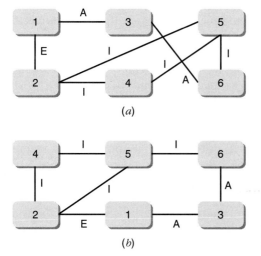

Figure 5.5   Closeness preferences layout: (a) Initial layout. (b) Final layout.

can never be completely reduced to just one such objective, but where the cost of movement is significant, this approach produces reasonable first approximations. The objective is to minimize the costs of interrelations among operations by locating those operations that interrelate extensively close to one another. If we label one of the departments i and another department j, then the cost of moving materials between departments i and j depends on the distance between i and j, D_{ij}.

In addition, the cost will usually depend on the amount or volume moving from i to j, such as trips, cases, volume, weight, or some other such measure, which we will denote by V_{ij}. Then, if the cost of the flow from i to j per-unit amount per-unit distance is C_{ij}, the total cost of i relating with j is $C_{ij}V_{ij}D_{ij}$. Note that C, V, and D may have different values for different types of flows and that they need not have the same values from j to i as from i to j, since the flow in opposite directions may be of an entirely different nature. For example, information may be flowing from i to j, following a certain paperwork path; but sheet steel may flow from j to i, following a lift truck or conveyor belt path.

Adding the flows from i to every one of N possible departments, we find that the total cost of department i interrelating with all other departments is

$$\sum_{j=1}^{N} C_{ij}V_{ij}D_{ij}$$

(It is normally assumed that $C_{ii}V_{ii}D_{ii} = 0$, since the distance from i to itself is zero.) Adding together the costs for all the departments results in the total cost.

$$TC = \sum_{i=1}^{N}\sum_{j=1}^{N} C_{ij}V_{ij}D_{ij}$$

Our goal is to find the layout that minimizes this total cost. This may be done by evaluating the cost of promising layouts or, as in the following simplified example, by evaluating *all possible* layouts.

The section of a business school containing the administrative offices of the operations management department is illustrated in Figure 5.6. Each office is approximately 10 feet by 10 feet, so the walking distance (D) between adjacent offices (i.e., offices 1 and 2, and offices 2 and 3) is 10 feet, whereas the distance between diagonal offices (offices 1 and 3) is 15 feet.

The average number of interpersonal trips made each day is given in a travel or load matrix (Table 5.4). According to Table 5.4, each day the assistant makes 5 trips to the chairperson's office and 17 trips to the secretary's office. Thus, the assistant would travel 305 feet (10 feet × 5 trips + 15 feet × 17 trips) each day. Assuming that the chairperson is paid approximately twice as much as the secretary and the junior administrative assistant, determine if the current arrangement is best (i.e., least costly) in terms of transit time and, if not, what arrangement would be better.

For convenience, the offices are numbered in Figure 5.6. Before calculating total costs of all possible arrangements, some preliminary analysis is worthwhile. First, because of special utility connections, restrooms are usually not considered relocatable. In addition, the relocation of the restrooms in this example would not achieve any result that could not be achieved by moving the other offices instead.

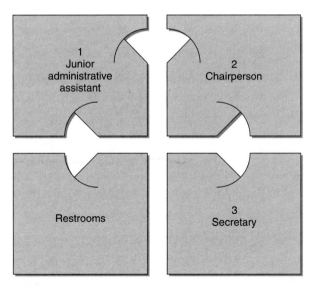

Figure 5.6 Office layout.

Second, many arrangements are mirror images of other arrangements and thus need not be evaluated, since their cost will be the same. For example, interchanging offices 1 and 3 will result in the same costs as the current layout. The essence of the problem, then, is to *determine which office should be located diagonally across from the restrooms.* There are three alternatives: chairperson, assistant, or secretary.

Now, let us evaluate each of the three possibilities as the "diagonal office"—first the chairperson, then the assistant, and last the secretary. The costs will simply be denoted as 1 for the assistant and the secretary or 2 for the chairperson (who earns twice as much as the others). As noted, the V_{ij} "volumes" will be the number of trips from i to j taken from the load matrix, and the distances will depend on who has the diagonal office across from the restrooms. The calculations for each arrangement are shown here.

1. Chairperson: $TC = 1(5)10 + 1(17)15 + 2(10)10 + 2(5)10 + 1(13)15 + 1(25)10$
$$= 1050$$

2. Assistant: $TC = 1(5)10 + 1(17)10 + 2(10)10 + 2(5)15 + 1(13)10 + 1(25)15$
$$= 1070$$

3. Secretary: $TC = 1(5)15 + 1(17)10 + 2(10)15 + 2(5)10 + 1(13)10 + 1(25)10$
$$= 1025 \text{ (lowest)}$$

*T*ABLE 5.4 • **Load Matrix, V_{ij} (Trips)**

	To		
From	1 Assistant	2 Chairperson	3 Secretary
1 Assistant	—	5	17
2 Chairperson	10	—	5
3 Secretary	13	25	—

To better understand these calculations, consider the current arrangement in which the chair has the office diagonal to the restrooms. In this case, the assistant must travel 305 feet each day, as was explained earlier. Each day the chairperson would have to travel 150 feet: (10 feet × 10 trips to the assistant) + (10 feet × 5 trips to the secretary). Finally, the secretary would have to travel 445 feet each day: (15 feet × 13 trips to the assistant) + (10 feet × 25 trips to the chair). Since the chairperson is paid twice as much as the secretary and assistant, we weight the chairperson's travel distance as twice that of the other two workers. Using this weighting scheme provides a total cost of the current office arrangement of 1050: that is, 305 + (2 × 150) + 445. The best arrangement is to put the secretary in the office diagonal to the restrooms for a relative cost of 1025. Again, if faced with an actual layout task, a computer package could be used.

Cellular Production

Cellular production is a relatively new type of transformation system that many firms have recently been adopting. It combines the advantages of the job shop and flow shop to obtain the high variety possible with the job form and the reduced costs and short response times available with the flow form. Figure 5.7 contrasts the job shop with cellular production. The job shop in Figure 5.7*a* has separate departments for welding, turning, heat treat, milling, and forming. This type of layout provides flexibility to produce a wide range of products simply by varying the

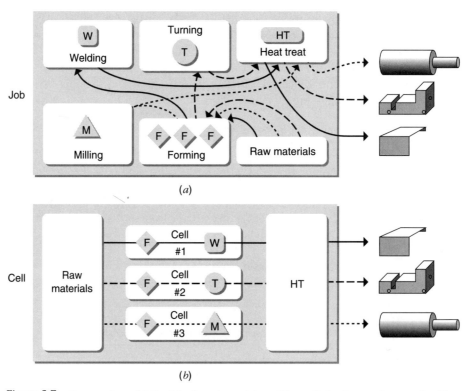

Figure 5.7   Conversion of (*a*) a job shop layout into (*b*) a cellular layout for part families.

sequence in which the products visit the five processing departments. Also, flexibility is enhanced, as machines are easily substituted for one another should a specified machine be busy or nonoperational.

Figure 5.7*b* shows cellular production. The cellular form is based on **group technology**, which seeks to achieve efficiency by exploiting similarities inherent in parts. In production, this is accomplished by identifying groups of parts that have similar processing requirements. Parts with similar processing requirements are called *part families*. Figure 5.8 provides an example of how a variety of parts can be organized into part families.

After the parts are divided into families, a **cell** is created that includes the human skills and all the equipment required to produce a family. Since the outputs are all similar, the equipment can be set up in one pattern to produce the entire family and does not need to be set up again for another type of output (as is necessary in a job shop). Some cells consist of just one machine producing a complete product or service. Other cells may have as many as 50 people working with dozens of machines.

A facility using cells is generally organized on the basis of *teams*. That is, a team is completely responsible for conducting the work within its cell. The team members usually schedule and inspect the work themselves, once they know when it is due. Occasionally, work must be taken outside a cell for a special treatment or process that is unavailable within the cell, but these operations are minimized whenever possible.

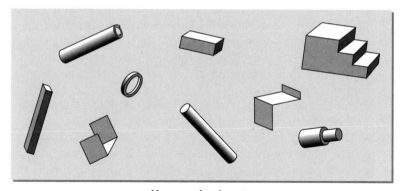

Unorganized parts

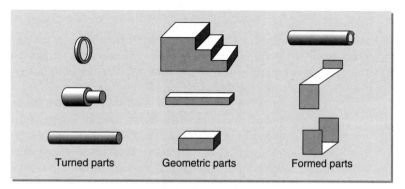

Turned parts   Geometric parts   Formed parts

Parts organized by families

Figure 5.8   Organization of miscellaneous parts into familes

The families are derived from one of a number of different approaches. Sometimes the basis is the machines that are needed to produce the output, or the families may be based on the size of the equipment, the quality required, the skills needed, or any other overriding consideration. This is called the *classification* stage. Items are classified into families—sometimes by simple inspection and other times by complex analysis of their routing requirements, production requirements, part geometry, and the like. It is generally not feasible to classify all the outputs into one of a limited number of families, so at some point all the miscellaneous outputs are placed in a "remainder" cell, which is operated as a mini-job shop.

Advantages of Cellular Production

Organizations adopt the cellular form to achieve many of the efficiencies associated with products that are mass-produced using flow transformation systems in less repetitive job shop environments. However, not all the advantages of a full flow shop or a full job shop can be obtained, because not enough high-volume equipment can be purchased to obtain the economies of scale that flow shops enjoy. And because the equipment is dedicated to part families, some of the variety afforded by job shops is lost.

One of the most important advantages of the cellular form is reduced machine setup times. In the job shop, when a worker completes the processing of one batch, the machine is set up for the next batch. Because a wide variety of parts typically flow through each department in a job shop, the next batch of parts processed by the worker will likely be different from the one just completed. This means that the worker may have to spend several hours or more simply setting up and preparing the machine for the next batch of parts. In cellular production, machine setup times are minimized because each cell processes only parts that have similar (or identical) setup and processing requirements. It is extremely desirable to minimize machine setup times, because setup time takes away from the amount of time machines can be used to produce the outputs.

Decreasing machine setup times provides several benefits. First, as we have just noted, when setup times decrease, the amount of time equipment is available to process parts increases. Second, increased capacity means that the company can produce at a given level with fewer machines. Reducing the number of machines used not only reduces the costs of equipment and maintenance, but also reduces the amount of floor space needed. Third, shorter setup times make it more economical to produce smaller batches. For instance, if the setup time is four hours, it would not be efficient to produce a small number of parts using a particular machine, only to spend another four hours to set it up for the next batch. However, if the machine required only a few minutes of setup time, it might be practical to produce a few parts on the machine.

There are numerous benefits associated with producing parts in small batches. To begin, producing small batches enhances an organization's flexibility in responding to changes in product mix. Also, reducing the size of batches leads to reductions in work-in-process inventory. Less inventory means that less space is needed to store it and less capital is tied up in it. Also, product lead times are shorter, and shorter lead times facilitate more accurate forecasting and may also provide a competitive advantage.

Another major advantage of the cellular form is that parts are produced in one cell. Processing the parts in one cell simplifies control of the shop floor. To illustrate this, compare the amount of effort required to coordinate the production activities in the job shop and the cellular layout shown in Figure 5.7. Producing parts in a single cell also reduces the amount of labor and equipment needed to move materials because travel distances between successive operations are shorter. Additionally, producing the parts in one cell provides an opportunity to increase the workers' accountability, responsibility, and autonomy. Finally, reducing material handling and increasing the workers' accountability typically translates into reduced defects. In a job shop, it is difficult to hold the workers accountable for quality because the product is processed in several different departments and the workers in one department can always blame problems on another department.

A unique advantage of the cell form is that it maximizes the inherent benefits of the team approach. In a flow shop, there is little teamwork, because the equipment does most of the work; the labor primarily involves oversight and maintenance. Job shops are organized by department, and this allows for some teamwork—but not in terms of specific jobs, because everyone is working on a different job. In a cell, all the workers are totally responsible for completing every job. Thus, the effect is to enrich the work, provide challenges, encourage communication and teamwork, meet due dates, and maintain quality.

An additional advantage for manufacturers is the minimal cost required to move to cellular production. Although some cells may be highly automated, with expensive special-purpose equipment, it is not necessary to invest any additional capital in order to adopt the cellular form. It requires only the movement of equipment and labor into cells. Or, with even less trouble—though with some loss of efficiency—the firm can simply designate certain pieces of equipment as dedicated to a single part family, but not relocate them. The term used in this case is *virtual cell* or *logical cell*, since the equipment is not physically adjoining but is still reserved for production of only one part family.

Another form of cellular production is called a mini-plant. Here, the cell not only does the manufacturing but also has its own industrial engineer, quality manager, accountant, marketing representative, and salesperson, and almost all the other support services that a regular plant has. Only far-removed services, such as R&D and human resources, are not dedicated to the mini-plant. The entire facility of the firm is thus broken down into a number of mini-plants, each with its own general manager, production workers, and support services so that it can operate as an independent profit center.

Disadvantages of Cellular Production

Some disadvantages of the cellular form are those of the flow shop and the job shop, but they are not as serious. As in a flow shop, if a piece of equipment should break down, it can stop production in the cell; but in a cell form—unlike a flow shop, where that might be the only piece of equipment in the facility—work might, if permissable, temporarily be shifted to other cells to get a job out.

However, obtaining balance among the cells when demands for a product family keep changing is a problem that is less in both flow and job shops. Flow shops are relatively fixed in capacity and they produce a standard output, so there is no question of balance. Job shops simply draw from a pool of skilled labor for whatever job comes in. With cells, by contrast, if demand for a family dries up, it may be necessary to break up that cell and redistribute the equipment, or reform the families. In the short run, though, labor can generally be assigned to whatever cell needs it, including the remainder cell.

Of course, volumes are too small in cellular production to allow the purchase of the high-volume, efficient equipment that flow shops use. The cellular form also does not allow for the extent of customization usually found in job shops, since the labor pool has largely been disbursed to independent cells (although the remainder cell may be able to do the work). Moreover, the fostering of specialized knowledge associated with various operational activities is reduced because the workers who perform these activities are spread out and therefore have limited opportunities to collaborate.

Cellular Layout

Cellular production creates teams of workers and equipment to produce families of outputs. The workers are cross-trained so that they can operate any of the equipment in their cell, and they take full responsibility for the proper performance or result of the outputs. Whenever feasible, these outputs are final products or services. At other times, particularly in manufacturing, the outputs are parts that go into a final product. If the latter is the case, it is common to group the cells closely around the main production or assembly line so that they feed their output directly into the line as it is needed.

In some cases, a *nominal* (or *virtual*) *cell* is formed by identifying certain equipment and dedicating it to the production of families of outputs, but without moving the equipment into an actual, physical cell. In that case, no "layout" analysis is required at all; the organization simply keeps the layout it had. The essence of the problem, then, is the identification of the output families and the equipment to dedicate to each of them.

It is more common for an organization to actually form physical cells. When physical cells are created, the layout of the cell may resemble a sort of mini-flow shop, a job shop, or a mix of these, depending on the situation. Thus, we will direct our attention here to the formation of the part or product families and their associated equipment, leaving the issues of physical layout to be addressed in the discussions of the flow shop and job shop.

In practice, organizations often use the term cell to include a wide range of very different situations: a functional department consisting of identical machines, a single machine that automatically performs a variety of operations, or even a dedicated assembly line. Earlier, we also referred to the portion of a shop that is not associated with a specific part family as a cell: a *remainder cell*. Nevertheless, we do not consider all these groups as part of what we are calling cellular production.

Organizations that formally plan their shop layouts typically choose to group their equipment on the basis of either the function it performs (i.e., job shops) or the processing requirements of a product or group of products (i.e., flow shops). As we discussed, the purpose of grouping equipment on the basis of its function is to maximize flexibility, whereas the purpose of grouping it on the basis of processing requirements is to maximize efficiency.

Companies that adopt cellular manufacturing typically create a *pilot cell* initially to experiment with the cellular approach, and therefore most of the equipment in the shop remains in functional departments at this stage. As these firms gain experience with the cell and become convinced that it is beneficial, they begin a phase of implementing additional cells. This can be referred to as the *hybrid stage* because as the shop is incrementally converted to cells, a significant portion of the facilities are still arranged in functional departments. At some point, the formation of additional cells is terminated and the firm may or may not have the majority of its equipment arranged in cells. Often companies stop creating new cells when the volume of the remaining parts is insufficient to justify forming additional cells. To clarify the concept of a cellular layout based on product families and machine cells, we next present a detailed example based on one of the more common approaches to cell formation.

Methods of Cell Formation

There are a variety of ways to determine what outputs should constitute a family and be produced in the same cell. Sometimes a family is dictated by the size or weight of the output; for example, huge pieces of steel may require an overhead crane to lift them onto the machines for processing. Sometimes electronic parts have special requirements for quality, such as being produced in a "clean room" or being welded in an inert gas environment. Sometimes it is obvious what family a part belongs in simply by looking at it and seeing how it was made (i.e., by what machines).

Most commonly, some form of manual determination based on human judgment is used. One relatively simple approach involves taking photographs of a sample of the parts and then manually sorting these photographs into families based on the geometry, size, or other visual characteristics of the parts. Another approach is to sort the parts based on the drawing name. A more sophisticated manual procedure is called ***production flow analysis*** (PFA). In this approach, families are determined by evaluating the resource requirements for producing the outputs. Outputs that have the same complete set of resource needs are grouped into a single family. It should then be possible to cluster a set of the necessary resources together in a cell to produce that family. However, this is not always the case, because there may not be enough of all resources to place each one in each of the cells that needs it or low levels of usage may not justify placing each resource in each cell. In these cases the resources can be shared between cells or additional resources acquired. For example, maternity wings at many hospitals are set up as cells having their own dedicated doctors, nurses, and even operating rooms. However, typically the amount of time the anesthesiologists are needed in the maternity wing does not justify dedicating anesthesiologists to the unit. Thus, the anesthesiologists split their time supporting several hospital units. At other times, even if there are sufficient quantities of the resources to assign each to the appropriate cells, two or three such resources may be needed in one cell to handle its capacity requirements while half a resource or less is needed in another cell. These difficulties are handled case by case.

The essence of PFA is to determine the *resource-output matrix* and then identify the outputs (parts or services) with common resource requirements. In manufacturing operations, the matrix is based on information contained in the part routings and is formed by listing all the parts (outputs) across the top and all the machines (resources) down the side. Then 1's are written in the matrix wherever a part uses a machine. For example, Table 5.5 shows a matrix with seven parts that together require

TABLE 5.5 ● Original Machine-Part Matrix

Machines	Parts						
	1	2	3	4	5	6	7
1		1			1		
2	1			1			1
3	1		1			1	
4		1					
5			1			1	
6	1						1

six machines. The objective is to reorder the parts and machines so that "blocks" of 1's that identify the cells are formed along the diagonal, as shown in Table 5.6. Similar resource-output matrices could be developed for service organizations. For example, a hospital might identify type of treatment as the output (e.g., maternity, cardiac, oncology) and the resources as the equipment required (X-ray, respirator, defibrillator, heart monitor). Once the treatment-equipment matrix was developed, it could be reordered to identify the resources needed to set up dedicated treatment cells.

Note that it is acceptable for an output not to use every resource in a cell and for a resource not to process every output. However, no output should interact with a resource *outside* of its cell. Thus, in Table 5.6, part 1 is listed as needing machine 3, but this is problematic. In this case, if we could duplicate machine 3, we could put it in both cell 1 and cell 2. Or we might consider putting machine 3 in cell 2 and sending component 1 to cell 2 after it is finished in cell 1 (but this violates our desire to produce cell-complete parts). Or we could remove part 1 from the families and put it in a remainder cell (if there are other components and machines not listed in Table 5.5 within the facility).

The general guidelines for reordering the matrix by PFA are as follows:

- Incompatible resources should be in separate cells.
- Each output should be produced in only one cell.
- Any investment in duplicate resources should be minimized.
- The cells should be limited to a reasonable size.

TABLE 5.6 ● Reordered Matrix

Machines	Parts						
	7	4	1	3	6	2	5
6	1		1				
2	1	1	1				
3			1	1	1		
5				1	1		
1						1	1
4						1	

Cell 1: machines 6, 2 (parts 7, 4, 1). Cell 2: machines 3, 5 (parts 3, 6). Cell 3: machines 1, 4 (parts 2, 5).

Another, less common method of cell formation is *classification and coding*. With classification and coding, an alphanumeric code is assigned to each part on the basis of design characteristics, processing requirements, or both. Parts with similar codes can be identified and grouped into families.

Project Operations

Project operations are of large scale and finite duration; also, they are nonrepetitive, consisting of multiple, and often simultaneous, tasks that are highly interdependent. However, the primary characteristics of the tasks are their limited duration and, if the output is a physical product, their immobility during processing. Generally, staff, materials, and equipment are brought to the output and located in a nearby *staging area* until needed. Projects have particularly limited lives. Resources are brought together for the duration of the project: some are consumed, and others, such as equipment and personnel, are deployed to other uses at the conclusion of the project. Typically, the output is unique (a dam, product development, a presidential campaign, a trial).

In designing a processing system, a number of considerations may indicate that the project form is appropriate. One of these is the rate of change in the organization's outputs. If one department must keep current on a number of markets that are rapidly changing, the typical organization would quickly fall behind its competition. The project form offers extremely short reaction times to environmental or internal changes and would thus be called for. In addition, if the tasks are for a limited duration only, the project form is indicated. Finally, the project form is chosen when the output is of a very large scale with multiple, interdependent activities requiring close coordination. During the project, coordination is achieved through frequent meetings of the representatives of the various functional areas on the project team.

One of the advantages of the project form, as noted earlier, is its ability to perform under time and cost constraints. Therefore, if performance time or cost is crucial for an output, the project form is most appropriate. However, in high-technology areas the project form, having a mixed personnel complement of different functional specialists (engineers, scientists, theoreticians, technicians, etc.), may be less capable than transformation systems in which operations are organized by specialty areas. In these other designs, a number of specialists can be brought together to solve a problem. In addition, specialized resources (such as staff and equipment) often cannot be justified for a project because of their low utilization; hence, generalized resources must be used instead. The project form of transformation processes is discussed in more detail in Chapter 10.

$\mathscr{S}$ELECTION OF A TRANSFORMATION SYSTEM _____

This section addresses the issue of selecting the appropriate transformation system, or mix of systems, to produce an output. From the preceding discussion, it should be clear that the five transformation systems are somewhat simplified extremes of what is likely to be observed in practice. Few organizations use one of the five forms in a pure sense; most combine two or more forms. For example, in manufacturing computer keyboards, some parts and subassemblies are produced in job shops or cells but then feed into a flow shop at the final assembly line, where a batch of one model is produced. Then the line is modified to produce a batch of another model. Even in "custom" work, jobs are often handled in groups of generally common items throughout most of their processing, leaving minor finishing details such as the fabric on a couch or the facade of a house to give the impression of customizing.

Although services typically take the form of a job shop, the emphasis has recently been on trying to mass-produce them (using cells or flow shops) so as to increase volume and reduce unit costs. Some examples are fast-food outlets, multiphasic medical screening, and group life insurance. Even with services we often find combined forms of process design: McDonald's prepares batches of Big Macs but will accept individual custom orders. Burger King uses a conveyor assembly line for its Whoppers but advertises its ability to customize its burgers to suit any taste.

The problem for the operations manager is to decide what processing form is most appropriate for the organization, considering long-run efficiency, effectiveness, lead time, capacity, quality, and flexibility. Selection may be even more difficult because, as mentioned previously, it is possible to combine processing forms to attain efficiency in some portions of the production process and flexibility in other portions. It is clear that the trade-offs must be well understood by the manager, and the expected benefits and costs must be well known.

Considerations of Volume and Variety

One of the most important factors in the design of a transformation system is establishing the volume and variety of outputs the organization will produce. High volumes tend to indicate that highly automated mass production will be necessary. High variety, on the other hand, implies the use of skilled labor and general-purpose tools and facilities.

A related consideration here is whether the output will be make-to-stock or make-to-order. A ***make-to-stock*** item is produced in batches of some size that is economical (for the firm) and then stocked (in a warehouse, on shelves, etc.). As customers purchase them, the items are withdrawn from stock. A ***make-to-order*** item is usually produced in a batch of a size set by the customer (sometimes just one) and is delivered to the customer upon its completion. Generally, make-to-stock items are produced in large volumes with low variety, whereas make-to-order items are produced in low volumes with high variety. (Quite often, *every* item is different.)

Clearly, services will not normally be of a type that can be stocked, even if every service is identical (e.g., a physical examination). Also, exceptions to these generalizations are abundant. Automobiles, for example, are made to order, but are produced in high volume and with high variety. (However, autos are really *assembled* to order; the assembly components are produced to stock.) And general-purpose machine shops often produce high volumes of low-variety items for specific customers.

Figure 5.9*a* illustrates these points as they relate to the various transformation systems. The horizontal axis shows volume, as measured by the batch size, and the left vertical axis shows the variety of outputs. Essentially, no organizations operate

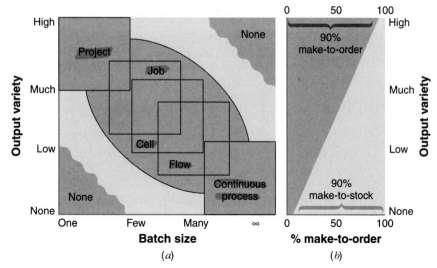

Figure 5.9 Effect of output characteristics on transformation systems.

in the upper right or lower left segments of this grid. Organizations making a single unit of output that varies each time (such as dams and custom-built machines) use the project form or sometimes the job shop. Some services also fall into this region, as indicated by the upper left tip of the oval. Job shop and cellular systems, however, are mainly used when a considerable variety of outputs are required in relatively small batches. This is particularly characteristic of services. When the size of a batch increases significantly, with a corresponding decrease in variety, then a flow shop is appropriate. Some services also fall into this category. Last, when all the output is the same and the batch is extremely large (or essentially infinite, as in the ore, petrochemical, and food and drink industries), the continuous process is appropriate. Very few services exist here.

Note the overlap in the different forms. This means for example, that on occasion some organizations will use a flow shop for outputs with smaller batches or larger variety, or both, than the outputs of organizations using a job shop. There are many possible reasons for this, including economic and historical factors. The organization may also simply be using an inappropriate transformation system. The point is that the categories are not rigid, and many variations do occur. Many organizations also use hybrids or combinations of systems, such as producing components to stock but assembling finished products to order, as in the auto industry.

Note in Figure 5.9b the general breakdown of make-to-order and make-to-stock with output variety and size of batch. Project forms (high variety, unit batch size) are almost always make-to-order, and continuous processing forms (no variety, infinite batch size) are almost always make-to-stock, though exceptions occasionally occur.

Product and Process Life Cycle

In Chapter 2 we described the life cycle of an output: how long it takes to develop, bring to market, and catch on; how quickly it grows in popularity; how different versions are developed for different market segments; how the output reaches market saturation; how price competition emerges. A similar life cycle occurs in the production system for an output. As a result, a project form of transformation system may be used for the development of a new output, may evolve into a job shop or cellular layout as a market develops, and finally may evolve into a flow shop as full standardization and high volumes develop. (We assume here that a continuous process is not appropriate for the output.) We briefly elaborate on this production life cycle.

In the R&D stage, many variations are investigated during the development of a product. As the output is being developed, prototypes are made in small volumes in a relatively inefficient, uncoordinated manner typically in a job shop. As demand grows and competitors enter the market, price competition begins and a cellular or flow system, with its high volume and low variable costs, becomes preferred. At the peak of the cycle, demand may increase to the point where such a system is justified.

This progress is illustrated in Figure 5.10, which presents a breakeven analysis for each of four transformation systems. The dark bold line illustrates the lowest-cost system for each stage of the life cycle. At the stage of project development and initiation (R&D and initial production), the cost of fixed equipment is nil, and labor is the predominant contributor to high variable costs. In the expansion stage, the job shop allows some trade-off of equipment for labor with a corresponding reduction in variable unit costs, thus leading, at these volumes, to a reduction in overall unit costs. Finally, at high volumes characterizing maturity, a nearly complete replacement of expensive labor with equipment is possible, using cellular form and the flow shop.

Be advised, however, that not all outputs can or should follow this sequence. The point is that the transformation system should evolve as the market and output evolve. But many organizations see their strength in operating a particular

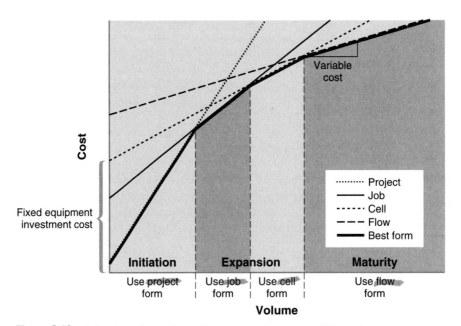

Figure 5.10   Selection of transformation systems by stage of life cycle.

transformation system, such as R&D or low-cost production of large volumes. If their outputs evolve into another stage of the life cycle in which a different transformation system form is preferable, they drop the output (or license it to someone else) and switch to another output more appropriate to their strengths.

Failing to maintain this focus in the organization's production system can quickly result in a "white elephant"—a facility built to be efficient at one task but being inefficiently used for something else. This can also happen if the organization, in an attempt to please every customer, mixes the production of outputs that require different transformation systems. Japanese plants are very carefully planned to maintain one strong focus in each plant. If an output requiring a different process is to be produced, a new plant is acquired or built.

Service Processes

As with the design of transformation systems for products, the design of transformation systems for services depends heavily on knowing exactly what characteristics of a service are important. We will consider three main characteristics of a service: its *facilitating good*, its *explicit benefits*, and its *implicit*, or *psychological, benefits.* Knowing the importance of each of these allows the designer to make the necessary trade-offs in costs and benefits to offer an effective yet reasonably priced service.

Service transformation systems are frequently implemented with little development or pretesting. This is often the major reason why so many of them fail. Consider the extensive development and testing of the McDonald's fast-food production system, of airline reservations systems, and of many life insurance policies. Each of these examples also illustrates the many hours of training required to use equipment and procedures properly and efficiently. Yet most new service firms frequently fail to train their personnel adequately, once again inviting failure.

One important service element that is usually missing from product design is extensive customer contact during the delivery of the service. This presents both problems and opportunities. For one thing, the customer will often add new inputs to the delivery system or make new demands on it that were not anticipated when it was designed. In addition, customers do not arrive at smooth, even increments of time but instead tend to bunch up, as during lunch periods, and then complain when they have to wait for service. Furthermore, the customers' biased perception of the server, and the server's skills, can often influence their satisfaction with the quality of the service. Obviously, this can either be beneficial or harmful, depending on the circumstances.

On the other hand, having the customer involved in the delivery of a service can also present opportunities to improve it. Since customers know their own needs best, it is wise to let them aid in the preparation or delivery of the service— as with automatic teller machines, salad bars, and pay-at-pump gas stations. In addition to improving the quality of the service, this can save the firm money by making it unnecessary to hire additional servers. However, the customer can also negligently—and quickly—ruin a machine or tool, and may even sue if injured by it, so the service firm must carefully consider how much self-service it is willing to let the customer perform.

Professor Richard Chase of the University of Southern California (Chase and Tansik 1983) devised a helpful way to view this customer contact when designing service delivery systems. Chase's suggestion is to evaluate whether the service is, in general, high-contact or low-contact, and what portions of the service, in particular, are each. The value of this analysis is that the service can be made both more efficient and more effective by separating these two portions and designing them differently. For example, the high-contact portions of the service should be handled by workers who are skilled at social interaction, whereas the low-contact portion should employ more technical workers and take advantage of labor-saving equipment. For example, a bank might have a back office where checks are encoded separately from the front office, where customers deposit them. In this back office, equipment and efficiency are the critical job elements, whereas in the front office, interpersonal skills and friendliness are critical.

Whenever possible, the low-contact portion of a service should be decoupled from the high-contact portion so that it may be conducted with efficiency, whereas the high-contact portion is conducted with grace and friendliness. Close analysis of the service tasks may also reveal opportunities for decreasing contact with the customer—through, for example, automated teller machines, phone service, self-service, or the Web, if this is appropriate—with a concomitant opportunity for improving both the efficiency and level of service. In particular, allowing customers to use the Web to obtain service (e.g., obtain account information, place orders) offers them convenient access, 24 hours per day, 365 days per year, and immediate attention (i.e., no longer being placed on hold for the next available representative).

Similarly, there may be some opportunities for increasing the amount of customer contact, such as phone or mail follow-ups after service, that should be exploited to improve the overall service and its image. The service provider should thoroughly investigate these opportunities.

NEW TRANSFORMATION TECHNOLOGIES AND REENGINEERING

Many new technologies, materials, and production methods are revolutionizing service and manufacturing operations. We are constantly bombarded with terms and concepts related to the "factory of the future" and the "office of the future." Most of these systems (though not all) are, of course, due to the advent of the computer and its inexpensive power. Organizations must be careful, however, not to use this new tool simply to automate their existing manual procedures. One of the main advantages of computerization is its ability to aid in the execution of tasks that at one time could be done only inefficiently. If operations are not reorganized to use the computer's power and flexibility efficiently, most of that advantage will be lost. It is commonly said, "Simplify and systemize before you computerize." For example, a manufacturer of helicopter engines that we are familiar with was having a problem controlling its inventory. Its solution to the problem was to purchase expensive automated equipment to store and handle the inventory. Unfortunately, the new automated equipment created more problems than it solved. After reflecting on its predicament, company managers commented that they would have been better off had they improved the efficiency of the operation by eliminating inventory in the first place and not simply thrown technology at the problem.

Taking this concept one step further, many companies are formally designing their business processes. With business process design (BPD), also known as reengineering, companies first determine their customers' needs. Then, on the basis of these needs and the capabilities offered by new technologies, the organization develops work processes to meet the needs. It is somewhat surprising that many organizations have never questioned the appropriateness of their processes, even though the technology available today is vastly different from the technology that was available when these processes were first developed.

A study by Battelle Laboratories of firms that achieve a return of more than 50 percent on investment found that the primary tangible factor common to these firms was a significant technological advantage over their competitors. The importance of technology may come as a surprise, since what we hear about success in business usually involves advertising or financial manipulation. In the next three subsections we describe some of these technologies, first for services, then for products, and last, for reengineering.

Office and Service Technologies

The computer has had a dramatic effect on the service industries, probably even more than in the manufacturing industries. As general examples, consider the optical scanner at the grocery checkout counter, the electronic cash transfer systems in the banks, the mail-sorting systems at the post office, or the energy control systems in buildings that regulate heat, water, and air conditioning.

As true as this may be for services in general, it is particularly true of services that are information-intensive. Here the computer has wrought a veritable revolution in the way of doing business. The impact of the computer has perhaps been greatest in the banking industry, with its automatic teller machines and electronic transfers of funds. However, the operations of other information-intense businesses have also been dramatically altered. Examples here would include reservations systems for hotels, airlines, rental cars, and so on; security systems; telecommunications; multiphasic screening; electronic classrooms; and on and on.

One area that is receiving an enormous amount of attention is the Internet, especially its graphical component the World Wide Web or, simply, the Web. However, a similar revolution is beginning within organizations as they develop similar private networks, called *intranets*. According to Forrester Research, in early 1996 22 percent of the Fortune 1000 companies used intranets—which is remarkable, given that virtually none of these organizations *had* intranets in 1994. Because intranets allow data to be exchanged freely among all users with access to the network, regardless of whether they are using Windows-based PCs, Apple Macintoshes, or UNIX workstations, intranets solve a number of problems for information managers.

There is little doubt that the Internet revolution will profoundly affect the way business is conducted. To illustrate this, consider the increasing number of "E" words that are becoming part of everyday language such as e-mail, e-cash, e-money, e-form, e-shops, e-Apps®, e-commerce, e-tickets, and e-trade. It is widely acknowledged that the Web offers organizations enormous opportunities to dramatically improve both efficiency and effectiveness. For example, organizations can update promotional and pricing materials instantaneously when these materials are stored electronically on a Web server. This is not typically possible with printed materials. Furthermore, providing access to promotional materials via the Web can greatly reduce the costs of distribution and printing while at the same time increasing international exposure. Finally, these promotional materials can be greatly enhanced by the inclusion of hypertext links and even audiovisual material.

Federal Express set up a Web server for its customers in late 1994. By early 1996 12,000 customers each day were using this service to access FedEx's package-tracking database. This provides the customer with a much higher level of service (they no longer have to wait for the next available customer service representative) and saves FedEx about $2 million annually. On the basis of the success of its public Web site, FedEx decided to equip its 30,000 office personnel with Web browsers to access the company's intranet.

In more sophisticated applications, a manager may query a database through a *decision support system* (DSS) to obtain specific information or a printed report. The DSS may use *artificial intelligence* (AI) or an *expert system* (ES) to analyze preexisting data, collect and process external data, or network to another database through telecommunications.

Artificial intelligence is the part of the field of computer science that focuses on making computers behave like, or emulate, humans. To emulate humans, AI systems manipulate symbols rather than data. In addition, they use networks, rules, and processing procedures rather than algorithms. By using such relationships, AI systems can represent and manipulate abstract ideas and activities. With these abilities, AI systems can make assumptions when needed and can reason inductively, correcting their mistakes as they go by changing their rule systems. This makes them excellent for relatively straightforward decisions in which the data may change but the process is constant. AI will become especially useful in services where single decisions are relatively frequent but not extremely complex, such as repairing autos or handling paperwork. AI can also act as an interpreter between workers and other computerized systems, telling the human what the computerized system needs and acting as a general interface and facilitator.

Expert systems are one type of artificial intelligence and have, to date, received most of the attention in this area. These systems are individually designed to capture the expertise of particular individuals or groups with respect to one task or field. Thus, an expert system allows less experienced workers to have the expertise needed to help them make decisions. Quite a few expert systems have been devised for design, testing, repair, and automation.

What will be the effect of all this technology on jobs and the work force? It is clear that the technology will eliminate the simpler rote jobs, just as it is now doing in manufacturing. New technologies also open up new jobs, however. A hundred years ago, if we had told the farmers that, by 1990, only one person in a thousand would work on a farm, they too would have asked what the unemployed farmers would do. Obviously, the standard of living rose, new jobs opened up, the work week was reduced, and other such changes accommodated the exodus from the farm. Undoubtedly, that will happen again.

Manufacturing Technologies

Numerical control (NC) is one of the oldest technologies available in manufacturing. As was discussed in Chapter 4, NC allows a machine to operate automatically through coded numerical instructions. Until recently, these instructions were on punched paper tape, which directed the operations of a machine (e.g., a player piano) in the same way that an operator would. When the punched tape was replaced by a computer system attached to the machine, the operation—called *computer numerical control* (CNC)—was much more efficient. More recently, larger computers have been directing the activities of multiple machines through *direct numerical control* (DNC) and material-handling systems such as robots and carts as well, orchestrating their functions and movements to produce the desired parts and goods in much less time.

Clearly, such systems are very expensive. One might think that to justify the expense of these systems, relatively high volumes of standard products would need to be made on them. However, this is directly contrary to their purpose, which is to capitalize on their flexibility and produce *small* batches of a high variety of products. (Nevertheless, the net result of producing a large amount of goods to pay for the expensive equipment is still the goal; it is simply done through greater variety.)

Robots have come of age. Initially used for fairly simple tasks such as welding and spray-painting, these machines have increased tremendously in ability in the last few years. They have much more sophisticated sensors and can perform very complex and difficult tasks, not only in production but also in assembly. A wide variety of robots have been developed to perform a number of highly varied tasks: painting, welding, positioning, lifting, assembly, handling materials, drilling. They are particularly valuable for jobs that are either uncomfortable for a human to perform (too hot, too dirty, and so forth) or too dangerous (because of nuclear contamination, corrosive chemicals, poisonous fumes, or the like).

When augmented by a *vision* system, as is now happening more frequently, a robot can perform an even broader array of tasks. This would include sorting through parts to select the proper one, picking up a randomly oriented part without damaging it, inspecting a part for dimensional accuracy or flaws, and other such tasks. Clearly, when one technology is wedded to another, such as robots to vision, tremendous increases in capability are possible.

Flexible manufacturing systems (FMSs) are also now in the limelight. Virtually unmanned, these systems include a series of identical machining centers; an automated, computer-controlled materials-handling system; and other possible peripherals such as a wash station, a coordinate measuring machine, a grinder, a storage rack, a robot, and loading and unloading stations. The materials management system is typically a series of automated guided vehicles (carts) for transporting pallets of materials, guided by a towline, rails, or an embedded wire in the floor. The carts, machines, cranes, and robots are programmed and supervised by a host computer, which interfaces with the plant computer when it needs additional data or is feeding data back.

The advantages of the FMS are those of cellular production (less space, faster response, low variable costs, and so on), as well as those of NC: consistency, quality, minimal labor expense, preprogrammed machining instructions (no blueprint reading). In spite of their name, FMSs are "flexible" only in a limited sense. For example, most of them are machining systems. None of them could produce toasters or motorcycles. Thus, their flexibility is only relative to what is normally produced with such machines. Although FMSs have given significant improvements in productivity, quality, space requirements, labor, and capacity, the cost of these systems is extremely high—in the millions of dollars—and not all of them have been successful. Therefore, to make them productive in any firm, planning is essential.

Business Process Design (Reengineering)

In addition to formally designing transformation systems, many organizations are now formally designing all their ~~important business processes~~. Indeed, very few topics are creating as much interest and controversy in business today as ***business process design*** (BPD). It is perhaps most commonly referred to as ***reengineering***, but a wide variety of other names are also frequently used, such as *business process reengineering, business process engineering, business process innovation,* and ~~*business process design*~~ or *redesign.* To compound the confusion, often managers incorrectly use terms such as *downsizing* and *restructuring* interchangeably with BPD.

To illustrate the widespread interest in BPD, we can note that in a study of large industrial companies conducted by Pitney Bowes Management Services, 83 percent of the responding companies indicated that they had experience with reengineering. Furthermore, two independent studies conducted by "big six" firms found that 75 to 80 percent of large U.S. companies had increased or would be increasing their commitment to BPD in the foreseeable future. Michael Hammer, who coined the term *reengineering,* found that the number of articles with this word in the title increased to more than 800 in 1994, from 10 in 1990.

To help put BPD in perspective, consider that the roots of the functional organization date back to the late 1700s, when Adam Smith proposed his concept of the division of labor in *An Inquiry into the Nature and Causes of the Wealth of Nations* (1776). Referring to the 17 operations required to produce a pin, Smith argued that assigning one task to each of 17 workers would be more efficient and would produce more pins than having 17 workers each autonomously perform all 17 tasks.

Although there have been dramatic advances in technology since Smith first proposed the division of labor, it is only recently that organizations have begun to challenge the concept and look for better ways to organize and integrate work. Indeed, ~~if you were to compare how companies are organized today and how they were organized 20 or 30 years ago, you would find that little has changed~~ in their organizational structures. This is true despite technological advances such as personal computers, fax machines, cellular phones, laser printers, the World Wide Web, compact disks, spreadsheets, word processors, client-server computing, groupware, E-mail, and cable modems, to name a few.

Initially, when these technologies were first adopted by organizations, the dramatic improvements in performance that were expected did not materialize. One popular explanation for this is that organizations were not taking advantage of the capabilities the new technologies offered. Rather, companies were simply using technology to speed up and automate existing practices. Clearly, if an activity or a set of activities is not effective to begin with, performing it faster and with less human intervention does not automatically make it effective.

For instance, one major financial institution reported that more than 90 steps were required for an office worker to get office supplies. These steps mostly involved filling out forms and getting the required signatures. Given the capabilities of information technology, it is certainly true that these steps could be automated and speeded up. For example, a computer system could be developed to generate all the forms automatically and then automatically E-mail them to the appropriate person for authorization. However, is automating all these steps the best solution?

Might it not make more sense to eliminate most of them? Consider that even if the forms are generated and dispatched faster, valuable managerial time is still being used to look over and approve these requests every time an employee needs a pad of paper or ballpoint pen. Indeed, when the cost of the controls is weighed against the benefits, it might be much more effective to give employees access to the supply cabinet to retrieve their own supplies as needed. Dr. Hammer uses the term *paving cow paths* to describe organizations that simply adopt a new technology without considering the capabilities it offers to perform work in entirely new and better ways.

The Nynex example at the beginning of this chapter provides a glimpse of several major themes associated with BPD. First, BPD's primary objective is improved customer service. This was clearly illustrated by Nynex's four core processes, as each began with the word *customer*. This brings us to a second theme associated with BPD, a concern with making *quantum* improvements in performance rather than small, *incremental* improvements. Nynex's goal to lower its operating expenses by 35 to 40 percent certainly represents a quantum improvement, as does its expected 1025 percent internal rate of return.

A third important theme of BPD is the central role of technology. When many of the new information technologies were initially adopted by companies, the expected improvements in organizational efficiency and effectiveness often did not materialize. On closer examination, it was discovered that many companies were adapting new technology to fit current business practices rather than attempting to take advantage of the capabilities offered by the technology to perform activities in perhaps entirely different and better ways. The early 1990s marked the beginning of the reengineering movement—companies started to consider the capabilities that technology offered in relationship to the way work was performed and organized.

Michael Hammer and Steven Stanton, in their book *The Reengineering Revolution* (New York: Harper Business, 1995), define reengineering as "the fundamental rethinking and *radical redesign* of business *processes* to bring about *dramatic* improvements in performance" (p. 3). The keywords *radical, redesign, process,* and *dramatic* are particularly important to understanding the concept of reengineering or BPD. The word *radical* is used to signify that the purpose of BPD is to *profoundly* change the way work is performed, not to make *superficial* changes. It has to do with understanding the foundation upon which work is based and eliminating old ways that no longer make sense. In other words, it refers to *reinventing* the way work is performed and organized, not simply improving it. Radically changing work is often best accomplished by starting with a clean slate and making no assumptions about how work activities are performed.

The second keyword, *redesign*, denotes the fact that BPD is concerned with the design of work. Typically people think of design as being primarily applicable to products. However, the way work is accomplished can also be designed. In fact, Hammer and Stanton point out that having intelligent, capable, well-trained, motivated employees is of little value if work is badly designed to begin with.

The third keyword is *process*. Although all organizations perform processes, it was not until recently that they began organizing work on the basis of these processes. Partly as a result of total quality management (TQM, discussed in Chapter 3), companies began to focus more on meeting customers' needs. As they did this, they soon realized that customers are not particularly interested in the individual activities that are performed to create a product or service. Rather, they are more concerned about the final result of these activities. Of course, since companies were not organized on the basis of their processes, they were not managed on the basis of processes either. Therefore, no one was assigned responsibility for the entire process that created the results of interest to the customer. Using the scenario of product design, a typical company would have departmental managers to oversee market research, manufacturing, and customer service. However, there was no manager responsible for ensuring that the results of all these activities were meeting customers' requirements. We use the term ***process-centered*** to refer to companies that have organized their work activities on the basis of specific value-creating processes.

The last keyword is ***dramatic***. BPD is concerned with making quantum improvements in performance, not small or incremental improvements. Thus, BPD focuses on achieving breakthroughs in performance. A company that lowers its lead time by 10 percent from the previous year does not exemplify a dramatic improvement. On the other hand, a company that reduces its lead time from three weeks to three days does.

To illustrate these concepts, consider the experiences of IBM Credit Corporation. IBM Credit is in the business of financing purchases of IBM office equipment. Numerous companies—including General Motors, Ford, Chrysler, and General Electric—are in the lending business. These companies have found that operating financial units can be extremely profitable in addition to offering customers a higher level of service.

Originally, IBM Credit was organized into functional departments. The steps involved in processing a credit request are shown in Figure 5.11. The process began when an IBM sales rep closed a deal and the customer wanted to finance the purchase through IBM Credit. In this case the sales rep would relay the pertinent information to one of 14 order loggers at IBM Credit. The order loggers sat in a conference room and manually wrote down on pieces of paper the information supplied by the sales reps. Periodically during the day, the pieces of paper were carted upstairs to the credit department. Employees in the credit department entered the pertinent information into a computer to check the borrower's creditworthiness. The results of this check were then recorded on another piece of paper.

Next, the documents would be transferred to the business practices department. This department would modify the standard loan covenant in response to specific requests by customers. The business practices department used its own computer system. After being processed in the business practices department, the documents were transported to the pricing department, where pricers entered the data into a program running on a personal computer to determine the appropriate interest rate. Finally, the entire dossier was transported to an administrator, who converted all the information into a "quote letter." The quote letter was then sent by Federal Express to the field sales rep.

The sales reps were extremely dissatisfied with this process. First of all, the entire process took an average of six days and sometimes as long as two weeks. What salesperson wants to give his or her customers two weeks to think over a purchase? On top of this, when a sales rep called to check on the status of a customer's credit request, often the request could not even be located.

As a result of complaints from the sales reps, a manager at IBM Credit decided to investigate the problem. The first thing this manager wanted to determine was how much work time actually went into processing a credit request. To determine this, the manager walked an actual request through the entire process. First, he

Figure 5.11
Processing credit requests at IBM credit.

recorded the time it took to log an actual order. Then, he took the order that was just called in and personally carried it to the credit department. Arriving at the credit department, he selected a worker at random and told the worker to stop what he or she was currently working on and perform the credit check. After repeating this in the other departments, the manager determined that the actual processing time of a credit request was about 90 minutes. Thus, out of an average of six days, each application was being processed only about 90 minutes, indicating a significant opportunity for improvement.

IBM Credit's approach to improving this process was to combine all these activities into one job called a *deal structurer.* Thus, one worker handled all the activities required to process a credit request, from logging the information to writing the quote letter. As a result of using deal structurers, turnaround times were reduced to an average of four hours. Furthermore, with a small reduction in head count, the number of deals processed by IBM Credit increased 100 times (not 100 percent). Do these results qualify as dramatic?

Given these results, you may wonder why IBM Credit had ever adopted a functional organizational structure in the first place. To answer this, let's put ourselves in the shoes of a manager at IBM Credit. Suppose we were asked to develop an organization to process credit requests. One requirement that might occur to us is that the process should be able to handle any possible type of credit request. Given this requirement, if you look again at Figure 5.11, you will see that IBM Credit's original functional arrangement accomplishes this objective. For example, no matter how difficult checking a particular borrower's creditworthiness might be, the process could handle it, because everyone in the credit department was a highly trained specialist. The same is true of all the other departments. However, another important question is: How often will this specialized knowledge be needed? In other words, what percent of the credit requests are relatively routine and what percent require deep, specialized knowledge? As IBM found out, the vast majority of credit requests could be handled relatively routinely.

Another explanation for why IBM Credit originally created a functional organization relates to the technology that was available at the time. A key ingredient that allowed IBM Credit to move to the deal-structurer model was advances in technology. For example, spreadsheets, databases, and other decision support tools were adopted so that the deal structurers could quickly check interest rates, access standard clauses, and check the creditworthiness of the borrowers. In effect, the new technology allowed the deal structurers, who had only general knowledge, to function as though they had the specialized knowledge of an expert in a particular discipline.

EXPAND YOUR UNDERSTANDING _____

1. When a line cannot be perfectly balanced, some people will have more work time than others within each cycle. What might be a solution for this situation?

2. A current sociological trend is to move away from paced lines. Yet increasing automation is pushing workers to match their work pace to that of machines and computers. How can both of these trends be happening at the same time?

3. If a job shop was being laid out in a third world country, how might the procedure be different? What other factors might enter in that would not exist in an industrialized country? Might the layout also differ among industrialized countries such as Europe and Japan? How about a flow shop?

4. In highly automated facilities, firms frequently increase the job responsibilities of the skilled workers who remain after automation has replaced the manual laborers, although there is less potential for applying their skills. Workers complain that they are under increased pressure to perform but have less control over the automated equipment. Is this ethical on the part of the companies involved? What approach would be better?

5. Cellular production is often conducted in a U-shaped (horseshoe-shaped) cell, rather than the rectangular cells shown in Figure 5.7b. What might be the advantages of this U shape?

6. What benefits would a nominal cell obtain, and not obtain, compared with a physical cell?

7. A number of firms are moving toward mini-factories. What advantages might this offer over straight cellular production?

8. If efficiency, variety, and so on are the important measures of the low-contact, or no-contact portion of a service, what are the important measures of the high-contact portion?

9. As the process life cycle changes with the product life cycle, should a firm change along with it or move into new products more appropriate to its existing process? What factors must be considered in this decision?

10. In Figure 5.9, showing the five transformation systems, why don't firms operate in the regions marked "none"?

APPLY YOUR UNDERSTANDING
Paradise State University

Paradise State University (PSU) is a medium-sized private university offering both undergraduate and graduate degrees. Students typically choose Paradise State because of its emphasis on high levels of interaction and relatively small classes. University policy prohibits classes with more than 75 students (unless special permission is obtained from the provost), and the target class size is 25 students. All courses are taught by tenure-track faculty members with appropriate terminal degrees. Faculty members teach two courses each semester.

The Business School at PSU offers only an MBA degree in one of six areas of concentration: accounting, finance, general management, management information systems (MIS), marketing, and operations management (OM). The MBA program is a one-year (two-semester) lockstep program. Since the Business School does not offer undergraduate business courses, students entering the program are required to have completed all the undergraduate business prerequisites from an accredited university. The faculty is organized into six functional departments. The table below lists the number of faculty members in each department and the average number of students each year who choose a particular concentration. Students are not permitted to have double concentrations, and PSU does not offer minors at the graduate level.

Department	Faculty	Number of Students per Year
Accounting	8	100
Finance	6	40
General Management	7	70
MIS	10	150
Marketing	6	50
OM	10	30

The number of courses required by each concentration in each department are listed in the table below. For example, a student concentrating in accounting is required to take 4 accounting classes, 1 finance class, 1 management class, 1 MIS course, 1 marketing class, and 2 OM classes.

Concentration	Number of Courses Taken in Respective Departments					
	Accounting	Finance	Management	MIS	Marketing	OM
Accounting	4	1	1	1	1	2
Finance	1	4	1	1	1	2
General Management	1	1	4	1	1	2
MIS	1	1	1	4	1	2
Marketing	1	1	1	1	4	2
OM	1	1	1	1	1	5

Questions

1. How many students must each department teach each semester? Given the target class size—25 students—are there enough faculty members?

2. Conceptually, how could the cellular production approach be applied to the Business School?

3. What would be the advantages and disadvantages of adopting a cellular approach at the Business School? As a student, would you prefer a functional organization or a cellular organization? As a faculty member, what would you prefer?

4. On the basis of the information given, develop a rough plan detailing how the Business School faculty might be assigned to cells.

Valley State University's Medical Clinic

Valley State University operates a walk-in medical clinic to meet the acute medical needs of its 13,000 students, 1200 faculty and staff members, and covered relatives. Patients arriving at the clinic are served on a first-come, first-served basis.

As part of a new total quality management program, Valley State conducted an in-depth four-month study of its current operations. A key component of the study was a survey, distributed to all students, faculty, and staff. The purpose of the survey was to identify and prioritize areas most in need of improvement. An impressive 44 percent of the surveys were returned and deemed usable. Follow-up analysis indicated that the people who responded were representative of the population served by the clinic. After the results were tabulated, it was determined that the walk-in medical clinic was located at the bottom of the rankings, indicating a great deal of dissatisfaction with the clinic. Preliminary analysis of the respondents' comments indicated that people were reasonably satisfied with the treatment they received at the clinic but were very dissatisfied with the amount of time they had to wait to see a caregiver.

Upon arriving at the clinic, patients receive a form from the receptionist requesting basic biographical information and the nature of the medical condition for which treatment is being sought. Completing the form typically requires 2 to 3 minutes. After the form is returned to the receptionist, it is time-stamped and placed in a tray. Student workers collect the forms and retrieve the corresponding patients' files from the basement. The forms typically remain in the tray for about 5 minutes before being picked up, and it takes the student workers approximately 12 minutes to retrieve the files. After a patient's file is retrieved, the form describing the medical problem is attached to it with a paper clip, and it is placed in a stack with other files. The stack of files is ordered according to the time stamps on the forms.

When the nurse practitioners finish with their current patient, they select the next file from the stack and escort that patient to one of the treatment rooms. On average, files remain in the stack for 10 minutes, but this varies considerably depending on the time of day and the day of the week. On Monday mornings, for example, it is common for files to remain in the stack for 30 minutes or more.

Once in the treatment room, the nurse practitioner reads over the form describing the patient's ailment. Next, the nurse discusses the problem with the patient while taking some standard measurements such as blood pressure and temperature. The nurse practitioner then makes a rough diagnosis, based on the measurements and symptoms, to determine if the ailment is one of the 20 that state law permits nurse practitioners to treat. If the condition is treatable by the nurse practitioner, a more thorough diagnosis is undertaken and treatment is prescribed. It typically takes about 5 minutes for the nurse practitioners to make the rough diagnosis and another 20 minutes to complete the detailed diagnosis and discuss the treatment with the patient. If the condition (as roughly diagnosed) is not treatable by the nurse practitioner, the patient's file is placed in the stack for the on-duty MD. Because of the higher cost of MDs versus nurse practitioners, there is typically only one MD on duty at any time. Thus, patients wait an average of 25 minutes for the MD. On the other hand, because of their higher training and skill, the MDs are able to diagnose and treat the patients in 15 minutes, despite the fact that they deal with the more difficult and less routine cases. Incidentally, an expert system for nurse practitioners is being tested at another clinic that—if shown to be effective—would initially double the number of ailments treatable by nurse practitioners and over time would probably increase the list even more, as the tool continued to be improved.

Questions

1. Develop a flow chart for the medical clinic that shows the times of the various activities. Is the patients' dissatisfaction with the clinic justified?

2. What probably are the patients' key requirements for the clinic?

3. What assumptions are being made about the way work is performed and treatment administered at the clinic?

4. Redesign the process of treating patients at the clinic using technologies you are familiar with, to better meet the patients' needs as listed in question 2.

X-Opoly, Inc.

X-Opoly, Inc., was founded by two first-year college students to produce a knockoff real estate board game similar to the popular Parker Brothers' game Monopoly®. Initially, the partners started the company just to produce a board game based on popular local landmarks in their small college town, as a way to help pay for their college expenses. However, the game was a big success and because they enjoyed running their own business, they decided to pursue the business full-time after graduation.

X-Opoly has grown rapidly over the last couple of years, designing and producing custom real estate trading games for universities, municipalities, chambers of commerce, and lately even some businesses. Orders range from a couple of hundred games to an occasional order for several thousand. This year X-Opoly expects to sell 50,000 units and projects that its sales will grow 25 percent annually for the next five years.

X-Opoly's orders are either for a new game board that has not been produced before, or repeat orders for a game that was previously produced. If the order is for a new game, the client first meets with a graphic designer from X-Opoly's art department and the actual game board is designed. The design of the board can take anywhere from a few hours to several weeks, depending on how much the client has thought about the game before the meeting. All design work is done on personal computers.

After the design is approved by the client, a copy of the computer file containing the design is transferred electronically to the printing department. Workers in the printing department load the file onto their own personal computers and print out the board design on special decals, 19.25 inches by 19.25 inches, using high-quality color inkjet printers. The side of the decal that is printed on is usually light-gray, and the other side contains an adhesive that is covered by a removable backing.

The printing department is also responsible for printing the property cards, game cards, and money. The money is printed on colored paper using standard laser printers. Ten copies of a particular denomination are printed on each 8.5-inch by 11-inch piece of paper. The money is then moved to the cutting department, where it is cut into individual bills. The property cards and game cards are produced similarly, the major difference being that they are printed on material resembling posterboard.

In addition to cutting the money, game cards, and property cards, the cutting department also cuts the cardboard that serves as the substrate for the actual game board. The game board consists of two boards created by cutting a single 19-inch by 19.25-inch piece of cardboard in half, yielding two boards each measuring 19.25 inches by 9.5 inches. After being cut, game boards, money, and cards are stored in totes in a work-in-process area and delivered to the appropriate station on the assembly line as needed.

Because of its explosive growth, X-Opoly's assembly line was never formally planned. It simply evolved into the 19 stations shown in the following table.

Station Number	Task(s) Performed at Station	Time to Perform Task
1	Place plastic money tray in box bottom. Take two dice from bin and place in box bottom in area not taken up by tray.	10 seconds
2	Count out 35 plastic houses and place in box bottom.	35 seconds
3	Count out 15 plastic hotels and place in box bottom.	15 seconds
4	Take one game piece from each of eight bins and place them in box bottom.	15 seconds
5	Take one property card from each of 28 bins. Place rubber band around property cards and place cards in box bottom.	40 seconds
6	Take one orange card from each of 15 bins. Place rubber band around cards and place cards in box bottom.	20 seconds
7	Take one yellow card from each of 15 bins. Take orange cards from box and remove rubber band. Place yellow cards on top of orange cards. Place rubber band around yellow and orange cards and place cards in box bottom.	35 seconds
8	Count out 25 $500 bills and attach to cardboard strip with rubber band. Place money in box bottom.	30 seconds
9	Count out 25 $100 bills. Take $500 bills from box bottom and remove rubber band. Place $100 bills on top of $500 bills. Attach rubber band around money and place in box bottom.	40 seconds
10	Count out 25 $50 bills. Take $500 and $100 bills from box bottom and remove rubber band. Place $50 bills on top. Attach rubber band around money and place in box bottom.	40 seconds
11	Count out 50 $20 bills. Take money in box and remove rubber band. Place $20 bills on top. Attach rubber band around money and place in box bottom.	55 seconds
12	Count out 40 $10 bills. Take money in box and remove rubber band. Place $10 bills on top. Attach rubber band around money and place in box bottom.	45 seconds
13	Count out 40 $5 bills. Take money in box and remove rubber band. Place $5 bills on top. Attach rubber band around money and place in box bottom.	45 seconds
14	Count out 40 $1 bills. Take money in box and remove rubber band. Place $1 bills on top. Attach rubber band around money and place in box bottom.	45 seconds
15	Take money and remove rubber band. Shrink wrap money and place back in box bottom.	20 seconds
16	Take houses, hotels, dice, and game pieces and place in bag. Seal bag and place bag in box.	30 seconds
17	Place two cardboard game board halves in fixture so that they are separated by ¼-inch. Peel backing off of printed game board decal. Align decal over board halves and lower it down. Remove board from fixture and flip it over. Attach solid blue backing decal. Flip game board over again and fold blue	90 seconds

(continued)

Station Number	Task(s) Performed at Station	Time to Perform Task
	backing over front of game board, creating a ¼ -inch border. Fold game board in half and place in box covering money tray, game pieces, and cards.	
18	Place game instructions in box. Place box top on box bottom. Shrink-wrap entire box.	30 seconds
19	Place completed box in carton.	10 seconds

Questions

1. What kind(s) of transformation system(s) does X-Opoly use?

2. What would be involved in switching the assembly line over from the production of one game to the production of another?

3. What is the cycle time of the 19-station line? What is its efficiency?

4. What is the line's maximum capacity per day, assuming that it is operated for one 8-hour shift less two 15-minute breaks? Assuming that X-Opoly operates 200 days per year, what is its annual capacity? How does its capacity compare with its projected demand?

5. On the basis of the task descriptions, develop a precedence graph for the assembly tasks. (Assume that tasks performed in the 19 stations cannot be further divided.) Using these precedence relationships, develop a list of recommendations for rebalancing the line in order to improve its performance.

6. What would be the impact on the line's capacity and efficiency if your recommendations were implemented?

EXERCISES

1. Given the following machine-component matrix, form cells using PFA.

Machines	Components						
	1	2	3	4	5	6	7
1		1			1		
2				1		1	
3			1	1			
4		1			1		1
5	1						1

2. **a.** Given the following load matrix, find the best layout.

Department	Department					
	1	2	3	4	5	6
1	—	4	6	2	0	7
2		—	3	5	1	3
3			—	2	6	5
4				—	5	2
5					—	3

b. Resolve part a if the rates are $4 from odd to even departments, $5 from even to odd, $6 from odd to odd, and $7 from even to even.

3. An office is laid out as in the following table. The office manager is considering switching departments 2 and 6 to reduce transport costs. Should this be done? (Use rectangular distances. Assume that offices are 10 feet on a side.) What is the difference in annual cost, assuming a 250-day work year?

1	2	3
4	5	6

Daily Trip Matrix

From	To					
	1	2	3	4	5	6
1	x	40	x	x	x	40
2	30	x	20	30	60	0
3	x	70	x	x	x	20
4	x	0	x	x	x	30
5	x	10	x	x	x	0
6	40	50	20	0	10	x

Trip Cost (to any department) per Foot From					
1	2	3	4	5	6
$0.02	$0.03	$0.01	$0.03	$0.02	$0.02

4. Relayout the office in Exercise 3 given the following desired closeness ratings.

Department	1	2	3	4	5	6
1		I	A	X	O	U
2			X	E	I	O
3				O	X	I
4					I	E
5						A
6						

5. Demand for a certain subassembly in a toy manufacturing facility is 96 items per eight-hour shift. The following six tasks are required to produce one subassembly.

Task	Time Required (minutes)	Predecessor Tasks
a	4	—
b	5	a
c	3	a
d	2	b
e	1	b, c
f	5	d, e

What is the required cycle time? Theoretically, how many stations will be required? Balance the line. What is the line's efficiency?

6. An assembly line has the following tasks (times shown in minutes).

   a. Six assemblies are required per hour. Balance the line.

   b. What is the efficiency of the line?

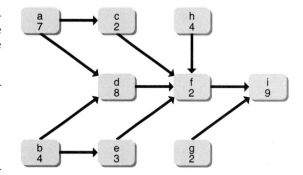

BIBLIOGRAPHY

Bradley, T. "Fender Blenders." *1988–1989 Guitar Buyers' Guide*. 129–133.

Business Week. "He's Gutsy, Brilliant, and Carries an Ax" (May 9, 1994): 62–66.

Bylinski, G. "The Digital Factory." *Fortune* (November 14, 1994): 92–107.

Chase, R. B., and W. K. Erikson. "The Service Factory." *Academy of Management Executive* (August 1988): 191–196.

Chase, R. B., and D. A. Tansik. "The Customer Contact Model for Organization Design." *Management Science*, vol. 29, no. 9 (September 1983): 1037–1050.

Ferras, L. "Continuous Improvements in Electronics Manufacturing." *Production and Inventory Management Journal* (Second Quarter 1994): 1–5.

Francis, R. L., and J. A. White. *Facility Layout and Location: An Analytical Approach*. Englewood Cliffs, N.J.: Prentice-Hall, 1987.

Gerwin, D. "Do's and Don'ts of Computerized Manufacturing." *Harvard Business Review* (March–April 1982): 107–116.

Hammer, M. "Reengineering Work: Don't Automate, Obliterate." *Harvard Business Review* (July–August 1990): 104–112.

Hammer, M. *Beyond Reengineering*. New York: Harper Business, 1996.

Hayes, R. H., and S. C. Wheelwright. "Link Manufacturing Process and Product Life Cycles." *Harvard Business Review* (January–February 1979): 133–140.

Kilpatrick, D. "Riding the Real Trends in Technology." *Fortune* (February 19, 1996): 57.

Levasseur, G. A., M. M. Helms, and A. A. Zink. "A Conversion to a Cellular Manufacturing Layout at Steward, Inc." *Production and Inventory Management Journal* (Third Quarter 1995): 37–42.

Stoner, D. L., K. J. Tice, and J. E. Ashton. "Simple and Effective Cellular Approach to a Job Machine Shop." *Manufacturing Review*, vol. 2, no. 2 (June 1989): 119–128.erity, J. W. "A Company That's 100% Virtual." *Business Week* (November 21, 1994): 85.

CHAPTER 6

Capacity and Location Planning

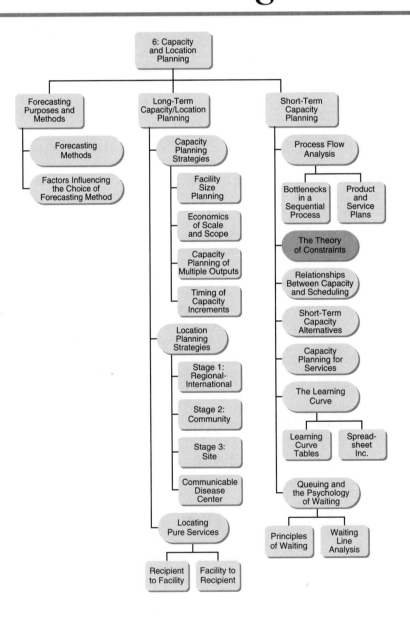

In this chapter our attention turns to translating the forecast of demand into capacity requirements for the organization's various resources. After overviewing the purposes and methods of forecasting, the chapter discusses various measures of capacity. Next, we discuss issues related to long-term capacity planning including location planning strategies. This is followed by a discussion of short-term capacity planning including process flow analysis, the theory of constraints, and how humans' ability to learn affects capacity planning. The chapter concludes with a discussion of the theory and psychology of waiting lines.

$\mathscr{I}$NTRODUCTION

- As is typical of a service business, fast-food chains such as Burger King must respond to sharp increases in demand but still keep costs low. Building up inventory to handle surges in demand is barely helpful, since the maximum allowed shelf life of its products is 10 minutes. And during the lunchtime rush, hamburger production may have to jump from 40 an hour to 800 an hour. To accommodate this high variability, Burger King has designed its facilities and processes for flexible capacity. For example, the drive-through, which accounts for almost half of its business, may be staffed by only one person during slow periods. This person takes the order, assembles it, and makes change. But during high-demand periods the production space is large enough to accommodate five people, who divide up the duties. In addition, opening a second drive-through window allows customers with special orders to pull forward if their order isn't ready at the first window, thereby permitting following customers to proceed with their service. By this and other techniques designed to reduce the average transaction time from 45 to 30 seconds, sales during peak demand periods have been increased 50 percent. Keeping costs low while meeting highly variable demand requires careful planning and management. For example, Burger King's award-winning restaurant design, the "BK-50," is 32 percent smaller and costs 27 percent less to build than the previous design, yet it can handle 40 percent more sales with less labor (Filley 1983).

- You might be surprised to learn that the semiconductor industry is taking a lesson from the steel industry. After all, the semiconductor industry is on the leading edge of technology, whereas the steel industry is decidedly mature. However, these industries have an important characteristic in common: both tend to require factories that are large and expensive (i.e., in excess of $1 billion). However, in the late 1980s steelmakers began to abandon economies of scale as a rationale for building large factories and began to develop smaller production facilities called minimills. Now chip makers are adopting a similar approach: they are constructing smaller and more automated wafer fabrication factories. One reason for this is that shorter product life cycles will make it virtually impossible to recoup the estimated $2 billion it will cost to build a conventional wafer fab in 1998. It takes 22 to 30 months to recapture the investment in a conventional wafer fabrication facility, but it is projected that it will take only 10 months to recoup the development costs of a so-called minifab. Another important benefit associated with the minifabs is that because equipment can be grouped in clusters, the time required to complete the 200 processing steps can be reduced from the current 60 to 90 days to 7 days. This is particularly important because studies indicate that getting a new chip to market a few months earlier can result in as much as $1 billion in added revenues (Port 1994).

- In the early 1990s Mercedes-Benz began investigating the feasibility of producing a luxury sports-utility vehicle, referred to as the Multi-Purpose Vehicle (MPV). Faced with increasing international competition, Mercedes deviated from its established procedures and staffed the project team with young product planners, engineers, and marketers. The team was charged with finding a site outside of Germany to build the MPV (up to this time, all Mercedes automobiles had been built in Germany). The team initially narrowed the search for the new facility to North America, because the combined costs of labor, shipping, and components would be lowest in this region. Costs were particularly important since the MPV was to be priced about the same as a fully loaded Jeep Grand Cherokee, yet Mercedes would operate its plant at a much lower volume than producers such as Chrysler.

  After further analysis, the team decided to limit the search to sites in the United States in order to be close to the primary market and to avoid the penalties associated with currency fluctuations. The team identified 100 possible sites in 35 states. As it began analyzing the sites, its primary concern was the cost of transportation. Since the MPV was going to be built only in the United States and half of its output would be exported, the team focused on sites near Atlantic or Gulf seaports, major highways, and rail lines. Also, workers' ages and mix of skills were considered. Eventually, the original list of sites was pared down to three sites in North Carolina, South Carolina, and Alabama. All three finalists were evaluated as relatively equal in terms of business climate, education levels, transportation, and long-term operating costs. According to the managing director, the decision to locate the new facility in Alabama came down to a perception on the part of Mercedes that Alabama was the most dedicated to the project (Woodruff and Templeman 1993).

- A geographic information system (GIS) is used to view and analyze data on digital maps as opposed to analyzing the same data printed out in massive tables that require reams of paper. One upscale clothing retailer with stores in Eau Claire and Green Bay, Wisconsin, analyzed its sales data on a map of the central part of the state. The map showed that each store drew the majority of its customers from a 20-mile radius. The map also highlighted an area between Eau Claire and Green Bay where only 15 percent of the potential customers had actually visited either store. Management's conclusion was that a new store in Wausau was needed to reach this untapped market. To take another example, at Super Valu (the nation's largest supermarket wholesaler), analysts would spread out paper maps and compare them with demographic data. Now, using a GIS, the same information is displayed on the screen of a personal computer, making it much easier to read and analyze (Tetzeli 1993).

- In industries such as fashion, which are characterized by highly volatile demand, the combined costs of stockouts and markdowns can be greater than total manufacturing costs. One approach to forecasting in these highly volatile industries is to determine what can and cannot be predicted well. Products in the "predictable" category are made farthest in advance, saving manufacturing capacity for the "unpredictable" products so that they can be produced closer to their actual selling season. Using this approach, Sport Obermeyer, a producer of fashionable skiwear, increased its profits between 50 percent and 100 percent over a three-year period in the early 1990s (Fisher, Hammond, Obermeyer, and Raman 1994).

As we will discuss in more detail throughout this chapter, *capacity* represents the rate at which a transformation system can create outputs. As is illustrated by the example of Burger King, capacity planning is as important to service organizations as it is to manufacturing organizations such as semiconductor manufacturers. These examples also illustrate other important issues associated with capacity planning. In Burger King's case, the transformation system was designed so that capacity could be quickly adjusted to match a highly variable demand rate throughout the day. The case of the semiconductor industry demonstrates the enormous cost often associated with expanding capacity. To further complicate matters, shorter product life cycles mean that organizations have less time to recoup their investment, especially when the next generation of products makes the current products obsolete.

Based on the demand forecast, capacity of the facility, and the characteristics of the output (e.g., its weight, materials), we can next determine the most economical way to obtain the inputs needed to produce and deliver the output to the customers. This includes considerations regarding the location of the facility relative to suppliers and potential customers.

The example of Mercedes-Benz illustrates two important characteristics of decisions about location: they are often done in stages, and multiple criteria are often considered. Decisions typically start off very broadly and, as additional information is collected, become narrower and more specific. In the case of Mercedes, the location for the new facility was specified broadly as someplace in North America. Then it was sequentially narrowed to the United States, to 100 sites within the United States, to three states, and finally to a site in Alabama. As regards the criteria used to compare locations, Mercedes considered factors such as labor cost, shipping cost, accessibility to transportation, the age and skill of the work force, and the state government's dedication to the project.

In this chapter we first briefly discuss the role of forecasting, not only for long-term capacity planning but also in terms of short-term capacity needs, and then go into detail about long-term capacity/location strategies. Over the long term, capacity and location are interwoven considerations, as will be described more extensively in the supply-chain management discussion in Chapter 9. Following the long-term discussion, we move into a description of short-term capacity alternatives, but here we are largely past the point of making a location decision. In this section, we also discuss process flow analysis, the learning curve, and issues specifically relevant to service capacity requirements.

$\mathscr{F}$ORECASTING PURPOSES AND METHODS

There is usually a close relationship between competing successfully and being able to predict key aspects of the future accurately. Clearly, it is not practical to try to plan without some prediction of the future. Even planning a simple party requires predicting how many people will show up, how much they will eat and drink, what kind of snacks and beverages they will enjoy, and how long they will stay. A business introducing a new product needs to predict the demand for the product, how prices and advertising will affect this demand, how competitors will respond, and so on.

Thus, we see that an accurate estimate of demand for the output is crucial to the efficient operation of the production system and, hence, to managing the organization's resources. For example, a supermarket chain that is contemplating the addition of a new store must have a reasonable estimate of demand in order to determine how big the store and the parking lot should be, what ancillary departments (such as a bakery, pharmacy, deli, and bank) should be included, and how many shopping carts and checkout lanes should be specified in the plans. Once the facility is constructed, a more specific, perhaps weekly, forecast of demand will be needed so that the manager will be able to schedule workers and order merchandise. The same is true for decisions about capacity, scheduling, and staffing in a product organization. Capacity (obtaining the proper level of resources) and scheduling (the timing of resource usage) both require forecasting, whether or not it be a formal procedure.

As an aside, it is worth noting that it is not only demand for the output that can be forecast. The tools of forecasting can also be used to predict the development of new technology, national and international economic conditions, and even many factors internal to the organization such as changes in lead time, scrap rates, cost trends, personnel growth, and departmental productivity. Here, however, we will restrict our discussion to the uses of forecasting for long- and short-term capacity planning.

Forecasts are used in organizations for four primary purposes.

1. To decide whether demand is sufficient to justify entering the market. If demand exists but at too low a price to cover the costs that an organization will incur in producing an output, then the organization should reject the opportunity.

2. To determine long-term (2- to 5-year) capacity needed, in order to design facilities. An overall projection of demand for a number of years in the future serves as the basis for decisions related to expanding, or contracting, capacity to meet the demand. Since there is competition, even in the not-for-profit

sector, an organization is courting disaster if it produces inefficiently, because of excess idle capacity, or insufficiently to meet demand, because of too little capacity.

3. To determine midterm (3-month to 18-month) fluctuations in demand, in order to avoid shortsighted decisions that will hurt the company in the long run. To illustrate, if a company planned its staffing solely on the basis of its weekly forecast, each week it might adjust the level on the basis of a forecast for the coming week. Thus, in some weeks it might lay off workers only to rehire them in the following week. Such weekly adjustments would most likely lower morale and productivity. A better approach is to base staffing on a longer-term perspective.

4. To ascertain short-term (1-week to 3-month) fluctuations in demand for the purposes of production planning, work force scheduling, materials planning, and other such needs. These forecasts support a number of operational activities and can have a significant effect on organizational productivity, bottlenecks, master schedules, meeting promised delivery dates, and other such issues of concern to top management and to the organization as a whole.

Forecasting Methods

Forecasting methods can be grouped in several ways. One classification, illustrated in Figure 6.1, distinguishes between formally recognized forecasting techniques and informal approaches such as intuition, spur-of-the-moment guesses, and seat-of-the-pants predictions. Our attention here will obviously be directed to the formal methods.

In general, qualitative forecasting methods are often used for long-range forecasts, especially when external factors (e.g., the Asian Crisis) may play a significant role. They are also of use when historical data are very limited or nonexistent, as in the introduction of a new product or service.

Some of the most significant decisions made by organizations, frequently strategic decisions, are made on the basis of *qualitative* forecasts. These often concern either a new product or service or long-range changes in the nature of the organization's outputs. In both cases, relevant historical data on demand are typically not available.

Qualitative forecasts are made using information such as telephone or mail surveys of consumers' attitudes and intentions, consumer panels, test marketing in limited areas, expert opinion and panels, and analyses of historical demand for similar products or services—a method known as *historical analogy*. One example of historical analogy would be the use of demand data for CD-Roms to predict the demand curve for DVDs.

A special type of expert panel is called *Delphi*. The RAND Corporation developed the Delphi method as a group technique for forecasting the demand for new or contemplated products or services. The intent was to eliminate the undesirable effects of interaction between members of the group (such as loud and dominating individuals) while retaining the benefits of their broad experience and knowledge. The method begins by having each member provide individual written forecasts, along with any supporting arguments and assumptions. These forecasts

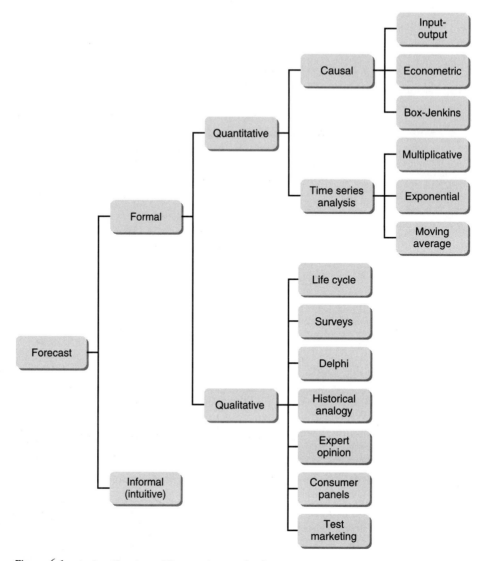

Figure 6.1   A classification of forecasting methods.

are submitted to a Delphi researcher, who edits, clarifies, and summarizes the data. These data are then provided as feedback to the members, along with a second round of questions. This procedure continues, usually for about four rounds, when a consensus among panel members can often be reached on some of the issues.

Another qualitative device often used in forecasting is called *life-cycle analysis*. Experienced managers who have introduced several new products are often able to estimate how long a product will remain in each stage of its life cycle. This forecast, coupled with other market information, can produce reasonably accurate estimates of demand in the medium to long range.

Quantitative forecasting methods are generally divided between methods that simply project the past history or behavior of the variable into the future (*time series analysis*) and those that also include external data (*causal*). Time series analysis is the simpler of the two and ranges from just using an average of the past data to using regression analysis corrected for seasonality in the data. Simple projection techniques are obviously limited to, and primarily used for, very short-term forecasting. Such approaches often work well in a stable environment but cannot react to changing industry factors or changes in the national economy.

Causal methods, which are usually quite complex, include histories of external factors and employ sophisticated statistical techniques. Many "canned" computerized forecasting packages are available for the quantitative techniques, both time series analysis and causal.

Factors Influencing the Choice of Forecasting Method

What method is chosen to prepare a demand forecast depends on a number of factors. First, if the forecast must be very accurate, highly sophisticated methods are usually needed. Typically, long-range (two- to five-year) forecasts require the least accuracy and are only for general (or aggregate) planning, whereas short-range forecasts require greater accuracy and are for detailed operations.

Second, if the data are available, one of the quantitative forecasting methods can be used. Otherwise, nonquantitative techniques are required. Attempting to forecast without a demand history is almost as hard as using a crystal ball. The demand history need not be long or complete, but some historical data should be used if at all possible.

Third, the greater the limitation on time or money available for forecasting, the more likely it is that an unsophisticated method will have to be used. In general, management wants to use a forecasting method that minimizes not only the cost of making the forecast but also the cost of an *inaccurate* forecast; that is, management's goal is to minimize the total forecasting costs. Costs of inaccurate forecasting include the cost of over- or understocking an item, the costs of under- or overstaffing, and the intangible and opportunity costs associated with loss of goodwill because a demanded item is not available.

Fourth, with the advent of computers, the cost of statistical forecasts based on historical data and the time required to make such forecasts have been reduced significantly. It has therefore become more cost-effective for organizations to conduct sophisticated forecasts.

Once a forecast of demand has been developed, it is translated into capacity requirements for the organization's various resources. Thus, the demand forecast is an important input to both long-term and short-term capacity planning. We discuss these topics in turn in the remainder of this chapter.

$\mathcal{L}$ONG-TERM CAPACITY/ LOCATION PLANNING

Capacity is generally taken to mean the maximum *rate* at which a transformation system produces outputs or processes inputs, though the rate may be "all at once." Table 6.1 lists measures of capacity for a number of production systems. Notice

*T*ABLE 6.1 • Examples of Measures of Capacity

Production System	Measure of Capacity in Terms of Outputs Produced	Measure of Capacity in Terms of Inputs Processed
airline	available seat miles per year	reservation calls handled per day
hospital	babies delivered per month	patients admitted per week
supermarket	customers checked out per hour	cartons unloaded per hour
post office	packages delivered per day	letters sorted per hour
university	graduates per quarter	students admitted per year
automobile assembly plant	autos assembled per year	deliveries of parts per day

that since capacity is defined as a rate, measures should be clear about the *time dimension*. For instance, how meaningful is it to know that a hospital can perform 25 surgeries? Without knowing whether this is all at once, per day, per week, or possibly per month, the number is relatively meaningless.

As illustrated in Table 6.1, airlines often measure their capacity in *available seat miles* (ASMs) per year. One ASM is 1 seat available for 1 passenger for 1 mile. Clearly, the number of planes an airline has, their size, how often they are flown, and the route structure of the airline all affect its ASMs, or capacity. However, we may also talk about the capacity of a single plane, such as a 550-seat jumbo, and here we clearly mean "all at once." Nevertheless, this capacity measure is not very useful without knowing to what use the plane may be put, such as constantly being in the air generating ASMs or used as an occasional backup. As can be seen, ASMs more easily convert into profitability measures. Similarly, an elementary measure of a hospital's capacity is often simply the number of beds it has (for the full year is implied). Thus, a 50-bed hospital is "small" and a 1000-bed hospital is "large." And a restaurant may measure its capacity in tables (per hour), a hotel in rooms (per night), and a public service agency in family contacts (per weekday).

Notice that these measures of capacity do not recognize the multiple types of outputs with which an organization may, in reality, be concerned. ASMs say nothing about the freight capacity of an airline, but freight may be a major contributor to profits. Similarly, number of beds says nothing about outpatient treatment, ambulance rescues, and other services provided by a hospital. Thus, capacity planning must often consider the capacity to produce multiple outputs. Unfortunately, some of the outputs may require the same organizational resources, as well as some very specialized resources.

The provision of adequate capacity is clearly a generic problem, common to all types of organizations, but in pure service organizations capacity is a special problem because the output cannot normally be stored for later use. A utility, for example, must have capacity available to meet peak power demands, yet the *average* power demand may be much, much lower. Where the provision of the service is by human labor, low productivity is a danger when staffing is provided to meet the demand peaks.

Another characteristic of capacity is that, frequently, a variety of restrictions can limit it. For example, the capacity of a fast-food restaurant may be limited not only by the number of order-takers on duty but also by the number of cooks, the number of machines to prepare the food, the amount of food in stock, the space in the restaurant, and even the number of parking spaces outside. Any one of these factors can become a ***bottleneck*** (discussed in a later section of the chapter) that limits the restaurant's normal operating capacity to something less than its theoretical or design capacity.

In addition, during the production process there are often natural losses, waste (avoidable), scrap (unavoidable), defects, errors, and so on that again limit the capacity of a system. These losses are considered in a measure known as the ***yield*** of the process: the amount of output of acceptable quality emerging from a production system compared with the amount that entered it. ***Yield management***, also known as ***revenue management***, is a somewhat different topic but of high interest these days, particularly in services. However, it is more related to schedule management and is thus deferred to our discussion in Chapter 7.

In the process of trying to forecast the long-run capacity needs for the organization, the issue of location of the facility, or facilities, cannot be ignored because the demand may well be a function of *where* the facility is located. And if there are multiple facilities, the capacity needs for any one will certainly depend on how many others are serving the same geographic needs. Moreover, transportation may also be a factor if there is a facilitating good, or product, involved, as well as inventories, warehouses, and other such matters that concern ***supply chain management***. In these days of intense worldwide competition, supply chain management is taking on significantly more importance, as it accounts for a greater and greater proportion of the total cost of all outputs. Although we discuss the interplay between capacity and location in this chapter, we defer the larger discussion of supply chain management to Chapter 9.

Capacity Planning Strategies

Issues of capacity planning over the long run relate primarily to the strategic issues of initiating, expanding, and contracting the major facilities used in producing the output. Note the interdependence of the capacity decision with the location decision. Every capacity decision requires a corresponding location decision. For example, expanding an existing facility defines the location of the new capacity to be an existing facility. This section will discuss capacity planning strategies in terms of facility size, economies of scale and scope, timing of capacity increments, and capacity for multiple outputs. The following section will then discuss the location aspects and relationships.

Facility Size Planning

Figure 6.2 illustrates the issue of facility size in terms of capacity and unit cost. Product cost curves are shown for five sizes of production facilities. When plants are operated at their lowest-cost production level (A, B, or C), the larger facilities will generally have the lowest costs, a phenomenon known as *economies of scale*. However, if production levels must be set at a value other than the lowest-cost level, the advantage of a larger facility may be lost. For example, point D is characterized by congestion and excessive overtime, and point E by idle labor and low equipment utilization. Points F and G illustrate some of the diseconomies of scale, as described next.

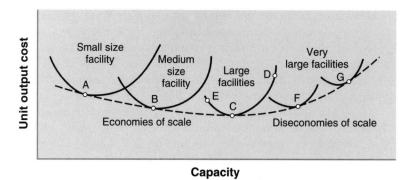

Figure 6.2   Envelope of lowest unit output costs with facility size.

Economies of Scale and Scope

Obtaining lower unit costs through the use of larger facilities is known as ***economies of scale***. Primarily, the economy comes from spreading the required fixed costs—land, administration, sales force, facilities, and such other factors— over a larger volume of products or services, although there are also economies obtained through stronger purchasing power and learning curve effects (discussed in a later section). However, as illustrated by points F and G in Figure 6.2, there is a limit to the benefits that can be obtained, because the inherent inefficiencies of large facilities begin to counter their economic benefits. This occurs through increased bureaucracy, poor communication, long lines of responsibility and authority, and the like. Many manufacturers now have a corporate policy that no plant will be larger than 200 to 250 workers, often considered an optimum size.

Managers frequently think in terms of economies of scale when making decisions about where to produce new products or services, or whether or not to extend their line of products and services. However, the focus lost through adding these new production requirements can jeopardize the competitive strength of a firm. Managers would be well advised to examine more closely where the economies are expected to come from: sometimes it is from higher volumes, sometimes from the use of common technology, sometimes from availability of off-peak capacity. If the source of the economy results in offsetting diseconomies of scale, as a result of loss of focus or for other reasons, the firm should not proceed.

An allied concept related to the use of many of the advanced, flexible technologies such as programmable robots is called ***economies of scope***. The phrase implies that economies can also be obtained with flexibility by offering variety instead of volume. However, upon closer examination it is not clear why being flexible offers any particular economies. The real reason for economies of scope derives from the same economies as those of scale—spreading fixed costs among more products or services—but the scale is now obtained over many small batches of a wide variety of outputs, rather than large batches of only a few standard outputs.

Capacity Planning for Multiple Outputs

Realistically, organizations are not always expanding their capacity. We usually focus on this issue because we are studying firms in the process of growth, but even successful organizations often reduce their capacity. Major ways of contracting capacity are to divest the firm of operations, lay off workers, and sell or lease equipment and facilities. Most organizations, however, try to contract only capacity that is inefficient or inappropriate for their circumstances, owing in part to a felt responsibility to the community. If it appears that organizational resources are going to be excessively idle in the future, organizations often attempt to add new outputs to their current output mix rather than contracting capacity (the latter frequently being done at a loss). This entails an analysis of the candidate output's life and seasonal demand cycles.

It is traditional in fire departments to use the slack months for building inspections, conducting fire prevention programs, giving talks on safety, and other such activities. The large investment in labor and equipment is thus more effectively utilized throughout the year by adoption of an *anticyclic* output (an output counter to the fire cycle)—fire prevention. For much the same reasons, many fire departments have been given the responsibility for the city or county's medical rescue service (although rescue alarms are not entirely anticyclic to fire alarms).

Clearly, many organizations, such as the makers of greeting cards, fur coats, swimming pool equipment, and fireworks, face this cyclic difficulty. A classic case of **seasonality** is that of furnace dealers. For the last 100 years all their business typically was in the late autumn and winter, as illustrated in Figure 6.3. With the rapid acceptance of air conditioning in the 1950s and 1960s, many furnace dealers eagerly added this product to their output mix. Not only was it conceptually along the same lines (environmental comfort) and often physically interconnected with the home furnace but, most important, it was almost completely anticyclic to the seasonal heating cycle. As shown in Figure 6.3, the addition of air conditioning considerably leveled dealers' sales throughout the year in comparison with furnace sales alone.

In a similar manner, and for much the same reasons, organizations add to their mix outputs that are anticyclic to existing output **life cycles.** Figure 6.4 illustrates the expected life cycles of an organization's current and projected outputs. Total

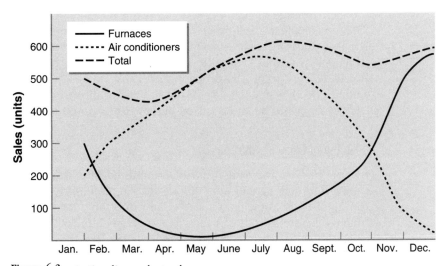

Figure 6.3   Anticyclic product sales.

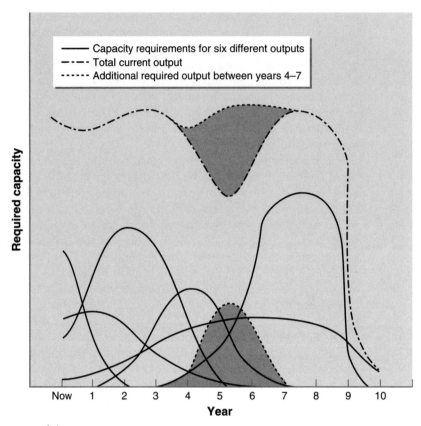

Figure 6.4   Forecast of required organizational capacity from multiple life cycles.

required capacity is found by adding together the separate capacities of each of the required outputs. Note the projected dip in required capacity five years in the future, and, of course, beyond the eight-year R&D planning horizon.

The message of Figure 6.4 should be clear to the organization—an output with a three-year life cycle (appearing similar to the shaded area) is needed between years 4 and 7 in order to maintain efficient utilization of the organization's available capacity. A priority output development program will have to be instituted immediately. At this point it is probably too late to develop something through R&D; a more effective strategy, especially in light of the relatively low volume and short life cycle, might be an extension of an existing output.

Timing of Capacity Increments

Once the best alternative for obtaining the desired capacity has been determined, the timing and manner must still be chosen. A number of approaches are illustrated in Figure 6.5. Sometimes there is an opportunity to add capacity in small increments (Figure 6.5a) rather than as one large chunk (Figure 6.5b), such as an entire plant. Clearly, small increments are less risky, but they do not offer an opportunity to upgrade the entire production system at one time, as a single chunk does. Other

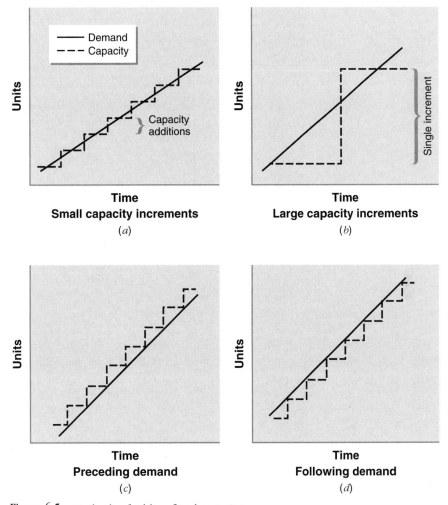

Figure 6.5 Methods of adding fixed capacity.

choices are to add capacity before the demand has arisen (Figure 6.5*c*) or after (Figure 6.5*d*). Adding capacity before demand occurs upstages the competition and enhances customers' loyalty but risks the cost of the capacity if the expected demand never materializes. Adding capacity after demand arises will encourage the competition to move into the market and take away part of your share. Clearly, the most appropriate strategy must be carefully evaluated for the situation at hand.

Location Planning Strategies

Having determined capacity requirements, we next discuss the most economical way to obtain the inputs needed to produce and deliver the output to the customer. This includes determining the location of the facility relative to suppliers and potential customers. Although we are discussing capacity and location planning sequentially, as noted earlier, these decisions are typically considered simultaneously since every capacity decision requires a location decision (e.g., where to add the new capacity or which plant should be closed).

In general, the decision about location is divided into three stages: regional (including international), community, and site. Sources of information for these stages are chambers of commerce, realtors, utilities, banks, suppliers, transportation companies, savings and loan associations, government agencies, and management consultants who specialize in relocation. For some pure service organizations (e.g., physicians), only the site selection stage may be relevant because they are already focused on a specific region and community.

Stage 1: Regional–International

In the regional–international stage, an organization focuses on what part of the world (e.g., North America, Europe, Pacific rim) or perhaps in what region of a country (e.g., Southwest, Midwest, Northeast) it wants to locate its new facility. In the example at the beginning of the chapter, Mercedes-Benz initially decided that its new facility should be located in North America and subsequently further narrowed the region to sites in the United States. There are four major considerations in selecting a national or overseas region for a facility: *proximity, labor supply, availability of inputs,* and *environment.*

To minimize transportation costs and provide acceptable service to customers, the facility should be located in a region in close *proximity* to customers and suppliers. Although methods of finding the location with the minimum transportation cost will be presented later in this chapter, a common rule of thumb within the United States is that the facility should be within 200 miles of major industrial and commercial customers and suppliers. Beyond this range, transportation costs begin to rise quickly.

The region should have the proper *supply of labor* available and in the correct proportions of required skills. One important reason for the past expansion of American firms abroad was the availability of labor at wage rates much lower than rates at home. Currently, this disparity has been reduced significantly because of increased wages abroad. However, the real consideration should be, not wage rates, but the productivity of domestic labor relative to productivity abroad. This comparison would thus involve level of skills, use of equipment, wage rates, and even work ethics (which differ even between regions within the United States) to determine the most favorable labor supply in terms of output per dollar of wages and capital investment. The organization of the labor pool should also be given consideration—that is, whether all the skills are unionized or whether there is an open shop. Some states have passed *right-to-work laws* that forbid any requirement that all employees join a union in order to work in an organization. Often, these laws result in significantly lower wage rates in these states.

The region selected for location of the facility should have the necessary *inputs* available. For example, supplies that are difficult, expensive, or time-consuming to ship and those that are necessary to the organization (i.e., no reasonable substitutes exist) should be readily available. The proper type (rail, water, highway, air) and supply of transportation; sufficient quantities of basic resources such as water, electricity, gas, coal, and oil; and appropriate communication facilities should also be available. Obviously, many American industries are located abroad in order to use raw materials (oil, copper, etc.) available there.

The regional *environment* should be conducive to the work of the organization. Not only should the weather be appropriate, but the political, legal, and social climate should also be favorable. The following matters should be considered:

1. Regional taxes
2. Regional regulations on operations (pollution, hiring, etc.)
3. Barriers to imports or exports
4. Political stability (nationalization policies, kidnappings)
5. Cultural and economic peculiarities (e.g., restrictions on working women)

These factors are especially critical in locating in a foreign country, particularly an underdeveloped country. Firms locating in such regions should not be surprised to find large differences in the way things are done. For example, in some countries governmental decisions tend to move slowly, with extreme centralization of authority. Very little planning seems to occur. Events appear to occur by "God's will" or by default. The pace of work is unhurried, and at times discipline, especially among managers, seems totally absent. Corruption and payoffs often seem to be normal ways of doing business, and accounting systems are highly suspect. Living conditions for the workers, especially in urbanized areas, are depressing. Transportation and communication systems (roads, ports, phone service) can be incomplete and notoriously unreliable. Attempting to achieve something under such conditions can, understandably, be very discouraging. When locating in such countries, a firm should allow for such difficulties and unexpected problems. In such an environment, Murphy's law thrives.

A model to help make the regional/national location decision is the CVD model we described for helping with the job shop layout in Chapter 5. In this case, we are interested in the total of all the supply costs into the facility and all the distribution costs out to customers. The procedure is to select some initial site for the facility that appears to be good and then sum the products of the transportation rate (C), the volume or weights (V), and the distance (D) over all the locations. Then we can simply consider placing the facility in another site and see if the cost is less, and so on. If all the sites are prespecified, then the site with the lowest cost is deemed best (at least on this one measure).

DILBERT ©United Feature Syndicate. Reprinted with permission.

Stage 2: Community

After the region of a new facility has been decided on, candidate communities within the region are identified for further analysis. Many of the considerations made at the regional–international stage should also be considered at this next stage. For example, the availability of acceptable sites, attitudes of the local government, regulations, zoning, taxes, labor supply, the size and characteristics of the market, and the weather would again be considered. In addition, the availability of local financing, monetary inducements (such as tax incentives) for establishing operations there, and the community's attitude toward the organization itself would be additional factors of interest to the organization.

Last, the preferences of the organization's staff should play a role in selecting a community. These would probably be influenced by the amenities available in the community such as homes, religious congregations, shopping centers, schools and universities, medical care, fire and police protection, and entertainment, as well as local tax rates and other costs. Upper-level educational institutions may also be of interest to the organization in terms of opportunity for relevant research and development. For example, it is no coincidence that major IBM plants are located in Lexington, Kentucky; Denver, Colorado; and Austin, Texas, which are also sites of major state universities.

The standard "breakeven" or "cost-volume-profit" model can be helpful for this stage of the location decision, except that there is no revenue line and there are multiple costs lines, each representing a different community's costs. We assume that the problem is to choose from among a set of predetermined communities, on the basis of a range of fixed and variable costs rather than just distribution cost, as calculated by the CVD model just given. That is, distribution cost may be considered, but it is only one factor (perhaps fixed, perhaps variable with output volume) among many that need to be considered to make a decision. Although the relevant *factors* for comparison between the communities may be known (e.g., labor costs, taxes, utility charges, etc.), their values may be uncertain, particularly if they are a function of the output rate of the facility being located. The various alternatives for location are then compared by graphing total operating costs for each alternative at different levels of demand, as in Figure 6.6.

This is accomplished by dividing the total operating cost into two components—fixed costs that do not vary with the demand for the output (e.g., land, buildings, equipment, property taxes, insurance) and variable costs such as labor, materials, and transportation—and plotting them on the axes of a graph. At the demand point E (the intersection of the two lines) the costs for the two alternatives are the same; for demand levels in excess of E, community 2 is best, and for levels less than E, community 1 is best. Thus, if the range of uncertainty concerning the output volume is entirely *above* point E, the manager need not be concerned about which community to choose—community 2 is best. Similar reasoning holds for any uncertainty existing entirely *below* point E—community 1 is best.

If the range of uncertainty is closely restricted to point E, then either community may be selected because the costs will be approximately the same in either case. However, if the range of uncertainty is broad and varies considerably from point E in both directions, then the breakeven chart will indicate to the manager the extra costs that will be incurred by choosing the wrong community. Before selecting either community, the manager should probably attempt to gather more information, to reduce the range of uncertainty in demand.

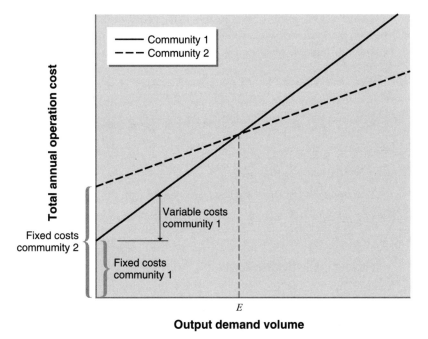

Figure 6.6   Breakeven location model

Stage 3: Site

After a list of candidate communities is developed, specific sites within them are identified. The *site*—the actual location of the facility—should be appropriate to the nature of the operation. Such matters as size; adjoining land; zoning; community attitudes; drainage; soil; the availability of water, sewers, and utilities; waste disposal; transportation; the size of the local market; and the costs of development are considered. The development of industrial parks in some communities has alleviated many of the difficulties involved in choosing a site, since the developer automatically takes care of most of these matters. Before any final decision is made, a cash-flow analysis is conducted for each of the candidate sites; this includes the cost of labor, land, taxes, utilities, transportation, and so on.

A model that can help with the site selection is the *weighted score model*. This approach can combine cost measures, profit measures, other quantitative measures, and qualitative measures to help analyze multiple locations (as well as any other multi-criteria decision). Deciding on a location, whether for products or services, is complicated by the existence of multiple criteria such as executives' preferences, maximization of facility use, and customers' attitudes. These and other criteria may be very difficult to quantify, or even measure qualitatively; if they are important to the decision, however, they must be included in the location analysis.

Locations can be compared in a number of ways. The most common is probably just managerial intuition: which location best satisfies the important criteria? The weighted score model is a simple formalization of this intuitive process that is useful as a rough screening tool for locating a single facility. In this model a weight is assigned to each factor (*criterion*), depending on its importance to the manager. The most important factors receive proportionately higher weights. Then a score is assigned to each of the alternative locations on each factor, again with higher scores representing better results. The product of the weights and the scores then gives a set of weighted scores, which are added up for each location. The location with the highest weighted score is considered best. In quantitative terms:

$$\text{Total weighted score} = \sum_i W_i S_i$$

where

i = index for factors

W_i = weight of factor i

S_i = score of the location being evaluated on factor i

The following example illustrates the method.

Communicable Disease Center

A county health department is investigating three possible locations for a specialized control clinic that will monitor acquired immune deficiency syndrome (AIDS) and other sexually transmitted diseases (STDs). The county director of public health is particularly concerned with four factors.

1. The most important consideration in the treatment of STDs is ease of access for those infected. Since they are generally disinclined to recognize and seek treatment, it is foolish to locate a clinic where it is not easily accessible to as many patients as possible. This aspect of location is probably as much as 50 percent more important than the lease cost of the building.

2. Still, the annual cost of the lease is not a minor consideration. Unfortunately, the health department is limited to a very tight budget, and any extra cost for the lease will mean that less equipment and staff are available to the clinic.

3. For some patients it is of the utmost importance that confidentiality be maintained. Thus, although the clinic must be easily accessible, it must also be relatively inconspicuous. This factor is probably just as important as the cost of the lease.

4. The director also wants to consider the convenience of the location for the staff, since many of the physicians will be donating their time to the clinic. This consideration is the least important of all, perhaps only half as important as the cost of the lease.

The three locations being considered are a relatively accessible building on Adams Avenue, an inconspicuous office complex near the downtown bus terminal, and a group of public offices in the Civic Center, which would be almost rent-free.

The director has decided to evaluate (score) each of these alternative locations on each of the four factors. He has decided to use a 4-point scale on which 1 represents "poor" and 4 represents "excellent." His scores and the weights (derived from the relative importance of the four factors) are shown in Table 6.2. The problem now is somehow to use this information to determine the best location for the clinic.

$\mathscr{T}$ABLE 6.2 • Potential Clinic Sites

W: Weight	F: Factor	A: Adams Avenue	B: Bus Terminal Complex	C: Civic Center
			Potential Locations	
2	1. Annual lease cost	1	3	4
3	2. Accessibility for patients	3	3	2
2	3. Inconspicuousness	2	4	2
1	4. Accessibility for personnel	4	1	2

Note: Factor scoring scale: 1, poor; 2, acceptable; 3, good; 4, excellent.

To determine the weighted score for each location, we multiply each score by the weight for that factor and then the sum over all factors for each location, as illustrated in Table 6.3. Since higher scores indicate better ratings, the location with the largest score—B, the office near the bus terminal—is best, followed by C, the Civic Center.

Quebec City, Canada, provides a good example of almost exactly this process (Price and Turcotte 1986). The Red Cross Blood Donor Clinic and Transfusion Center of Quebec City in Canada was located in a confined spot in the downtown area and wanted to expand in another location. The center's main activities affecting the choice of a new location were receiving donors, delivering blood and blood products throughout the community and the province of Quebec, and holding blood donor clinics over the same region.

Accordingly, the criteria for a site were identified as:

- Highway access for both clinics and blood deliveries
- Ability to attract more donors as a result of improved accessibility and visibility
- Convenience to both public and private transportation
- Ease of travel for employees
- Internal floor space
- Lot size
- Acceptability of the site to management and governmental authorities involved in the decision

$\mathscr{T}$ABLE 6.3 • Comparison of Site Factors by the Weighted Score Method

Factor	Weight	A	B	C
		Sites:		
1	2	2 × 1 = 2	2 × 3 = 6	2 × 4 = 8
2	3	3 × 3 = 9	3 × 3 = 9	3 × 2 = 6
3	2	2 × 2 = 4	2 × 4 = 8	2 × 2 = 4
4	1	1 × 4 = 4	1 × 1 = 1	1 × 2 = 2
Total		19	24	20

$\mathcal{T}_{\text{ABLE}}$ 6.4 • Comparison of Quebec City's Site Factors

Site	Road Access	Bus Access	Proximity	Availability	Rank
1	0.4	0.0	0.4	0.7	1
2	0.2	0.2	0.3	0.7	2
3	0.3	0.3	0.2	0.0	4
4	0.0	0.4	0.1	0.0	5
5	0.1	0.1	0.0	0.7	3

The analysis of the problem was very complicated, owing to conflicting requirements and the unavailability of data. Nevertheless, five sites were finally identified and evaluated on the basis of four final criteria. The five sites were then ranked on each of these criteria, and a scoring model was constructed to help management determine the best location. The weights were to be determined by management, and they could be modified to determine if changing them would have any effect on the best location. The final scores and rankings, assuming equal weights across the four criteria, are shown in Table 6.4.

Locating Pure Services

Although all the material presented so far applies equally to services and product firms, some situations unique to service organizations are worth noting. Two that we will look at in detail here involve the recipient coming to the facility, as in retailing, and the facility going to the recipient, as with "alarm" services.

Recipient to Facility

In recipient-to-facility situations, the facility draws customers or recipients from an area surrounding it, possibly in competition with other, similar facilities. Research has found that under these circumstances the drawing power of retail facilities is proportional to the size of the facility and inversely proportional to the square (or cube, in some cases) of the average recipient's travel time. This assumes that all other factors—such as price and quality—are equivalent or insignificant. This type of relationship is known as a *gravity* method because, like gravity, it operates by drawing nearby objects in.

Next, consider the situation of public services such as health clinics, libraries, and colleges. Apart from the difficulty of framing a location model is the probably more significant problem of choosing a measure, or measures, of service: number of recipients served (a "surrogate" measure), change in the recipient's condition (a direct measure of benefit), quantity of services offered (another surrogate), and so on. Some measures recommended in the literature on health clinics, which can be used for trial-and-error procedures, are:

1. *Facility utilization:* Maximize the number of visits to the facilities.
2. *Travel distance per citizen:* Minimize the average distance per person in the region to the nearest clinic.

3. *Travel distance per visit*: Minimize the average distance per visit to the nearest clinic.

No one measure has been found to work best for all cases of deciding on a location.

Facility to Recipient

Facility-to-recipient situations are common among the urban "alarm" services: fire, police, and ambulance. Again, the problem of measuring a service appropriately involves such factors as number of recipients served, average waiting time for service, value of property saved, and number of service facilities. Two general cases are encountered in this problem, whether a single- or multiple-facility service is being located:

1. High-density demand for services where multiple vehicles are located in the same facility and vehicles are often dispatched from one alarm directly to another
2. Widely distributed demand for services where extreme travel distances require additional facilities

Typical of situation 1 are fire companies and ambulances. Results in these cases have been basically the same. There is a significant drop-off in the returns to scale as more units are added to the system. Typically, the first three or four will improve all measures by up to 80 percent of the maximum improvement. Each additional unit gains less. A second common finding is that optimally located facilities yield only about a 15 percent improvement over existing or evenly dispersed facilities. Last, incremental approaches to selecting additional locations provide slightly poorer service than a total relocation analysis of all the facilities.

$\mathscr{S}$HORT-TERM CAPACITY PLANNING

In the short term, capacity planning is primarily related to issues of scheduling, labor shifts, balancing of resource capacities, and other such issues instead of location decisions. We will look into a variety of such approaches in this section.

Process-Flow Analysis

Earlier, we discussed some factors that might limit the output of a production system, such as bottlenecks in the system and yield considerations like scrap and defects. Here we will introduce some other terms relating to the use of a production system. One capacity measure that is commonly used is ***utilization***, which is simply the actual output relative to some expected, design, or normal output rate. For example, if a machine runs 4 hours a day in an American plant and the maintenance and setup time are usually 2 hours a day, the utilization for that day might be reported as $4/6 = 67\%$, which is considered to be fairly high utilization for a machine in a job shop. However, if the machine was in a Japanese plant, the utilization would probably be reported as 4/24 = 17%, since the machine could, in theory, have been used for all 24 hours in the day! Clearly, utilization figures do not mean much unless one knows what the "normal" or expected output rate is based on. (When labor utilization measures are used for wage payment plans, this "normal" definition is often a heated subject of union negotiations. For example, should mandated "breaks" be included in the base or not? Should sick time be included? Lunch? Inactivity due to lack of materials to work on? And so on.) An advantage of basing the utilization on 24 hours is that this shows how much more could be done with the resource if it were needed. On the other hand, most managers would not like hearing that their expensive machinery was only being 17 percent utilized!

Bottlenecks in a Sequential Process

Another, major concept in operations is that of *efficiency versus capacity (output rate)*. **Efficiency** is defined as output divided by input. Here we measure output as minutes of work embodied in the item being produced and input as minutes of resource time spent overall in producing the item. Normally, we expect that the amount of productive capacity and the capital investment to gain this capacity will be proportional. In the case of one worker, or one machine that produces the output, this is generally true. But when many workers or machines, or both, are required to produce the output (as is usually the case), such a simple correspondence may not exist.

For example, if rubber balls are molded in one machine run by one worker (and both machine and worker are constantly busy with this task) at the rate of 100 per hour, and a capacity of 1000 per hour is required, then the resource investment translates directly—10 machines and 10 workers will generally be needed. If a *sequential* process is involved, however, the resource investment does not translate so directly into the required output. For example, assume that King Sports Products produces a variety of tennis rackets *sequentially* on four machines, and the times required on each machine for one typical racket are as shown in Figure 6.7. Note in this figure that the ***throughput time*** for each racket is 4 + 3 + 10 + 2 = 19 minutes, which also represents the work embodied in each finished tennis racket.

To minimize the cost of equipment, King could use one of each machine with a resulting capacity or output rate (based, of course, on the *slowest* machine's processing time, 10 minutes) of 6 units per hour. That is, since every item must go through *each* of the machines, in order, every racket must wait for machine C, the

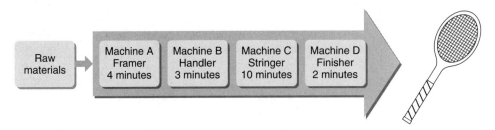

Figure 6.7   King Sports production process.

bottleneck, to finish before it can proceed. During this wait, the first, second, and fourth machines will be idle 6, 7, and 8 minutes, respectively, out of every 10-minute cycle. Since the output in this process embodies 19 minutes of work, whereas the input consists of four machines that have each spent 10 minutes with that item at their machine (not all of which is productive), this gives an overall efficiency of only 47.5 percent:

$$\text{efficiency} = \frac{\text{output}}{\text{input}} = \frac{4 + 3 + 10 + 2}{4(10)} = \frac{19}{40} = 47.5\%$$

Note that it does not matter whether the bottleneck is at the end of the sequence, at the beginning, or in the middle. The process is still slowed, on average, to the output rate of the slowest machine. The capacity of this process is thus 6 units per hour, and the **cycle time of the process** is 10 minutes, or ⅙ of an hour—the capacity/output rate and the cycle time are always reciprocals. The process cycle time can be visualized as the time between items coming off the end of the production line, whereas the throughput time can be visualized as the time you would spend in the production process if you attached yourself to the item being produced and rode along through the production process—there is often no relationship between them! And the final output work time is the productive time the item spends in the process.

If King is willing to invest in another, fifth machine, it should purchase another machine of type C, since that is the bottleneck. Then it could run machines C_1 and C_2 concurrently and put out two units every 10 minutes, obtaining an "effective" machine C processing time of 5 minutes for the machines by staggering their production. Note that machine C is still the bottleneck in the production process so this effective 5-minute machine processing time is once again the cycle time for the system. The effect of this single investment would be to *double* the capacity/output rate to 12 units per hour (5-minute cycle time) and increase the system efficiency to

$$\frac{4 + 3 + 10 + 2}{5(5)} = \frac{19}{25} = 76\%$$

Note in this efficiency calculation that the work output per racket is always 19 minutes, regardless of the number of machines; only the input changes. Now the input is five machines running at a 5-minute cycle time. Continuing in this manner results in the data shown in Table 6.5 and sketched in Figure 6.8. In developing Table 6.5, the next machine added was always the machine that currently had the longest machine time. For example, when there were six machines, machine A had the longest machine time. Thus, the seventh machine added was a machine A.

Note from the table and figure that efficiency of production does not always increase when machines are added, although the general trend is upward. This is because some systems are fairly well "balanced" to begin with. (For example, the cycles across the machines are quite even with 7 machines, 2, 3, 3.33, 2; and even more so at 10 machines. Also note that the addition of only one extra machine at such points does not pay for itself.) If points of high efficiency are reached "early" (as machines are added), these points will tend to be natural operating solutions. For example, a tremendous gain in efficiency (and in output percentage) is reaped by adding a fifth machine to the system. Further additions do not gain much. The next largest gain occurs when the tenth machine is added to the system.

$\mathscr{T}_{ABLE}$ 6.5 • Return to King for Using More Machines

Number of Machines	Type of Next Machine	Machine Times (minutes)				Cycle Time (min)	Total Hourly Output	Efficiency (percent)
		A	B	C	D			
4	—	4	3	10	2	10	6	47.5
5	C	4	3	5	2	5	12	76.0
6	C	4	3	3.33	2	4	15	79.2
7	A	2	3	3.33	2	3.33	18	81.4
8	C	2	3	2.5	2	3	20	79.2
9	B	2	1.5	2.5	2	2.5	24	84.4
10	C	2	1.5	2	2	2	30	95.0
11	D	2	1.5	2	1	2	30	86.0
12	A	1.33	1.5	2	1	2	30	79.2
13	C	1.33	1.5	1.67	1	1.67	36	87.5
14	C	1.33	1.5	1.43	1	1.5	40	90.5

Although this analysis describes the general trade-offs of the system, no mention has been made of demand. Suppose that demand is 14 units per hour. Then, to minimize risk but still keep an efficient system, King might use 5 machines and either work overtime, undersupply the market, or use a number of other strategies, as will be discussed later. Similarly, for a demand of 25 to 35 per hour, the use of 10 machines would be appropriate.

Product and Service Flows

With the role of a bottleneck in a production process in mind, let us now consider the more general procedure of conducting a process-flow analysis, also known as a "mapping" or "blueprinting" in service systems. The purpose of conducting a process flow analysis is normally to identify bottlenecks, inventory buildup points,

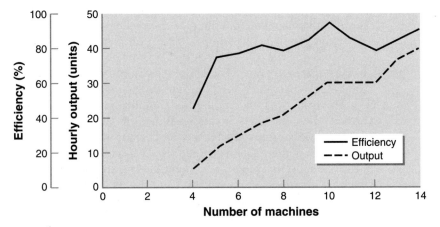

Figure 6.8   Efficiency and output increase when machines are being added.

and time delays in a production process. When used for a service process, it also typically illustrates potential failure points in the process and the *line of visibility* that divides those activities a customer perceives from those that are conducted out of the customer's sight (the "backroom," as in an auto repair shop, where operations can be conducted with efficiency). Standard nomenclature is to use rectangles for tasks/activities, triangles for storage or waiting points, diamonds for decision points, and arrows for flows. An activity changes the characteristics of a product or service, whereas a flow simply indicates the next step in the process, which may involve a change in position.

A simplified process-flow diagram for a manufactured unit is shown in Figure 6.9. The inputs, on the left, consist of raw material delivered by truck once a day and parts also delivered by truck once a day, both of which immediately go into different storage facilities (with different capacities). Assembly of each unit requires one fabricated component of 25 pounds and two purchased parts. The capacities of each of the stages in the production process are as labeled. The output demand is currently 120 units a day, giving rise to the flows shown on the arrows, but management anticipates an increase of perhaps as much as a third in the near future. Their concern is whether the system can handle this increase in demand. The plant runs one 8-hour shift a day.

As we see from the calculated flows shown on the arrows, there is currently excess capacity in the early stages of the production system up to assembly. (*Note*: Current process cycle time is 4 minutes.) At 20 units/hour, assembly could just handle the anticipated demand of 120 × 1.33 = 160 units a day. However, the raw material storage facility, which can only hold 3500 pounds (enough to produce 140 units a day), is the bottleneck in the system, since we need 160 × 25 pounds/unit = 4000 pounds of storage. Perhaps we could change our system to deliver a portion of the truckload directly to fabrication, or run out 500 pounds to fabrication as the raw material is unloaded from the truck so there is enough space for the full required two-ton delivery. Note that any activity or storage could have been the bottleneck in the process. What's more, even if we increase the capacity of the storage facility, the bottleneck will shift to the packaging

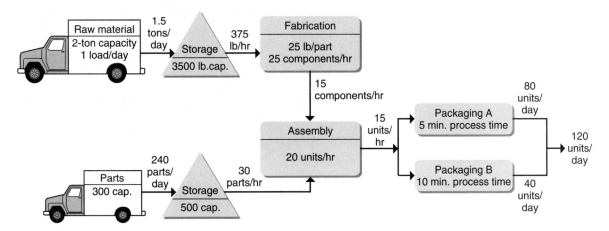

Figure 6.9 Process flow for manufactured unit.

machines, being able to produce only 12 units per hour from A and another 6 per hour from B, for a total of 18 per hour, or 144 units a day. And if their capacity is increased, the bottleneck will shift to the 300-part truck delivery because we will need $160 \times 2 = 320$ parts delivered each day. As you can see, the bottleneck shifts around the facility as we solve one problem after another. However, the process-flow diagram allows us to *anticipate* such shifts and head them off before they become real problems.

In a similar manner, Figure 6.10 presents a flow diagram for a photocopy service. Since products are not usually produced in a service, the diagram is often called a service "map" or "blueprint" and shows the process times more prominently instead. Note the "line of visibility" in the diagram that divides what the customer sees from the backroom operations, and the potential failure points.

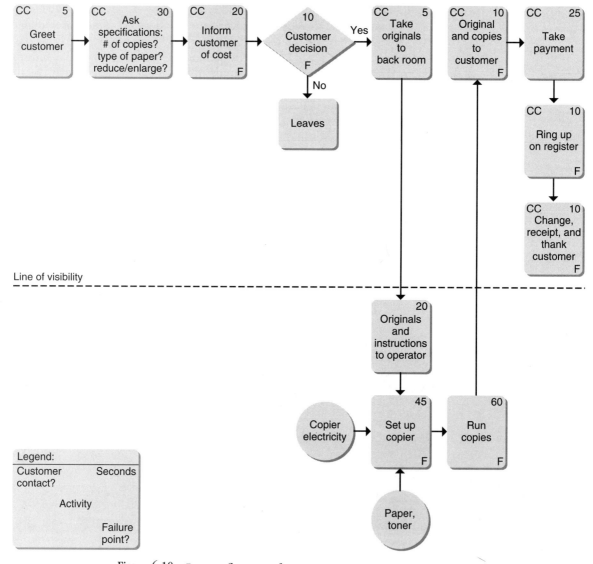

Figure 6.10   Process-flow map for a service.

The Theory of Constraints

Related to this topic of process-flow analysis, bottlenecks, and balancing the flows in a production system is the **theory of constraints** (Goldratt 1990). The theory of constraints was originally used in a proprietary package called *optimized production technology* (OPT), which is based on an alternative way of capacity planning. The basic procedure is first to identify bottleneck workstations in the shop, schedule them to keep them fully utilized, and then schedule the non–bottleneck workstations to keep the bottlenecks busy so that they are never waiting for work. The following nine guidelines capture the essence of the theory:

1. *Flows rather than capacities should be balanced throughout the shop.* The objective is to move material quickly and smoothly through the production system, not to balance capacities or utilization of equipment or human resources.

2. *Utilization of a non–bottleneck is determined by other constraints in the system, such as bottlenecks.* Non–bottleneck resources do not restrict the amount of output that a production system can create. Thus, these resources should be managed to support the operations of those resources (i.e., the bottlenecks) that do constrain the amount of output. Clearly, operating a non–bottleneck resource at a higher rate of output than the bottleneck resource does nothing to increase the output produced by the entire production system.

3. *Utilizing a workstation (producing when material is not yet needed) is not the same as activation.* Traditionally, managers have not made a distinction between using a resource and activating it. However, according to the theory of constraints, a resource is considered activated only if it is helping the entire system create more output. If a machine is independently producing more output than the rest of the system, the time the machine is operated to produce outputs over and above what the overall system is producing is considered utilization, not activation.

4. *An hour lost at a bottleneck is an hour lost for the whole shop.* Since the bottleneck resource limits the amount of output the entire system can create, time when this resource is not producing output is a loss to the entire system that cannot be made up. Lost time at a bottleneck resource can result because of down time for maintenance or because the resource was starved for work. For example, if a hair stylist is idle for an hour because no customers arrive, this hour of lost haircuts cannot be made up, even if twice as many customers as usual arrive in the next hour.

5. *An hour saved at a non–bottleneck is a mirage.* Since non–bottlenecks have plenty of capacity and do not limit the output of the production system, saving time at these resources does not increase total output. The implication for managers is that timesaving improvements to the system should be directed at bottleneck resources.

6. *Bottlenecks govern shop throughput and work-in-process inventories.*

7. *The transfer batch need not be the same size as the process batch.* The size of the *process batch* is the size of the batch produced each time a job is run.

Often, this size is determined by trading off various costs, as is done with the economic order quantity (EOQ) model discussed in Chapter 8. On the other hand, the size of the *transfer batch* is the size of the batch of parts moved from one work center to another work center. Clearly, parts can be moved in smaller batches than the process batch. Indeed, considerable reductions in batch flow times can often be obtained by using a transfer batch that is smaller than the process batch. For example, assume that a manufacturer produces a part in batches of 10. This part requires three operations, each performed on a different machine. The operation time is 5 minutes per part per operation. Figure 6.11 demonstrates the effect on flow time when a process batch of 10 units is reduced to a transfer batch of 1 unit. Specifically, in Figure 6.11a the transfer batch is the same size as the process batch, and a flow time of 150 minutes results. In Figure 6.11b the 1-unit transfer batch reduces flow time to 60 minutes. The reason for long flow time with a large transfer batch is that in any batch the first part must always wait for all the other parts to complete their processing before it is started on the next machine. In Figure 6.11a, the first part in the batch has to wait 45 minutes for the other nine parts. When the transfer batch is reduced to 1 unit, the parts in the batch do not have to wait for the other parts in the process batch.

8. *The size of the process batch should be variable, not fixed.* Because the economics of different resources can vary, the process batch does not need to be the same size at all stages of production. For example, consider an item that is produced on an injection molding machine and then visits a trimming department. Since the time and cost to set up injection molding equipment are likely to be very different from the time and cost to set up the trimming equipment, there is no reason why the batch size should be the same at each of these stages. Thus, batch size at each stage should be determined by the specific economics of that stage.

Time	5	10	15	20	25	30	35	40	45	50	55	60	65	70	75	80	85	90	95	100	105	110	115	120	125	130	135	140	145	150
Opn 1	P1	P2	P3	P4	P5	P6	P7	P8	P9	P10																				
Opn 2											P1	P2	P3	P4	P5	P6	P7	P8	P9	P10										
Opn 3																					P1	P2	P3	P4	P5	P6	P7	P8	P9	P10

(a)

Time	5	10	15	20	25	30	35	40	45	50	55	60
Opn 1	P1	P2	P3	P4	P5	P6	P7	P8	P9	P10		
Opn 2		P1	P2	P3	P4	P5	P6	P7	P8	P9	P10	
Opn 3			P1	P2	P3	P4	P5	P6	P7	P8	P9	P10

(b)

Figure 6.11   Transfer batch size and its effect on flow time. (*a*) Transfer batch size equals process batch size. (*b*) Transfer batch size equals one part.

9. *A shop schedule should be set by examining all the shop constraints simultaneously.* Traditionally, schedules are determined sequentially. First the batch size is determined. Next lead times are calculated and priorities set. Finally, schedules are adjusted on the basis of capacity constraints. The theory of constraints advocates considering all constraints simultaneously in developing schedules. The theory also argues that lead times are the result of the schedules and therefore cannot be determined beforehand.

The critical aspect of these guidelines is the focus on bottleneck workstations, not overloading the workstations, and the splitting of batches in order to move items along to the next workstation when desirable. A five-step process is recommended for implementing the theory of constraints:

1: **Identify the system's constraint(s).** Usually the process-flow diagram will help identify the constraints, but the ultimate constraint may in fact be sales representatives' time, capital available for investment, mandated policies such as a single shift, or even demand in the marketplace.

2: **Exploit the constraint.** Find ways to maximize the return per unit of the constraint. An example here would be to use the scarce resource to produce as much of the highest profit item as possible.

3: **Subordinate all else to the constraint.** The objective here is to make sure the constraint is always productive and that something else isn't drawing resources away from the constraint. For example, perhaps inventories should be built in front of a scarce machine or worker.

4: **Elevate the constraint.** Again, find ways to make the constraint as productive as possible, such as extra maintenance; saving time on the constraint by using other, perhaps less-efficient machines more intensively; or even obtaining more of the constraint.

5: **If the constraint is no longer a bottleneck, find the next constraint and repeat the steps.** As illustrated in the process-flow manufacturing example, once a bottleneck has been eliminated, something else becomes the bottleneck—perhaps another machine or storage facility, or perhaps the demand in the marketplace.

Relationship between Capacity and Scheduling

An important aspect of capacity worth emphasizing in the earlier discussions is its close tie to scheduling. That is, poor scheduling may result in what appears to be a capacity problem, and a shortage of capacity may lead to constant scheduling difficulties. Thus, capacity planning is closely related to the scheduling function, a topic to be discussed in Chapter 7. The difference is that capacity is oriented primarily toward the *acquisition* of productive resources, whereas scheduling concerns the *timing* of their use. However, it is often difficult to separate the two, especially where human resources are involved, such as in the use of overtime or the overlapping of shifts.

As a simple example, suppose that an organization has to complete within two weeks the two customers' jobs shown in Table 6.6. The table shows the sequential

$\mathscr{T}$ABLE 6.6 • Sequential Operations Required for Two Jobs

Job	Operations Resource Needed	Time Required (hours)
1	A	10
	C	10
	A	30
	B	20
	C	5
2	B	15
	A	10
	C	10
	A	10
	B	10

processing operations still to be completed and the times required. (The operations resources may be of any form—a facility, a piece of equipment, or a specially skilled worker.) In total, 60 hours of resource A are needed, 45 hours of B, and 25 hours of C. It would appear that two weeks (80 hours) of capacity on each of these three resources would be sufficient, and additional capacity would, therefore, be unnecessary.

Figure 6.12 shows the resource requirements of the two jobs plotted along a time scale. Such a chart is called a **Gantt chart** and can be used to show time schedules and capacities of facilities, workers, jobs, activities, machines, and so forth. In Figure 6.12*a* each job was scheduled on the required resource as soon as it finished on the previous resource, whether or not the new resource was occupied with the other job. This infeasible schedule is called **infinite loading** because work is scheduled on the resource as if it had infinite capacity to handle any and all jobs. Note that in this way capacity conflicts and possible resolutions can be easily visualized. Shifting the jobs to avoid such conflicts—this is called **finite loading**—gives the longer but feasible schedule shown in Figure 6.12*b*.

The first resource conflict in Figure 6.12*a* occurs at 20 hours, when job 1 finishes on resource C and next requires resource A, which is still working on job 2. The second conflict, again at A, occurs at 35 hours, and the third, on B, at 50 hours. It is quickly seen that deferring one job for the other has drastic consequences for conflicts of resources later on as well as for job completion times. Another consideration, not specified here, is whether an operation can be stopped to let another job pass through (this is called *operation splitting*) or, once started, must be worked on until completion.

Short-Term Capacity Alternatives

The problem of short-term capacity is to handle unexpected but imminent actual demand, either less than or more than expected, in an economic manner. It is known, of course, that the forecast will not be perfect; thus, managers of resources must plan what short-term capacity alternatives to use in either case. Such considerations are usually limited to, at most, the next six months, and usually much less, such as the next few days or hours.

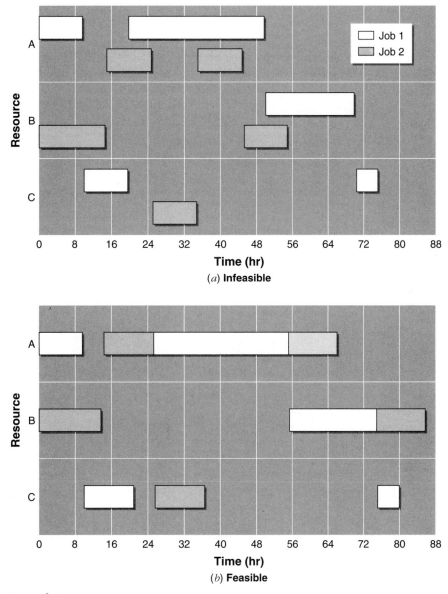

Figure 6.12   Gantt charts for capacity planning and scheduling.

Some alternatives for obtaining short-run capacity are categorized in Table 6.7. Each of the techniques in the table has advantages and disadvantages. The first set of alternatives concerns simply trying to increase the resource base. The use of overtime is expensive (time and a half), and productivity after eight hours of work often declines. It is a simple and easily invoked approach, however, that does not require additional investment, so overtime is one of the most common alternatives. The use of extra shifts requires hiring but no extra facilities. However, productivity of second and third shifts is often lower than that of the first shift. Part-time hiring can be expensive and is usually feasible for only low or unskilled work. Floating

$\mathcal{T}$ABLE 6.7 • **Techniques for Increasing Short-Run Capacity**

I.   Increase resources
   1.   Use overtime
   2.   Add shifts
   3.   Employ part-time workers
   4.   Use floating workers
   5.   Lease workers and facilities
   6.   Subcontract

II.   Improve resource use
   7.   Overlap or stagger shifts
   8.   Cross-train the workers
   9.   Create adjustable resources
   10.   Share resources
   11.   Schedule appointments/reservations
   12.   Inventory output (if feasible) ahead of demand
   13.   Backlog or queue demand

III.   Modify the output
   14.   Standardize the output
   15.   Offer complimentary services
   16.   Have the recipient do part of the work
   17.   Transform service operations into inventoriable product operations
   18.   Cut back on quality

IV.   Modify the demand
   19.   Partition the demand
   20.   Change the price
   21.   Change the promotion
   22.   Initiate a yield/revenue management system

V.   Do not meet demand
   23.   Do not supply all the demand

workers are flexible and very useful, but of course also cost extra. Leasing facilities and workers is often a good approach, but the extra cost reduces the profit, and these external resources may not be available during the high-demand periods when they are most seriously needed. Subcontracting may require a long lead time, is considerable trouble to implement, and may leave little, if any, profit.

The second set of techniques involves attempts to find ways to improve the utilization of existing resources. For daily demand peaks (seen especially in services, as discussed in the next section), shifts can be overlapped to provide extra capacity at peak times, or staggered to adjust to changes in demand loads. Cross-training the workers to substitute for each other can effectively increase labor flexibility. And there may be other ways to make labor and other resources adjustable also. A similar alternative is to simply share resources whenever possible. Especially for services, appointment and reservation systems, if feasible, can significantly smooth out daily demand peaks. If the output can be stocked ahead of time, as with a product, this is an excellent and very common approach to meeting capacity needs. If recipients are willing, the backlogging of demand to be met later during slack periods is an excellent strategy; a less accurate forecast is needed and investment in finished goods is nil. However, this may be an open invitation to competition.

Modifying the output is a creative approach. Doing less customization, allowing fewer variants, offering complimentary services, and encouraging recipients to do some assembly or finishing tasks themselves (as at self-service gasoline stations and fast-food restaurants), perhaps with a small price incentive, are frequently employed and are excellent alternatives.

Attempting to alter the demand, partition it, or shift it to a different period is another creative approach. Running promotions or price differentials ("off-peak" pricing), or both, for slack periods is an excellent method for leveling demand, especially in utilities, telephones, and similar services. Prices are not easily increased above normal in high-demand periods, however. One formal method of partitioning both the demand and the resource supply is known as yield or revenue management, a subject we will discuss in more detail in Chapter 7. Last, the manager may simply decide not to meet the market demand—again, however, at the cost of inviting competition.

In actuality, many of these alternatives are not feasible except in certain types of organizations or in particular circumstances. For example, when demand is high, subcontractors are full, outside facilities and staff are already overbooked, second-shift workers are employed elsewhere, and marketing promotion is already low-key. Thus, of the many possible alternatives, most firms tend to rely on only a few, such as overtime and, for product firms, stocking up ahead of demand.

So far we have primarily discussed increasing capacity in the short run, but firms also have a need to *decrease* short-run capacity. This is more difficult, however, and most such capacity simply goes unused. If the output involves a product, some inventory buildup may be allowed in order to make use of the available capacity; otherwise, system maintenance may be done (cleaning, fixing, preprocessing, and so on).

Capacity Planning for Services

Capacity planning is often much more difficult for pure service operations than for products, and with a service there is a clearer distinction between long- and short-run capacity planning. For services, the more difficult aspects of providing capacity occur in the short run, usually because the demand for a service is subject to daily peaks and valleys, and the output cannot be stored ahead of time to buffer this fluctuation. For example, doctors' offices see demand peaks at 9 A.M. and 1 P.M., and college classes see it at 10 A.M. Or there may be weekly peaks, monthly peaks, or yearly peaks, such as Friday's demand on banks to deposit (or cash) paychecks, and the first-of-the-month demand on restaurants when Social Security checks arrive in the mail. Some services, such as fire departments, experience multiple peaks, as illustrated in Figure 6.13*a*, which shows the regular *daily* cycle of fire alarms, with a peak from 3 to 7 P.M.; and Figure 6.13*b*, which shows the *yearly* cycle of fire alarms, with a peak in April.

As noted earlier with regard to products, frequently it is not clear whether a problem is a matter of scheduling or capacity; this is particularly true with services. The primary problem is matching availability of staff to demand in terms of timing and skills, both on a daily basis and over the longer term (such as weekly and monthly). Service organizations have developed many novel approaches to this problem as just briefly described: split shifts, overlapping shifts, duty tours (e.g., 48 or 72 hours for firefighters), part-time help, overbooking, appointment systems, and on-call staff. Some of these approaches will be considered in more detail in Chapter 7. However, for services, a favorite alternative is to share capacity with neighboring units by pooling resources such as generators, police patrols, or hotel

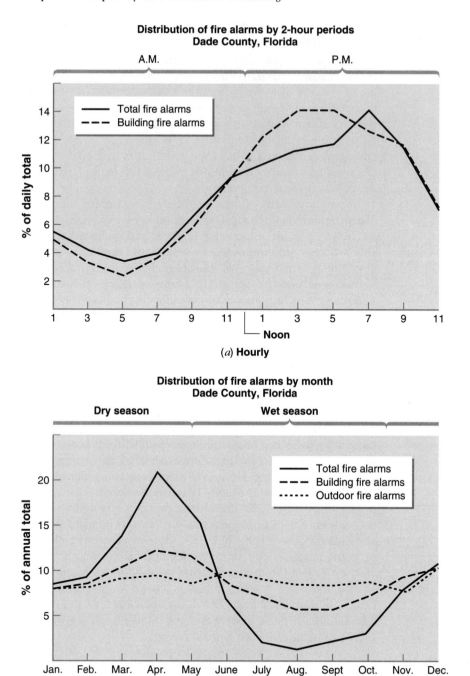

Figure 6.13   Fire alarm histories: (*a*) hourly and (*b*) monthly.

rooms. When one organization is temporarily overloaded, the neighbor absorbs the excess demand. Another favorite approach for some services that has even been too successful is that of shifting the demand to off-peak periods. When AT&T offered lower phone rates after 5 P.M., it found that it had to raise the Sunday-night 5–11 P.M. rate owing to excessive shifted demand.

In many situations, it is almost impossible to measure an organization's capacity to produce a service, because the service is so abstract. Thus, a more common approach is to measure *inputs* rather than outputs, and assume (perhaps with regular checkups) that the production system is successful at transforming the inputs into acceptable services (outputs). For example, organizations that offer plays, art exhibits, and other such intangible services do not measure their patrons' pleasure or relaxation; rather, they measure number of performances, number of actors and actresses, and number of paintings (or painting-days, since many exhibits have a rotating travel schedule). Even fire departments do not attempt to measure their capacity by the number of fires they can extinguish; instead, they use the number of engines or companies they can offer in response to a call, the service or response time, or the number of firefighters responding.

Clearly, this manner of measuring service capacity can leave a lot to be desired. Do more paintings give greater satisfaction? Do higher-quality paintings give greater satisfaction? Might there be other factors that are equally or more important, such as the crowd, the parking facilities, or the lighting on the paintings? Is a hospital where more deaths occur providing worse service? Is a hospital with more physicians on staff providing better service?

The Learning Curve

An extremely important aspect of capacity planning, and an important operations concept in and of itself, is the ***learning curve*** effect—the ability of humans to increase their productive capacity through "learning." This issue is particularly important in the short-term start-up of new and unfamiliar processes such as those involving new technologies (e.g., learning to use a new software program), and always occurs in the production ramp-up of new models of automobiles, planes, computers, etc. Thus, the characteristic of slow, possibly error-prone output initially, followed by better, faster production, should be of major concern to marketing and sales—which are often trying to market the output or have promised a certain volume to a customer by a set date; to accounting—which is checking productivity and yield rates in order to determine a fair cost for the output; and to finance—which is concerned with the timing of cash flows related to purchases, labor, and revenues.

The improvement with experience is not necessarily due to learning alone, however. Better tools, improvements in work methods, upgraded output designs, and other such factors also help increase productivity. Hence, such curves are also known as *improvement curves, production progress functions, performance curves*, and *experience curves*. The learning curve effect, from this viewpoint, also affects long-term capacity and is often factored into 5- and 10-year planning processes, another issue of interest to marketing and accounting, as well as finance. The Japanese, in particular, count on increasing the long-term capacity of a facility through the workers' development of better work methods and improvements in tools.

The derivation of the learning curve began in the airframe manufacturing industry during the 1930s, when it was found that the labor-hours needed to build each successive airplane decreased relatively smoothly. In particular, the learning curve law was found to be:

Each time the output doubles, the labor hours decrease to a fixed percentage of their previous value.

In the case of plane production, this percentage was found to be 80 percent. Thus, when the first plane of a series required 100,000 labor-hours to produce, the second took 80,000 labor hours, the fourth took 80,000 × 0.80 = 64,000, the eighth 64,000 × 0.80 = 51,200, and so on. This type of mathematical relationship is described by the *negative exponential function*,[1] illustrated for airplanes in Figure 6.14.

A number of factors affect the learning curve rate, but the most important are the complexity of the task and the percentage of human, compared with mechanical, input. The greatest learning—sometimes at a rate as high as 60 percent—occurs for highly complex tasks consisting primarily of human inputs. A task that is highly machine-automated clearly leaves little opportunity for learning. (Thus, a rate close to 100 percent would apply, because only the human can learn.) In airframe manufacturing the proportion of human effort is about 75 percent, and an 80 percent learning rate applies. For similar work of the same complexity and ratio of human-to-machine input, approximately the same rate will apply.

But learning curves are not limited to manufacturing, or even to product-oriented organizations. These curves apply just as well to hairdressing, selling, finding

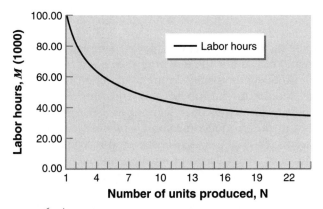

Figure 6.14   80 percent learning curve for airplane production.

---

[1]The function is as follows: $M = mN^r$

where

        M = labor-hours for the Nth unit

        m = labor hours for first unit

        N = number of units produced

        r = exponent of curve corresponding to learning rate

          = log(learning rate)/0.693

Two forms of the learning curve relationship are used in the literature. In one form M corresponds to the cumulative *average* labor-hours of all N units, and in the other form M corresponds to the *actual* labor-hours to produce the Nth unit. The second interpretation is more useful for capacity planning and will be used here. For example, then, a learning rate of 90 percent would mean that each time production doubled from, say, N_1 to N_2, unit N_2 would require 90 percent of the labor hours that N_1 required. The log here is the "natural" log (the base e), and 0.693 is the natural log of 2.0. But base 10, or any other base, may be used if divided by the log of 2.0 to the same base. That is, r = log [rate]/log 2.0.

a parking space, and preparing pizza. As indicated, they also apply to *groups* of individuals, and *systems* that include people and machines, as well as to individuals.

The primary question, of course, is what learning rate to apply. If previous experience is available, this may give some indication; if not, a close watch of the time it takes to produce the first few units should give a good indication. Let us illustrate the use of the learning curve, and some learning curve tables, with a simple example.

Learning Curve Tables

It is not usually necessary to solve the learning curve equation every time you run across a learning situation. First, the general law already stated will usually suffice for most purposes. Secondly, the solution to the equation for various learning rates, assuming that the first item took 1 time unit, has already been calculated and tabulated in Tables 6.8 and 6.9. These tables provide the percentage of time the *N*th unit will require relative to what the first unit required (Table 6.8) and the cumulative amount of time that the first *N* units will take relative to what the first unit took (Table 6.9).

To use Tables 6.8 and 6.9, you multiply the values given in these tables by the labor-hours actually required for the first unit in your situation to get the time for the *N*th unit, or the cumulative time for units 1 through *N*, respectively. Returning to our example—the 80 percent learning curve for airplanes—we see in Table 6.8 that unit 2 (left-hand column) under "80%" will require 0.8 of what unit 1 required (100,000 labor-hours), that unit 4 will require 0.64, that unit 8 will take 0.512, and so forth. In addition, we also see that unit 3 will take 0.7021 and unit 6, for example, 0.5617 (i.e., 0.5617 × 100,000 or 56,170 labor-hours). The *total* labor-hours to produce two, four, or eight planes can be found by adding the necessary values together, or by looking at Table 6.9, where this has already been done. Again, reading under "80%" for 2, 4, and 8 units, we get 1.8, 3.142, and 5.346 × 100,000 respectively, for 180,000, 314,200, and 534,600 labor-hours, cumulative. We next illustrate the use of the learning curve tables with a simple example, followed by a more complex example.

Following the engineering specifications for the assembly of a new motor, a production team was able to assemble the first (prototype) motor in 3.6 hours. After more practice on the second and third motors, the team was able to assemble the fourth motor in 1.76 hours. What is the team's learning rate, and how long will the next motor probably take?

Here the actual individual assembly times are given, so we can use Table 6.8, which tabulates *the ratio of what the *N*th unit took relative to the first unit.* First, we need to find the ratio from the given data and then locate that value somewhere in the table. Our ratio for the fourth motor would be: 1.76/3.6 = 0.49. Next, we turn to Table 6.8 and scan across row "4" under the "Units" column. We find the value 0.49 under "70%," so this is our learning rate for the team (which is pretty good, by the way).

To find out how long the next (fifth) motor will take, we drop down the "70%" column to the next row that corresponds to the fifth unit. (*Note:* The rows are not always in increments of 1. For example, at 10 they jump by 2, and at 100 by 20.) At the fifth row the value is 0.4368, which, when multiplied by what the first unit took (3.6 hours), gives: 0.4368 × 3.6 = 1.57 hours. Remember: The tabulated values as-

$\mathcal{T}$ABLE 6.8 • Unit Values of the Learning Curve

Example: Unit 1 took 10 hours. 80% learning rate. What will unit 5 require?
Solution: Unit 5 row, 80% column value = 0.5956. Thus, unit 5 will take 10 (0.5956) = 5.956 hours.

Units	\multicolumn{8}{c}{Improvement Ratios}
	60%	65%	70%	75%	80%	85%	90%	95%
1	1.0000	1.0000	1.0000	1.0000	1.0000	1.0000	1.0000	1.0000
2	0.6000	0.6500	0.7000	0.7500	0.8000	0.8500	0.9000	0.9500
3	0.4450	0.5052	0.5682	0.6338	0.7021	0.7729	0.8462	0.9219
4	0.3600	0.4225	0.4900	0.5625	0.6400	0.7225	0.8100	0.9025
5	0.3054	0.3678	0.4368	0.5127	0.5956	0.6857	0.7830	0.8877
6	0.2670	0.3284	0.3977	0.4754	0.5617	0.6570	0.7616	0.8758
7	0.2383	0.2984	0.3674	0.4459	0.5345	0.6337	0.7439	0.8659
8	0.2160	0.2746	0.3430	0.4219	0.5120	0.6141	0.7290	0.8574
9	0.1980	0.2552	0.3228	0.4017	0.4930	0.5974	0.7161	0.8499
10	0.1832	0.2391	0.3058	0.3846	0.4765	0.5828	0.7047	0.8433
12	0.1602	0.2135	0.2784	0.3565	0.4493	0.5584	0.6854	0.8320
14	0.1430	0.1940	0.2572	0.3344	0.4276	0.5386	0.6696	0.8226
16	0.1296	0.1785	0.2401	0.3164	0.4096	0.5220	0.6561	0.8145
18	0.1188	0.1659	0.2260	0.3013	0.3944	0.5078	0.6445	0.8074
20	0.1099	0.1554	0.2141	0.2884	0.3812	0.4954	0.6342	0.8012
22	0.1025	0.1465	0.2038	0.2772	0.3697	0.4844	0.6251	0.7955
24	0.0961	0.1387	0.1949	0.2674	0.3595	0.4747	0.6169	0.7904
25	0.0933	0.1353	0.1908	0.2629	0.3548	0.4701	0.6131	0.7880
30	0.0815	0.1208	0.1737	0.2437	0.3346	0.4505	0.5963	0.7775
35	0.0728	0.1097	0.1605	0.2286	0.3184	0.4345	0.5825	0.7687
40	0.0660	0.1010	0.1498	0.2163	0.3050	0.4211	0.5708	0.7611
45	0.0605	0.0939	0.1410	0.2060	0.2936	0.4096	0.5607	0.7545
50	0.0560	0.0879	0.1336	0.1972	0.2838	0.3996	0.5518	0.7486
60	0.0489	0.0785	0.1216	0.1828	0.2676	0.3829	0.5367	0.7386
70	0.0437	0.0713	0.1123	0.1715	0.2547	0.3693	0.5243	0.7302
80	0.0396	0.0657	0.1049	0.1622	0.2440	0.3579	0.5137	0.7231
90	0.0363	0.0610	0.0987	0.1545	0.2349	0.3482	0.5046	0.7168
100	0.0336	0.0572	0.0935	0.1479	0.2271	0.3397	0.4966	0.7112
120	0.0294	0.0510	0.0851	0.1371	0.2141	0.3255	0.4830	0.7017
140	0.0262	0.0464	0.0786	0.1287	0.2038	0.3139	0.4718	0.6937
160	0.0237	0.0427	0.0734	0.1217	0.1952	0.3042	0.4623	0.6869
180	0.0218	0.0397	0.0691	0.1159	0.1879	0.2959	0.4541	0.6809
200	0.0201	0.0371	0.0655	0.1109	0.1816	0.2887	0.4469	0.6757
250	0.0171	0.0323	0.0584	0.1011	0.1691	0.2740	0.4320	0.6646
300	0.0149	0.0289	0.0531	0.0937	0.1594	0.2625	0.4202	0.6557
350	0.0133	0.0262	0.0491	0.0879	0.1517	0.2532	0.4105	0.6482
400	0.0121	0.0241	0.0458	0.0832	0.1453	0.2454	0.4022	0.6419
450	0.0111	0.0224	0.0431	0.0792	0.1399	0.2387	0.3951	0.6363
500	0.0103	0.0210	0.0408	0.0758	0.1352	0.2329	0.3888	0.6314

Source: Albert N. Schreiber, Richard A. Johnson, Robert C. Meier, William T. Newell, and Henry C. Fischer, *Cases in Manufacturing Management* (New York: McGraw-Hill, 1965), p. 464. Reprinted by permission of McGraw-Hill, © 1965.

$\mathcal{T}_{ABLE}$ 6.9 • Cumulative Values of the Learning Curve

Example: Unit 1 took 10 hours. 80% learning rate. What will be the total hours required to produce the first five units?
Solution: Unit 5 row, 80% column: value = 3.738. Thus, the first five units will require 10 (3.738) = 37.38 hours.

	Improvement Ratios							
Units	60%	65%	70%	75%	80%	85%	90%	95%
1	1.000	1.000	1.000	1.000	1.000	1.000	1.000	1.000
2	1.600	1.650	1.700	1.750	1.800	1.850	1.900	1.950
3	2.045	2.155	2.268	2.384	2.502	2.623	2.746	2.872
4	2.405	2.578	2.758	2.946	3.142	3.345	3.556	3.774
5	2.710	2.946	3.195	3.459	3.738	4.031	4.339	4.662
6	2.977	3.274	3.593	3.934	4.299	4.688	5.101	5.538
7	3.216	3.572	3.960	4.380	4.834	5.322	5.845	6.404
8	3.432	3.847	4.303	4.802	5.346	5.936	6.574	7.261
9	3.630	4.102	4.626	5.204	5.839	6.533	7.290	8.111
10	3.813	4.341	4.931	5.589	6.315	7.116	7.994	8.955
12	4.144	4.780	5.501	6.315	7.227	8.244	9.374	10.62
14	4.438	5.177	6.026	6.994	8.092	9.331	10.72	12.27
16	4.704	5.541	6.514	7.635	8.920	10.38	12.04	13.91
18	4.946	5.879	6.972	8.245	9.716	11.41	13.33	15.52
20	5.171	6.195	7.407	8.828	10.48	12.40	14.61	17.13
22	5.379	6.492	7.819	9.388	11.23	13.38	15.86	18.72
24	5.574	6.773	8.213	9.928	11.95	14.33	17.10	20.31
25	5.668	6.909	8.404	10.19	12.31	14.80	17.71	21.10
30	6.097	7.540	9.305	11.45	14.02	17.09	20.73	25.00
35	6.478	8.109	10.13	12.72	15.64	19.29	23.67	28.86
40	6.821	8.631	10.90	13.72	17.19	21.43	26.54	32.68
45	7.134	9.114	11.62	14.77	18.68	23.50	29.37	36.47
50	7.422	9.565	12.31	15.78	20.12	25.51	32.14	40.22
60	7.941	10.39	13.57	17.67	22.87	29.41	37.57	47.65
70	8.401	11.13	14.74	19.43	25.47	33.17	42.87	54.99
80	8.814	11.82	15.82	21.09	27.96	36.80	48.05	62.25
90	9.191	12.45	16.83	22.67	30.35	40.32	53.14	69.45
100	9.539	13.03	17.79	24.18	32.65	43.75	58.14	76.59
120	10.16	14.11	19.57	27.02	37.05	50.39	67.93	90.71
140	10.72	15.08	21.20	29.67	41.22	56.78	77.46	104.7
160	11.21	15.97	22.72	32.17	45.20	62.95	86.80	118.5
180	11.67	16.79	24.14	34.54	49.03	68.95	95.96	132.1
200	12.09	17.55	25.48	36.80	52.72	74.79	105.0	145.7
250	13.01	19.28	28.56	42.08	61.47	88.83	126.9	179.2
300	13.81	20.81	31.34	46.94	69.66	102.2	148.2	212.2
350	14.51	22.18	33.89	51.48	77.43	115.1	169.0	244.8
400	15.14	23.44	36.26	55.75	84.85	127.6	189.3	277.0
450	15.72	24.60	38.48	59.80	91.97	139.7	209.2	309.0
500	16.26	25.68	40.58	63.68	98.85	151.5	228.8	340.6

Source: Albert N. Schreiber, Richard A. Johnson, Robert C. Meier, William T. Newell, and Henry C. Fischer, *Cases in Manufacturing Management* (New York: McGraw-Hill, 1965), p. 465. Reprinted by permission of McGraw-Hill, © 1965.

sume that the first unit took only 1 hour (or minute, or day, or whatever the measure is), so if the first unit took something other than "1," you need to multiply the table value by the actual time it took to produce the first unit.

Next, let us consider a more complex, real-life problem that also requires the use of the cumulative table, Table 6.9.

Spreadsheet, Inc.

Spreadsheet, Inc., has just entered the growing software training market with a contract from a financial organization to teach spreadsheet modeling techniques to the organization's 10 managers, for purposes of financial and pension planning. The lesson for the last manager has just ended, and the organization, considering the first 10 lessons highly successful, has engaged Spreadsheet to give the same lessons to its staff of 150 agents. The lesson for the first manager was highly experimental, requiring 100 hours in all, but careful analysis and refinement of the techniques have gradually decreased this time to the point where the average time for all 10 initial lessons was just under half that value, 49 hours each. To properly staff, schedule, plan, and cost out the work for the 150 lessons, Spreadsheet needs to know how many hours of lessons will be required.

To begin, we can use Table 6.9 to determine the learning rate: the average of 49 hours each, times 10 managers, gives 490 hours, cumulative. This is 4.9 times what the first manager required (490 hours/100 hours). Finding the value 4.9 in Table 6.9 for 10 units will then give the learning curve rate applying to these complex lessons. Reading across the 10-unit row, we find 4.931 (close enough) under the "70%" column. (On occasion, interpolation between columns may be necessary, or alternatively the exact quantities can be calculated directly using the formula. Spreadsheets can greatly facilitate the task of manually calculating time estimates based on the learning curve formula.)

Assuming that the lessons are continuous and the teaching techniques are not forgotten (an important assumption), we can look further down the "70%" column in Table 6.9 to find the value corresponding to the *total* number of lessons to be given: 10 + 150 = 160. This value, 22.72, is then multiplied by the amount of time required for the first lesson (100 hours) to give a grand total of 2272 hours for the 160 lessons. Since the initial 10 managers required a total of 490 hours by themselves, the second group, consisting of the agents, will require 2272 − 490 = 1782 hours. The time phasing of this 1782 hours is also available, if desired, from Table 6.8.

The learning curve is only a theoretical construct, of course, and therefore it only approximates actual learning. A more realistic, and typical, learning pattern is illustrated in Figure 6.15. Initially, actual labor hours per unit vary around the theoretical curve until a "learning plateau" is reached at, perhaps, the tenth unit. At this plateau no significant learning appears to occur, until there is a breakthrough. Learning typically involves a number of such plateaus and breakthroughs. At about 30 units, production is halted for a period of time and "forgetting" occurs, rapidly at first but then trailing off. When production is resumed, relearning occurs very quickly (as when someone relearns to ride a bicycle after 40 years) until the original efficiency is reached (at about 33 units). If the conditions are the same at this time as for the initial part of the curve, the original learning curve rate will then hold. After sufficient time passes, the improvement due to learning becomes trivial

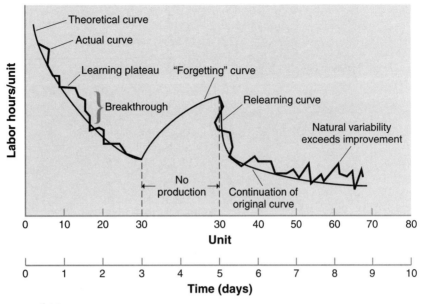

Figure 6.15 Typical pattern of learning and forgetting.

in comparison with natural variability in efficiency, and at that point we say that learning has ceased.

Queuing and the Psychology of Waiting

An important element in evaluating the capacity of operations to produce either products or services concerns the waiting lines, backlogs, or *queues*, that tend to build up in front of the operations. Queuing theory provides a mechanism to determine several key performance measure of an operating system based on the rate of arrivals to the system and the system's capacity (specified as the system's service rate). With an unpaced production line, for example, buffer inventory between operations builds up at some times and disappears at other times, owing to natural variability in the difficulty of the operations.

In the production of services, this variability is even greater because of both the amount of highly variable human *input* and the variable *requirements* for services. What is more, the "items" in queue are often people, who tend to complain and make trouble if kept waiting too long. Thus, it behooves the operations manager to provide adequate service to keep long queues from forming. This costs more money for service facilities and staffs. But long queues cost money also, in the form of in-process inventory, unfinished orders, lost sales, and ill will. Figure 6.16 conceptually illustrates, as a function of the capacity of the service facility, the trade-offs in these two costs.

1. *Cost of waiting*: In-process inventory, ill will, lost sales. This cost decreases with service capacity.

2. *Cost of service facilities*: Equipment, supplies, and staff. This cost increases with service capacity.

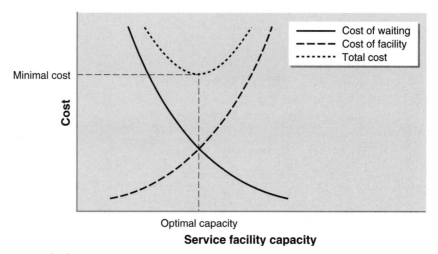

Figure 6.16   The relevant queuing costs.

Principles of Waiting

At some point the total of the two costs in Figure 6.15 above is minimized, and it is at this point that managers typically wish to operate. However, before investing resources in adding expensive service facilities, a topic we address soon, the manager may find it worthwhile trying to reduce the cost of waiting instead. Given that perceptions and expectations may have more to do with customer satisfaction than actual waiting time, David Maister (1984) has formulated eight insightful "principles" of waiting which, if addressed carefully, may be more effective in reducing the overall cost of waiting to the organization than adding service facilities.

1. **Unoccupied time feels longer than occupied time.** Give customers something to do while waiting, hopefully something that will facilitate the service that is to come. An example is having customers key in their Social Security number while waiting on the phone so the representative will have their file on screen as they answer the call.

2. **Pre-service waiting feels longer than in-service waiting.** Using staging areas to complete portions of the service, such as taking a patient's temperature and blood pressure, communicates to them that the service has begun.

3. **Anxiety makes waiting seem longer.** Offer information to relieve anxiety, or distracters (even music, mirrors) to allay anxiety.

4. **Uncertain waiting is longer than known, finite waiting.** Provide cues, or direct announcements, to indicate how soon the service will be coming or finishing (especially in the case of a painful procedure).

5. **Unexplained waiting is longer than explained waiting.** Keep customers informed about why they are being delayed, and how long it will be before they can be serviced.

6. **Unfair waiting is longer than fair waiting.** Make sure that priority or express customers are handled in a manner transparent to other customers, and treated out of sight, if possible.

7. **Solo waiting is longer than group waiting.** In part this reflects principles 1 (someone else to talk to), 3 (seeing and talking to others can reduce anxiety), and 5 (other waiting customers may communicate reasons for the waiting), as well as the general principle that there is more security in groups.

8. **The more valuable the service, the longer it is worth waiting for.** The use of marketing and other means to increase the perception of the value of the service will reduce the impatience with waiting.

Waiting Line Analysis

The formation of waiting lines, also known as queues, is a very common phenomenon in operations. People wait for service, items wait for repair, products wait for processing, and so on. Managers often desire to know how long the wait will be and how much the wait will be decreased if they add resources to the service process such as additional servers or productivity-enhancing equipment. The basic problem facing the manager is to find the best trade-off between the cost of service facilities and the cost of waiting, usually customer ill will.

The analysis of these queues to determine the waiting time and other queue characteristics can sometimes involve sophisticated mathematical techniques. Here we will consider only the most basic queuing situations and derive the characteristics for these queues through fairly simple graphs and equations. Given an arriving population and a service facility (or facilities) with a certain speed of service, queuing theory will determine, given certain assumptions, the expected (average) length of the queue, the number of people or items in the queue, the idle time of the facility, and other such criteria of service facility performance.

The structure of the queuing system to be considered here is illustrated in Figure 6.17. It is assumed that the arrivals wait in *one* queue (or take a number for service or add their names to a list) and, as they come to the front of the line, go to the next available service facility. (This system is called first come, first served, FCFS, and is commonly adopted for reasons of fairness.) The arrivals are assumed to come at random, with the average rate λ (arrivals per unit time).

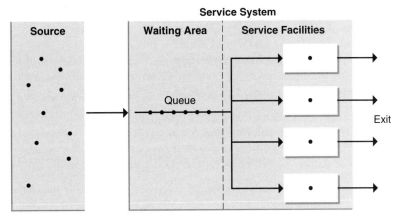

Figure 6.17   Queuing system structure.

Service is also assumed to be random, with the average μ (services per unit time when there is a queue). Note in Figure 6.17 that the queue, as normally interpreted, does *not* include the arrival(s) currently being serviced at the service facility(ies).

If the service can be performed *before* the recipient arrives and then stored until his or her arrival (and the demand rate is less than the service rate), a continuing queue will not form. For example, if punch is being served as a refreshment at a party where people arrive for refreshments, on the average, every 4 seconds and it takes 4 seconds to pour a drink, there will never be a permanent queue. This is because even when people are not coming for a drink the server keeps on pouring drinks; then, when a batch of people all come at once, the drinks are ready. However, if mixed drinks are being served so that the mix cannot be poured *until the person gives his or her order*, a queue will tend to form under exactly the same conditions.

In some situations the recipients do *not* arrive randomly but are *scheduled*, as in medicine and dentistry. If possible, appointments in such a case should be scheduled so that the first recipient has the most *definite* required service time and the last recipient the most *variable* service time. For similar types of recipient needs, the variability is often proportional to the expected length of service. That is, a 10-minute appointment may run 5 to 15 minutes, but a 4-hour appointment may run 3½ to 4½ hours. Scheduling in this manner then minimizes the potential wait for all *subsequent* recipients.

To use queuing theory, some basic assumptions must be satisfied.

- ***The system is in "steady state."*** The time to reach steady state is usually a small fraction of an on-going service system and may be ignored. However, some systems, such as fast-food restaurants, may always be in transient (nonsteady) states such as 9:00 A.M. start-up, 11:30 A.M.–12:30 P.M. lunch rush, and the 5:30 P.M.–6:30 P.M. dinner rush. In these cases queuing theory can be used to study the system at specific times such as the lunch hour rush but these results cannot be generalized to other times. Typically, systems that are always in a transient state are studied under the most demanding conditions to see how they perform under these demanding conditions. If this is not acceptable, computer simulation can be used to study these systems.

- ***First come, first served "priority discipline" must be used.*** We assume people (or items) are served in the order they join the queue and only one queue exists, even if there are multiple service facilities.

- ***An unlimited source exists.*** We assume we never run out of recipients from the source.

- ***Unlimited queue space is available.*** We assume there is sufficient space in the (single) queue to hold any recipient who desires service.

- ***Standard queue behavior prohibits:***

  Balking—refusing to join the queue

  Reneging—leaving the queue before being served

  Jockeying—switching between multiple queues as their lengths vary

  Cycling—returning to the queue following service (e.g., children with playground equipment)

- ***Arrivals and service are random.*** As stated earlier, the random arrivals occur at the average rate λ and the services at the average rate μ when the system is busy.

The assumption of random arrivals and services results in a particular distribution of arrival and service rates known as the Poisson distribution. With the assumptions already given, these distributions allow us to find a number of useful characteristics that describe the queue and the service process. The most important characteristic of a queue is its expected (average) length, L_q. This characteristic is presented in Figure 6.18 as a function of two parameters of the queuing situation.

- K—the number of servers or service facilities, known as "channels" (four shown in Figure 6.17) in the service system
- λ/μ—the "utilization" of the facility (If the arrival rate λ exceeds the service rate of a single server μ, the queue will grow indefinitely unless more than one server is available.)

Note in Figure 6.18 that as curves of constant K reach values $\lambda/\mu = K$ (near the top of the chart), the length of the queue, L_q, gets larger. This is because the arrivals tend to fully utilize the capacity of the system. For example, if the arrival rate is twice that of the service rate, this will keep two servers busy full time.

When there is only one service facility (i.e., $K = 1$), L_q can be calculated as

$$L_q = \frac{\lambda^2}{\mu(\mu - \lambda)}$$

Once a value for L_q is found using either Figure 6.18 or this formula, many other interesting characteristics describing the system can be derived from it.

1. The *average number of items in the system*, both in the queue and in service combined, L. The number being served, on the average, is simply the utilization of the service facility, λ/μ. Thus,

$$L = L_q + \frac{\lambda}{\mu}$$

2. The *expected waiting time in the queue*, W_q. This is *not*, as might be expected, simply the average length of the queue times the service time. Rather, another relationship is used: the average *length* of the queue will equal the average *waiting time* multiplied by the average *arrival rate*: $L_q = W_q\lambda$. Rearranging terms

$$W_q = \frac{L_q}{\lambda}$$

3. The *expected total time in the system*, W. This will be the queuing time plus the service time, $1/\mu$.

$$W = W_q + \frac{1}{\mu}$$

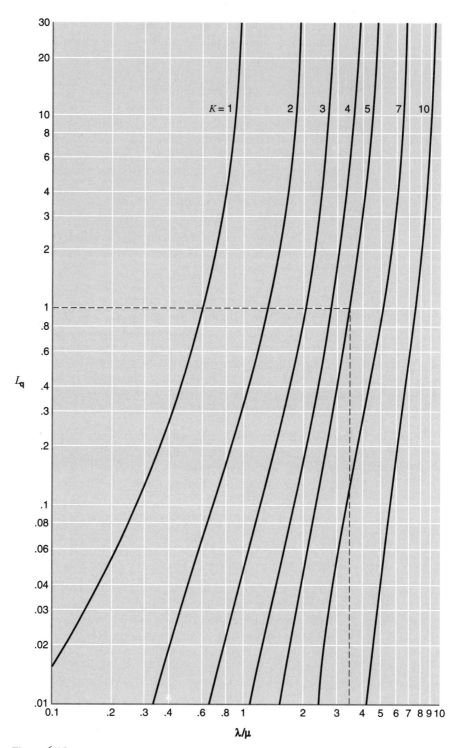

Figure 6.18   Multichannel queue.

4. For service systems composed of a single server (channel) we can determine the *probability of n items occupying the system* (both queuing and in service).

$$P_n = \left(\frac{\lambda}{\mu}\right)^n \left(1 - \frac{\lambda}{\mu}\right) \text{ for } K = 1$$

Note that when $n = 0$, this reduces to the *probability that the system is empty.*

$$P_0 = 1 - \frac{\lambda}{\mu} \text{ for } K = 1$$

The *probability that the system is busy*, otherwise known as the *utilization* of the facility, is thus $1 - P_0$ or

$$P_{busy} = \frac{\lambda}{\mu} \text{ for } K = 1$$

One of the most confounding aspects of waiting line analysis is that it defies normal expectations. For example, if a service system with one server results in an average queue length of 12 recipients, then most people expect that adding a second server will cut the queue in half, to 6 recipients. But consider the following situation. A one-person service facility can serve, on the average, 10 customers per hour and customers arrive, on the average, every 7.5 minutes. What will happen if a second server is added?

$$\lambda = \frac{60}{7.5} = 8/\text{hr}, \quad \mu = 10/\text{hr}, \quad \frac{\lambda}{\mu} = 0.8, \quad K = 1$$

From Figure 6.18, $L_q = 3$, approximately. If a second server is added, then reading from Figure 6.18 at $K = 2$ and $\lambda/\mu = 0.8$, we find $L_q = 0.14$. That is, the expected line length reduces by

$$\frac{3.0 - 0.14}{3.0} = 0.95$$

or 95 percent. This is much greater than just one-half (50 percent). The reasons stem from the randomness of the arrivals and the fact that services cannot be produced during idle periods and stored for use in busy periods. A second server is no help when the facility is idle or only one customer is being served, but when *groups of people* arrive, the second server is a *great* help. Let us consider an example now of a more complex managerial situation.

The warehouse for a furniture store is trying to estimate the best number of work crews to employ. The crews can each load, on the average, four trucks per hour but cost $100 per hour in total wages. (Only one crew can work on a truck at one time.) On the other hand, the idle time of trucks is charged at $160 per hour. If the trucks arrive every 20 minutes, on the average, how many crews should the warehouse employ? (Assume loading and arrival rates are random.)

$$\lambda = 60/20 = 3/hr$$

$$\mu = 4/hr$$

$$\frac{\lambda}{\mu} = 0.75$$

One crew. From Figure 6.18 at the intersection of $\lambda/\mu = 0.75$ and $K = 1$, we find $L_q = 2.3$. Hence: $W_q = 2.3/3 = 0.77$ hours per truck. At three trucks per hour, the total hourly waiting cost of the trucks is

$$0.77 \times 3 \times \$160 = \$370$$

$$\underline{+ \;\$100} \text{ (cost of one crew)}$$

Total $470/hr

Two crews. From Figure 6.18 at $K = 2$: $L_q = 0.12$

$$W_q = \frac{0.12}{3} = 0.04$$

waiting cost of trucks: $0.04 \times 3 \times \$160 \;\; = \$ \; 20$

cost of two crews: $\underline{\$200}$

Total $220/hr

Three or more crews. The most that can now be saved from the cost of waiting trucks is $20, so clearly it is not worthwhile to add another $100 crew. The best answer is, therefore, *two* crews.

EXPAND YOUR UNDERSTANDING

1. What impact might the Internet, the World Wide Web, and intranets have on using the Delphi method?

2. Why might a decision maker choose a qualitative forecasting method when extensive historical demand data are available?

3. Frequently, simple models such as breakeven are much more appealing to management than more sophisticated models (such as linear programming). Why might this be so?

4. Exactly what decreases in unit cost occur with larger facilities as a result of economies of scale? Might any costs increase with size of a facility?

5. Why has the concept of economies of scope never arisen before? What does advanced technology have to do with it?

6. How ethical is it for airlines, hotels, and other service providers to overbook their limited-capacity facilities intentionally, knowing that at some point they will have to turn away a customer with a "guaranteed" reservation?

7. Does the concept of bottlenecks apply to services as well as products?

8. What elements would be measured if a product firm were to measure its capacity by its inputs, as some service firms do?

9. Does the learning curve continue downward forever?

10. Which measures used to locate pure service organizations are direct measures of benefit and which are surrogate measures of benefit? Can you think of better direct measures? Why aren't they used?

11. Would the failure points, line of visibility, and processing times used in service maps be useful in process flow diagrams for products?

12. When might an organization not use all three stages of the location selection process described here?

13. Might the breakeven model be used for the national or site stage of location? Might the weighted score model be useful in the national or community stage of location? What factors would be used in these models at other stages?

14. Does the theory of constraints apply to services as well as to products?

15. Are the principles of waiting captured in the 23 capacity techniques of Table 6.7? Which ones?

APPLY YOUR UNDERSTANDING _____
Exit Manufacturing Company

The planning committee of Exit Manufacturing Company (made up of the vice presidents of marketing, finance, and production) was discussing the plans for a new factory to be located outside of Atlanta, Georgia. The factory would produce exterior doors consisting of prehung metal over Styrofoam insulation. The doors would be made in a standard format, with 15 different insert panels that could be added by retailers after manufacture. The standardization of construction was expected to create numerous production efficiencies over competitors' factories that produced multidimensional doors. Atlanta was felt to be an ideal site because of its location—in the heart of the sunbelt, with its growing construction industry. By locating close to these growing sunbelt states, Exit would minimize distribution costs.

The capital cost for the factory was expected to be $14 million. Annual maintenance expenses were projected to total 5 percent of capital. Fuel and utility costs were expected to be $500,000 per year. An analysis of the area's labor market indicated that a wage rate of $10 per hour could be expected. It was estimated that producing a door in the new facility would require 1.5 labor-hours. Fringe benefits paid to the operating labor were expected to equal 15 percent of direct labor costs. Supervisory, clerical, technical, and managerial salaries were forecast to total $350,000 per year. Taxes and insurance would cost $200,000 per year. Other miscellaneous expenses were expected to total $250,000 per year. Depreciation was based on a 30-year life with use of the straight-line method and a $4 million salvage value. Sheet metal, Styrofoam, adhesive for the doors, and frames were projected to cost $12 per door. Paint, hinges, doorknobs, and accessories were estimated to total $7.80 per door. Crating and shipping supplies were expected to cost $2.50 per door.

Exit's marketing manager prepared the following price-demand chart for the distribution area of the new plant. Through analysis of this data, the committee members felt that they could verify their expectation of an increase from 15 to 25 percent in the current market share, owing to the cost advantage of standardization.

Average Sales Price ($/door)	Area Sales (in units)
$90	40,000
$103	38,000
$115	31,000
$135	22,000

Questions

Develop a breakeven capacity analysis for Exit's new door and determine:

a. Best price, production rate, and profit.

b. Breakeven production rate with the price in a.

c. Breakeven price with the production rate in a.

d. Sensitivity of profits to variable cost, price, and production rate.

Stafford Chemical, Inc.

Stafford Chemical, Inc., is a privately held company that produces a range of specialty chemicals. Currently, its most important product line is paint pigments used by the automobile industry. Stafford Chemical was founded more than 60 years ago by Phillip Stafford in a small town north of Cincinnati, Ohio, and is currently run by Phillip's grandson, George Stafford. Stafford has more than 150 employees, and approximately three-quarters of them work on the shop floor. Stafford Chemical operates out of the same plant Phillip built when he founded the company; however, it has undergone several expansions over the years.

Recently, a Japanese competitor of Stafford Chemical by the name of Ozawa Industries announced plans to expand its operations to the United States. Ozawa, a subsidiary of a large industrial Japanese company, decided to locate a new facility in the United States to better serve some of its customers: automobile manufacturers who have built assembly plants there.

The governor of the state in which Stafford Chemical operates has been particularly aggressive in trying to persuade Ozawa Industries to locate in a new industrial park located about 30 miles from Stafford's current plant. She has expressed a willingness to negotiate special tax rates, to subsidize workers' training, and to expand the existing highway to meet Ozawa's needs. In a recent newspaper article, she was quoted as saying:

> Making the concessions I have proposed to get Ozawa to locate within our state is a good business decision and a good investment in our state. The plant will provide high-paying jobs for 400 of our citizens. Furthermore, over the long run, the income taxes that these 400 individuals will pay will more than offset the concessions I have proposed. Since several other states have indicated a willingness to make similar concessions, it is unlikely that Ozawa would choose our state without them.

George Stafford was outraged after being shown the governor's comments.

> I can't believe this. Stafford Chemical has operated in this state for over 60 years. I am the third generation of Staffords to run this business. Many of our employees' parents and grandparents worked here. We have taken pride in being an exemplary corporate citizen. And now our governor wants to help one of our major competitors drive us out of business. How are we supposed to compete with such a large industrial giant? We should be the ones who are getting the tax break and help with workers' training. Doesn't 60 years of paying taxes and employing workers count for something? Where is this governor's loyalty? It seems to me that the state should be loyal to its long-term citizens, the ones who care about the state and community they operate in—not some large industrial giant looking to save a buck.

Questions

1. How valid is George Stafford's argument? How valid is the governor's argument? Is Stafford Chemical being punished because it was already located within the state?

2. How ethical is it for states and local governments to offer incentives to attract new businesses to their localities? Are federal laws needed to keep states from competing with one another?

3. Does the fact that Ozawa is a foreign company alter the ethical nature of the governor's actions? What about Ozawa's size?

4. What are George's options?

EXERCISES _____

1. Three professors are grading a combined final exam. Each is grading different questions on the test. One professor requires 3 minutes to finish his or her portion, another takes 6 minutes, and the third takes 2 minutes. Assume there is no learning curve effect.

   a. What will their hourly output be?

   b. If there are 45 tests to grade, how long will the grading take?

   c. If each professor were to grade the exams separately in 18 minutes, how long would it take to grade the 45 tests? How long if another professor (who also required 18 minutes) joined them?

d. If another professor pitches in just to help the second professor, how long will it take the four of them to grade the tests?

e. If a fifth professor offers to help, what might happen?

2. A toy firm produces drums sequentially on three machines A, B, and C with cycle times of 3, 4, and 6 minutes, respectively.

a. Determine the optimum efficiency and output rates for adding one, two, ..., six more machines.

b. Assume now that two identical lines are operating, each with machines A, B, and C. If new machines can be shared between the lines, how should one, two, and then three new machines be added? What are the resulting efficiencies and outputs of the two lines? Is it always best to equally share extra machines between the two lines?

3. If the production system for a product has a utilization of 80 percent and a yield of 75 percent, what capacity is needed to produce 1000 units a year?

4. If unit 1 requires 6 labor hours and unit 5 requires 1.8324, what is the learning rate? What will unit 6 require? What have the first five units required in total?

5. A production lot of 25 units required 103.6 hours of effort. Accounting records show that the first unit took 7 hours. What was the learning rate?

6. If unit 1 required 200 hours to produce and the labor records for an Air Force contract of 50 units indicate an average labor content of 63.1 hours per unit, what was the learning rate? What total additional number of labor-hours would be required for another Air Force contract of 50 units? What would be the average labor content of this second contract? Of both contracts combined? If labor costs the vendor $10 per hour on this second Air Force contract and the price to the Air Force is fixed at $550 each, what can you say about the profitability of the first and second contracts, and hence the bidding process in general?

7. All the reports you wrote for one class had three sections: introduction, analysis, conclusion. The times required to complete these sections (including typing, etc.) are shown below in hours.

Report	Introduction	Analysis	Conclusion
1	1.5	6	2
2	—	(lost data)	—
3	1	3	0.8

The class requires 5 reports in all. You are now starting report 4 and, although you are working faster, you can afford to spend only 1 hour a day on these reports. Report 5 is due in one week (7 days). Will you be done in time?

8. Use the CVD model to evaluate the following three locations in terms of access to five destinations. Site I is located 313, 245, 188, 36, and 89 feet, respectively, from the five destinations; site II, 221, 376, 92, 124, and 22 feet; and site III, 78, 102, 445, 123, and 208 feet.

9. Reevaluate exercise 8 if the number of trips to each of the destinations is, respectively, 15, 6, 12, 33, and 21.

10. Choose the best coat on the basis of two factors, price and quality, if price is 50 percent more important than quality. Only the rankings are available for each factor (where 1 is best).

Coat:	1	2	3	4	5	6	7	8	9
Cost (rupees):	2	5	3	1	7	8	9	4	6
Quality:	6	3	4	8	1	7	9	5	2

11. The location subcommittee's final report to the board has focused on three acceptable communities. Table 15b in the appendix to the report indicates that the cost of locating in communities 1, 2, and 3 is approximately $400,000, $500,000 and $600,000 per year (respectively), mortgaged over 30 years. Paragraph 2 on page 39 of the report indicates that the variable cost per unit of product will increase 15 percent in community 1 but decrease 15 percent in community 3, owing to differences in labor rates. As plant manager, you know that variable costs to date have averaged about $3.05 per unit and sales for the next decade are expected to average 20 percent more than the last 10 years, during which annual sales varied between 40,000 and 80,000 units. Which location would you recommend?

12. Nina is trying to decide in which of four shopping centers to locate her new boutique. Some cater to a higher class of clientele than others, some are in an indoor mall, some have a much greater volume than others, and, of course, rent varies considerably. Because of the nature of her store, she has decided that the class of clientele is the most important consideration. Following this, however, she must pay attention to her expenses; and rent is a major item—probably 90 percent as important as clientele. An indoor, temperature-controlled mall is a big help, however, for stores such as hers, where 70 percent of sales are from passersby slowly strolling and window-shopping. Thus, she rates

this as about 95 percent as important as rent. Last, a higher volume of shoppers means more potential sales; she thus rates this factor as 80 percent as important as rent. As an aid in visualizing her location alternatives, she has constructed the following table. "Good" is scored as 3, "fair" as 2, and "poor" as 1. Use a weighted score model to help Nina come to a decision.

	Location			
	1	2	3	4
Class of clientele	Fair	Good	Poor	Good
Rent	Good	Fair	Poor	Good
Indoor mall	Good	Poor	Good	Poor
Volume	Good	Fair	Good	Poor

13. The emergency room of a local hospital employs three doctors. Emergency patients arrive randomly at the average rate of 3.5 per hour. Service is good and averages about 1/2 hour per patient, so the hospital is considering reducing the number of doctors to two. What effect would this have on patient waiting time?

14. Jim sells tickets at a counter where the customers randomly arrive, on the average, every 2 minutes. He finds that he can serve no more than 10 customers per hour. For management to maintain an average queue length of no more than one customer, how many more ticket sellers must they provide to help Jim?

15. City Bank is trying to determine how to staff its teller windows so that the average number of customers waiting for service in the single line ("cattle stall") queue does not exceed eight. On average, one customer arrives every minute and one teller can service 20 customers an hour. On the average, how long will a customer have to wait in the cattle stall? Find the utilization of the facility. How many square feet of space will be required if every teller needs 50 square feet and every waiting customer requires 15 square feet?

BIBLIOGRAPHY

APICS. *Certification Study Guide: Capacity Management.* Washington, D.C.: American Production and Inventory Control Society, 1980.

Filley, R. D. "Putting the 'Fast' in Fast Foods: Burger King." *Industrial Engineering* (January 1983): 44–47.

Fisher, M. L., J. H. Hammond, W. R. Obermeyer, and A. Raman. "Making Supply Meet Demand in an Uncertain World." *Harvard Business Review* 72 (May–June 1994): 83–93.

Francis, R. L., and J. A. White. *Facilities Layout and Location: An Analytical Approach.* Englewood Cliffs, N.J.: Prentice-Hall, 1987.

Georgoff, D. M., and R. G. Murdick. "Manager's Guide to Forecasting." *Harvard Business Review* 64 (January–February 1986): 110–120.

Goldratt, E. M. *Theory of Constraints,* 2nd rev. ed. Croton-on-Hudson: North River Press, 1990.

Harvard Business School. "A Glossary of TOM Terms." Harvard Reprint No. 9–687–019, Sept. 1994.

Heskett, J. "Note on Service Mapping." Harvard Reprint No. 9–693–065, Nov. 1992.

Johnson, J. C., and D. F. Wood. *Contemporary Physical Distribution and Logistics,* 3rd ed. New York: Macmillan, 1986.

Maister, D. H. "The Psychology of Waiting Lines." Harvard Reprint No. 9–684–064, May 1984.

Marshall, P. W. "A Note on Process Analysis (Abridged)." Harvard Reprint No. 9–689–032, Sept. 1994.

Port, O. "Huh? Chipmakers Copying Steelmakers?" *Business Week* (August 15, 1994): 97–98.

Price, W. L., and M. Turcotte. "Locating a Blood Bank." *Interfaces* (September–October 1986): 17–26.

Tetzeli, R. "Mapping for Dollars." *Fortune* (October 18, 1993): 91–96.

Vollmann, T. E., W. L. Berry, and D. C. Whybark. *Manufacturing Planning and Control Systems,* 2nd ed. Homewood, Ill.: Irwin, 1988.

Willis, R. E. *A Guide to Forecasting for Planners and Managers.* Englewood Cliffs, N.J.: Prentice-Hall, 1987.

Woodruff, D., and J. Templeman. "Why Mercedes Is Alabama Bound." *Business Week* (October 11, 1993): 138–139.

CHAPTER 7

Schedule Management

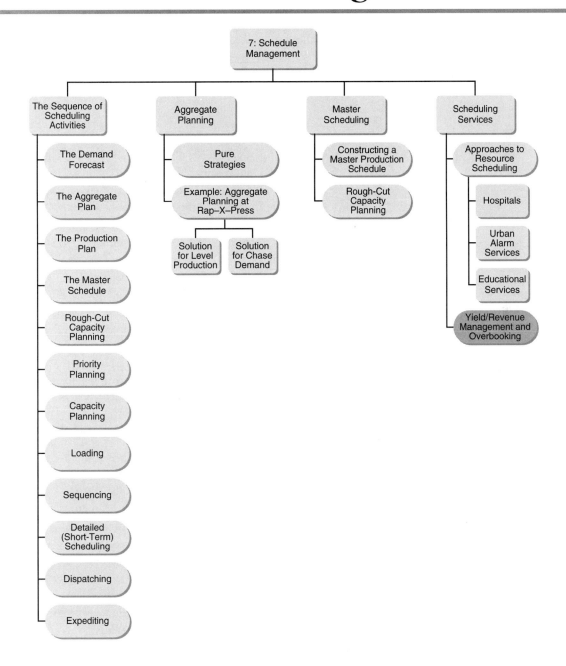

In this chapter we add the dimension of time to our previously static picture of the organization, transforming it into a running, operating set of activities that are producing and supplying outputs to live, demanding customers. Here we are concerned with ensuring that the right tasks are conducted at the right time on the right items to produce the output—that is, scheduling. We begin the chapter with a broad overview of the sequence of scheduling activities and then discuss the topics of aggregate planning and master scheduling in more detail. The chapter concludes with a discussion of scheduling services including the topic of yield/revenue management and overbooking.

$\mathcal{I}$NTRODUCTION

- At the Henry Ford Hospital, the aggregate scheduling problem is to match available capital, workers, and supplies to a highly variable pattern of demand. The hospital has 903 beds arranged into 30 nursing units, with each nursing unit containing 8 to 44 beds. For purposes of planning, each of the nursing units is treated as an independent production facility. However, a number of factors complicate the aggregate planning process at the hospital. First, as noted, demand exhibits a high degree of variability. For example, while the average number of occupied beds in 1991 was 770, in one eight-week period it was 861 and in another it was 660. A second complicating factor is the large penalty incurred by the hospital for HMO patients who require care but cannot be admitted because a bed is not available. In these cases, not only does the hospital lose the revenue from the patient, but it must also pay another hospital for the patient's stay. A third complication is the tight labor market for registered nurses, making it difficult and expensive to change the rate of production. On average, it takes the hospital 12 to 16 weeks to recruit and train each nurse, at a cost of approximately $7600 per nurse. A final complication is the high costs associated with idle facilities. The hospital estimates that the cost of one eight-bed patient module exceeds $35,000 per month (Schramm and Freund 1993).

- Package Products, in Pittsburgh, Pennsylvania, produces folding carton packing for the bakery and deli industries. A key aspect of Package Products' strategy is to be recognized by its customers for quality, reliability, and service. Significant growth during the 1990s greatly complicated the task of managing the company's operations. In addition, its customers were becoming more demanding, and the marketplace was becoming more competitive. To gain better control over its operations, Package Products implemented a finite capacity scheduling (FCS) software package. Before it acquired the FCS system, a Gantt chart was maintained manually to schedule jobs. Problems with the manual system included chronic capacity shortages and the fact that key data resided in the heads of people who were scattered throughout the organization. Two criteria used for selecting the FCS software package were that it should work with the company's existing business system and that it should not be a "black box," claiming to provide optimal schedules that no one could really understand. Through the use of the FCS program, overtime has been substantially reduced, on-time delivery has been improved by 32 percent, and backorders have been reduced by 53 percent. Additionally, customer service can now respond to customers' inquiries in an average of 22 seconds—versus taking overnight previously (Trail 1996).

These examples illustrate the considerations and complications associated with developing aggregate and detailed production plans and schedules. Developing an aggregate production plan is important because without taking a sufficiently long-term view of the organization, we may end up making short-run decisions that adversely affect the organization in the long run. For example, during one period at the Henry Ford Hospital, a decision was made to reduce the staff. However, shortly after the staff was reduced, it was determined that more staff was needed, and thus new staff members were recruited. The net result was that the hospital incurred both the costs associated with reducing its staff and the costs associated with recruiting and training a new staff a short time later. A better approach would have been to compare the costs of reducing and hiring staff with the costs of having too large a staff for a short time period. Of course, the only way to accomplish this is to look far enough into the future to estimate if and when demand will pick up again.

Problems with productivity are often attributable, in large part, to poor management of the schedule: ensuring that the *right* tasks are conducted at the *right* time on the *right* items to produce the output—which is, in a sense, a matter of "orchestration," more generally known as *scheduling*. Scheduling is an important component of the overall product supply chain that addresses issues managers must face on a daily basis: where each input (material, machine, worker) must be, when it must be there, what form it must be in, how many must be available, and other such details.

Scheduling for continuous process and flow shops is not anywhere near the problem that it is for job shops. This is because scheduling is largely *built into* the transformation process when the facility is designed and therefore need not (in fact *cannot*) be constantly changed. To reschedule these facilities, beyond just increasing or decreasing the rate of input, requires a rebalancing of the entire flow through the production system. At the other extreme, the scheduling of project operations is probably the most important single planning activity in the successful management of projects. Because of the extent of this topic, we will defer its treatment to Chapter 10.

In this chapter we begin with a look at the generic sequence of the scheduling activities in product firms, since these functions are better developed and more common in product firms than in service organizations. Following this, we look at the first major activity in the sequence of activities: aggregate planning. The aggregate plan forms the foundation for all other scheduling and materials management. Two pure strategies—level production and chase demand—are described and illustrated with an example. Next, we consider the major task of master scheduling and discuss its purpose, procedures, and results, briefly noting the role of rough-cut capacity planning in validating the feasibility of the master production schedule. Finally, we consider the problem of detailed scheduling for services and the common procedure of overbooking to reduce the opportunity costs of the expensive resources.

THE SEQUENCE OF SCHEDULING ACTIVITIES

In most organizations a department (or an individual) is specifically responsible for scheduling operations. In product organizations, this function is frequently called production planning and control, or some similar name. The breadth of this department's responsibility varies considerably; for example, it may consist only of planning gross output levels or may include all the scheduling activities illustrated in Figure 7.1.

This figure does not describe a *standardized* scheduling system, such as might exist in an available computer package; rather, it shows a complex of activities and terms that are often grouped under *scheduling*. Many of these have become major activities only since the advent of computerized scheduling. Before that, they were simply a matter of individual judgment (as some of them still are). Let us look at the scheduling activities in the Figure and their interrelationships; in the following sections of the chapter we will then look more intensively at some of the major activities and describe some approaches to dealing with them.

The Demand Forecast

As we described in Chapter 6, the foundation that supports scheduling is, in most cases, the forecast of demand for the upcoming planning horizon. In some industries, however, only minimal forecasting is needed because customers place orders a year or more ahead of the time when the output will be needed. For example, in the airframe industry, airlines may place orders years ahead of time because of long lead times and backlogs of orders. In these situations, organizational operations are scheduled on the basis of actual orders instead of forecasted demand.

Most organizations do not operate in such a favorable environment, however, and their success often hinges on the accuracy of their forecasts of demand. In these cases the concepts and techniques of forecasting briefly overviewed in Chapter 6 are especially relevant for scheduling.

It might be noted that forecasts over different periods are used for different purposes. For example, long-range forecasts (i.e., 2 to 5 years) are used more for facility and capacity planning than for any scheduling function. In the range of 3 to 18 months, forecasts are used for aggregate planning, as described later, and detailed forecasts for the next few months are particularly crucial in near-term scheduling such as loading and sequencing.

The Aggregate Plan

The **aggregate plan** is a preliminary, approximate schedule of an organization's overall operations that will satisfy the demand forecast at minimum cost. The

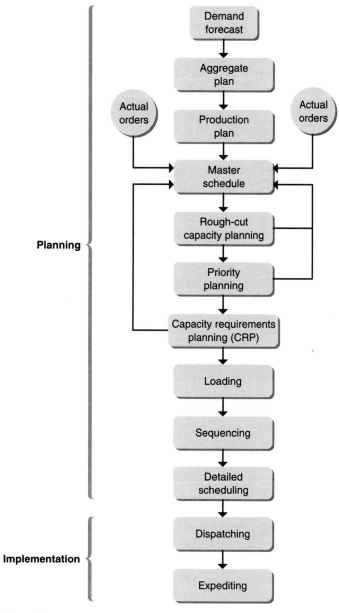

Figure 7.1   Relationship of scheduling activities.

planning horizon, the period over which changes and demands are taken into consideration, is often one year or more and is broken into monthly or quarterly periods. This is because one of the purposes of aggregate planning is to minimize the effects of shortsighted, day-to-day scheduling, in which small amounts of material may be ordered from a supplier and workers laid off one week, only to be followed by reordering more material and rehiring the workers the next week. By taking a longer-term perspective on use of resources, short-term changes in requirements can be minimized with a considerable saving in costs.

In minimizing short-term variations, the basic approach is to work only with "aggregate" units (i.e., units grouped or bunched together). Aggregate resources are used, such as total number of workers, hours of machine time, and tons of raw materials, as well as aggregate units of output—gallons of product, hours of service delivered, number of patients seen, and so on—totally ignoring the fact that there may be differences between these aggregated items. In other words, neither resources nor outputs are broken down into more specific categories; that occurs at a later stage.

On occasion, the units of aggregation are somewhat difficult to determine, especially if the variation in output is extreme (as when a manufacturer produces dishwashers, clothes washers, and dryers). In such cases, *equivalent units* are usually determined; these are based on value, cost, worker-hours, or some similar measure. For the appliance manufacturer, the aggregate plan might be: January, 5000 "appliances"; February, 4000 "appliances"; and so on.

The resulting problem in aggregate planning is to minimize the long-run costs of meeting forecasted demand. The relevant costs include hiring and laying off workers, storing finished goods (if a product is involved), paying wages and overtime, covering the expense of shortages and *back orders*, and subcontracting. As it turns out, the use of inventory to buffer production against variations in demand is an extremely important managerial option. In service organizations this option is usually not available, since services—such as plane trips and patient care—cannot be inventoried. The result is an increased cost of producing the service, with an increase in its price. Aggregate planning is discussed in considerably more detail later in this chapter.

The Production Plan

The result of managerial iteration and changes to the aggregate plan is the organization's formal ***production plan*** for the planning horizon used by the organization (e.g., one year). Sometimes this plan is broken down (i.e., *disaggregated*) one level into major output groups (still aggregated)—for example, by models but not by colors. In either case, the production plan shows the resources required and changes in output over the future: requirements for hiring, limitations on capacity, relative increases and decreases in inventories of materials, and output rate of goods or services.

The Master Schedule

The driving force behind scheduling is the master schedule, also known in industry as the ***master production schedule*** (MPS). There are two reasons for this:

1. It is at this point that *actual* orders are incorporated into the scheduling system.

2. This is also the stage where aggregate planned outputs are broken down into individual scheduled items that customers actually want (called ***level zero items***). These items are then checked for feasibility against lead time (time to produce or ship the items) and operational capacity (if there is enough equipment, labor, etc.).

The actual scheduling is usually iterative, with a preliminary schedule being drawn up, checked for problems, and then revised. After a schedule has been determined, the following points are checked:

- Does the schedule meet the production plan?
- Does the schedule meet the end item demand forecasts?
- Are there conflicts in the schedule involving priority or capacity? (See the next two scheduling activities.) "Rough-cut capacity planning" (discussed next), based on the MPS, derives weekly work-center loads and compares them with capacities available.
- Does the schedule violate any other constraints regarding equipment, lead times, supplies, facilities, and so forth?
- Does the schedule conform to organizational policy?
- Does the schedule violate any legal regulations or organizational or union rules?
- Does the schedule provide for flexibility and backups?

Problems in any one of these areas may force a revision of the schedule and a repeat of the previous steps. The result is that the master schedule then specifies *what end items* are to be *produced in what periods* to *minimize costs* and gives some measure of assurance that such a plan is *feasible*. Clearly, such a document is of major importance to any organization—it is, in a sense, a blueprint for future operations. Master scheduling is discussed in more detail later in this chapter.

Rough-Cut Capacity Planning

As a part of checking the feasibility of the master schedule, a simple type of ***rough-cut capacity planning*** is conducted. Historical ratios of workloads per unit of each type of product are used to determine the loads placed on the work centers by all the products being made in any one period. Then the loads are assumed to fall on the work centers in the same period as the demands; that is, the lead times are not used to offset the loads. If a work center's capacities are not overloaded (underloads are also checked), it is assumed that sufficient capacity exists to handle the master schedule, and it is accepted for production. Capacity planning was discussed in Chapter 6 but will be brought up again in Chapter 8.

Priority Planning

The term *priority planning* relates not to giving priorities to jobs (a topic included under *sequencing*), but rather to determining *what material* is needed *when*. For a master production schedule to be feasible, the proper raw materials, purchased materials, and manufactured or purchased subassemblies must be available when needed, with the top priority going to immediate needs. The key to production planning is the "needed" date. Years ago, scheduling concentrated on *launching orders*, that is, on when to *place* the order. Priority planning concentrates on when the order is actually needed and schedules *backward* from that date. For example, if an item is needed on June 18 and requires a two-week lead time, then the order is released on June 4 and not before. Why store inventory needlessly?

The systems that have been devised for accomplishing this task are inventory control systems based on lead times and expected demands. The classic order-point inventory systems are most appropriate for organizations *producing to stock* (e.g., flow shops). These are called *order-point systems* because new orders for materials are sent out when the inventory on hand reaches a certain low point. For organizations that *produce to order* (e.g., many job shops), requirements for materials are known with near-certainty because they are tied to specified outputs. For example, every car requires four wheel covers—the number of wheel covers depends only on the number of cars. Computerized ***materials requirements planning*** (MRP) systems anticipate needs, consider lead times, release purchase orders, and schedule production in accord with the master schedule. If insufficient lead time exists to produce or obtain the necessary materials, or other problems arise, the master schedule must be revised or other arrangements made. These inventory systems are discussed in greater detail in Chapter 8.

Capacity Planning

The inventory control system and master schedule drive the ***capacity requirements planning*** (CRP) system, described in Chapter 8. This system projects job orders and demands for materials into requirements for equipment, work force, and facility and finds the total required capacity of each over the planning horizon. That is, during a given week, how many nurses will be required, how many hours of a kidney machine, how many hours in operating rooms?

This may or may not exceed *available* capacity. If it is within the limits of capacity, then the master schedule is finalized, work orders are released according to schedule, orders for materials are released by the priority planning system, and *load reports* are sent to work centers, listing the work facing each area on the basis of the CRP system. Note that external lead times (often longer than internal lead times) from suppliers have already been checked at the stage of priority planning, so the master schedule can indeed now be finalized.

If the limits of capacity are exceeded, however, something must be changed. Some jobs must be delayed, or a less demanding schedule must be devised, or extra capacity must be obtained elsewhere (e.g., by hiring more workers or using overtime). It is the task of production planning and control to solve this problem.

Loading

Loading means deciding which jobs to assign to which work centers. Although the capacity planning system determines that sufficient gross capacity exists to meet the master schedule, *no actual* assignment of jobs to work centers is made. Some equipment will generally be superior for certain jobs, and some equipment will be less heavily loaded than other equipment. Thus, there is often a "best" (fastest or least costly) assignment of jobs to work centers.

Sequencing

Even after jobs have been assigned to work centers, the *order* in which to process the jobs—their ***sequencing***—must still be determined. Unfortunately, even this seemingly small final step can have major repercussions on the organization's workload capacity and on whether or not jobs are completed on time. A number of priority rules have been researched, and some interesting results are available in the literature.

Detailed (Short-Term) Scheduling

Once all this has been specified, detailed schedules itemizing specific jobs, times, materials, and workers can be drawn up. This is usually done only a few days in advance, however, since changes are always occurring and detailed schedules become outdated quickly. It is the responsibility of production planning and control to ensure that when a job is ready to be worked on, all the items, equipment, facilities, and information (blueprints, operations sheets, etc.) are available as scheduled. This topic is also discussed later.

Dispatching

All the previous activities constitute schedule *planning*; no production per se has taken place yet. **Dispatching** is the physical *release* of a work order from the production planning and control department to operations. The release may be manual—from the *dead load file*, as it is called—or through a computerized master scheduling system.

Expediting

Once production planning and control has released a job to operations (or the *shop floor*, as it is sometimes called), the department usually has no more responsibility for it, and it is the production manager's task to get the job done on time. This task is known as **expediting**. When jobs fall behind schedule, managers have historically tended to use expediters to help push these "hot" jobs through the operations. Of course, expediting can be done more proactively, by monitoring the progress of jobs to ensure that they stay on schedule.

Before computerized scheduling techniques were available, extensive use of expediters was common (and it still is in many organizations). The problem was the impossibility of the scheduling task facing production planning and control. Not only could it not determine a good production schedule; it often could not even tell when insufficient capacity existed. Production managers thus relied heavily on expediters to gather all the necessary materials together (often cannibalizing parts from other jobs) in order to get important jobs completed. Of course, this further delayed the remaining jobs, so that more and more jobs tended to become "hot."

Commonly, yellow tags were used to label "hot" jobs until, pretty soon, all the jobs had yellow tags. To identify "especially hot" jobs, then, red tags were used. After a while the operations area resembled a rainbow, whereupon no new orders were accepted, the backlog was worked off, and the cycle started from scratch.

It may be presumed that a clear indication of the failure of a scheduling system is the existence of a great many expediters. One problem with the informal scheduling system, of course, was a lack of *deexpediting* (delaying jobs that had dropped in priority) to reflect changes in required due dates and thus, in priorities

DILBERT ©United Feature Syndicate. Reprinted with permission.

and schedules. Deexpediting has now been built into the computerized manufacturing resource planning (MRP II) and scheduling systems that are now so common in industry.

Aggregate Planning

The problem of aggregate planning arises in the following context. Managers have a month-to-month forecast of total demand for all outputs (combined) for the next year or so. They are expected to capitalize on this demand by supplying whatever portion of it will maximize long-run profitability. That is, not all the demand need be satisfied if attempting to fill it will result in lower overall profits. But a loss of market share might result, which, in turn, may reduce long-run profitability.

The managers have a set of productive facilities and workers with some maximum capacity to supply demand. There may also be some finished output available in inventory to help meet the demand, but there may, as well, be backorders of unsatisfied demand. They must decide how to employ the resources at their disposal to best meet the demand. If excess capacity is available, they may lease it out, sell it, or lay off workers. If insufficient capacity is available, but only for a short time in the future, they may employ overtime or part-time workers, subcontract work, or simply not meet the demand.

As discussed in Chapter 6, there are a number of ways of changing the capacity available to a manager to meet demand at minimum cost, such as:

1. Overtime
2. Additional or fewer shifts
3. Hiring or laying off workers (including part-time)
4. Subcontracting
5. Building up inventories during slack periods
6. Leasing facilities or workers, or both
7. Backlogging demand
8. Changing demand through marketing promotions or pricing
9. Undersupplying the market

Each of these strategies has advantages and disadvantages and perhaps certain restrictions on its use (such as legal or union regulations, or limitations on a public facility). The managers must plan their strategy carefully, because a shortsighted strategy, such as laying off workers when they will be needed again later, can be very expensive to rectify. However, an excessively long-range perspective may also be incorrect: a worker may be kept idle for a year when it would be much cheaper to lay off and then rehire the worker. Note that some of these alternatives (e.g., overtime, hiring, and layoffs) assume that equipment and facilities are already available and that there are not three shifts working seven days a week. If this is not the case, then additional facilities and equipment may also need to be acquired.

Pure Strategies

There are two aggregate planning strategies, known as *pure strategies*, which, though rarely used in practice because of their expense, give managers a starting point to improve upon and also a feel for some upper limits on cost:

1. *Level production.* With a level production strategy, the same amount of output is produced each period. Inventories of finished goods (or backlogged demand) are used to meet variations in demand, at the cost of investment in inventory or the expense of a shortage (stockout). The advantage is steady employment with no work force expenses. Since service outputs cannot generally be inventoried, this strategy, for a service firm, normally results in a constant but poorly utilized work force (e.g., repair crews, firefighters) of a size large enough to meet peak demand. If the service firm uses a smaller work force, it risks losing some demand to a competitor.

2. *Chase demand.* In this strategy, production is identical to the expected demand for the period in question. This is typically obtained either through overtime or hiring and laying off. (Again, this assumes sufficient equipment and facilities.) The advantage of this policy is that there are no costs entailed by inventories of finished goods, except perhaps for buffer stock (also called *safety stock*, as discussed in Chapter 8), and no shortage costs, including loss of goodwill. Service firms use this strategy by making use of overtime, split shifts, overlapping shifts, call-in workers, part-time workers, and so on.

The vast majority of firms often achieve lower costs than the costs of these two pure strategies by using *hybrid* (mixed) strategies that include overtime, hiring and layoffs, subcontracting, and the like. Product firms also have the option of trading off investment in inventories of finished goods for changes in capacity level or vice versa. (For example, a product firm can build up inventory ahead of demand rather than acquiring all the capacity needed to meet peak demand.) We demonstrate with an example.

Example: Aggregate Planning at Rap-X-Press

Rap-X-Press is a new local express pickup and delivery business. Sarah Primes is responsible for determining and acquiring the personnel Rap-X-Press will need in

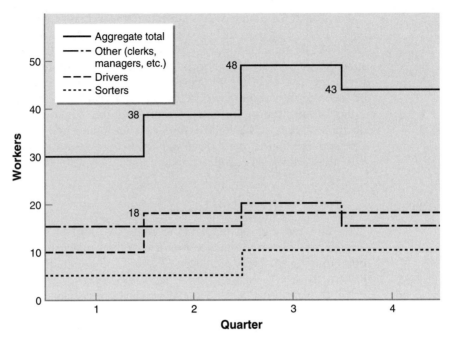

Figure 7.2   Personnel needed by Rap-X-Press.

the coming year. Sarah has determined the firm's needs for each quarter in each of the three major personnel categories shown in Figure 7.2. The sum of the three categories gives the aggregate personnel needs.

In trying to determine a hiring schedule for next year, Sarah must make a judgment concerning whether the increased need for personnel is simply seasonal or, instead, represents permanent growth in the market. Essentially, will the number of drivers needed in the first quarter of the year following that shown in Figure 7.2 drop back to 10, or will it remain at 15? If the need will decrease, Sarah might want to use overtime, or temporary drivers and sorters, in quarters 3 and 4, for example. However, if the growth in demand is permanent, she may decide to hire permanent workers.

Suppose the average salary for Rap-X-Press is $5000 per quarter per employee, but the cost of lost sales, including goodwill, when there are insufficient employees is estimated to be $6000 per quarter per employee. The cost of using overtime in place of hiring a worker is $8000 per quarter. What would be the total annual cost for a level production strategy of 40 workers? What would be the cost for a chase demand strategy employing 30 workers? 40 workers?

Solution for Level Production

The analysis for the level production strategy at 40 workers is given in Figure 7.3. Two sets of costs are incurred: the cost of having excess workers in the first two periods (totaling $60,000), and the cost of being short in the last two periods (totaling $66,000), for a grand total over the year of $126,000. Note that if the level of starting workers is raised (to, say, 45) or lowered (to, say, 35), the two costs will change, giving a different total annual cost. Thus, with a level production strategy

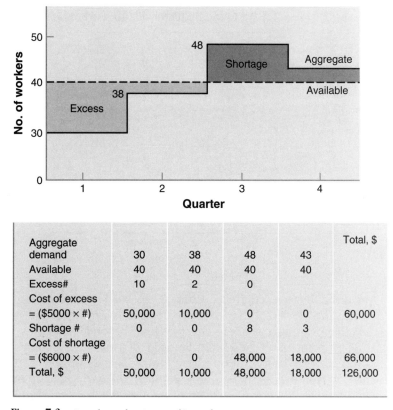

Aggregate demand	30	38	48	43	Total, $
Available	40	40	40	40	
Excess#	10	2	0		
Cost of excess = ($5000 × #)	50,000	10,000	0	0	60,000
Shortage #	0	0	8	3	
Cost of shortage = ($6000 × #)	0	0	48,000	18,000	66,000
Total, $	50,000	10,000	48,000	18,000	126,000

Figure 7.3   Level production at 40 workers.

in a simplistic setting such as this, there may be an optimal number of employees to keep on the payroll.

Solution for Chase Demand

Table 7.1 gives the cost calculations for the chase demand strategy using overtime with 30 workers. As can be seen, there is no excess employee cost, but the overtime cost is overwhelming: $312,000 total for the year. In Table 7.2, overtime is used, assuming a starting work force of 40. In this case, an excess employee cost is

TABLE 7.1 • Cost of Chase Demand with 30 Workers

Quarter	1	2	3	4	Total $
Aggregate demand	30	38	48	43	
Available	30	30	30	30	
Overtime #	0	8	18	13	
Overtime cost = ($8000 × #)	0	64,000	144,000	104,000	312,000

$\mathcal{T}_{ABLE}$ 7.2 • Cost of Chase Demand with 40 Workers

Quarter	1	2	3	4	Total $
Aggregate demand	30	38	48	43	
Available	40	40	40	40	
Overtime #	0	0	8	3	
Overtime cost = ($8000 × #)	0	0	64,000	24,000	88,000
Excess #	10	2	0	0	
Cost of excess = ($5000 × #)	50,000	10,000	0	0	60,000
Total cost					148,000

incurred, but the required overtime is so much less that the total cost for the year drops to $148,000. Although chase demand is a much better strategy with 40 workers than with 30, it is not as cheap as level production.

The point of all these calculations is to show the potential complexity of the problem. The best solution for any firm depends on the costs of overtime, shortage, ill will, excess staffing, hiring and layoffs (which were not considered here), and the other alternatives open to the firm (such as subcontracting). But the best solution depends not only on the set of costs facing a firm, but also on the expected (and actual) demand rates over the year. Given the risk that demand forecasts may be in error, managers may choose a staffing strategy that is more expensive relative to the forecast in order to protect themselves against the risk of being in error (such as having inadequate staff to handle a potential explosion in demand).

Ohio National Bank (ONB), one of the largest banks in Ohio at the time, employed 1800 people who provided a full range of banking services. (ONB is now integrated into BancOhio National Bank.) The management of ONB was seeking ways to better schedule its full and part-time encoders while reducing the number of unencoded checks at the end of each day (Krajewski and Ritzman 1980). Existing methods of scheduling were unable to give an accurate estimate of either the number of encoders needed at any given time or the time when a set of encoders would finish the day's work. As a result, some checks went unencoded at the end of the work day, increasing the bank's float costs, or last-minute overtime was required to complete the encoding, which irritated the encoders, increased turnover and personnel costs, and reduced productivity and morale.

ONB's existing schedule consisted of 33 full-time encoders from 11 A.M. to 8 P.M., 2 part-time encoders from 12 noon to 5 P.M., and 2 more part-time encoders from 5 P.M. to 10 P.M. every day of the week. This fixed schedule did not accommodate variability in the volume of checks arriving, and the full-time encoders frequently had to work overtime to complete all the work. It was clearly necessary to do a better job of matching the work force to the expected volumes.

This was done by designing a computer program to schedule the encoders' shifts. It consisted of two primary models. The first model used simple linear regression to predict expected hourly volumes on the basis of past data about arrivals by hour of the day, day of the week, day of the month, and month of the year. The second model used linear programming to determine the optimal number of full- and part-time encoders to schedule for each shift to minimize the sum of weekly regular-time wages, overtime wages, and float costs. The major data required for this second model are definitions of shifts, volumes of checks, encoder productivities, costs, number of encoding machines, and any limits on the number of encoders and the amount of overtime. The output consisted of three reports: shift assignments, hourly clerks on hand, and the costs of the schedule.

The general solution for ONB was to use 2 full-time encoders from 11 A.M. to 8 P.M. and 33 part-time encoders from 1 to 6 P.M. all week, plus 27 part-time encoders from 6 to 10 P.M. on Mondays, Tuesdays, and Fridays. This schedule was estimated to save ONB almost $80,000 per year. Regular use of the program indicated that the encoding was completed by 10 P.M. about 98 percent of the time, whereas it had rarely been achieved in the past. Moreover, unexpected overtime and poorly defined work schedules ceased to be a significant cause of turnover.

MASTER SCHEDULING

As briefly described earlier, aggregate planning leads to the firm's production plan. Disaggregating the production plan into individual end items results in the master production schedule (MPS). The master production schedule shows how many of what end items (or assemblies, in the case of a make-to-order firm) to produce when. If the production plan is stated, as it sometimes is, in dollars or pounds or some other such measure, it will have to be converted into units of production in the MPS.

Because it is the final word about what the company will actually build and when, the MPS also acts as upper management's "handle" on the production system. By altering the MPS, management can alter inventory levels, lead times, capacity demands, and so on. Such power is a two-edged sword, however. If management attempts to overload the MPS in order to produce more output than can realistically be made, the shop will jam up with work to be done and will not get anything out. In creating the MPS, limits on capacity must be carefully observed; they cannot be ignored by using a master schedule that is only top management's "wish list."

In the traditional functional organization, the main players in creating the master schedule are sales and operations, each representing one of two primary objectives of master scheduling:

1. **Sales:** To schedule finished goods to meet delivery needs
2. **Operations:** To maintain efficient utilization of work centers by not overloading or underloading them

If these objectives cannot be met—because of, say, a capacity limitation in a work center—then the production plan may have to be revised.

In addition to limiting work to what can realistically be done, the MPS also includes other functions. First, it buffers the forecast by "smoothing" demand over time, reducing capacity-constrained peaks, and raising low-demand idle periods. It also subtracts existing inventories of products from the forecasts so that the shop doesn't make products that already exist in inventory. And it "batches" demands over time into convenient and economical groups for production so that scarce facilities and equipment aren't wasted.

As noted earlier, the MPS is based both on firm orders, received through salespersons or directly from the customer, and on end item forecasts of future demand for which orders have not yet been received. In addition to the forecast demands, extra demands, such as demand for spares and parts, are added to the MPS. Then these requirements are all summed by the delivery time period to make up the total demand facing the organization over the planning horizon. As more firm orders come in, they continue to replace or "consume" the forecasted orders, as shown in Figure 7.4. The items still remaining in the forecast that have not been replaced by firm orders are considered *available to promise* by sales.

The MPS is usually stated in terms of weekly periods, or *buckets*, as they are called. Some firms use days, and some even use hours. Nevertheless, the disaggregation of the quarterly, or monthly, production plan into MPS buckets is still the same. The planning horizon may extend for a year or more, but it must extend at least as long as the longest lead time item in the product. Otherwise, the demands cannot be placed on the schedule. For example, if you maintained a 12-month MPS and had a component that took 15 months to obtain, you wouldn't be able to schedule the delivery of orders taken today (and due to be delivered in 16 months or so).

In some situations (such as make-to-order firms), final products are assembled to order from existing components, modules, or assemblies that have been pro-

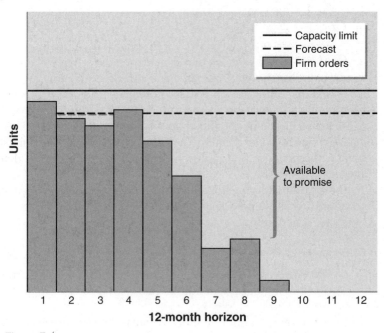

Figure 7.4   Orders replacing the forecast in the master schedule.

duced at some earlier time. That is, the assemblies are produced to stock and scheduled on the MPS, but the final products are produced to order and scheduled on a separate final assembly schedule. This is shown in Figure 7.5. Note that the final demands total to the MPS, but the specific *combination* of components was unknown until the actual orders arrived. Automobiles, some computers, and pre-fabricated homes are made this way. And some restaurants prepare meals in this way, to meet peak demand periods with only one cook or only a few workers.

An MPS is needed for both job shops and flow shops, although the detailed issues of scheduling are different, as will be seen later. That is, both require a production schedule that satisfies customers' demands but doesn't exceed the limits of capacity. Nevertheless, just because aggregate capacity may be satisfied for a workstation or facility, certain scheduling aspects may limit the use of that capacity and thereby pose another problem for the MPS, if not the entire production plan. We will discuss these kinds of problems later.

Although we appear to discuss master scheduling as a static process, in reality it is very dynamic, changing continually and being reworked weekly. It is best visualized as a rolling schedule that is replanned every week, the previous week being deleted and a new week being added at the end of the planning horizon.

The MPS itself includes four separate periods in the planning horizon that serve four unique purposes, as shown in Figure 7.6. First, there is usually an immediately upcoming *frozen* period, delineated by a *time fence*, during which orders can no longer be changed because critical subcomponents have already been ordered, produced, or installed. This frozen period is usually stated as one month because many products are assembled in the last two or three weeks before delivery. Up

Master schedule

Week	1	2	3	4
Chrome cylinders	10	15	12	8
Cast-iron cylinders	25	28	22	17
4" pistons	20	24	18	15
5" pistons	15	19	16	10

Week 1: Final assembly schedule based on firm orders

Cyl.	Piston	Mon	Tu	Wed	Th	Fr	Total
Ch	4"	1	2	1	2	1	7
CI	4"	2	3	3	3	2	13
Ch	5"	1	0	1	0	1	3
CI	5"	2	3	2	3	2	12

20 – 4" ⊢ 10 Ch
— 25 CI
15 – 5"

Figure 7.5 Master and final assembly schedules: custom pumps division.

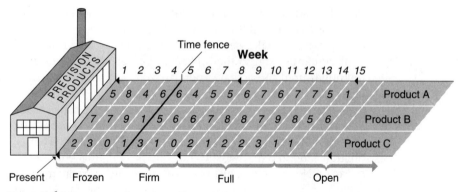

Figure 7.6   Four periods in the rolling MPS.

until assembly, the components are still being made in the shop, and changes may still be possible in their manufacture or assembly.

Following this time is a *firm* period of just a few weeks when changes may be taken, but only if they are exceptional. These changes may require approval from a senior manager. The next period is called *full* because the forecast has been fully consumed, so no more orders can be taken. However, changes may be taken in existing orders. Last is the *open* period, when there are still items available to promise.

Rough-Cut Capacity Planning

Rough-cut capacity planning uses historical ratios to distribute a load of products across the various workstations (or work centers). The ratios give the number of work hours needed in each station to produce one of each of the products required.

After the workloads are distributed, on the basis of the initial master schedule, they are totaled and compared against the capacity available at each of the workstations. If a workstation is overloaded, some action must be taken; either additional capacity must be found (e.g., overtime or subcontracting) or the master schedule must be changed. Underloads are also checked in order to keep the workstations well utilized. If an underload exists, more work may be added through changes in the master schedule, or capacity (e.g., workers) may be shifted out of that workstation.

$\mathscr{S}$CHEDULING SERVICES

In this section we consider the scheduling of pure services. Much of what was said previously applies to the scheduling of services as well as products, but here we consider some scheduling issues of particular relevance to services.

Up to now we have dealt primarily with situations where the jobs (or recipients) were the items to be loaded, sequenced, or scheduled. There are, however, many operations for which scheduling of the jobs themselves is either inappropriate or impossible, and it is necessary to concentrate instead on scheduling one or more of the input resources. Therefore, the staff, the materials, or the facilities are scheduled to correspond, as closely as possible, with the expected arrival of the jobs. Such situations are common in service systems such as supermarkets, hospitals, urban alarm services, colleges, restaurants, and airlines.

In the scheduling of jobs we were primarily interested in minimizing the number of late jobs, minimizing the rejects, maximizing the throughput, and maximizing the utilization of available resources. In the scheduling of resources, however, there may be considerably more criteria of interest, especially when one of the resources being scheduled is staff. The desires of the staff regarding shifts, holidays, and work schedules become critically important when work schedules are variable and not all employees are on the same schedule. In these situations there usually exist schedules that will displease everyone and schedules that will satisfy most of the staff's more important priorities—and it is crucial that one of the latter be chosen rather than one of the former.

Approaches to Resource Scheduling

The primary approach to the scheduling of resources is to match availability to demand (e.g., 7 P.M.–12 A.M. is the high period for fire alarms). By so doing, we are not required to provide a continuing high level of resources that are poorly utilized the great majority of the time. However, this requires that a good forecast of demand be available for the proper scheduling of resources. If demand cannot be accurately predicted, the resulting service with variable resources might be worse than using a constant level of resources.

Methods of increasing resources for peak demand include using overtime and part-time help and leasing equipment and facilities. Also, if multiple areas within an organization tend to experience varying demand, it is often helpful to use *floating* workers or combine departments to minimize variability. On occasion, new technologies, such as 24-hour automated tellers and paying bills by telephone, can aid the organization.

As mentioned previously, the use of promotion and advertising to shift *demand* for resources is highly practical in many situations. Thus, we see *off-peak pricing* in the utilities and communication industries, summer sales of snowblowers in retailing, and cut rates for transportation and tours both in off-peak seasons (fall, winter) and at off-peak times (weekends, nights). Let us now consider how some specific service organizations approach their scheduling problems.

Hospitals

There are multiple needs for scheduling in hospitals. Although arrivals of patients (the jobs) are in part uncontrollable (e.g., emergencies), they are to some extent controllable through selective admissions for hernia operations, some maternity cases, in-hospital observation, and so on. With selective admissions, the hospital administrator can smooth the demand faced by the hospital and thereby improve service and increase the utilization of the hospital's limited resources.

Very specialized, expensive equipment such as a kidney machine is also carefully scheduled to allow other hospitals access to it, thus maximizing its utilization.

By sharing such expensive equipment among a number of hospitals, more hospitals have access to modern technology for their patients at a reasonable level of investment.

Of all the scheduling in hospitals, the most crucial is probably the scheduling of nurses, as illustrated in the following example describing Harper Hospital (Filley 1983). This is because (1) it is mandatory, given the nature of hospitals, that nurses always be available; (2) nursing resources are a large expense for a hospital; and (3) there are a number of constraints on the scheduling of nurses, such as number of days per week, hours per day, weeks per year, and hours during the day.

Like many other hospitals, Harper Hospital of Detroit was under heavy pressure from Blue Cross, Medicare, and Medicaid to provide more health care at less cost. In addition, it needed to achieve more economies of scale from a merger that had taken place some years before. It also desired to improve its patient care. One target to help achieve these goals was a better system for scheduling nurses.

Previously, nurses were scheduled on the basis of strict bed counts, problems with inadequate staffing during the prior day, and requests for extra help. What was developed was a *patient classification system* (PCS) that incorporated labor standards to determine what levels of nursing were needed. At the end of each shift, designated nurses evaluated each area's patients by their condition and assigned them to a "care level" ranging from minimal to intensive. An hour before the next shift begins, the patients' needs for care are added up—accounting for new admissions, checkouts, and returns from surgery—to determine the total levels of care required. Given the levels in each area, nursing labor standards are used to determine how many nurses are needed on the next shift.

As a result of the new system, both the quality of patient care and the nurses' satisfaction went up. Annual labor savings from the new system were estimated as exceeding $600,000. Harper has further fine-tuned the PCS system and now recalibrates its standards every two years.

Urban Alarm Services

In urban services that respond to alarms—such as police, fire, and rescue services—the jobs (alarms) appear randomly and must be quickly serviced with sufficient resources. Otherwise, extreme loss of life or property may result. In many ways this problem is similar to that of a hospital, since the cost of staffing personnel is a major expense, but floating fire companies and police SWAT units may be utilized where needed, and some services (such as fire inspection) can be scheduled to help *smooth* demand.

Sometimes a major difference vastly complicates some of these services (particularly fire): ***duty tours*** of extended duration, as opposed to regular shifts, run over multiple days. These tours vary from 24 to 48 hours in teams of two to four members. Common schedules for such services are "two (days) on and three off" and "one on and two off," with every fifth tour or so off as well (for a running time off, every 3 weeks, of perhaps 3 + 2 + 3 = 8 days). Because living and sleeping-in are considered part of the job requirements, the standard workweek is in excess of 40 hours—common values are 50 and 54 hours. Clearly, the scheduling of such duty tours is a complex problem, not only because of the unusual duration of the tours but also because of the implications concerning overtime, temptations of "moonlighting," and other such issues.

Educational Services

Colleges and universities have scheduling requirements for all types of transformations: intermittent (such as counseling), continuous (English 1), batch (committee meetings), and project (regional conferences). In some of these situations the jobs (students) are scheduled, in some the staff (faculty administrators) are scheduled, and in others the facilities (classrooms, convention centers) are scheduled.

The primary problem, however, involves the scheduling of classes, assignment of students, and allocation of facilities and faculty resources to these classes. To obtain a manageable schedule, three difficult elements must be coordinated in this process:

1. Accurate forecast of students' demand for classes
2. Limitations on available classroom space
3. Multiple needs and desires of the faculty, such as

   - Number of "preparations"
   - Number of classes
   - Timing of classes
   - Level of classes
   - Leave requirements (sabbatical, maternity, etc.)
   - Release requirements (research, projects, administration)

Because of the number of objectives in such scheduling problems, a variety of multicriteria approaches have been used to aid in finding acceptable schedules, including simulation, goal programming, and interactive modeling.

In summary, the approach to scheduling services is usually to match resources and forecasted demand. Since demand cannot be controlled, it is impossible to build up inventory ahead of time, and backordering is usually not feasible. Careful scheduling of staff, facilities, and materials is done instead, with (limited) flexibility achieved through floating part-time and overtime labor and off-peak rates to encourage leveling of demand. The best schedule is often not the one that optimizes the use of resources or minimizes lateness for the expected demand, but rather the one that gives acceptable results under all likely operating conditions. As described in Chapter 6, an important aspect of scheduling services is the queues that tend to build up if capacity is inadequate. Here, queuing theory and psychology concerning waiting can be profitably applied.

Yield/Revenue Management and Overbooking

Yield management, also sometimes called *revenue management,* is the attempt to allocate the fixed capacity of a service (although the process is now being used by retailers and manufacturers, also) to match the highest revenue demand in the marketplace. It appears that American Airlines was one of the first to develop this technique but its use has spread to hotels, cruise lines, and other services who hold a fixed capacity for revenue-producing customers, jobs, items, and so on. As described by Kimes (1989), yield management is most appropriate under the following circumstances.

1. **Fixed capacity:** There is only a limited, indivisible number of capacity openings available for the period. There is no flexibility in either dividing up the capacity or in finding additional capacity.

2. **Perishable capacity:** Once the period passes, the capacity can no longer be used for that period. There is essentially no salvage value for the capacity.

3. **Segmentable market:** The demand for the capacity must be segmentable into different revenue/profit classes, such as business versus pleasure, Saturday night stayover or not, deluxe and budget, and so on.

4. **Capacity sold in advance:** The capacity is sold by reservation. Using yield management techniques, certain classes of capacity are held back for certain, more profitable classes of reservations or periods of the season. If the profitable classes fail to fill by a certain time point, some of the capacity is then released for the next lowest profit class. This procedure cascades down through both reservation classes and time points as the period in question approaches.

5. **Uncertain demand:** Although demand for each of the reservation classes may be forecast, the actual demand experienced in each of the classes for each of the time periods is uncertain.

6. **Low marginal sales cost, high marginal capacity addition cost:** The cost to add a unit of capacity is extremely high but the cost to sell (rent) a unit of it for the period in question is low.

The technique used to determine how to allocate capacity among the different classes is similar to that used for **overbooking**. Overbooking is an attempt to reduce costs through better schedule management, as illustrated by Scandinavian Airlines (Alstrup et al. 1989). Scandinavian Airlines (SAS) operates a fleet of DC-9 aircraft with 110 seats each. If SAS accepts reservations for only these 110 seats, "no-shows" (passengers who fail to show up for a flight) will refuse to pay for their reservations and SAS can lose from 5 to 30 percent of the available seats. If there are 100 flights every day, these no-shows can cost the airline as much as $50 million a year. To avoid this loss, all airlines overbook flights by accepting a fixed percentage of reservations in excess of what is actually available.

The management of SAS decided to develop an automated overbooking system to include such factors as class, destination, days before departure, current reservations, and existing cancellations. The objective of the system was to determine an optimal overbooking policy for the different classes on each flight, considering the costs of ill will, alternative flight arrangements, empty seats, and upgrading or downgrading a passenger's reserved class.

A number of interesting findings were made in the process of conducting the study. For example, an early finding was that the probability that a reservation would be canceled was independent of the time the reservation was made. When the system was completed, it was tested against the heuristics used by experienced employees who had a good "feel" for what the overbooking rate should be. It was

$\mathcal{T}$ABLE 7.3 • Demand for Flights

No. of No-Shows	Relative Frequency
4	0.10
3	0.20
2	0.35
1	0.25
0	0.10
	1.00

found that the automated system would increase SAS's net revenue by about $2 million a year.

To better understand the situation and demonstrate the solution approach, let us assume that the number of seats on a plane is fixed at 28. How many reservations should the airline accept, given the chances described in Table 7.3 of no-shows? For example, if 32 reservations are accepted, the probability that only 30 passengers show up is 35 percent.

Suppose that a profit of $50 is made for each passenger carried, but a cost is incurred if a passenger with a reservation has to be turned away. This cost could be a free ticket, ill will, passage on another airline, or whatever. If the cost is low—say, less than the profit—then it will be to the airline's advantage to overbook quite a bit (although possibly not all the way to 32, since there would then be a 90 percent chance of having an overbooking cost). On the other hand, suppose that the cost is very high—much more than the profit. Then the airline would be very reluctant to overbook much at all, out of fear of having to pay one or more costs of overbooking. Table 7.4 gives the probabilities of demand for each set of overbookings accepted, as specified in the previous paragraph. Assume that turning a passenger away costs the airline $20, how many reservations should be accepted? Suppose the cost is $100.

Using the probabilities of no-shows (shown in Table 7.3), we can calculate the costs and profits according to Table 7.5. (There is no sense in accepting more than

$\mathcal{T}$ABLE 7.4 • Demand Probabilities
  with Reservations

Relative Frequency	Reservations				
	28	29	30	31	32
0.10	24	25	26	27	28
0.20	25	26	27	28	29
0.35	26	27	28	29	30
0.25	27	28	29	30	31
0.10	28	29	30	31	32
1.00					

32 reservations, because this will definitely fill the plane.) Here we see that the total profit is $1359. The process is repeated for 31 reservations, and the calculations are given in Table 7.6. Continuing with 30, 29, and 28 reservations (it makes no sense to accept fewer than 28 reservations), we get the values shown in Table 7.7. Clearly, the maximum profit is obtained with 31 reservations. If the turnaway cost is raised to $100, the results are shown in Table 7.8. Now the highest profit is obtained with 29 reservations.

$\mathcal{T}$ABLE 7.5 • Expected Profit with 32 Reservations

	Demand					
	28	29	30	31	32	Total
Probabilities	0.10	0.20	0.35	0.25	0.10	
Seats filled (S)	28	28	28	28	28	
Profit: $50 S	1400	1400	1400	1400	1400	
Turnaways (T)	0	1	2	3	4	
Cost: $20 T	0	20	40	60	80	
Net profit	1400	1380	1360	1340	1320	
Expected net profit	140	276	476	335	132	$1359

$\mathcal{T}$ABLE 7.6 • Expected Profit with 31 Reservations

	Demand					
	27	28	29	30	31	Total
Probabilities	0.10	0.20	0.35	0.25	0.10	
Seats filled (S)	27	28	28	28	28	
Profit: $50 S	1350	1400	1400	1400	1400	
Turnaways (T)	0	0	1	2	3	
Cost: $20 T	0	0	20	40	60	
Net profit	1350	1400	1380	1360	1340	
Expected net profit	135	280	483	340	134	$1372

$\mathcal{T}$ABLE 7.7 • Expected Profit at $20 Turnaway Cost

Reservations	Expected Profits
32	$1359
31	$1372 (best)
30	$1371
29	$1345.5
28	$1302.5

$\mathcal{T}$ABLE 7.8 • Expected Profit at $100 Turnaway Cost

Reservations	Expected Profits
32	$1195
31	$1280
30	$1335
29	$1337.5 (best)
28	$1302.5

EXPAND YOUR UNDERSTANDING

1. Why go through the process of aggregating forecasts to produce an aggregate plan, which is then disaggregated into the actual product or service master schedule? Why not just use the individual forecasts to produce the master schedule?

2. Describe the role of sales in setting the master schedule. Is its only concern to get as much produced as possible? What else may sales be concerned about when it helps set the schedule?

3. A lot of scheduling seems to be the straightforward manipulation of data, applying ratios, batching lots, meeting deadlines, converting pounds to units, and so on. Couldn't all this be done by computer? What would be hard to do by computer?

4. Describe any of your experiences with level production or chase demand. Do these concepts apply only to businesses? Where else might you see them?

5. Suppose you are a production scheduler and receive a notice from sales that a customer has canceled an order that was in the frozen portion of the master schedule. Would you go ahead and build the product anyway because the schedule is frozen? Or would you immediately stop work on the order? If you stopped work, what good is having a frozen schedule that really is not frozen?

6. In what way is rough-cut capacity planning actually "rough"? What does it ignore?

7. How ethical is it to overbook (and guarantee) limited service capacity in a restaurant? What about a hospital, where lack of service could have serious, perhaps fatal, consequences?

8. Many services, such as airlines, conduct their scheduling in two stages. First, an overall macro schedule is constructed and optimized for costs and service to the customer. This schedule is then considered to be the baseline for detailed scheduling to attempt to achieve. The second, detailed stage is then a real-time schedule to adjust the macro schedule for any necessary changes, emergencies, and so on. Describe how this might work for airlines, hospitals, schools, and urban alarm services. What serious problems might arise with this approach?

APPLY YOUR UNDERSTANDING
Grassboy, Inc.

Grassboy, Inc., produces a line of lawn mowers in a variety of engine sizes and cutting widths. In an effort to deal with the highly seasonal nature of its demand, Grassboy forecasts demand for the next eight quarters. The forecast for the next eight quarters is given in the following table.

Quarter	Demand Forecast
1	5000
2	7500
3	15,000
4	5000
5	6000
6	8000
7	16000
8	5500

Grassboy has a single production line that can assemble 7000 units per quarter per shift using regular time and can assemble an additional 25 percent using overtime. The assembly line can be operated for either one or two shifts; however, the union contract permits making changes to the number of shifts only at the beginning of a quarter. The company is permitted to send the workers home early without pay if its plans call for producing less than 7000 units in a given quarter. The cost of adding a shift is $7500, and the cost of eliminating a shift is $14,000. Grassboy also has identified several overseas manufacturers that can produce as many of its lawn mowers as needed as subcontractors.

On average, the cost of producing a single lawn mower is $25 per mower using regular time and $33 using overtime. The delivered cost of mowers produced by subcontractors is $49. Grassboy's cost of holding a lawn mower in inventory for one quarter is $4, and the cost of backordering a unit is $12 per quarter. Inventory costs are calculated on the basis of average inventory held during the quarter (i.e., the average of the quarter's beginning and ending inventory). Backorder costs are calculated on the basis of the ending backorder position in a given quarter.

Grassboy was operating with one shift in the quarter just ending and expects to end the quarter with 750 units in inventory.

Questions

1. Develop an aggregate plan that calls for a constant level of employment that meets the fluctuations in demand by using inventory, backorders, overtime, subcontracting, or some combination of these. Assume that all demand must be met by the eighth quarter.

2. Develop an aggregate plan that meets the fluctuations in demand by adjusting the number of shifts.

3. What are the advantages and disadvantages of the aggregate schedules you developed? Which one would you recommend to Grassboy's management?

EXERCISES

1. How many workers are needed with level production to meet quarterly demands of 45, 65, 50, and 40 if each worker can produce 5 units a quarter? Recalculate your answer if there are already 20 units in inventory. Recalculate again assuming that there are 20 inventory units but also that 10 units are required as safety stock.

2. Currently, 2 workers can each produce 10 units a quarter. Find the long-run average annual cost of using overtime (at $20/unit) and undertime (at $10/unit) to chase quarterly demands of 40, 60, 30, and 20.

3. Use the same data as in Exercise 2 but use hiring and layoffs, at a cost of $30 each, to chase demand.

4. Find the costs of inventory and backordering with level production to meet quarterly demands of 20, 50, 30, and 40. Inventory costs $10/unit/quarter, and backordering costs $15/unit/quarter.

5. Demand forecasts of the year for your product for each quarter are 120, 140, 110, and 90, with this pattern repeating in the future as far as can be told.

The current workforce is 11, and each worker can produce 10 units in a quarter. Inventory costs are $10 per unit per quarter, whereas shortage costs with backordering are $13 per unit per quarter. Hiring and layoff costs $100 per worker, but idle workers cost $150 a quarter. Cost to produce units on overtime is an additional $15 each. Find the best long-term production plan if all demand must be met.

6. A restaurant has 30 tables. If it accepts N reservations, the probability that N will arrive is 0.1; N–1 is 0.2; N–2 is 0.3; and N–3 is 0.4. If each unfilled table costs $20 but a customer turned away costs $10, find how many reservations to accept. Solve again, assuming that a customer turned away costs $25.

7. The Arms Hotel has 56 rooms. An unfilled room represents $50 a night in lost profit, whereas every turnaway due to a filled room costs $30 in ill will. If N reservations are accepted, the probability of N, N–1, and N–2 guests actually showing up is 0.2, 0.5, 0.3, respectively. How many reservations should be accepted?

BIBLIOGRAPHY

Alstrup, J., S.-E. Andersson, S. Boas, O. B. G. Madsen, and R. V. V. Vidal. "Booking Control Increases Profit at Scandinavian Airlines." *Interfaces* (July–August 1989): 10–19.

Collier, D. A. *Service Management: Operating Decisions*. Englewood Cliffs, N.J.: Prentice-Hall, 1987.

Filley, R. D. "Cost Effective Patient Care: Harper-Grace Hospitals." *Industrial Engineering* (Jan. 1983): 48–52.

Goldratt, E. Y., and J. Cox. *The Goal*. New York: North River, 1984.

Greene, J. H., ed. *Production and Inventory Control Handbook*, 2nd ed. New York: McGraw-Hill, 1987.

Kimes, S. E. "Yield Management: A Tool for Capacity-Constrained Service Firms." *Journal of Operations Management*, vol. 8, no. 4 (Oct. 1989): 348–363.

Krajewski, L. J., and, L. P. Ritzman. "Shift Scheduling in Banking Operations: A Case Application." *Interfaces* (April 1980): 1–7.

Lovelock, C. "Strategies for Managing Capacity-Constrained Service Organizations." *Service Industries Journal* (Nov. 1984).

Orkin, E. B. "Boosting Your Bottom Line with Yield Management." *Cornell Hotel and Restaurant Administration Quarterly* (Feb. 1988): 52–56.

Schramm, W. R., and Freund, L. E. "Application of Economic Control Charts by a Nursing Modeling Team." *Industrial Engineering* (April 1993): 27–31.

Tho, R. "An Inventory Depletion Overbooking Model for the Hotel Industry." *Journal of Travel Research* (Spring 1985): 24–30.

Trail, D. T. "Package Products Capitalizes on Data." *APICS—The Performance Advantage* (August 1996): 38–41.

Vollmann, T. E., W. L. Berry, and D. C. Whybark. *Manufacturing Planning and Control Systems*, 2nd ed. Homewood, Ill.: Irwin, 1988.

CHAPTER 8

Materials Management

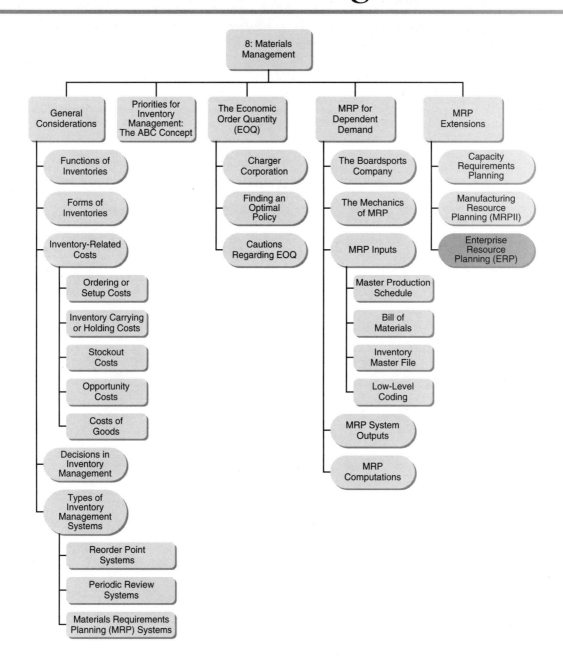

CHAPTER IN PERSPECTIVE

Materials management deals with determining how much and when to order to support the production plan. After discussing the functions and forms of inventory, inventory-related costs, and types of inventory management systems, the ABC classification system for prioritizing inventory items is overviewed. Next, the economic order quantity (EOQ) model is discussed for independent demand items and materials requirements planning for dependent demand items. The chapter concludes with some extensions to material requirements planning including capacity requirements planning (CRP), manufacturing resource planning (MRP II), and enterprise resource planning (ERP).

INTRODUCTION

- A custom-designed inventory management system has helped transform Mothers Work, Inc., from a small mail-order company to the dominant retailer of maternity clothes. The inventory system provides details down to the level of individual garments and gives managers a comprehensive picture of the entire inventory pipeline. The system provides daily reports on what is and what isn't selling, and how long before more product can be purchased or made. Also, Mothers Work uses the system to test market fashions in stores before committing itself to large production runs. In addition, monitoring daily sales figures allows the company to produce more of hot-selling styles in two weeks or less and to speed new ideas from the design table to stores. Other retail stores are often restricted to selling styles selected six months in advance. Having the ability to wait until the last possible moment before ordering or producing garments greatly minimizes the need to mark down slow-selling styles and helps maintain sufficient inventory levels of styles the customers desire (Bird 1996).

- Electronic commerce (e-commerce) is no longer simply a management buzzword; it is fundamentally changing the way products are bought and sold. Over the last decade large companies such as Wal-Mart, General Motors, Eastman Kodak, and Baxter International have been developing private computer networks for controlling the flow of goods across the value chain. Still evolving, these private networks are moving to the public Internet. One major advantage of these networks is that less time and money is spent reentering information into different computer systems. Campbell Soup, for example, estimates that 60 percent of the orders it receives contain mistakes. As a result, salespeople spend 40 percent of their time fixing these problems instead of selling. With these and other savings, it is estimated that e-commerce will reduce the costs of processing a purchase order from $150 to $25. As another example, Fruit of the Loom developed a system to link its 50 wholesalers to its central warehouse. With the system, its central inventory becomes virtual inventory for the wholesalers. For example, if a silk-screener needs black T-shirts for a coming concert and the wholesaler is low, Fruit of the Loom's central warehouse is notified and the T-shirts are shipped from there directly to the customer (Verity 1996).

- Courtaulds Films produces plastic films used to package food products, such as candy bars and potato chips. Its plants, located in England and France, are operated 24 hours a day 7 days a week and supply food manufacturers worldwide. The company uses 60 types of raw material to produce 40 types of film and offers a total of 12,500 make-to-order end products. At the end of the 1980s, 25 percent of its deliveries were shipped late because its production planning and scheduling system was unable to handle the complexity inherent in this situation. In an effort to reach a goal of 95 percent on-time shipments, managers at Courtaulds visited the Formica Company and learned about its manufacturing resource planning (MRP II) system. By the early 1990s, Courtaulds had implemented its own MRP II system and distinguished itself as a class A user. The employees now take a great deal of pride in their excellent on-time performance (Goddard 1992).

- Recording for the Blind & Dyslexic (RFB&D) is the only national nonprofit organization that loans textbooks in recorded or computerized formats to individuals who cannot read standard print because of a visual, perceptual, or other physical disability. When RFB&D was about to move from its existing facility in New York to a new facility in New Jersey, it took the opportunity to design and implement a new, integrated production system utilizing high technology materials-handling automation. RFB&D faces the difficult situation of having to satisfy, with extremely limited resources, an annual increase in demand for its books of 3 to 5 percent. Moreover, fast response is critical because many requests are for textbooks needed for classes that are soon to begin.

   With limited space, only limited inventories of recordings can be maintained, and access must be swift and reliable. RFB&D's goals were to achieve a lead time of no more than two working days and to reduce the production cost per book served. Before the move and installation of the system, performance was 333 books per day. This had to be increased 28 percent, at the same cost per book or less. Thus, RFB&D turned to a version of MRP known as resource requirements planning (RRP). This new software was teamed with new or upgraded hardware to achieve RFB&D's goals. Specifically, automated carousels were obtained for fast storage and retrieval of the 45,000 most active titles. Six hundred feet of overhead conveyors were added to connect all workstations. The speed of the machines that copied master recordings to cassettes was doubled. An automated sorting system was added for returned cassettes, and a bar code reader was installed for computer processing of mailed and returned cassettes. The results were gratifying: 27 percent more books could be produced, unit costs were reduced 16 percent (representing nearly $500,000, or 13 percent of RFB&D's annual budget), and 97 percent of the orders were mailed within five working days. (Almost half of those were mailed within 24 hours.) (Jarkon and Nanda 1985).

In Chapter 7, we discussed the dynamics of scheduling operations. In this chapter we continue our discussion by looking at the uses of inventories, and the means of determining the best levels of inventories to hold. The chapter considers both purchased and internally produced inventories. Although we describe various functions of inventories, the material in the chapter focuses largely on cycle inventories that are replenished on a regular basis in "lots" or batches—that is, where the production of the materials is not produced by a continuous or flow process.

Our focus then shifts to managing the inventory of dependent-demand items. *Dependent-demand* items are so named because their demand is derived from (depends on) the demand for independent-demand items (usually finished goods). Although the calculations involved in managing dependent-demand items are not very complicated, the quantity of data can be overwhelming, as the Courtaulds example illustrates. Therefore, materials management systems for dependent-demand items typically require a computer.

The examples in the introduction illustrate a number of other important issues related to managing dependent-demand items. First, Courtaulds Films illustrates how computers can help an organization cope with the complexity of managing a large number of materials. RFB&D and Courtaulds illustrate a second important issue—the increasing emphasis many organizations are placing on reducing lead times and meeting delivery schedules. Finally, both RFB&D and Courtaulds demonstrate the importance of integrating the materials management system with the rest of the organization, especially with the production scheduling system.

From Chapter 7, as well as the earlier examples, it is clear that the materials management systems must fit closely with the scheduling systems. In fact, such systems are typically known as *production and inventory control systems*. This tie has become closer with the development of computerized production planning and control systems, since the management of tremendous quantities and varieties of materials is not the problem for computers that it was for manual systems. This has allowed the two systems to be joined, for both substantial savings in costs and significant improvement in the control of materials and operations, thereby resulting in higher productivity, adherence to promised due dates, and other such benefits.

GENERAL CONSIDERATIONS

Although inventory is inanimate, the topic of inventory and inventory control can arouse completely different sentiments in the minds of people in various departments within an organization. The salespeople generally prefer large quantities of inventory to be on hand. In this way they can meet customers' requests without having to wait. Customer service is their primary concern. The accounting and financial personnel see inventory in a different light. High inventories do not translate into high customer service in the accountant's language; rather, they translate into large amounts of tied-up capital that could otherwise be used to reduce debt or for other more economically advantageous purposes. From the viewpoint of the operations manager, inventories are a tool that can be used to promote efficient operation of the production facilities. Neither high inventories nor low inventories, per se, are desirable; inventories are simply allowed to fluctuate so that production can be adjusted to its most efficient level. And top management's concern is with the "bottom line"—what advantages the inventories are providing versus their costs.

Functions of Inventories

There are many purposes for holding inventory but, in general, inventories have five basic functions. Be aware that inventories will not generally be identified and segregated within the organization by these functions and that not all functions will be represented in all organizations.

1. ***Transit inventories***: Transit inventories exist because materials must be moved from one location to another. (These are also known as ***pipeline inventories***.) A truckload of merchandise from a retailer's regional warehouse to one of its retail stores is an example of transit inventory. This inventory results because of the transportation time required.

2. ***Buffer inventories***: Another purpose of inventories is to protect against the uncertainties of supply and demand. Buffer inventories—or, as they are sometimes called, ***safety stocks***—serve to cushion the effect of unpredictable events. The amount of inventory over and above the average demand requirement is considered to be buffer stock held to meet any demand in excess of the average. The higher the level of inventory, the better the customer service—that is, the fewer the ***stockouts*** and ***backorders***. A stockout exists when a customer's order for an item cannot be filled because the inventory of that item has run out. If there is a stockout, the firm will usually backorder the item immediately, rather than wait until the next regular ordering period.

3. ***Anticipation inventories***: An anticipated future event such as a price increase, a strike, or a seasonal increase in demand is the reason for holding anticipation inventories. For example, rather than operating with excessive overtime in one period and then allowing the productive system to be idle or shut down because of insufficient demand in another period, inventories can be allowed to build up before an event to be consumed during or after the event. Manufacturers, wholesalers, and retailers build anticipation inventories before occasions such as Christmas and Halloween, when demand for specialized products will be high.

4. ***Decoupling inventories***: It would be a rare production system in which all equipment and personnel operated at exactly the same rate. Yet if you were to take an inspection tour through a production facility, you would notice that most of the equipment and people were producing. Products move smoothly even though one machine can process parts five times as fast as the one before or after it. An inventory of parts between machines, or fluid in a vat, known as decoupling inventory, acts to disengage the production system. That is, inventories act as shock absorbers, or cushions, increasing and decreasing in size as parts are added to and used up from the stock. Even if a preceding machine were to break down, the following machines could still produce (at least for a while), since an in-process inventory of parts would be waiting for production. The more inventories management carries between stages in the manufacturing and distribution system, the less coordination is needed to keep the system running smoothly. Clearly, there is an optimum balance between inventory level and coordination in the operations system. Without decoupling inventories, each operation in the

plant would have to produce at an identical rate (a paced line) to keep the production flowing smoothly, and when one operation broke down, the entire plant would come to a standstill.

5. **Cycle inventories**: Cycle inventories—or, as they are sometimes referred to, *lot-size* inventories—exist for a different reason from the others just discussed. Each of the previous types of inventories serves one of the major purposes for holding inventory. Cycle inventories, on the other hand, result from management's attempt to minimize the total cost of carrying and ordering inventory. If the annual demand for a particular part is 12,000 units, management could decide to place one order for 12,000 units and maintain a rather large inventory throughout the year or place 12 orders of 1000 each and maintain a lower level of inventory. But the costs associated with ordering and receiving would increase. Cycle inventories are the inventories that result from ordering in batches or "lots" rather than as needed.

Forms of Inventories

Inventories are usually classified into four forms, some of which correspond directly with the previous inventory functions but some of which do not.

1. *Raw materials*: Raw materials are objects, commodities, elements, and items that are received (usually purchased) from outside the organization to be used directly in the production of the final output. When we think of raw materials, we think of such things as sheet metal, flour, paint, structural steel, chemicals, and other basic materials. But nuts and bolts, hydraulic cylinders, pizza crusts, syringes, engines, frames, integrated circuits, and other assemblies purchased from outside the organization would also be considered part of the raw materials inventory.

2. *Maintenance, repair, and operating supplies*: Maintenance, repair, and operating (MRO) supplies are items used to support and maintain the operation, including spares, supplies, and stores. Spares are sometimes produced by the organization itself rather than purchased. These are usually machine parts or supplies that are crucial to production. The term *supplies* is often used synonymously with *inventories*. The general convention, and the one that we will adopt in this book, is that supplies are stocks of items used (consumed) in the production of goods or services but are not directly a part of the finished product. Examples are copier paper, staples, pencils, and packing material. Stores commonly include both supplies and raw materials that are kept in stock or on shelves in a special location.

3. *Work-in-process*: **Work-in-process (WIP)** inventory consists of all the materials, parts, and assemblies that are being worked on or are waiting to be processed within the operations system. Decoupling inventories are an example of work-in-process. That is, they are all the items that have left the raw materials inventory but have not yet been converted or assembled into a final product.

4. *Finished goods*: The **finished goods** inventory is the stock of completed products. Goods, once completed, are transferred out of work-in-process

inventory and into the finished goods inventory. From here they can be sent to distribution centers, sold to wholesalers, or sold directly to retailers or final customers.

As you can see from this discussion, the inventory system and the operations system within an organization are strongly interrelated. Inventories affect customer service, utilization of facilities and equipment, capacity, and efficiency of labor. Therefore, the plans concerning the acquisition and storage of materials, or "inventories," are vital to the production system.

The ultimate objective of any inventory system is to make decisions regarding the level of inventory that will result in a good balance between the purposes for holding inventories and the costs associated with them. Typically, we hear inventory management practitioners and researchers speaking of *total cost minimization* as the objective of an inventory system. If we were able to place dollar costs on interruptions in the smooth flow of goods through the operations system, on not meeting customers' demands, or on failures to provide the other purposes for which inventories exist, then minimization of total costs would be a reasonable objective. But, since we are unable to assign costs to many of these subjective factors, we must be satisfied with obtaining a good balance between the costs and the functions of inventories.

Inventory-Related Costs

There are essentially five broad categories of costs associated with inventory systems: ordering or setup costs, inventory carrying or holding costs, stockout costs, opportunity costs, and cost of goods. This section looks at these costs in turn.

Ordering or Setup Costs

Ordering costs are costs associated with outside procurement of material, and *setup costs* are costs associated with internal procurement (i.e., internal manufacture) of parts of material. Ordering costs include writing the order, processing the order through the purchasing system, postage, processing invoices, processing accounts payable, and the work of the receiving department, such as handling, testing, inspection, and transporting. Setup costs also include writing orders and processing for the internal production system, setup labor, machine downtime due to a new setup (i.e., cost of an idle, nonproducing machine), parts damaged during setup (e.g., actual parts are often used for tests during setup), and costs associated with employees' learning curve (i.e., the cost of early production spoilage and low productivity immediately after a new production run is started).

Inventory Carrying or Holding Costs

Inventory *carrying* or *holding* costs have the following major components:

- Capital costs
- Storage costs
- Risk costs

Capital costs include interest on money invested in inventory and in the land, buildings, and equipment necessary to hold and maintain the inventory, an item of special interest to both financial and top management. These rates often exceed 20 percent. If these investments were not required, the organization could invest the capital in an alternative that would earn some return on investment.

Storage costs include rent, taxes, and insurance on buildings; depreciation of buildings; maintenance and repairs; heat, power, and light; salaries of security personnel; taxes on the inventory; labor costs for handling inventory; clerical costs for keeping records; taxes and insurance on equipment; depreciation of equipment; fuel and energy for equipment; and repairs and maintenance. Some of these costs are variable, some fixed, and some "semifixed."

Risk costs include the costs of obsolete inventory, insurance on inventory, physical deterioration of the inventory, and losses from pilferage.

Even though some of these costs are relatively small, the total costs of carrying items in inventory can be quite large. Studies have found that for a typical manufacturing firm, the cost is frequently as large as 35 percent of the cost of the inventoried items. A large portion of this is the cost of the invested capital.

Stockout Costs

If inventory is unavailable when customers request it, a situation that marketing detests, or when it is needed for production, a stockout occurs. Several costs are associated with each type of stockout. A stockout of an item demanded by a customer or client can result in lost sales or demand, lost goodwill (which is very difficult to estimate), and costs associated with processing back orders (such as extra paperwork, expediting, special handling, and higher shipping costs). A stockout of an item needed for production results in costs for rescheduling production, costs of down time and delays caused by the shortage, the cost of "rush" shipping of needed parts, and possibly the cost of substituting a more expensive part or material.

Opportunity Costs

Often capacity and inventory costs can be traded off for one another. For example, capacity costs can be incurred because a change in productive capacity is necessary or because there is a temporary shortage of or excess in capacity. Why would capacity be too great or too small? If, for example, a company tried to meet seasonal demand (or any fluctuations in demand) by changing the level of production rather than by allowing the level of inventory to rise or fall, capacity would have to be increased during high-demand periods and lie idle during low-demand periods. Also, capacity problems are often due to scheduling conflicts. These commonly arise when multiple products have to be produced on the same set of facilities.

Opportunity costs include the overtime required to increase capacity; the human resource management costs of hiring, training, and terminating employees; the cost of using less skilled workers during peak periods; and the cost of idle time if capacity is *not* reduced during periods when demand decreases. The trade-offs in these costs were considered earlier, in Chapter 7, with regard to aggregate planning.

Cost of Goods

Last, the goods themselves must be paid for. Although they must be acquired sooner or later anyway, *when* they are acquired can influence their cost considerably, as through quantity discounts.

Decisions in Inventory Management

The objective of an inventory management system is to make decisions regarding the appropriate level of inventory and changes in the level of inventory. To maintain the appropriate level of inventory, decision rules are needed to answer two basic questions:

1. When should an order be placed to replenish the inventory?
2. How much should be ordered?

The decision rules guide the inventory manager or computerized materials management system in evaluating the current state of the inventory and deciding if some action, such as replenishment, is required. Various types of inventory management systems incorporate different rules to decide "when" and "how much." Some depend on time and others on the level of inventory, but the essential decisions are the same. Even when complexities, such as uncertainty in demand and delivery times, are introduced, deciding "how many" and "when to order" still remains the basis of sound inventory management.

Types of Inventory Management Systems

All inventory systems can be classified as one of three varieties, based on the approach taken to deciding "when to order":

1. Reorder point systems
2. Periodic review systems
3. Materials requirements planning (MRP) systems

Before we discuss these three systems, let us consider a simplified inventory management situation, to provide a background.

Consider a distributor of bottled water imported from a spring in the Swiss Alps. The distributor sells 1000 five-gallon bottles per month to residential customers in the southeast. Demand for the five-gallon bottles is constant throughout the year. Suppose that the distributor has a policy of ordering 2000 bottles per order and that it has just received a shipment of 2000, bringing its inventory level to 2000.

The distributor sells 1000 five-gallon bottles per month, and therefore the beginning inventory of 2000 units will be depleted by the end of the second month. To avoid "stocking out," an order must be placed and shipment received before the end of the second month. To keep the costs of carrying inventory as low as possible, it is desirable to schedule receipt of the order at the time that the previous inventory is exhausted. Assuming this perfect scheduling and "instantaneous replenishment" (the entire order quantity is received when the inventory level reaches zero), we can graph the inventory level as it changes over time as in Figure 8.1.

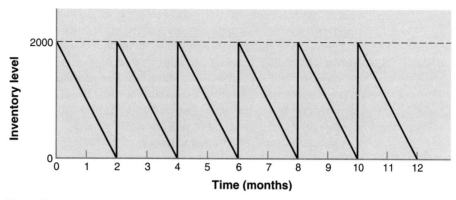

Figure 8.1   Fluctuations in inventory.

Inventory is used at the rate of 1000 per month, and orders are received so that the inventory level is replenished before a stockout can occur. No stockouts occur, and the inventory level never exceeds the order quantity of 2000. While beyond the scope of this book, we note that more sophisticated models are not dependent on the unrealistic assumptions of constant demand and instantaneous replenishment. For now, let us turn to a discussion of the three types of inventory control systems.

Reorder Point Systems

In reorder point systems an inventory *level* is specified at which a replenishment order for a fixed quantity of the inventory item is to be placed. Whenever the inventory on hand reaches the predetermined inventory level—the ***reorder point***—an order may be placed for a prespecified amount if there are no current outstanding orders, as illustrated in Figure 8.2. Note in the figure that the demand

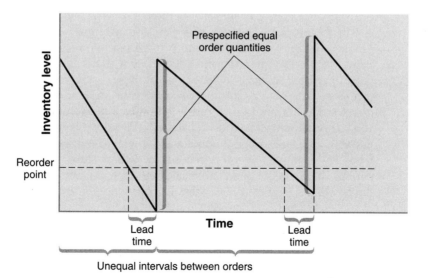

Figure 8.2   A reorder point system.

rates between cycles are not necessarily the same, which is true in general for any time periods. The reorder point is established so that the inventory on hand at the time an order is placed is sufficient to meet demand during the **lead time** (i.e., the time between placement of an order and receipt of the shipment). The quantity of inventory to be ordered is often based on the **economic order quantity (EOQ)** (one answer to the question "how much to order"), an approach illustrated later in this chapter. But other rules for deciding "how much," such as ordering a "six-week supply," are also used in reorder point systems.

A simplified and much-used variation of the reorder point system is the **two-bin** system, in which parts are stored in two bins—one large and one small. The small bin usually holds sufficient parts to satisfy demand during the replenishment lead time. Parts are used from only the large bin, until it is empty. At that time, a replenishment order is placed, and parts from the small bin are used until the replenishment order is received.

Many variations of two-bin systems have been developed. In some systems it is simply the responsibility of the employee who removes the last item from the large bin to place a requisition for materials with the purchasing department or with the supervisor. In others, a completed requisition is placed at the bottom of the larger bin and needs to be picked up and submitted only when the last item is removed. In others, a card is affixed to a wrapped quantity of items in the small bin. When these items are opened, the card is removed and sent to data processing to generate an order. The advantage of the two-bin system is that no detailed real-time records of inventory use (a **perpetual inventory system**) must be kept, and inventory need not be continually recounted to determine whether or not a reorder should be placed.

This latter point is important. A perpetual inventory system requires either a manual card system or a computerized system to keep track of daily usage and daily stock levels. Also, each day the cards or the computer file must be "searched" to find all items that have fallen to or below the reorder point. Note that these clerical functions remove the burden of assessing proper inventory levels from the people who use the inventory. Perpetual systems run into problems when those who use the inventory fail to report its use. Management controls over the inventory system must be fairly rigid to ensure that perpetual records remain accurate and, in turn, result in the proper placement of orders for inventory. This also requires a regular physical check of the inventory to be sure that the records are accurate. A reorder point system could not perform adequately without either a two-bin system or perpetual inventory control. Without one of these, someone would have to record the inventory balances for all items each day in order to have accurate counts and, therefore, to know when to order. The recent development of real-time inventory control systems that include computerized order entry and invoicing has greatly eased the difficulties of the perpetual system and reduced the need for two-bin systems. For example, inventory records at grocery stores can be instantaneously updated as items are scanned at the cash registers. Of course, actual inventory may still not be what is expected due to shrinkage (theft), spoilage, damage, and such.

Periodic Review Systems

In **periodic review systems** the inventory level is reviewed at equal time intervals, and at each review a reorder may be placed to bring the level up to a desired quantity. Such a system is especially appropriate for retailers ordering families of goods. The amount of the reorder is based on a maximum level established for each inventory item. The quantity that should be reordered is the amount necessary to bring the *on-hand* inventory plus the *on-order* quantity, less the expected demand over the lead time, up to the maximum level:

$$\text{Reorder quantity} = \text{maximum level} - \text{on-hand inventory}$$
$$- \text{ on-order quantity} + \text{demand over lead time}$$

The on-hand inventory is the amount actually in stock. If the system allows backorders, then on-hand could be negative, at least in theory. If backorders are not used, then a stockout simply results in a zero on-hand quantity.

The on-order amount is the quantity for which purchase orders have been issued, but delivery has not yet been made. We deduct the on-order quantity (Q) to ensure that an order is not placed for the same goods. Figure 8.3 illustrates such an occurrence. Suppose that at review point A an order is simply placed for Q_A. At review point B, the first order has not arrived, so an order for Q_B is placed. No attention was paid to the on-order quantity. Now, some time later, Q_A is received, and then Q_B. At review point C, inventory exceeds the desired maximum.

In periodic review systems the *review period* (and therefore the *reorder period*) is fixed, and the *order quantity varies* (see Figure 8.4) according to the rule just given. This system is more appropriate when it is difficult to keep track of inventory levels and the cost of stockouts or safety stock is not excessive. Since inventory is not continuously tracked, there is a significant chance of stocking out. This possibility can be avoided by using safety stock.

In reorder point systems the *order quantity is fixed*, and the *reorder period varies* (see Figure 8.2). This system is best where a continuing watch of inventory levels is feasible and stockouts or safety stock would be expensive. If demand

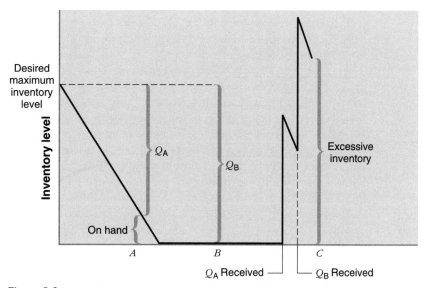

Figure 8.3   Periodic review system without considering on-order quantity.

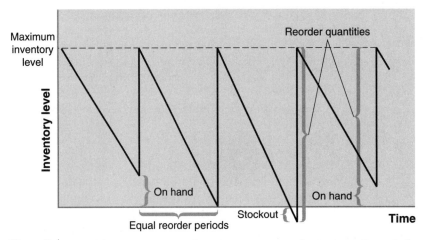

Figure 8.4   Periodic review system (assumes none on order at time of reorder).

increases during the period, the reorder point system would simply place an order sooner than normal. The periodic review system would review and place an order at the regularly scheduled time but for a quantity larger than normal. However, in both systems there is a risk of a stockout because the demand during the lead time may be greater than the amount on hand at the time the order is placed. As we will see, there are ways to compensate for this risk.

Note that it is not unusual for some organizations to use a reorder point system for some inventory items and a periodic review system for other items. For example, large grocery chains often carry inventories of some items such as canned vegetables in their own regional warehouses and rely on third-party distributors for other products such as cosmetic products. For the items available in the chain's own regional warehouse, orders are automatically submitted to the warehouse based on a reorder point system as items are scanned at the checkout. For the items supplied by the third-party distributors, orders are submitted at fixed times (e.g., once a week or once every other week) based on a physical count of what is actually on the store's shelves, what is already on order, and any special promotions that may be run.

Another type of periodic review inventory situation is that of the single-period, minimal-salvage-value problem. This situation is faced by vendors who stock a certain amount of material for an upcoming period of uncertain demand and then must resupply for the next period, a situation commonly known as the ***newsboy problem***. More specifically, a semi-perishable commodity is purchased in some order size before demand is known and is then either sold or scrapped, depending on the demand level. If an insufficient amount was ordered, the vendor loses the opportunity to have made additional profits. If too much was ordered, the vendor takes a loss (either a total loss or, if there is some salvage value, a partial loss) on the excess.

However, this problem is almost identical to that of the overbooking situation discussed in Chapter 7, except that these are products that are ordered ahead of time instead of reservations taken for the upcoming period. Nevertheless, the same type of solution approach is used: assuming one stocking/reservation level is chosen and then working out the expected value of the profits, trying the next level, and so on. Hence, we will not repeat the procedure here.

Materials Requirements Planning (MRP) Systems

The two systems discussed so far are appropriate for inventory items with fairly constant, and independent, demand. ***Independent demand*** means simply that demand for an item is not based on demand for some other item. Examples include clothing, furniture, automobiles, retail items, and supply-type items (paper, pencils) in a manufacturing or office environment. The most likely applications for the two previous systems are inventories of finished goods.

Conversely, ***dependent demand*** items are components, assemblies, and sub-assemblies of the finished item (called the *end item*), such as the bicycle tires on a bike, the lampshades, or any raw materials. These materials and parts are not usually subject to random demands from customers; they are subject primarily to the demands placed on them from the end items or assemblies they go into. Since demand for them depends on the demand for the end item, they do not require separate forecasts. For instance, Burger King does not need to forecast the demand for both hamburgers and hamburger buns, since the demand for hamburger buns depends on the demand for hamburgers (i.e., each hamburger requires one bun). Thus, we derive the demand for dependent demand items from the demand of end items, and control their inventory levels through materials requirements planning (MRP). As we will see, the MRP system considers how the product is made and how long it takes to make each of the items.

As with the perpetual and periodic inventory systems, MRP time-phases orders on the basis of lead times and minimum stocking levels, also. The size of an order can be based on an economic order quantity, six weeks' worth of stock, or any other such rule. In this regard it is not much different from the other inventory systems. However, in MRP it is not the stock level that is monitored but, rather, the demands of the parent product for the part. These expected future demands are updated continuously as the demands of the final product change, thus giving a better forecast.

PRIORITIES FOR INVENTORY MANAGEMENT: THE ABC CONCEPT

In practice, not all inventories need be controlled with equal attention. Some inventories are simply too small or too unimportant to warrant intensive monitoring and control. In addition, in implementing new inventory management systems, priorities must be developed to allow management to decide the order in which to include the inventoried items in the control system. One simple procedure that has been widely and successfully used is the ABC classification system.

The ***ABC classification system*** is based on the annual dollar purchases of an inventoried item. As can be seen from Table 8.1, a relatively small proportion of the total items in an inventory account for a relatively large proportion of the total annual dollar volume, and a large proportion of the items account for a small proportion of the dollars. This phenomenon is often found in systems in which large numbers of different items are maintained. It is also in evidence in marketing, where a small number of customers represent the bulk of the sales; in complaint

$\mathcal{T}$ABLE 8.1 • Inventory Value by Item

Annual Quantity Used	Percentage of Total Items	Annual Dollar Purchases	Percentage of Total Purchases
521	4.8	$15,400,000	50.7
574	5.3	6,200,000	20.4
1023	9.4	3,600,000	11.8
1145	10.5	2,300,000	7.6
3754	34.0	1,800,000	5.9
3906	36.0	1,100,000	3.6
10,923	100.0	$30,400,000	100.0

departments, where a large volume of complaints come from a relatively small group; and so forth.

The three classifications used in the ABC system are:

- A. *High-value items*: The 15 to 20 percent or so[1] of the items that account for 75 to 80 percent of the total annual inventory value.

- B. *Medium-value items*: The 30 to 40 percent of the items that account for approximately 15 percent of the total annual inventory value.

- C. *Low-value items*: The 40 to 50 percent of the items that account for 10 to 15 percent of the annual inventory value.

The classification is shown in Figure 8.5, which gives the cumulative distribution of the dollar value of inventory items. In practice, the A items are identified first, then the C items, and what is left is usually considered to represent the B items. Of course, at times it may be appropriate to reclassify an item on the basis of other criteria. For example, a B item that has especially long lead times or is considered

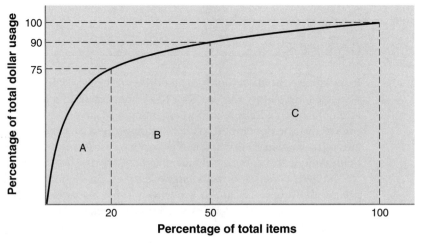

Figure 8.5   ABC inventory categories.

---

[1]The percentages are somewhat arbitrary and vary to suit individual needs.

critical can be elevated to category A. A common misconception is that the ABC classification is based on the dollar value of the individual items. In actuality, relatively costly items can still be classified as C if annual usage is low enough.

The ABC classification is management's guide to the priorities of inventory items. The A items should be subject to the tightest control, with detailed inventory records and accurate, updated values of order quantities and reorder points. B items are subject to normal control, with order quantities set by EOQ (as shown in the next section) but with less frequent updating of records and review of order quantities and reorder points. C items are subject to little control; orders are placed for a six-month to one-year supply so that relatively little control must be exercised and inventory records can be kept simple. Essentially, the time and effort saved by not controlling C items is used to tighten control of A items.

Johnson & Johnson's Devro Division uses very expensive, complex machinery in a 24-hour, 7-day continuous process to produce sausage casings for food processors in the United States, England, Australia, Canada, and Germany (Flowers and O'Neill 1978). To keep the equipment working and quickly repair any breakdowns, Devro maintains a large, expensive stock of more than 1000 spare parts. Previously, parts were ordered from a routine check of the stockroom, which resulted in excesses of some parts and shortages of others. For the shortages, air freight was used to expedite the deliveries, since normal lead times were too long.

To gain better control over these parts, Devro implemented a more formal inventory control, based on the ABC approach. To initiate the study, data were collected on each of the 1337 spare parts and a standard ABC analysis was conducted. The result was that 33 items were identified as class A (representing about 50 percent of total annual usage), 330 items as class B (representing 35 percent of usage), and the remaining 974 items as class C.

The A and B items were placed on perpetual inventory cards, and traveling requisitions were prepared for them beforehand. For traveling requisitions, departmental approval was required only once a year, so the requisition could go directly to purchasing for ordering.

The result has been a reduction in air freight charges of 46 percent and item-ordering time from three days to one day. The frequency of ordering the wrong part has also been reduced, and since all the necessary information is on the requisition, the crib room attendant is saving an hour a day. Last, owing to the consolidation of information, parts are now being ordered from the lowest-cost supplier and competitive bids are being sought on the items most frequently used.

The ABC concept is not only used for inventory control but is also frequently used to determine priorities for customer service and to decide on levels of safety stock. The concept is also known by other names, such as the *80–20 rule* and the *Pareto principle* (after the economist who discovered the effect).

$\mathscr{T}$HE ECONOMIC ORDER QUANTITY (EOQ)

The concept of **economic order quantity (EOQ)** applies to inventory items that are replenished in *batches* or *orders* and are not produced and delivered continuously. Although we have identified a number of costs associated with inventory decisions, only two categories, carrying cost and ordering cost, are considered in the basic EOQ model. Shortage costs and opportunity costs are not relevant, because shortages and changes in capacity should not occur if demand is constant, as we assume in this basic case. The cost of the goods is considered to be fixed and, hence, does not alter the decisions as to *when* inventory should be reordered or *how much* should be ordered.

More specifically, we assume the following in the EOQ model:

1. Rate of demand is constant (e.g., 50 units per day)
2. Shortages are not allowed
3. Lead times are known with certainty, so stock replenishment can be scheduled to arrive exactly when the inventory drops to zero
4. Purchase price, ordering cost, and per-unit holding cost are independent of quantity ordered
5. Items are ordered independently of each other

Let us return to the water distributor, which sells 1000 five-gallon bottles per month (30 days) and purchases in quantities of 2000 per order. Lead time for the receipt of an order is six days. The cost accounting department has analyzed inventory costs and has determined that the cost of placing an order is $60 and the annual cost of holding one five-gallon bottle in inventory is $10.[2]

Under its current policy of ordering 2000 per order, what is the water distributor's total annual inventory cost?

Its inventory pattern is represented by the "sawtooth" curve of Figure 8.6. For simplicity, let

$$Q = \text{order quantity}$$
$$U = \text{annual usage (demand)}$$
$$C_O = \text{cost to place one order}$$
$$C_H = \text{annual holding cost per unit}$$

To determine the total annual incremental cost of the distributor's current inventory policy, we must determine two separate annual costs: total annual holding cost and total annual ordering cost.

The *ordering* cost is determined by C_O, the cost to place one order ($60), and the number of orders placed per year. Since the distributor sells 12,000 five-gallon bottles per year and orders 2000 per order, it must place six (that is, 12,000/2000) orders per year, for a total ordering cost of $360 (6 orders per year $\times$ $60 per order). Using our notation, we write the annual ordering cost as

$$\text{annual ordering cost} = \frac{U}{Q} \times C_O$$

---

[2]Sometimes holding cost is given as a fixed value per year and other times as a percentage of the value of the inventory, especially when interest charges represent the major holding cost. Then $C_H = iC$ where C is the cost of the inventory item and i is the interest rate.

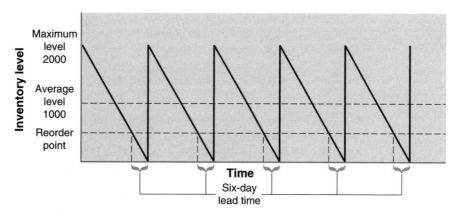

Figure 8.6 Water distributor's inventory pattern.

The annual holding cost is determined by C_H, the cost of holding one five-gallon bottle for one year ($10), and the number of bottles held as "cycle stock." Notice that the inventory level is constantly changing and that no single bottle ever remains in inventory for an entire year. On average, however, there are 1000 bottles in the inventory. Consider one cycle of the distributor's inventory graph, as shown in Figure 8.7. The inventory level begins at 2000 units and falls to 0 units before the next cycle begins. Since the rate of decline in inventory is constant (i.e., 1000 per month), the average level is 1000 units, or simply the arithmetic average of the two levels: (2000 + 0)/2 = 1000.

If, on the average, there are 1000 bottles in inventory over the entire year, then the annual inventory holding cost is $10,000 ($10 per unit × 1000 units). Or, in our general notation,

$$\text{annual holding cost} = \frac{Q}{2} \times C_H$$

Adding annual ordering cost and annual holding cost gives the following equation for total annual cost (TAC):

$$\text{TAC} = \left(\frac{U}{Q}\right) C_O + \left(\frac{Q}{2}\right) C_H$$

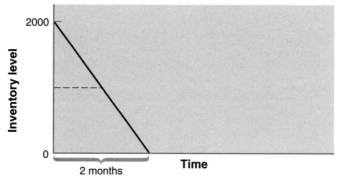

Figure 8.7 Water distributor's inventory graph.

For the water distributor, TAC is $360 + $10,000 = $10,360. Thus, its current inventory policy of ordering quantities of 2000 bottles is costing $10,360 per year. Is this the best policy, or can it be improved?

Finding an Optimal Policy

We can graph annual holding cost and annual ordering cost as a function of the order quantity, as shown in Figure 8.8. Since the annual holding cost is $(Q/2)C_H$, which can be written $(C_H/2)Q$, we see that holding cost is linear and increasing with respect to Q. Annual order cost is $(U/Q)C_O$, which can be rewritten as $(UC_O)/Q$. We can see that ordering cost is nonlinear with respect to Q and decreases as Q increases.

Now, if we add the two graphed quantities for all values of Q, we have the TAC curve shown in Figure 8.8. Note that TAC first decreases as ordering cost decreases but then starts to increase quickly. The point at which TAC is minimized is the optimal order quantity; that is, it gives the quantity Q that provides the least total annual inventory cost. This point is called the *economic order quantity* (EOQ), and for this inventory problem it happens to occur where the order cost curve intersects the holding cost curve. (The minimum point is not *always* where two curves intersect; it just happens to be so in the case of EOQ.) From Figure 8.8 we can see that EOQ is approximately 400 bottles per order.

We can compute an accurate value algebraically by noting that the value of Q at the point of intersection of the two cost lines is the EOQ. We can find an equation for EOQ by setting the two costs equal to one another and solving for the value of Q:

$$EOQ = \sqrt{\frac{2UC_O}{C_H}}$$

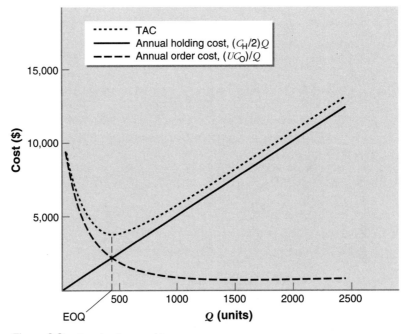

Figure 8.8 Graph of annual inventory costs.

For the water distributor, we can compute EOQ as

$$\text{EOQ} = \sqrt{\frac{2(12,000)60}{10}} = \sqrt{144,000} = 379.6$$

Obviously, since we cannot order a fraction of a bottle, the order quantity would be rounded to 380 units.

The total annual cost (TAC) of this policy would be:

$$\text{TAC} = \left(\frac{12,000}{380}\right)60 + \left(\frac{380}{2}\right)10 = 1894.74 + 1900 = \$3794.74$$

Note that this is an improvement in total annual cost of $6565.26 over the present policy of ordering 2000. Actual inventory situations often exhibit relative "insensitivity" to changes in quantity in the vicinity of EOQ. To the inventory manager, what this means is added flexibility in order quantities. If, for example, shipping and handling was more convenient or economical in quantities of 500 (perhaps the items are shipped on pallets in quantities of 250), the additional 120 units per order would cost the organization only an extra $145.26 per year.

Cautions Regarding EOQ

The EOQ is a computed minimum-cost order quantity. As with any model or formula, the GIGO rule (garbage in, garbage out) applies. If the values used in computing EOQ are inaccurate, then EOQ will be inaccurate—though, as mentioned previously, a slight error will not increase costs significantly. EOQ relies heavily on two variables that are subject to considerable misinterpretation. These are the two cost elements: holding cost (C_H) and order cost (C_O). In the derivation of EOQ, we assumed that by ordering fewer units per order the cost of holding inventory would be reduced. Similarly, it was assumed that by reducing the number of orders placed each year the cost of ordering could be proportionately reduced. Both assumptions must be thoroughly questioned in looking at each cost element that is included in both C_H and C_O.

For example, if a single purchasing agent is employed by the firm, and orders are reduced from 3000 per year to 2000 per year, does it stand to reason that the purchasing expense will be reduced by one-third? Unless the person is paid on a piecework basis, the answer is clearly no. Similarly, suppose we rent a warehouse that will hold 100,000 items and that we currently keep it full. If the order sizes are reduced so that the warehouse is only 65 percent occupied, can we persuade the owners to charge us only 65 percent of the rental price? Again, the answer is no. Clearly, then, when costs are determined for computations, only real, out-of-pocket costs should be used. Costs that are committed or "sunk," no matter what the inventory level or number of orders is, should be excluded.

Note also that C_H and C_O are *controllable* costs. That is, they can be reduced, if this is advantageous. This is exactly what the Japanese recognized. The problems they saw with holding inventory were:

- Product defects become hidden in the inventory, thereby increasing scrap and rework later in the production system, when defects are harder to repair. Just as important, the problem in the system that led to the defective part cannot be tracked down so easily later on.

- Storage space takes up precious room and separates all the company's functions and equipment, thereby increasing problems with communication. Space itself is extremely expensive in Japan (directly increasing the variable C_H).
- More inventory in the plant means that more control is needed, more planning is required, larger systems are required to move all that stock, and in general more "hassle" is created, which leads to errors, defects, missed deliveries, long lead times, and more difficulty in product changeovers.

Rarely do U.S. firms consider these real costs in the EOQ formula. More typically, these costs are considered part of the indirect, overhead, or "burden" costs that are assumed to be uncontrollable. Again, the message is: Be very careful about the values used in the EOQ formula.

Also, it should be noted that very small EOQ values (e.g., 2) will not usually be valid, because the cost functions are questionable for such small orders. Last, EOQ reorder sizes should not be followed blindly. There may not be enough cash just now to pay for an EOQ, or storage space may be insufficient.

MRP FOR DEPENDENT DEMAND

Many items, particularly *finished products* such as automobiles, televisions, and cartons of ice cream, are said to experience independent demand. That is, the demand for these items is unrelated to the demand for other items. For instance, in general there is no product that creates a demand for an automobile. However, every time an automobile is demanded, a demand for one steering wheel is created. Thus, the demand for steering wheels depends on and is derived from the demand for automobiles.

Independent demand appears to be random—that is, caused by chance events. Most *raw materials, components*, and *subassemblies* are dependent on demands for these finished goods and other assemblies and subassemblies. Furthermore, independent demand may occur at a constant rate over an inventory cycle. However, these items are usually produced or ordered in batches based on the economic order quantity model. Therefore, when a lot is ordered for production in the factory, all materials and components needed for production are ordered at the same time, creating a "lump" in demand for the dependent-demand items.

Examples of constant and lumpy demands are shown in Figure 8.9. In the case of constant demand, demand varies around the average (shown by the dashed line). Materials requirements planning (MRP) is a system designed specifically for the situation when "lumps" in demand are known about beforehand, typically because the demands are "dependent." For example, in a facility that produces wooden doors, reorders of (finished) doors may be based on a reorder point system. When the number of finished doors on hand reaches a prespecified reorder point, then an order is placed into production on the shop floor. Figure 8.10*a* illustrates this inventory time pattern where the demand for finished doors is relatively constant.

If a reorder point system similar to the one used in managing the inventory of finished doors was used in managing the inventory of lumber used to produce the doors, the pattern shown in Figure 8.10*b* would result. Notice that in Figure 8.10*b*

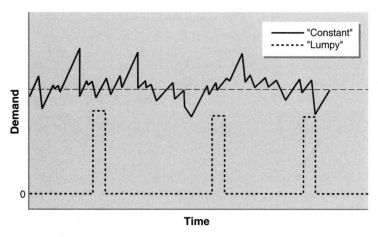

Figure 8.9   Constant and lumpy demands.

the normal inventory level is X units; when the inventory of finished doors in Figure 8.10*a* reaches its reorder point and a production order is released to the shop, a requisition for the required quantity of lumber is made against that inventory. The inventory level will drop by the quantity used in producing the lot, thus causing the raw materials inventory to fall below its reorder point. This triggers a re-

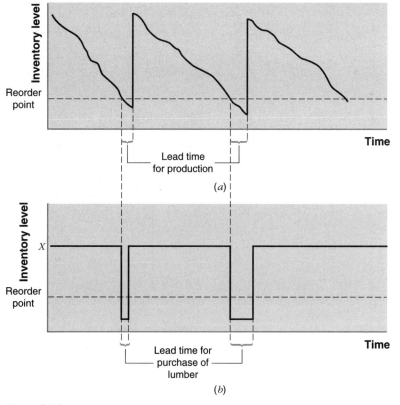

Figure 8.10   Relationship between finished item inventory and raw material/subassembly item inventory—reorder point approach. (*a*) Finished doors. (*b*) Lumber.

order for a quantity of lumber, resulting in replenishment of the inventory after its purchase lead time.

As you can see, the average inventory level for the lumber is quite high, and most of this inventory is being held for long periods of time without being used. A logical approach to help lower this level is to anticipate the timing and quantities of demands on the lumber inventory and then schedule purchases to meet this requirement. Figure 8.11 illustrates the results of this anticipation of demand. Figure 8.11*a* illustrates the same pattern of finished-product inventory as Figure 8.10*a*. Figure 8.11*b* depicts the scheduling of receipts of lumber just before the time when it is needed. The impact on average inventory level is obvious.

All reorder point systems assume (even though implicitly) that demand for each item in inventory is independent of the demand of other items in the inventory. These systems work well when the assumption holds but work rather poorly for items whose demand is dependent on higher-level items. Materials requirements planning is one method used for dependent inventory items.

However, dependent demand is not the only cause of lumpy demand. Demand can appear in lumps if only a small number of customers exist for the item and their

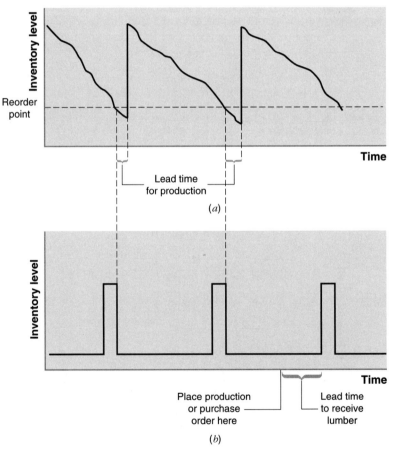

Figure 8.11   Relationship between finished item and subassembly/raw material item inventories—a requirements planning approach. (*a*) Finished doors. (*b*) Lumber.

purchasing habits are discontinuous. MRP is not a solution to the general problem of lumpy demand, since no basis exists for developing the materials plan unless the demand is *dependent* on something that a planner can either measure or forecast.

The availability and practicality of MRP systems are directly related to the advent of relatively inexpensive computer power. Without the computer, inventory professionals would simply be unable to perform all the calculations and maintain all the schedules necessary for requirements planning. A simple example will illustrate this point.

The Boardsports Company

The Boardsports Company produces a skateboard known as the Sidewalk Special. Its major components are one fiberglass board and two wheel assemblies. The lead time to assemble a Special from its two major components is one week. The first component, the board, is purchased and has a three-week delivery lead time. The second component, the wheel assembly, is assembled by Boardsports. Each wheel assembly is made up (with a one-week lead time) of one wheel mounting stand (manufactured by Boardsports with a four-week lead time), two wheels (purchased with a one-week lead time), one spindle (manufactured by Boardsports with a two-week lead time), and two chrome-plated locknuts (purchased with a one-week lead time). The product structure (or ***product tree***) is shown in Figure 8.12.

To produce an order for 50 Specials, the material requirements are computed as follows.

$$\text{Fiberglass boards: } 1 \times \text{number (no.) of Specials} = 1 \times 50 \ = \ 50$$
$$\text{Wheel assemblies: } 2 \times \text{no. of Specials} = 2 \times 50 \ = \ 100$$
$$\text{Wheels: } 2 \times \text{no. of wheel assemblies} = 2 \times 100 = 200$$
$$\text{Spindles:} 1 \times \text{no. of wheel assemblies} = 1 \times 100 = 100$$
$$\text{Wheel mount stand: } 1 \times \text{no. of wheel assemblies} = 1 \times 100 = 100$$
$$\text{Locknut: } 2 \times \text{no. of wheel assemblies} = 2 \times 100 = 200$$

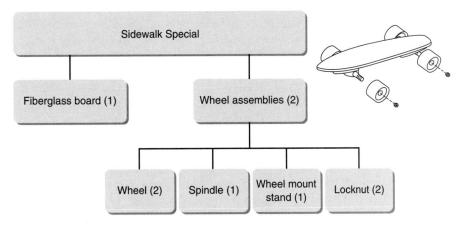

Figure 8.12   Skateboard product tree.

$\mathcal{T}$ABLE 8.2 • Demand for Sidewalk Specials

		Week								
		1	2	4	5	6	7	8	9	10
Sidewalk Specials										50
Boards	Date needed								50	
	Order date					50				
Wheel assembly	Date needed								100	
	Order date						100			
Wheels	Date needed							200		
	Order date						200			
Spindles	Date needed							100		
	Order date					100				
Mounting stands	Date needed							100		
	Order date			100						
Locknuts	Date needed							200		
	Order date						200			

(Boards row shows "3 week lead time" arrow from 50 in week 9 to 50 in week 6.)

Assume that according to the master schedule, an order for 50 Specials is due to be delivered in 10 weeks. The calendar in Table 8.2 illustrates the timing of due dates and the necessary order dates (assuming the lead times stated earlier) that must be met in order to deliver in the tenth week.

Note that MRP is a highly *logical* system. Knowing that 50 Specials must be shipped at the end of week 10 means that 50 boards must be placed on order for outside procurement at the end of week 6, that an order for 100 mounting stands must be placed in the shop at the end of week 4, and so forth. This is illustrated in the time-scaled assembly chart in Figure 8.13. (In essence, this is the product tree of Figure 8.12 laid on its side, with its components time-scaled to show their lead times.) Ordering in each week what will be needed rather than, say, an EOQ amount, is called **lot-for-lot** ordering.

Ordering later than these dates would result in late shipment (or working overtime and otherwise expediting the order), and ordering earlier would result in having inventory available (and occupying space, requiring paperwork, and incurring other holding costs) before it is needed (though perhaps at a savings in order costs). MRP looks at each end product and the dates when each is needed. From these due dates, needed dates for all lower-level items are computed, and from these due dates starting or order dates are determined.

The overall idea is simple, but consider the extreme complexity of operating an MRP system manually. In this simple example, with only one end product, the calculations and record keeping are straightforward. But for a large firm that manufactures hundreds of end items with thousands of intermediate components, only a computer can keep up with the processing volume.

This is an important point because MRP is not a revolutionary idea. The basic idea has been around for some time. It is and has been practiced for construction

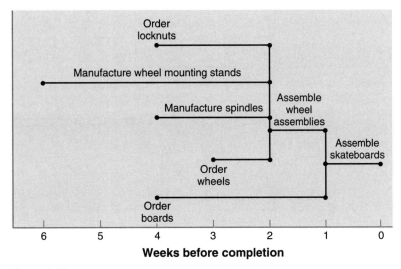

Figure 8.13 Time-scaled assembly chart for skateboard.

projects (from a single house to a mammoth skyscraper) that are scheduled according to a philosophy of having "the right materials to the right place at the right time." MRP has come of age in manufacturing and assembly operations because large-scale and relatively inexpensive computer power is available.

The Mechanics of MRP

Materials requirements planning is a management system for production and inventory. As such, it requires information about both production and inventory in order to produce its primary output—a schedule or plan for orders, both released and pending, which specifies actions to be taken now and in the future. Figure 8.14 illustrates the flows of information within an MRP system and indicates three primary inputs to the MRP system:

1. Master production schedule
2. Bill of materials file
3. Inventory master file

A major output from the MRP computer system is the planned order release report, although other reports—on changes, exceptions, and deexpediting—are also outputs.

Figure 8.14 shows in detail a portion of Figure 7.1. Here we are not concerned with the aggregate plan or the production plan, and the demand forecast is passed right through the master production schedule, which feeds the MRP system. However, MRP also requires other inputs that are not related to the major scheduling functions shown in Figure 7.1, such as current inventory levels and bills of material for the products. The MRP output reports shown in Figure 8.14 are, then, the inputs to the capacity planning function shown in Figure 7.1.

The relationship between materials planning and operations scheduling is, of necessity, intimate. Any attempts to design these two systems so that they operate independently will either fail outright or, at best, be grossly inefficient.

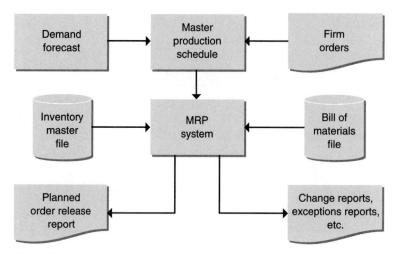

Figure 8.14 Schematic of MRP system.

MRP Inputs

As already indicated, the MRP inputs are the master production schedule, the bill of materials file, and the inventory master file.

Master Production Schedule

As discussed in Chapter 7, the master production schedule is based on actual customer orders and predicted demand. This schedule indicates exactly when each end item will be produced to meet the firm and predicted demand. That is, it is a time-phased production plan.

Bill of Materials

For each item in the master production schedule, there is a ***bill of materials (BOM)***. The bill of materials file indicates all the raw materials, components, subassemblies, and assemblies required to produce an item. The MRP computer system accesses the bill of materials file to determine exactly what items, and in what quantities, are required to complete an order for a given item.

Rather than simply listing all the parts necessary to produce one finished product, the BOM shows the way a finished product is put together from individual items, components, and subassemblies. For example, the product structure illustrated in Figure 8.15 would generate the BOM illustrated in Figure 8.16.

This BOM shows the finished product (sometimes called the ***parent item***) at the highest, or *zero*, level. Subassemblies and parts that go directly into the assembly of the finished product are called level 1 components, parts and subassemblies that go into level 1 components are shown as level 2, and so on. Thus, when a master production schedule shows a requirement for a given quantity of finished products for a certain due date, production planners can ***explode*** the BOM for that finished product to determine the number, due dates, and necessary order dates of subcomponents.

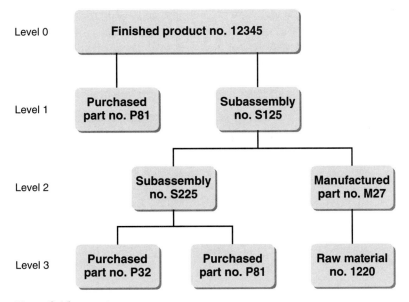

Figure 8.15   Product structure tree.

Exploding a BOM simply means stepping down through all its levels and determining the quantity and lead time for each item required to make up the item at that level. Note that if some items are manufactured internally, their lead time will be a function of the number of items to be produced rather than a fixed period. The result of exploding a BOM for a given product is a time-phased requirement for specific quantities of each item necessary to make the finished product. We exploded an order for skateboards earlier, although we had not formally introduced the notion of a bill of materials. A great deal of the time required to implement an MRP system is spent restructuring BOMs (so that they can be exploded properly) and verifying their accuracy. Clearly, exploding incorrect BOMs will only cause trouble further downstream.

Note in Figures 8.15 and 8.16 that purchased part No. P81 is used as both a level 1 and a level 3 component and is specifically identified in both locations in the product tree and bill of materials. Purchased part No. P81 could perhaps be a stainless steel nut and bolt assembly used to produce subassembly No. S225 and to complete the assembly of the finished product 12345 by being put together with

Level 1 Parts	Level 2 Parts	Level 3 Parts	Description	Quantity	Source
No. P81				1 lb.	Purchased
No. S125				1 lb.	Manufactured
	No. S225			1 lb.	Manufactured
		No. P32		1 lb.	Purchased
		No. P81		2 lb.	Purchased
	No. M27			1 lb.	Manufactured
		No. 1220		3 lb.	Purchased

Figure 8.16   Bill of materials (BOM) for a three-level product.

subassembly No. S125. We do not aggregate the number of P81s used to produce a single finished product (i.e., we not show part No. P81 as requiring 3 to produce finished product No. 12345), because aggregating would not allow us to identify the specific number of P81s necessary to produce a lot of S225 subassemblies. It would also preclude knowing how many P81s would be necessary to complete final assembly of S125 subassemblies into finished products.

Inventory Master File

The inventory master file contains detailed information regarding the number or quantity of each item on hand, on order, and committed to use in various time periods. The MRP system accesses the inventory master computer file to determine the quantity available for use in a given time period, and if enough are available to meet the needs of the order, it commits these for use during the time period by updating the inventory record. If sufficient items are not available, the system includes this item, as well as the usual lot size, on the planned order release report.

Low-Level Coding

In exploding the BOM, the requirements for the components are determined level by level. Thus, the requirements for the level 1 items are determined first. Next, the requirements for the level 2 items are computed, and so on. According to this logic, a problem can arise when a given component occurs on more than one level. The best-case scenario is that only the computational time increases, because the calculation is repeated several times. The worst-case scenario is that an error is made in determining the component requirements. To illustrate this, consider the product tree structure shown in Figure 8.17. The numbers in parentheses represent the number of components required. If we determine the requirements level by level, at level 1 we calculate that three B's are needed for each end item P. However, when we get to level 2 we calculate that six B's are needed (ignoring the three needed at level 1). One of two things can happen at level 2. Either we completely ignore the requirements at level 1 and conclude that only six B's are needed, or the program is smart enough to know that component B is also used in level 1. If the program is able to figure this out, then it can recalculate the number of B's needed at level 1 and add this to the number of B's needed at level 2.

An alternative approach is to use low-level coding in constructing the BOM. With low-level coding, the lowest level at which a component occurs is deter-

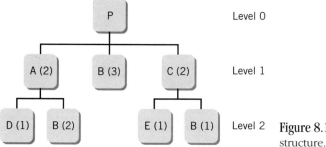

Figure 8.17 Original product tree structure.

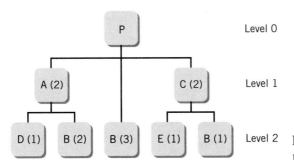

Figure 8.18 Low-level-coded product tree structure.

mined. Then, any other occurrences of this component are shifted down to this level. For example, in Figure 8.17, component B occurs on levels 1 and 2. Since level 2 is the lowest level at which component B occurs, all occurrences of component B are shifted down to level 2, as shown in Figure 8.18. Now, with the product tree structure shown in Figure 8.18, the requirements for component B need be calculated only one time at level 2. Note that low-level coding is often an iterative process because the product tree structure is constantly changing as various components are shifted to lower levels.

MRP System Outputs

Three specific outputs of the MRP system constitute the plan of action for released and pending orders:

1. Order action report
2. Open orders report
3. Planned-order release report

The *order action report* indicates which orders are to be released during the current time period and which orders are to be canceled. The *open orders report* shows which orders are to be expedited or deexpedited. This report is an exception report, listing only those open orders for which action is necessary. The *planned-order release report* is the time-phased plan for orders to be released in future time periods. It is this report that determines whether or not a master production schedule is feasible.

MRP Computations

An order for 100 of a finished product due 12 weeks from today may or may not be cause for action in the production-inventory system. If 1000 are currently on hand and planned order deliveries for 350 are scheduled between now and 12 weeks from now, 650 will be available from which the order for 100 can be shipped. But if 400 are available now and 350 will be shipped between now and the due date for the order of 100, action is necessary. The resulting MRP calculations are relatively straightforward:

- Process all items in the bill of materials level by level.
- For each item at a level:
  - Determine the time-phased gross requirements by summing planned order releases of its parent items multiplied by the quantity usage rate per parent item, for each period of the planning horizon.
  - Subtract on-hand and on-order amounts from gross requirements to determine the net requirements.
  - Apply the lot-sizing rule assumed to determine the lot size.
  - Offset the order release for lead time, yielding time-phased planned order releases.

MRP computations are based, in large part, on gross and net requirements. The order for 100 to be shipped in 12 weeks is a gross requirement. Actions, however, should be based on net requirements. In the first instance, the net requirement is -550 (i.e., $100 - 650$); thus, there is no production requirement. But in the second case, the net requirement in the twelfth week is 50 (i.e., $100 - 50$). Since there is a net requirement for 50 units, at least that quantity will have to be produced to meet the shipping requirement for 50. These quantities are based on the following two formulas:

Net requirements for planning period = gross requirements
for the planning period − planned on hand at planning period

and

Planned *on hand* at planning period = current on hand +
scheduled receipts prior to planning period − scheduled
requirements prior to planning period

Using the lead times available in the inventory file, we can calculate order release dates by backscheduling or time phasing from the due date by the amount of the lead time. Orders are scheduled to be received when needed to meet the due date or dates. If the net requirements for the planning period are positive, then an order must be scheduled to be received in time for use in the planning period. MRP answers the question of when to order by first determining when items are needed, and then scheduling an order release so that the items will be received just before that date. On the other hand, if the net requirements are negative or zero, no order is necessary.

Each component that goes into the production of the 100 parent items is scheduled in an analogous fashion. A planned-order release at one level generates requirements at the level below it. The differences in on-hand inventory at each level, the order quantities used at different levels, and the number of different finished products that use a particular component result in different order cycles for items at the various levels.

For example, suppose that in the order for 100 items in week 12, the planned on-hand quantity is 50 and the lead time for production (assembly) of level 1 items is three weeks. Then, an order for at least 50 (and possibly more, depending on the company's policy of ordering in standard reorder or lot sizes) would be placed

MRP for Dependent Demand

$\mathcal{T}_{ABLE}$ 8.3 • Zero-Level MRP

Week	1	2	3	4	5	6	7	8	9	10	11	12
Gross requirements	50			150			50	100				100
On hand 400	400	400	350	350	350	200	200	200	150	50	50	50
Net requirements	—	—	—	—	—	—	—	—	—	—	—	50
Planned-order receipts												50
Planned-order releases									50			
Lead time = 3 weeks												

in week 9. On the next MRP table, this order will show up in the row "Planned-order receipts." The materials requirements plan at level 0 of the product is shown in Table 8.3.

At level 1, a purchased hose may be required, and therefore a requirement plan must be developed for this item as well. But the same hose may be used on another product. Therefore, the requirements plan for the hose must incorporate the requirements generated from all items in which it is used. The MRP for the purchased hose is shown in Table 8.4. Lead time is four weeks. Notice the planned-order receipt of 50 units in week 2, resulting from a planned-order release four weeks previously.

But also notice the demand in week 10 for 200 of the hoses. Assume that these are required to produce subassemblies used in an entirely different end product. The requirements for both uses are aggregated, and an order is planned in week $10 - 4 = 6$ for 250. The order of 250 is for a standard reorder quantity.

This same procedure is followed at each level. All requirements from higher levels generate needs at lower levels. These needs are aggregated at each level for each item, and a requirements plan is established using the formulas and tables just discussed.

$\mathcal{T}_{ABLE}$ 8.4 • Level 1 MRP

Week	1	2	3	4	5	6	7	8	9	10	11	12
Gross requirements									50	200		
On hand	50	50	100	100	100	100	100	100	100	50	100	
Net requirements		—	—	—	—	—	—	—	—	150		
Planned-order receipts		50										
Planned-order releases						250						
Lead time = 4 weeks												

$\mathcal{M}$RP EXTENSIONS _____

Next, let us look at some derivatives of the MRP procedure.

Capacity Requirements Planning

Capacity requirements planning (CRP) is the process of determining workloads on each of the work centers due to the master schedule of final products. The workloads are typically stated in production-hours (or labor-hours, machine-hours, or both) required for each week in the future. In terms of complexity, this is at the other extreme from comparing the aggregate plan (discussed in Chapter 7) with existing capacity to see if there is a potential problem (*rough-cut capacity planning*).

There, the aggregate plan, or perhaps the master production schedule (MPS), was converted from units into equivalent workers, machine hours, or other critical dimensions of capacity, and overall capacity demands were compared with capacity limits. If the demands were close to, or higher than, the limits, overtime was scheduled, another shift (or partial shift) was added, subcontracting was initiated, and so on.

But this rough-cut planning ignored a number of factors: existing inventories, lead times, loads on individual work centers, and so on. In actuality, four different procedures are commonly used for capacity planning. In increasing order of complexity, they are:

- *Capacity using overall factors*: This is the basic rough-cut approach, based on the MPS and production standards that convert required units of finished goods into historical loads on each work center. The loads are assumed to fall into the same period as the finished goods in the MPS.

- *Bills of capacity*: This procedure again uses the MPS, but instead of historical ratios, it uses the bill of materials and the routing sheet. The routing sheet shows each work center, in order, needed to work on a part, the setup time required, and the run time required. With this information, all the work centers and their times needed to produce each required component to support the MPS can be identified. Then, multiplying by the number of units specified in the MPS gives the workloads at each work center for those periods.

- *Resource profiles*: This procedure is the same as bills of capacity, except lead times are included so the workloads fall in the correct periods.

- *Capacity requirements planning*: Finally, CRP uses the preceding information plus the MRP outputs to take the existing inventories and lot sizing into consideration as well. It also considers partially completed work, demands for service parts that are not usually included in the MPS, scrap adjustments, and so on.

The result of capacity planning is a tabular load report for each work center and each week in the future (as shown in Table 8.5) or a graphical load profile (as in Figure 8.19), which the manager can use to help plan for production requirements. The report or profile will indicate where capacity is inadequate for certain work centers and idle for others.

$\mathcal{T}$ABLE 8.5 • Tabular Load Report

			Work Center
Week	021	055	122
11	32 hr	74 hr	17
12	15	80	8
13	21	32	6
14	5	51	12
15	8	24	10
•	•	•	•
•	•	•	•
•	•	•	•

The imbalances may be corrected by a simple shift of personnel or equipment from one work center to another. Or perhaps work can be shifted in the schedule to smooth out the loads and balance the capacity demands. If not, overtime or another shift may be needed. Or it may be possible to alter the MPS, shifting some customers' orders earlier, to reduce excessive capacity demands. Of course, if none of these strategies are possible, it may be necessary to contact some customers to determine if a delay in their orders is acceptable.

Manufacturing Resource Planning (MRP II)

When the scheduling activities illustrated in Figure 7.1 are computerized and tied in with purchasing, accounting, sales, engineering, and other such functional areas,

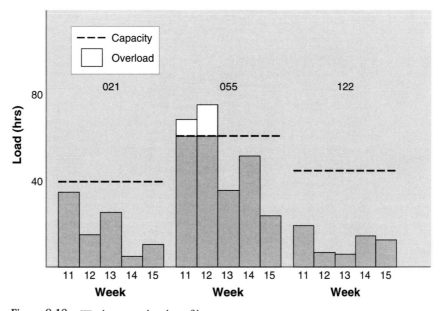

Figure 8.19   Work center load profiles.

the result is known as ***manufacturing resource planning (MRP II)***. A typical MRP II system is illustrated in Figure 8.20. The forecast and actual customer orders come into the master schedule, which drives the production system. Another major input to the production system is the engineering database, which includes bills of materials, engineering designs, drawings, and other such information required to manufacture and assemble the product.

At the bottom of Figure 8.20 is the actual build stage, where plant monitoring and control operates. This function receives additional information and gives information to plant maintenance. Cost accounting data are also collected at this stage. The process is completed with distribution requirements planning.

Clearly, all other company functions can also be tied to this system. Finance, knowing when items will be purchased and when products will be delivered, can properly project cash flows. Human resources (personnel) can similarly project requirements for hiring (and layoffs). And marketing can determine up-to-date customer delivery times, lead times, and so on.

A number of MRP II software packages are available, for all sizes of computers. Many, such as Micro-MRP, now run on microcomputers. Each of these packages operates in basically the same manner. First, it takes the sales forecast and basic engineering data for each product and, using an MRP subsystem, develops the time-phased materials requirements. Once this information is available, the

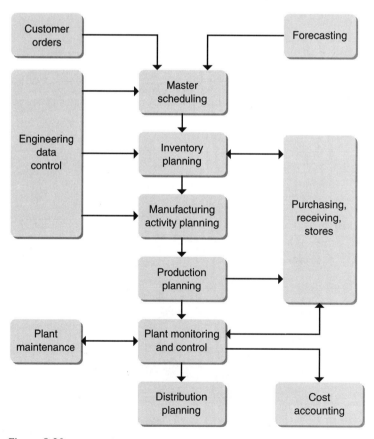

Figure 8.20   Typical MRP II system and its modules.

purchasing, capacity planning, and operations scheduling components take over to produce purchase-order requirements, route the product through operations, generate capacity requirements by individual operations, and load and schedule operations for production.

Requirements-based scheduling systems such as MRP II require a computer system for implementation because of their relatively large scale and complexity. The role of the computer is extremely important here. Again, the concept of requirements-based scheduling is not novel; it simply was previously too cumbersome to pursue in a clerically oriented system. Construction management has for years recognized the need for detailed requirements planning and scheduling. If material, labor, or equipment was at the job site in the wrong sequence or at the wrong time, not only would bottlenecks be unending, but wasted time and material losses from weather damage and theft would raise the cost of construction to unreasonable levels.

The computer has simply allowed all this clerical data processing and file handling to be accomplished more efficiently. Hence, what once was conceptually feasible but technically infeasible is now both technically and conceptually possible. And because of the speed of the computer, managers can perform as many simulations and "what if" experiments as they wish, in order to determine the best decision. The system simulates the impacts of the decision throughout the organization, predicting the results in terms of customer orders and due dates.

MRP has even been applied to services. For example, when NASA was planning on perhaps as many as 30 shuttle launches a year, it became aware that many scheduling conflicts were possible, given its limited, and expensive, resources (Steinberg, Lee, and Khumawala 1980). To handle the extensive demands of each launch, it had to design a flight operations planning schedule (FOPS), or calendar of resource readiness. The resource demands of different flights, of which there are eight varieties, had to be coordinated with the perhaps self-conflicting demands of individual flights. The approach taken to address this problem was a variant of MRP, called requirements planning.

To use the requirements planning approach for FOPS, a bill of requirements based on component activities needed for each flight was identified. Since some activities cannot proceed until other activities have been completed, a dependent-demand element is directly analogous to MRP, even though there are no inventories of materials to consider. It is also necessary to check how much "load" each activity places on the different departments in NASA in each time period. The schedule can be constructed either through infinite loading (not worrying about exceeding departmental capacities) or through finite loading, where excessive loads are shifted either earlier or later in time to remain within departmental capacities.

The flight schedule file represents the master production schedule in MRP because it identifies final "products" (launches) that must be completed without delays. Activities are scheduled backward from the flight schedule file as each is required. This gives the resulting schedule for all activities to support each flight. If there is a conflict for scarce resources, the earliest scheduled flight takes priority. Two primary resources are checked: labor and equipment. Each department must identify whether it is labor-constrained or equipment-constrained for the system to check. Each department then receives a weekly load profile summary that indicates its planned activities to support each launch. It also receives a summary of the required activities over the coming weeks. Through the use of the FOPS system, NASA has been able to effectively manage multiple, simultaneous schedules for its space shuttle launches.

Enterprise Resource Planning (ERP)

As we just discussed, MRP II extends MRP systems to share information with a variety of other functional departments outside the operations area including engineering, purchasing, customer-order entry, plant maintenance, and cost accounting. Thus, a key component of MRP II is storing operational information centrally and providing access to those departments that need it. Before MRP II systems, it was not uncommon for each functional department to maintain its own computer system. With these separate systems, the same information would be stored in several different databases throughout an organization. One problem with this approach is that it is difficult to update information consistently when it is stored in multiple locations. Indeed, it was frequently not even known how many different databases held a particular piece of information. Thus, it was common for the same information to have different values in each database. For example, the cost to produce a particular item would often have different values in the engineering, production, sales, and accounting databases.

The next stage in the evolution of information systems has been directed toward integrating all the business activities and processes throughout an entire organization. These information systems are commonly referred to as ***enterprise resource planning (ERP)*** systems. As the name suggests, the objective of these systems is to provide seamless, real-time information to all employees who need it, throughout the entire organization (or enterprise). In many cases, business process design (BPD, discussed in Chapter 5) has served as the impetus for developing and implementing these ERP systems.

Figure 8.21 illustrates a typical ERP system. As shown, ERP extends the idea of a central shared database to all areas within an organization. Using ERP, each area interacts with a centralized database and servers. With this approach, information is entered once at the source and made available to all employees needing it. Clearly,

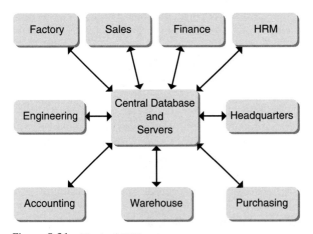

Figure 8.21   Typical ERP system.

this approach eliminates the incompatibility created when different functional departments use different systems, and it also eliminates the need for people in different parts of the organization to reenter the same information over and over again into separate computer systems.

One of the most popular ERP systems is SAP AG's R/3 system (Lieber 1995; White, Clark, and Ascarelli 1997). As of March 1997, more than 7000 companies had adopted it, and SAP's share of the ERP market was estimated to be 26 percent. Indeed, with sales of $2.4 billion in 1996, SAP is the world's fourth-largest software company, trailing only Microsoft, Oracle, and Computer Associates International. Examples of companies that use R/3 include Microsoft, Owens-Corning, IBM, Chevron, Colgate-Palmolive, Compaq Computer, and Analog Devices. Owens-Corning spent two years installing R/3 at a cost of $100 million. Chevron estimated that it also spent $100 million installing R/3 and expects the system to save it $50 million annually. Microsoft spent 10 months and $25 million installing R/3. In Microsoft's case, R/3 was used to replace 33 different financial tracking systems that were used in 26 of its subsidiaries. It expects to save $18 million annually.

A primary consideration in Owens-Corning's case was the need to provide buyers of its building products—including insulation, pipes, and roofing material—with one-stop shopping. R/3 facilitated this task by allowing the sales representatives to quickly see what products were available at any plant or warehouse. Analog Devices uses R/3 to integrate its international operations. For example, Analog uses R/3 to consolidate the products stored at its warehouses, thereby creating a worldwide order-processing system. Furthermore, the system calculates exchange rates automatically.

EXPAND YOUR UNDERSTANDING

1. Do any of the five functions and four forms of inventories still exist in service firms? If so, which ones, and why? If not, how are the functions served?

2. Contrast the functions and forms of inventories. Does every form exist for each function and vice versa, or are some more common?

3. How do you make the actual decision about identifying A and B items when you have the list of total annual inventory values? How do you decide where to draw the line? Is the process different from deciding between grades of A or B in a university class?

4. Suppose you determine an EOQ for a situation but you know the value is too low to last until the next time supplies arrive. What should you do? Should you order two EOQs?

5. Why are accurate records, particularly regarding bills of material and inventories, important for MRP?

6. Comparing Figures 8.10 and 8.11, what percentage of inventory reduction would you estimate has occurred? If this firm holds $1 million worth of lumber before MRP and values its capital at 20 percent, how much is the MRP conversion worth to it?

7. Another way to do lot sizing is to use the EOQ. Why not just do this, since it gives an optimal answer?

8. How might MRP be applied to services? Are the same inputs required? Will the outputs be the same?

9. MRP II and ERP are relatively new applications of computer technology. How difficult do you think each would be to implement in the typical firm? What aspects of these technologies might make them difficult? How long might each take to implement?

10. In many of today's firms, the customer's computer is tied to the supplier's computer over phone lines, so that purchase orders go directly into the supplier's planning system. What are the implications of this close relationship?

APPLY YOUR UNDERSTANDING _____
Andrew Jacobs and Company

Andrew Jacobs and Company employs approximately 280 people in the manufacture of a number of add-on appliances for residential heating and air conditioning units. The company began 15 years ago, producing a home humidifier, and has since expanded into dehumidifiers and air purifiers. It currently produces 30 different models, but because of heavy competition, engineering changes are constantly taking place and the product line is often changing. Each model is made up of between 40 and several hundred different parts, which range from purchased nuts and bolts and prefabricated subassemblies to internally manufactured components.

Andrew Jacobs purchases over 2500 parts and manufactures over 1000 parts and assemblies of its own. Many of the parts are used in several different models, and some parts—such as nuts and bolts—are used in over 75 percent of the finished products.

The finished goods inventory is kept relatively small. Sales are forecast on a month-to-month basis, and production is scheduled according to actual sales orders and the sales forecast. For this reason, production lots placed in the final assembly line are usually for relatively small quantities.

Rather than producing manufactured parts and subcomponents and purchasing other parts according to the sales forecast, parts, subassemblies, and purchased items are ordered on the basis of reorder point and economic order quantity. Since it is imperative to maintain accurate control of these raw materials and subassembly items, all parts and materials stored in the main supply area are controlled with the use of perpetual inventory cards, which are maintained by the scheduling department. Each card contains the reorder point, the economic order quantity, and the lead time for outside procurement or internal manufacture. Both receipt of new inventory into the main supply room and use of items from the supply room are recorded on the inventory card.

The scheduling department is responsible for checking the availability of inventory on the inventory cards. Approximately three weeks before a final assembly order is to be placed on the floor, the scheduler checks all the cards for parts needed in that assembly to determine whether issuing the number required to complete the assembly will reduce the inventory below the reorder point. If the scheduler determines that the projected final assembly order will result in hitting the reorder point, a production order or a purchase order is issued.

Physical inventories are taken every quarter, and usually a substantial number of small adjustments must be made. The quarterly physical inventory was suggested after a series of major inventory shortages occurred several years ago. The company's current policy allows any worker to enter the main supply area to remove needed parts. The workers are to fill out materials requisitions and to sign for all parts removed, but they are frequently in a rush and fail to complete the inventory requisitions accurately. There have been several cases where parts staged for final assembly of one product were removed and used on the assembly of another item.

To adjust for many of these problems, the production schedulers often add a safety factor to the reorder point when placing orders, and they have typically increased the order quantity from 10 to 25 percent over the economic order quantity. Their justification is that "it is less expensive to carry a little extra inventory than to shut down the production facility waiting for a rush order."

Questions

1. Evaluate and critique the existing system used by Andrew Jacobs and Company.

2. How might MRP work in a situation like this?

3. Beyond implementing a computerized MRP system, what other suggestions would you make to help alleviate Andrew Jacobs's problems?

EXERCISES

1. A firm maintains a maximum inventory level of 55 units, has a reorder point of 35 units, and is currently at 15 units with an outstanding order of 30 units. How many units should it order? Suppose its current inventory was 30 units? Assume that demand over the lead time is 5 units.

2. Categorize the following inventory items as type A, B, or C.

Unit Cost ($)	Annual Usage (Units)
10,000	4
7000	1
4000	13
1200	5
700	500
300	20
250	45
60	5,000
25	400
17	4,000
9	1,000
7	8,000
3	750
2	4,000
1	12,000

3. Frame-Up, a self-service picture framing shop, orders 3000 feet of a certain molding every month. The order cost is $40 and the holding cost is $0.05 per foot per year. What is the current annual inventory cost? What is the maximum inventory level? What is the EOQ?

4. The Corner Convenient Store (CCS) receives orders from its distributor in three days from the time an order is placed. Light Cola sells at the rate of 860 cans per day. (It can sell 250 days of the year.) A six-pack of Light Cola costs CCS $1.20. Annual holding cost is 10 percent of the cost of the cola. Order cost is $25.00. What is CCS's EOQ, and what is the reorder point?

5. It is time to consider reordering material in a periodic review inventory system. The inventory on hand is 100 units, maximum desired level of inventory is 250 units, usage rate is 10 units a day, reorder period is every two weeks (10 working days), lead time for resupply is 15 days, and amount on order is 250 units. How much should be ordered?

6. Wooden pencils are made in 1 week out of 4 parts: 2 wooden halves, the graphite, the metal cap, and the rubber eraser. Construct an MRP explosion for orders of 10 dozen in week 2, 30 dozen in week 3, and 15 dozen in week 5. There are currently 500 wooden halves on hand, 300 graphite rods, and 1500 metal caps, but no rubber erasers. All items are purchased with a 1-week lead time except the graphite, which takes 2 weeks. Use lot-for-lot sizing.

7. Product 101 consists of three 202 subassemblies and one 204 subassembly. The 202 subassembly consists of one 617, one 324 subassembly, and one 401. A 204 subassembly consists of one 500 and one 401. The 324 subassembly consists of one 617 and one 515.

   a. Prepare a product tree.

   b. Prepare an indented bill of materials.

   c. Determine the number of each subassembly or component required to produce fifty 101s.

8. Complete the MRP for item No. 6606 below.

Week	5	6	7	8	9	10	11	12	13	14	15	16	17
Gross requirement				100			50	30			80		
On hand 100													
Net requirement													
Planned-order receipts													
Planned-order releases													
Lead time = 3 weeks													

BIBLIOGRAPHY

APICS Dictionary, 8th ed. Falls Church, Va.: American Production and Inventory Control Society, 1995.

Bird, L. "High-Tech Inventory System Coordinates Retailer's Clothes with Customers' Taste." *Wall Street Journal* (June 12, 1996): B1, B5.

Bylinsky, G. "The Digital Factory." *Fortune* (November 14, 1994): 92–110.

Flores, B. E., and D. C. Whybark. "Implementing Multiple Criteria ABC Analysis." *Journal of Operations Management*, vol. 7, nos. 1–2 (October 1987): 79–85.

Flowers, A. D., and J. B. O'Neill II. "An Application of Classical Inventory Analysis to a Spare Parts Inventory." *Interfaces* (February 1978): 76–79.

Goddard, W. E. "Getting a Grip on Customer Service." *Modern Materials Handling* (September 1992): 41.

Gray, C. *The Right Choice: A Complete Guide to Evaluating, Selecting and Installing MRP II Software*. Essex Junction, Vt.: Wight, 1987.

Janson, R. L. *Handbook of Inventory Management*. Englewood Cliffs, N.J.: Prentice-Hall, 1989.

Jarkon, J. G., and R. Nanda. "Resource Requirements Planning Achieves Production Goals for Non-Profit Organization." *Industrial Engineering* (October 1985): 54–62.

Lieber, R. B. "Here Comes SAP." *Fortune* (October 2, 1995): 122–124.

Reid, R. A. "The ABC Method in Hospital Inventory Management: A Practical Approach." *Production and Inventory Management Journal* (Fourth Quarter 1987): 67–70.

Steinberg, E. E., B. Khumawala, and R. Scamell. "Requirements Planning Systems in the Health Care Environment." *Journal of Operations Management*, vol. 2, no. 4 (August 1982): 251–259.

Verity, J. W. "Invoice? What's an Invoice?" *Business Week* (June 10, 1996): 110–112.

Vollmann, T. E., W. L. Berry, and D. C. Whybark. *Manufacturing Planning and Control Systems*, 2nd ed. Homewood, Ill.: Irwin, 1988.

White, J. B., D. Clark, and S. Ascarelli. "This German Software Is Complex, Expensive, and Wildly Popular." *Wall Street Journal* (March 17, 1997): A1, A12.

CHAPTER 9

Supply Chain Management and Just-in-Time Systems

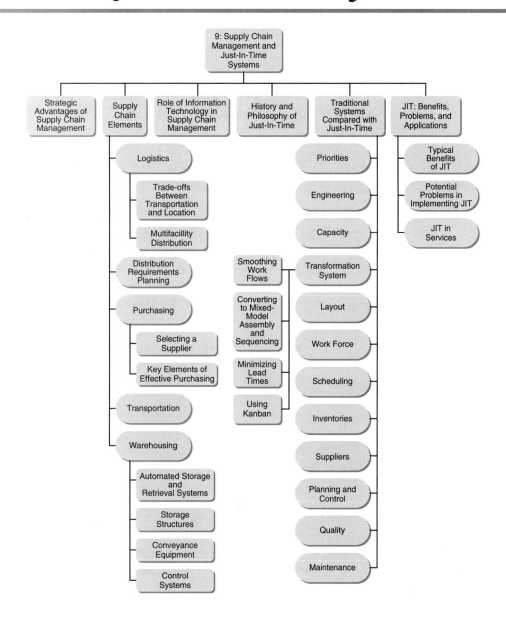

CHAPTER IN PERSPECTIVE

In this chapter we continue our discussion of materials management but enlarge the scope to include distribution, supply, purchasing, logistics, transportation, warehousing, and just-in-time (JIT) issues. This overall perspective is called supply chain management. Given the recency of the JIT philosophy, we spend additional time on this topic, including the history and philosophy of JIT, a comparison between traditional systems and JIT, and the benefits and problems associated with JIT.

INTRODUCTION

- Procter and Gamble developed its continuous replenishment program (CRP) to provide customers with quicker and more accurate stock replenishment. Two key aspects of the CRP were the elimination of nonvalue-adding costs and reduced cycle times. The program has succeeded in reducing inventory levels in customer warehouses from 19 to 6 days, increased inventory turnover from 19 to 60, reduced administrative costs by eliminating paperwork, and increased store service levels from 96.4 percent to 99.2 percent.

  With the CRP, orders originating from retail stores are transmitted via electronic data interchange (EDI) and collected at customer distribution centers. The orders received at the customer distribution centers are compared to on-hand inventory levels and sent on to the customer's headquarters where optimum order quantities are established. The order quantities are then sent to both the customer distribution centers and to Procter and Gamble's headquarters. P&G headquarters forwards the orders to the appropriate manufacturing plants. Once the product is produced at the plants, it is shipped to the customer distribution center and then on to the stores. (Poirier and Reiter 1996)

- Rio Bravo Electroicos' plant in Juárez, Mexico, assembles wiring harnesses for Delphi Packard Electric Systems, located in the United States. Rio Bravo is what is known as a maquiladora facility. Maquiladora facilities receive components from suppliers in the United States duty-free, perform assembly operations, and then export the products back to the United States or to other countries. Rio Bravo employs a pull production system. With this system, material needed to support the plant's 36 subassembly and assembly lines is replenished every 2 hours from materials stocked in the main storage area. The main storage area contains a 15-day supply of materials.

  One problem with operating a just-in-time delivery system across international boundaries is the possibility that a shipment will be stopped at customs. To eliminate this problem, Rio Bravo participates in a bilateral security program whereby products shipped to the United States do not require inspection as long as the shipments have been properly sealed in a secured area at the Mexican plant. Also, it must allow United States customs officials regular access to its facilities to review its operations (Auguston 1995).

- "Buick City" is the name General Motors has applied to the transformation of its automobile assembly facility in Flint, Michigan. This extensive 1.8-million-square-foot assembly plant is based on JIT and automation. A major part of the JIT program is a sophisticated computerized production control system that ties all the production robots and equipment to the material requirements planning and inventory control systems.

  With this system, in-plant inventories have been reduced to less than an hour's supply in some cases, and they never exceed more than 16 hours' worth. There are separate delivery schedules for more than 600 suppliers providing more than 4000 parts, each with only a 20-minute window for delivery. The Woodbridge Group, for example, delivers car seats in assembly order within 3½ hours of receiving an order. A continuous broadcast every 54 seconds from the assembly factory tells Woodbridge the sequence and specifications of the seats needed in the next 3 hours. Eighty-five separate point-of-use receiving dock doors have reduced dock-to-line delivery distances to less than 300 feet. Seven types of standard, bar-coded, returnable containers are used for all parts processed in the plant. Both the supplier and the factory's automatic receiving and dispatch equipment use the bar codes.

  Furthermore, the plant uses state-of-the-art materials handling equipment, including automated guided vehicles and more than 200 robots. The robots load and unload trucks and perform other manufacturing operations. In one application, a robot unloads car seats from a truck and passes them to an overhead conveyor. When they reach the end of the conveyor line, another robot takes them off and places them at their point-of-use on the assembly line. The robot that does the unloading also places the empty boxes returning on the conveyor back in the delivery truck. The primary benefits of this program include major reductions in the costs of labor, materials, damage to parts, and repairs. Even more significant are the improvements in the quality of the product (Sepehri 1988).

As these examples illustrate, ***supply chain management*** and ***just-in-time (JIT)*** have taken on the nature of a crusade in U.S. industry. Chapter 8 discussed the MRP approach to planning the ordering and production of materials. Supply chain management expands this concept to the entire value chain from receipt of the customer's order to delivery back to the customer. And as part of the supply chain, JIT is another approach for managing the delivery of materials. However, as we will see, JIT is much more than simply planning and scheduling the delivery of materials. Perhaps it is best described as a philosophy that seeks to eliminate all types of waste, including carrying excessive levels of inventory and long lead times. Before discussing JIT in detail, we begin with an overview of supply chain management.

$\mathscr{S}$TRATEGIC ADVANTAGES OF SUPPLY CHAIN MANAGEMENT

The term ***supply chain management*** as currently used in organizations typically includes the supply, storage, and movement of materials, information, personnel, equipment, and finished goods within the organization and between it and its environment. The objective of supply chain management is to integrate the entire process of satisfying the customer's needs all along the supply chain. This includes procuring different groups of raw materials from multiple sources (often through purchasing or recycling or recovery), transporting them to various processing and assembly facilities, and distributing them through appropriate distributors or retailers to the final consumer. Within this process are a great variety of activities such as packaging, schedule coordination, credit establishment, inventory management, warehousing, maintenance, purchasing, order processing, supplier selection and management, and so on.

As organizations have continued to reduce production costs and improve the quality, functionality, and speed of delivery of their products and services to customers, the costs and delays of distributing those goods and services are taking a greater and greater fraction of the total cost and time. For example, the cost of just physical distribution itself is now up to 30 percent of sales in the food industry. To achieve quick response with quality goods that accurately satisfy the need at the lowest possible cost requires taking a broad, long-range, integrated perspective of the entire customer fulfillment process instead of focusing on the little segments and pieces of the chain.

For instance, if each segment of the supply chain is acting in a way to optimize its own value, there will be discontinuities at the interfaces and unnecessary costs will result. If an integrated view is taken instead, there may be opportunities in the supply chain where additional expense or time in one segment can save tremendous expense or time in another segment. If a broad enough view is then taken, the savings in the one segment could be shared with the losing segment, so everyone would be further ahead. This broad, integrated view of the supply chain is more feasible these days due to the recent capabilities of advanced information technology and computer processing (e.g., bar codes, computerized manufacturing, the Internet, electronic funds transfer).

In the following sections, we will discuss the various elements of the supply chain that primarily affect cost, and sometimes also the speed of response. Later in the chapter, we focus more heavily on the just-in-time approach to value delivery, which has a primary benefit in response time but also may offer some cost savings as a spillover benefit.

$\mathcal{S}$UPPLY CHAIN ELEMENTS

As shown in Figure 9.1, the supply chain consists of the network of organizations that supply inputs to the business unit, the business unit itself, and the customer network. Note that the supplier network can include both internal suppliers (i.e., other operating divisions of the same organization) and external suppliers (i.e., operating divisions of separate organizations). Also, note how design activities cut across the supplier network and the business unit, and how distribution activities cut across the business unit and the customer network. This broader view of the entire process of serving customer needs provides numerous benefits. For example, it focuses management attention on the entire process that creates value for the customer, not the individual activities. When viewed in this way, information is

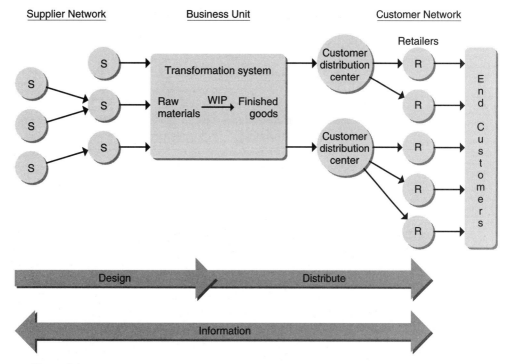

Figure 9.1   The supply chain.

more freely shared up and down the supply chain, keeping all parties informed of one another's needs. Furthermore, activities can be performed at the point in the supply chain where they make the most sense. To illustrate, instead of providing Johnson Controls with detailed specifications for car seats, Chrysler provides broad specifications and relies on Johnson Controls' expertise to design and manufacture its car seats.

In this section we will look at each of the major elements of the supply chain to better understand how they operate and interact to deliver value to the final customer. The major elements we consider here are the overall logistics of the process (particularly multifacility logistics), distribution requirements planning, purchasing, transportation, and warehousing. Obviously, materials management and scheduling are also important elements of the value chain, but these aspects were considered earlier in their own right. In the following section, we then turn to the task of integrating all these elements into a successful supply chain.

Logistics

In these days of intense worldwide competition, international production, and global distribution, logistics is taking on tremendous importance. Labor cost is dropping as a proportion of total output cost, as are manufacturing costs in general, but the costs of acquisition and distribution have remained about the same and now account, as noted above, for up to 30 percent of sales. Moreover, as quality and functionality become more standardized, speed of response is becoming particularly important in the final selection of a supplier.

Trade-offs between Transportation and Location

Outputs can be distributed to customers by transporting them, if there is a facilitating good, or by locating where the customers can easily obtain them. Since service outputs without a facilitating good are generally difficult, expensive, or even impossible to transport, service organizations distribute their output primarily by locating in the vicinity of their recipients. Examples of this approach are medical clinics, churches, playgrounds, restaurants, and beauty shops.

Advances in information and telecommunications technology have allowed some pure service organizations (i.e., those without a facilitating good) to reach their recipients through phone, cable, the Internet, or microwave links. Thus, stockbrokers, banks, and other such service providers may locate in areas removed from their customers or recipients but more economical in other respects, such as proximity to the stock exchange or the downtown business district.

Some pure service organizations, however, do attempt to transport their services, although frequently with a great deal of trouble. These instances occur when the nature of the service makes it (a traveling carnival, a home show) impractical to remain in one fixed location for an extended duration or, more commonly, when the service (mobile X-ray, blood donor vehicle, bookmobile) is deemed very important to the public but may otherwise be inaccessible.

Product organizations, on the other hand, can generally trade transportation costs for location costs more easily and, therefore, can usually minimize their logistics costs. This allows goods producers to locate in the best global locations for each stage in their supply chains. In some instances, however, even product organizations are forced into fixed locations. One of these instances concerns the nature of the firm's inputs, and the other concerns its outputs.

Processing Natural Resources

Organizations that process natural or basic resources as raw materials or other essential inputs to obtain their outputs will locate near their resource if one of the following conditions holds:

1. There is a large loss in size or weight during processing.
2. High economies of scale exist for the product. That is, the operating cost of one large plant with the same total capacity as two smaller plants is significantly less than the combined operating costs of the two small plants.
3. The raw material is perishable (as in fish processing and canning) and cannot be shipped long distances before being processed.

Examples of these types of industries are mining, canning, beer production, and lumber. In these cases the natural inputs (raw materials) are either voluminous or perishable, and the final product is much reduced in size, thus greatly reducing the cost of transportation to the recipients (either final users or further processors).

Immobile Outputs

The outputs of some organizations may be relatively immobile, such as dams, roads, buildings, and bridges. In these cases (referred to as *projects*) the organization locates itself at the construction site and transports all required inputs to that location. The home office is frequently little more than one room with a phone, secretary, files, and billing and record-keeping facilities.

Product organizations may also locate close to their market, not necessarily to minimize transportation costs of distribution, but to improve customer service. Being close to the market makes it easier for the recipient to contact the organization and also allows the organization to respond to changes in demand (involving both quantity and variety) from current and new recipients. As in war, the people on the front line are closest to the action and are able to respond to changing situations faster than those far away, simply because information about changes is available sooner and is generally more accurate.

Multifacility Distribution

Up to this point in our discussion of the trade-off between transportation and location, we have largely restricted our discussion to the single-facility situation in which, for example, one facility services a set of geographically dispersed recipients (Figure 9.2). The next level of complexity is multiple facilities such as national or global distribution centers, or assembly plants. Determining the best locations for multiple facilities is known as the ***multifacility location problem***. Franchises are a specialized form of branch facilities, as are warehouses, branch banks, and adult evening classes offered at local high schools and colleges.

The multifacility situation also involves issues of channel selection discussed in the marketing literature, such as the use of wholesalers, retailers, and factory representatives. These channels often have additional locations that must be considered in the overall distribution analysis.

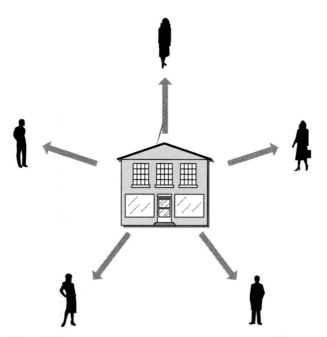

Figure 9.2   The problem of location with a single source and multiple recipients.

The analysis is complex because the best location–distribution pattern for each facility depends on the location–distribution patterns for each of the other facilities. Some of the major complications associated with multifacility distribution are described as follows.

1. *Multiple facilities:* First, more than one facility may produce the output for multiple recipients. That is, there may be a southeastern plant, a midwestern plant, and a western plant among which the output can be divided up to supply the customers. Three situations often arise in this case: locating one additional facility with N existing facilities already situated; locating (or relocating) all N facilities at once; and, last, once facilities are situated, determining the new allocation of outputs from them to the recipients.

   A special point about the location of all N facilities is that the problem cannot be solved by locating them one at a time. Rather, they must all be located at once, since changing the distribution pattern of any one facility will change the distribution patterns of some or all of the other facilities as well.

2. *Multiple stages:* There may also be multiple intervening staging points between the production facility and the recipients, such as factory warehouses, distribution centers, wholesalers, and retailers. This can be the case either with a single production facility or, as shown in Figure 9.3, with multiple production facilities.

3. *Unspecified sites:* Sometimes possible sites are identified beforehand, and the problem becomes one of selecting the best set of N sites from M locations. This may even be the case in the single-facility problem. If the sites are not determined in advance, the problem is clearly more complex.

4. *Unknown quantities:* The number of production facilities may also be unknown, and the problem is to determine not only *where* they should be located and *which recipients* they should serve but also *how many* facilities there should be. Obviously, this problem is very complicated. In addition, the number of intervening facilities at any stage (e.g., warehouses) may be unknown, as well as the *number* of stages, making for a significantly more complex problem.

5. *Multiple outputs:* So far, we have assumed that there is only one output; in fact, though, there may be any number. The problem arises when the distribution of demand among the recipients for the different outputs varies considerably, necessitating different solutions in the situations just given.

Distribution Requirements Planning

The concept of distribution requirements planning (DRP) follows naturally from our logistics discussion. The distribution process is illustrated in Figure 9.4, where retailers order from local warehouses, the warehouses are supplied from regional centers, and the regional centers draw from the central distribution facility, which gets its inventory directly from the factory.

Clearly, there are time lags in each chain of this process. Also, each distribution point has its own standard reorder quantity, storage capacity, safety stock level, and so on. Without planning by the factory or central distribution facility, orders

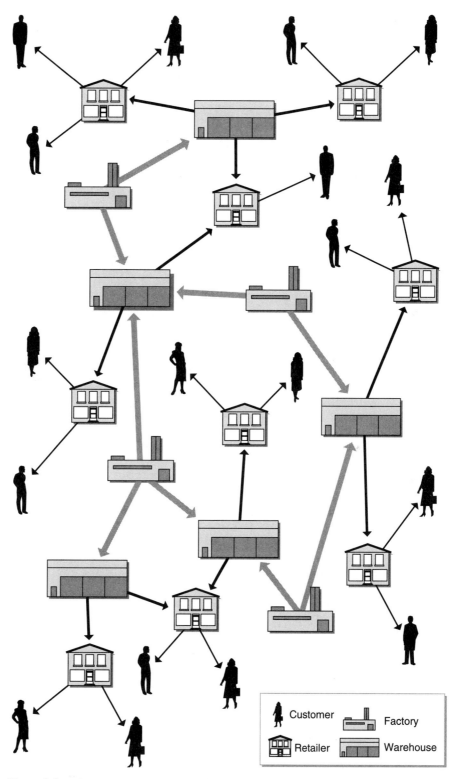

Figure 9.3   The multifacility problem.

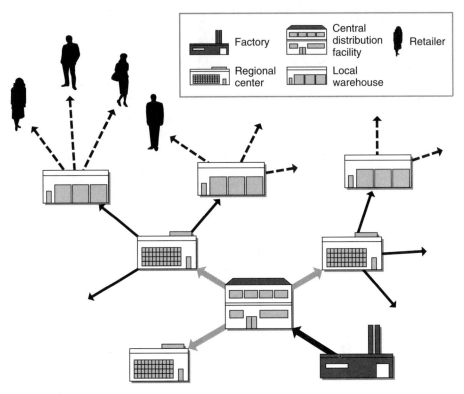

Figure 9.4   Distribution requirements planning situation.

can often bunch up, requiring high stocking levels to avoid shortages or stockouts. This is, of course, true throughout the system, so high inventory levels are held by each of the distribution points in the entire system.

By applying MRP to the distribution function, such demands are anticipated and orders are released ahead of time to avoid stockouts and their resultant high follow-on inventories. This process is shown in Table 9.1. In the appropriate distribution environment, factory orders are built up from lower levels in the distribution network, which provides significant advantages in scheduling and coordination. The DRP process is, however, vulnerable to poor forecasts at the lower levels. If local forecasts are incorrect, then demands placed on the factory will also be incorrect, and either excess stock, at an unnecessary cost, or shortages will result.

Purchasing

An organization depends heavily on purchasing activities to reliably obtain materials by the time they are needed in the product supply process. Purchasing must make some important trade-offs in this process. Particularly because of the current fierce price competition from abroad, purchasing activities—matching varying prices, qualities, quantities, and lead time to meet the needs of production; inventory control; quality control; and other operations activities—are crucial.

Manufacturing organizations spend about 55 percent of their revenues for outside materials and services (Tully 1995). It is perhaps somewhat surprising that, on aver-

$\mathcal{T}$ABLE 9.1 • The DRP Process

Local warehouse A   **Local warehouse B**

Week	11	12	13	14	15	16	17	18	19	
Carton requirements			83	16		17				Regional center I
On hand	90	90	90	7	21	21	4	4	4	(1 week lead time
Net requirement				9						Order size: 30)
Planned receipts										
Planned releases			30							

Regional center II

Week	11	12	13	14	15	16	17	18	19	
Carton requirements			30			60				Central distribution facility
On hand	10	10	10	30	30	30	20	20	20	(1 week lead time
Net requirement			20			30				Order size: 50)
Planned receipts										
Planned releases		50			50					

Week	11	12	13	14	15	16	17	18	19	
Carton requirements		50			50					Factory
On hand	90	90	40	40	40	190	190	190	190	(2 week lead time
Net requirements					10					Order size: 200)
Planned receipts										
Planned releases			200							

age, these companies spend only 6 percent of revenues on labor and 3 percent on overhead. And with factory automation increasing, the percentage of expenditures on purchases is increasing even more. In addition, with JIT programs at so many firms (discussed in greater detail later), "just-in-time purchasing" is even further increasing the importance of the purchasing and procurement, since delays in the receipt of materials, or receiving the wrong materials, will stop a JIT program dead in its tracks.

Thus, the purchasing system has a major potential for lowering costs and increasing profits—perhaps the most powerful within the organization. Consider the following data concerning a simple manufacturing organization.

$$
\begin{aligned}
\text{Total sales} &= \$10{,}000{,}000 \\
\text{Purchased materials} &= 7{,}000{,}000 \\
\text{Labor and salaries} &= 2{,}000{,}000 \\
\text{Overhead} &= 500{,}000 \\
\text{Profit} &= 500{,}000
\end{aligned}
$$

To double profits to $1 million, one or a combination of the following five actions could be taken.

1. Increase sales by 100 percent
2. Increase selling price by 5 percent (same volume)
3. Decrease labor and salaries by 25 percent
4. Decrease overhead by 100 percent
5. Decrease purchase costs by 7.1 percent

Although action 2 looks best, it may well be impossible, since raising prices almost always reduces the sales volume. In fact, raising prices often decreases the total profit (through lower volume). Alternative 5 is thus particularly appealing.

 Decreasing the cost of purchased material provides significant profit leverage. In the previous example, every 1 percent decrease in the cost of purchases results in a 14 percent increase in profits. This potential is often neglected in both business and public organizations. Indeed, a recent study found that a 5 percent reduction in total purchasing cost at a typical manufacturing organization increases net profit by 3 percent. The same manufacturer would have to cut payroll in half to achieve this same increase in profit. Furthermore, this logic is equally applicable to more service-oriented organizations. For example, investment firms typically spend 15 percent of their revenues on purchases.

Another common term for the purchasing function is *procurement*. Whereas "purchasing" implies a *monetary* transaction, "procurement" is simply the responsibility for acquiring the goods and services the organization needs. Thus, it may include, for example, scrap, as well as purchased materials. Procurement also allows the consideration of environmental aspects of obtaining and distributing products. For example, there is often the possibility of recovering certain materials through recycling or scrap purchases. And re-manufacturing of goods is an inexpensive alternative to virgin production. On the distribution side, the concept of *reverse logistics* is being practiced in Germany, where packaging must reverse the logistics chain and flow back to the producer who originated it for disposal or reuse.

Procurement by an organization is similar to purchasing by the individual consumer, except for the following differences:

1. The volume and dollar amounts are much larger.
2. The buyer may be larger than the supplier, whereas in consumer purchases the buyer is typically smaller than the supplier.
3. Very few suppliers exist for certain organizational goods, whereas many typically exist for consumer goods.
4. Certain discounts may be available for organizations.

Selecting a Supplier

Some of the general characteristics of a good supplier are as follows.

1. Deliveries are made on time and are of the quality and in the quantity specified. This maintains the consistent flow of processing for the purchasing organization.

2. Prices are fair, and efforts are made to hold or reduce the price.

3. Supplier is able to react to unforeseen changes such as an increase or decrease in demand, quality, specifications, or delivery schedules—all frequent occurrences in operations.

4. Supplier continually improves products and services.

Suppliers with all these characteristics are difficult to find. The purchasing function must recognize these criteria and not be swayed by considerations of cost or price alone.

The evaluation of suppliers should include four major areas:

1. Technical and engineering capability

2. Manufacturing strengths

3. Financial strengths

4. Management capability

Each of these four areas can be evaluated through generally available information and through meetings with the potential supplier. The supplier's technical and manufacturing capability can often be evaluated by meeting with engineering and manufacturing personnel, evaluating bids, touring plants, and using a trial order.

Financial strength is an important consideration, for even if a company is technically competent, it may not be financially sound enough to meet deliveries. An analysis of financial statements—including financial ratio analysis of ability to repay short- and long-term debt, profitability, and the general trend of the capitalization structure of the firm—should also be undertaken.

Management strength is paramount in long-term and high-dollar contracts. For example, the management of construction contractors for buildings, bridges, and highways or airframe manufacturers for aircraft must be evaluated to determine its ability to successfully complete the project. The technical capability may well exist, but managerial talent and organization may not be available to guide the project. Even for short-term arrangements, the ability of the supplier's management to control its own operations will lead to better prices, delivery, and quality.

Last, in these days of intense global competition, just-in-time, and six-sigma quality, the relationship between customers and their suppliers has changed significantly. More and more, customers are seeking a closer, more cooperative relationship with suppliers. They are cutting back the number of suppliers they do business with by a factor of 10 or 20, with those remaining getting the overwhelming volume of their business.

These single-sourcing arrangements are becoming close to partnerships, with the customer asking the supplier to become more involved even at the design stage, and asking for smaller, more frequent deliveries of higher-quality items. In some cases, suppliers are being certified or qualified so that their shipments do not need to be inspected by the customer—the items go directly to the production line.

In the not-too-distant past, when JIT was still novel, customers were using single-sourcing as a way to put pressure on their suppliers, forcing the supplier to stock inventories of items for immediate delivery rather than holding the stock themselves. Singing the praises of JIT—and insisting that the supplier implement JIT so that its deliveries could be made in smaller, more frequent batches—was often just a ploy to accommodate the customers' own sloppy schedules, because they never knew from week to week what they were going to need the following week. Although some firms may still be doing this, the majority are moving to JIT and quality first, and then bringing their suppliers along with them. In many cases, the customer is teaching the supplier how to implement effective JIT and quality programs, as exemplified by AlliedSignal (Tully 1995).

With annual sales exceeding $14 billion, AlliedSignal is a leading producer of auto parts and aerospace electronics. Allied works closely with its suppliers to reduce production costs, with impressive results. For example, in 1994 Allied increased its profits by 21 percent on a 6 percent increase in revenue by reducing its purchase costs. Allied uses a two-pronged approach to lower its purchasing costs. First, it demands a significant one-time price reduction when it enters into a "partnership agreement" with a new supplier. In addition, it requires that the supplier commit to lowering prices by 6 percent (adjusted for inflation) each year. To help the suppliers achieve these requirements, Allied increases its purchase volumes and helps the suppliers increase their operating efficiency. For example, Allied doubled its purchases from Mech-Tronics in return for an initial 10 percent price cut. Additionally, with Allied's help, Mech-Tronics was able to substantially improve its productivity.

Key Elements of Effective Purchasing

Organizations that are highly effective in purchasing follow three practices:

1. *They leverage their buying power.* The advantages associated with decentralization are typically not achieved when it comes to purchasing. For example, Columbia/HCA combines the purchases of its 200-plus hospitals to increase its overall purchasing power. By combining all of its purchases for supplies ranging from cotton swabs to IV solution, for instance, it was able to reduce purchasing costs by $200 million and boost profits by 15 percent.

2. *They commit to a small number of dependable suppliers.* Leading suppliers are invited to compete for an organization's business on the basis of set requirements, such as state-of-the-art products, financial condition, reliable delivery, and commitment to continuous improvement. The best one-to-three suppliers are selected from the field of bidders on the basis of the specified requirements. Typically, one- to five-year contracts are awarded to the selected suppliers. These contracts provide the supplier with the opportunity to demonstrate its commitment to the partnership. If a supplier is able to consistently improve its performance, the organization should reciprocate by increasing the volume of business awarded to that supplier and extending the contract.

3. *They work with and help their suppliers reduce total cost.* Often, organizations will send their own production people to a supplier's plant to help the supplier improve its operating efficiency, improve its quality, and reduce waste. Additionally, an organization may benchmark key aspects of a supplier's operation such as prices, costs, and technologies. If it is discovered that a supplier has slipped relative to the competition, the organization can try to help the supplier regain its lead. If the supplier is unable or unwilling to take the steps necessary to regain its leadership position, the organization may need to find a new partner.

Transportation

The four major **modes of transportation** are, historically, water, rail, truck, and air. Water is the least expensive mode and is good for long trips with bulky, nonperishable items. But it is very slow and of limited accessibility. It handles the majority of ton-miles of traffic. However, railroads handle the most total tons of traffic and are thus used for shorter hauls than water. They have many advantages: ability to handle small as well as large items, good accessibility, specialized services (e.g., refrigeration, liquids, cattle), and still a relatively low cost.

Trucking holds more advantages for short hauls with small volumes to specialized locations. Truck transport has grown at the expense of rail for several reasons such as growth of the national highway system, better equipment, and liberalized regulations.

Air transport is used for small, high-value, or perishable items such as electronic components, lobsters, optical instruments, and important paperwork. Its main advantage is speed of delivery over long distances. Thus, for the appropriate products, it can significantly reduce inventory and warehousing costs, with a corresponding improvement in customer service.

Taking all the pros and cons of each mode of transportation into consideration in planning is a complex task. Table 9.2 lists the major considerations that should be factored into the decision. Each particular situation may have additional factors to consider.

Independent of the specific mode of transport are additional transportation problems involving such considerations as the *number* of transporting vehicles, their capacities, and the *routes* that each vehicle will take. In general, these interrelated problems are frequently included as part of the *routing problem*.

Solving the routing problem involves finding the best number of vehicles and their routes to deliver the organization's output to a group of geographically dispersed recipients. When only one vehicle is serving all the recipients, the problem is known as the *traveling salesman problem*. In this problem a number of possible routes exist between the organization and all the recipients, but only a few or perhaps just one of these routes will minimize the total cost of delivery.

𝒯ABLE 9.2 • Factors to Consider in Transportation Decisions

- Cost per unit shipped
- Ability to fill the transporting vehicle
- Total shipment cost
- Protection of contents from theft, weather, and the like
- Shipping time
- Availability of insurance on contents, delivery, and so forth
- Difficulty of arranging shipment (governmental regulations, transportation to shipment site, and so on)
- Delivery accommodations (to customer's site, transfer to another transportation mode, extra charges)
- Seasonal considerations: weather, holidays, and so on
- Consolidation possibilities (among multiple products)
- Risk: to contents, to delivery promises, to cost, and the like
- Size of product being shipped
- Perishability of product during shipment.

In the routing and traveling salesman problems, certain procedures are available to minimize either the distance traveled or the cost, but quite often there are other considerations, such as balancing workloads among vehicles or minimizing idle or delay time.

Warehousing

A quiet revolution has been occurring in the warehouse in the last decade. A number of seemingly small improvements in various aspects of warehousing and materials handling have joined together with information technology to produce a true leap in productivity and performance. The following are the independent elements that have joined together:

- Computer hardware
- Computer software
- Scanning equipment
- Sortation devices
- Conveyance equipment
- Unit load concepts
- High-density automated storage and retrieval system (AS/RS)
- Warehouse construction
- Simulation modeling
- Management interest

The driving force behind many of these individual improvements, such as barcode labeling, simulation, and AS/RS is, of course, the development of the computer and associated software, particularly the microcomputer. Probably even more significant than the impact of the computer on each of the warehousing elements, however, has been the *tying together* of all the elements, again through the computer. We will look at these elements in closer detail.

Automated Storage and Retrieval Systems

There are four major components of AS/RS:

1. Storage and retrieval (S/R) equipment
2. Storage structures
3. Conveyance equipment
4. Control systems

Of the S/R equipment, there are two types, unit load systems and order-picking systems.

Unit Load

These are the relatively older, better-known systems such as high-rise stacker cranes for high-density palletized storage. Unit load warehousing systems now exceed 100-foot heights and have travel speeds up to 500 feet per minute (fpm) horizontally and 150 fpm vertically. Load capabilities are in the neighborhood of 2 tons. Aisle sizes have shrunk to the width of the standardized load plus only a few inches. The storage and retrieval equipment is mounted on a rail in the aisle with guidance provided at the top.

Recent developments in unit load systems include *deep lane storage*, which stores pallets two deep, thus eliminating half the aisles, and *rackless storage*, which accesses the material through an overhead monorail and thereby uses no aisles at all.

Order Picking

Order-picking systems fill small, partial loads of multiple items such as a retail store might order. These "less-than-unit-load" systems are of two types: in-aisle and out-of-aisle. The in-aisle systems consist of the person going to the part location and picking the part; the out-of-aisle systems bring the parts, or a container holding the parts, to the person at the end of the aisle. The latest innovation in in-aisle systems consists of a microprocessor controller that horizontally and vertically drives a "man-aboard crane" directly to the appropriate container from which the parts are picked.

Recent developments in out-of-aisle systems include microcomputer-controlled carousel loops that rotate the containers on the carousel until the proper container is accessible at the end of the loop. A second major innovation in out-of-aisle systems is the microprocessor-controlled miniload crane. These systems were originally devised for locating and retrieving manila folders in high-density information storage files, but have been adapted very successfully to small-parts retrieval.

In-aisle systems are less expensive to purchase and maintain and give the most flexibility. However, out-of-aisle systems make the best use of space and require fewer people. They also provide the best control.

Storage Structures

There is a tremendous interest in making better use of space, not just to reduce the cost of real estate and plant, but also to reduce the costs of utilities and maintenance. The resulting trend to high-density storage systems is referred to as "maximizing the cube," or in other words, using all the volume in the storage location, particularly the empty space so common *above* the storage bins. The S/R systems described in the previous section directly relate to this trend, particularly concepts such as rackless storage.

But even in the design of the structure there have been exciting innovations. The most recent is called a *rack supported* building, where the storage structure supports the walls and roof of the building. The result is a savings of more than 20 percent in costs and much higher utilization of space. An especially favorable aspect of such structures is that for tax purposes they are treated as depreciable equipment rather than buildings.

Conveyance Equipment

Both fixed-path and variable-path conveyance equipment have seen numerous innovations. One of the major innovations in the latter is the automated guided vehicle systems (AGVS). These self-loading and unloading vehicles now follow an *electronic* guidepath in the floor, for significant reliability improvements over their nonelectronic predecessors.

A major development in fixed-path systems has been in the area of sortation devices, particularly bar coding and its associated scanning equipment. Sortation equipment of the diverter type can now handle up to 120 items per minute and 100 pounds. Tile-sorting machines have reached speeds of 300 items per minute and 200 pounds.

Control Systems

As mentioned previously, this area has probably provided the major breakthrough for all the systems. The computer can be used for receiving, inspection, inventory counting, stock allocation, order picking, backordering, billing, scheduling, and numerous other warehousing functions. Its benefits include better space utilization, reliable control of equipment, higher warehouse productivity, better customer service, lower error rates, and better working conditions with higher worker morale as a result. These benefits are all in addition to the major benefit of simply better managerial control.

Since the mid-1970s, there has been a tremendous increase in the number of computer-controlled AS/RS systems, especially distributed systems with microcomputers tied to a plant computer, either by cable or by microwave radio. These microcomputers work independently but are directed and feed back to the host computer for information updates. They are dedicated in use, thereby performing independently and more reliably.

ROLE OF INFORMATION TECHNOLOGY IN SUPPLY CHAIN MANAGEMENT

In the not-too-distant past the primary means of communication between members of a particular supply chain was paper. Unfortunately, communicating via paper-based transactions is slow, often unreliable, and prone to errors. For example, Campbell Soup Company estimates that 60 percent of the fax and phone orders it receives contain errors (Verity 1996). As a result, salespeople often spend 40 percent of their time correcting these errors rather than making additional sales. To correct this problem, Campbell is investing $30 million in the redesign of its order-processing system. The company hopes the new system will increase the percentage of paperless orders it receives to 80 percent. Managers estimate the system will reduce costs by $18 million annually while at the same time reducing delivery times.

As Campbell Soup illustrates, information technology is a key ingredient to and perhaps the primary enabler of effective supply chain management. In today's highly competitive environment, effective use of information technology helps organizations reduce cycle times, adopt more responsive cross-functional organizational structures, and capture more timely information. The ultimate goal of such information systems is to make available to all participants in the supply chain all the information needed at the time it is needed. Such information includes the status of orders, product availabilities, and delivery schedules.

Electronic commerce (or e-commerce) is the term currently used to describe a variety of approaches for conducting business in a paperless environment. One problem with paper-based systems is the time and money that is wasted rekeying the same information into different computer systems. And of course, the more times the same information is entered, the more opportunities there are for making mistakes. Some analysts estimate that the use of e-commerce reduces the cost of processing a purchase order from $150 to $25. It has been further estimated that companies in the U.S. annually purchase $500 billion worth of goods electronically (Verity 1996).

One early approach to e-commerce was electronic data interchange (EDI). With EDI, business documents such as purchase orders and invoices are transferred between the computers of different organizations in a standard format. The benefits of EDI include faster access to information, improved customer service, reduced paperwork, less redundancy, and better order tracing.

Another important technology to supply chain management is bar coding and scanning. These identification technologies permit the rapid collection and dissemination of information throughout the supply chain. For example, Wal-Mart is well known for making available the point-of-sale information it collects to its supply chain partners. Federal Express uses the same technology to provide its customers with up-to-date tracking information on their packages.

Arguably the most significant information technology development to supply chain management is the Internet, and more specifically, its graphical component known as the World Wide Web (or Web). Without a doubt, the Web offers enormous opportunities for members of a supply chain to share information. Companies such as IBM, General Electric, Dun & Bradstreet, and Microsoft are rapidly developing products and services that will help make the Web the global infrastructure for electronic commerce (Verity 1996). However, a number of hurdles must be resolved before the Web will reach its ultimate potential including issues related to privacy and security.

In the remainder of this chapter our focus turns to the just-in-time technique for managing the schedules and delivery of materials.

HISTORY AND PHILOSOPHY OF JUST-IN-TIME

The concept of JIT was originally developed by the Toyota Motor Company in Japan in the mid-1970s, and it is still called the *Toyota system* by Japanese firms. To understand why JIT was developed, it is important to understand a little about the history and culture of Japan.

Japan is a small country with minimal resources and a large population. Thus, the Japanese have always been careful not to waste resources, including space (especially land), as well as time and labor. Waste is abhorrent because the country has so little space and so few natural resources to begin with. Therefore, the Japanese have been motivated to maximize the gain or yield from the few resources available. It has also been necessary for them to maintain their respect for each other in order to work and live together smoothly and effectively in such a densely populated space. As a result, their work habits tend to reflect this philosophy of minimizing waste and maintaining respect. JIT, an example of this philosophy, is based on three primary tenets:

1. Minimizing waste in all forms
2. Continually improving processes and systems
3. Maintaining respect for all workers

During production, the Japanese studiously avoid waste of materials, space, and labor. They therefore pay significant attention to identifying and correcting problems that could potentially lead to such waste. Moreover, operation and procedures are constantly being improved and fine-tuned so as to increase productivity and yield, further eliminating waste. Equal respect is paid to all workers, and the trappings of status are minimized so that respect among all can be maintained.

JIT takes its name from the idea of replenishing material buffers just when they are needed and not before or after. This eliminates the waste of having expensive materials sit idle while awaiting processing, as well as the waste of having expensive resources wait for late materials. It also avoids the problem of having unacceptable-quality items hidden in inventory until some later date; with JIT, all items and possible defects are immediately visible. However, JIT is much broader than its name suggests: it seeks to eliminate all types of waste, including scrap, defective products, unneeded space, unnecessary inventories, and idle facilities.

Translated into actions for operations, JIT means keeping work flows moving all the time from receipt in the plant to delivery to the customer, eliminating inventories, reducing travel distances, eliminating defects and scrap, making maximum use of precious space, and so forth. This philosophy is applied however and wherever it can be. Thus, JIT cannot be reduced to a "formula"; every firm may apply the philosophy differently.

By using JIT, Toyota was able to reduce the time needed to produce a car from 15 days to 1 day. In fact, JIT is best applied to a production system, such as automobile assembly, that would be considered repetitive, such as a flow shop. Although automobile assembly is not a flow shop in the sense that every item is identical, it is closer to a flow shop than to a job shop where every item, or lot, is completely different. The Japanese perception of JIT is to attempt to make the goods "flow like water" through the shop. Although this is more difficult for a job shop, the approach can still be used there with significant benefits.

Because of its broad nature and wide range of benefits—from increased market share to better quality to lower costs—JIT has become, for many companies, a major element in competitive strategy. The firms may adopt only particular or especially relevant elements of JIT, or add certain other aspects or programs to it, but it still plays a major role in their overall strategy. For instance, the inventory philosophy in many firms goes by the name zero inventories. At IBM, JIT is known as *continuous flow*, whereas at Hewlett-Packard it is called *stockless production*. In some plants it is even called *repetitive manufacturing*.

More recent adoptions of JIT have also stressed its second aspect: continuous improvements. That is, JIT is considered not simply a means of converting the transformation system from a sloppy, wasteful form (sarcastically referred to as *just-in-case*) to an efficient, competitive form, but also as producing continuing improvements throughout the system to keep the firm competitive and profitable in the future.

Yet to be seen in any significant form is the third aspect of JIT: "respect for people." This is probably the most basic and important of the three tenets. U.S. industry seems to be moving slowly in this direction, particularly with the adoption of production teams, quality circles (Chapter 3), and cellular manufacturing (Chapter 5). Nonetheless, U.S. firms and industries seem far behind the Japanese in obtaining respect and loyalty from their workers. This is probably because these firms and industries do not show respect for and loyalty to their employees in the first place.

Initially, in the early 1980s, JIT was greeted with a great deal of ambivalence in the United States. Typical of the sentiment at this time was, "It will never work here." However, this view abruptly changed when a number of domestic companies such as Hewlett-Packard and Harley-Davidson began demonstrating the significant benefits of JIT.

Next, we describe the most common characteristics of JIT systems and compare them with the more traditional just-in-case systems.

$\mathcal{T}$RADITIONAL SYSTEMS COMPARED WITH JUST-IN-TIME

Table 9.3 presents a dozen characteristics of JIT systems that tend to distinguish them from the more traditional systems historically used in U.S. industry. These characteristics range from philosophy and culture to standard operating procedures. The contrasts summarized in Table 9.3 are described in the following subsections.

Priorities

Traditionally, most firms want to accept all customer orders, or at least provide a large number of options from which customers may order. However, this confuses the production task, increases the chance of errors, and increases costs. With JIT, the target market is usually limited and the options are also limited. A wise JIT firm knows which customers it does *not* want.

In JIT firms the emphasis is on low cost but high quality within that limited market. This does not mean, however, that high performance or comfort is unavailable. For example, a car may have many accessories that would be considered luxury options on traditional cars, such as air conditioning, but are included as standard. By including these features as standard equipment, the production task is simplified and the product can be produced at lower cost. The primary options, if offered, would usually include mutually exclusive aspects such as color.

Thus, we see that right from the start the overall priorities of JIT firms are different from those of the traditional firm. This perspective is reflected in the approach

Table 9.3 • Comparison of Traditional Systems and JIT

Characteristic	Traditional	JIT
Priorities	Accept all orders Many options	Limited market Few options Low cost, high quality
Engineering	Customized outputs Design from scratch	Standardized outputs Incremental design Simplify, design for manufacturing
Capacity	Highly utilized Inflexible	Moderately utilized Flexible
Transformation system	Job shop	Flow shops, cellular manufacturing
Layout	Large space Materials handling equipment	Small space Close, manual transfer
Work force	Narrow skills Specialized Individualized Competitive attitude Change by edict Easy pace Status: symbols, pay, privilege	Broad skills Flexible Work teams Cooperative attitude Change by consensus Hard pace No status differentials
Scheduling	Long setups Long runs	Quick changeovers Mixed-model runs
Inventories	Large WIP buffers Stores, cribs, stockrooms	Small WIP buffers Floor stock
Suppliers	Many Competitive Deliveries to central receiving area Independent forecasts	Few or single-source Cooperative, network Deliveries directly to assembly line Shared forecasts
Planning and control	Planning-oriented Complex Computerized	Control-oriented Simple Visual
Quality	Via inspection Critical points Acceptance sampling	At the source Continuous Statistical process control
Maintenance	Corrective By experts Run equipment fast Run one shift	Preventive By operator Run equipment slowly Run 24 hours

JIT firms take to each of the other production characteristics as well. In one sense, their "strategy" for competing is different from that of the traditional firm, and this strategy permeates their production system.

Engineering

In line with the priorities, engineering in the JIT firm designs standard outputs and incrementally improves each design. The parts and subassemblies that make up each output are also standardized; over time they are further simplified and improved. More traditionally, engineers attempt to design custom outputs to satisfy unique customers, starting from scratch each time and designing new parts and subassemblies. The reason for the new parts and subassemblies is often that the engineers change and do not know what their predecessors have already designed. Yet even if the same engineers are doing the design work, they often design new parts when a previously designed, tested, and proven part would do—because they cannot afford the time to find the previous design.

Last, JIT designs usually include considerations about the manufacturability of the part or product. This is called ***design for manufacturability (DFM)*** or ***design for assembly (DFA)***. Too often, the traditional firm whips up an engineering design as quickly as it can (since it has had to start from scratch) and then passes the design on to manufacturing without giving a thought to how it can be made (sometimes it cannot). With this approach, poor quality and high costs often result and cannot be improved on the shop floor, since they were designed in from the start. If the product or part absolutely cannot be made, or perhaps cannot be assembled, then the design is sent back to engineering to modify, taking more time and costing more in engineering hours.

Capacity

In the traditional firm, excess capacities of all kinds are usually designed into the system ***just-in-case*** a problem arises and they are needed. These capacities may consist of extra equipment, overtime, partial shifts, and frequently, large work-in-process (WIP) inventories. All of them cost extra money to acquire and maintain, which eventually increases the cost of the product.

In the JIT firm, excess capacities are kept to a minimum to avoid inherent waste, particularly the WIP inventories, as will be noted later. In place of the excess capacities, tighter control is exerted over the production system so that conditions do not arise where significant additional capacity is needed in the first place.

Transformation System

Although JIT can be used profitably in the continuous process and project industries, it offers the most benefit in repetitive production. If the true market situation consists of unique products, then JIT may not have a lot to offer (although its three basic tenets and the various characteristics described earlier may still be of value). In these less repetitive cases, an MRP system may be most appropriate. However, in the common batch situation where the United States typically uses job shops, JIT can be used by smoothing flows, converting to mixed-model assembly and sequencing, minimizing lead times, and employing cellular manufacturing and product-line–based flow shops. Cellular manufacturing and flow shops were discussed in earlier chapters; the other concepts are described here.

Smoothing Work Flows

The Japanese have noticed that erratic flows in one part of a production system often become magnified in other parts of the system, not only further down the line but, because of scheduling, further *up* the line as well. This is due to the formation of queues in the production system, the batching of parts for processing on machines, the lot-sizing rules we use to initiate production, and many other similar policies. These disruptions to the smooth flow of goods are costly to the production system and waste time, materials, and human energy.

Another different aspect of JIT production is that the parts flow so quickly through the production system that the typical disposable packaging can become a major nuisance. Thus, manufacturers are turning to reusable, and generic, packages, totes, cartons, pallets, carriers, and other approaches that will perform a number of tasks such as protection and identification, as well as being carriers.

Note that early production or delivery is just as inappropriate as late delivery. The goal is *perfect* adherence to schedule—without this, erratic flows are introduced throughout the plant. With continuous, smooth flows of parts come continuous, level flows of work so there are no peak demands on workers, machines, or other resources. Then, once adequate capacity has been attained it will always be sufficient.

The Japanese therefore attempt to make the goods "flow like water," as they describe it. The first step in achieving this smooth flow is to master-schedule small lots of final products, but frequently. Every product will be produced at least once in a day, and often many times throughout the day. With many small lots master-scheduled for final assembly, multiple small lots of components must also be produced. This is achieved by mixed-model sequencing.

Converting to Mixed-Model Assembly and Sequencing

The mixed-model approach to assembly and sequencing is basically a matter of even production. With even production, items are produced smoothly throughout the day rather than in large batches of one item, followed by long shutdowns and setups and then by another large batch of another item. Let us demonstrate with an example.

Suppose three different models are being produced in a plant that operates two shifts, and the monthly demands are as given in Table 9.4. Dividing the monthly demand by 20 working days per month and then again by two shifts per day gives the daily production requirements per shift. A common divisor of the required production per shift of 20 A's, 15 B's, and 10 C's is 5. Using 5 as the common divisor means that we would produce five batches of each of these models each shift. Dividing the required production per shift of each model by five batches indicates that on each production cycle 4 units of A, 3 units of B, and 2 units of C will be produced. Assuming two 15-minute breaks per 8-hour shift (480 minutes), the production rate must be 45 units per 450 minute shift ($480 - 15 - 15 = 450$), or 10 minutes per unit (450 minutes per shift/45 units per shift). Since one cycle consists

$\mathscr{T}_{ABLE}$ 9.4 • Mixed-Model Assembly Cycle

Model	Monthly Demand	Required/Shift	Units/Cycle
A	800	$800/(20 \times 2) = 20$	4
B	600	15	3
C	400	10	2
Total	1800	45	9

of 9 units (4 A's, 3 B's, and 2 C's), the entire cycle will take 90 minutes. Thus, each production cycle of 4 A's, 3 B's, and 2 C's will be repeated five times each shift to produce the required 45 units.

One possible production cycle would be to produce the three models in batches using a sequence such as A–A–A–A–B–B–B–C–C. Alternatively, to smooth the production of the nine units throughout the production cycle, a sequence such as A–B–A–B–C–A–B–A–C might be used. Clearly, numerous other sequences are also possible. With daily production of all models, no erratic changes are introduced into the plant through customer demand, because some of every product is always available. When models are produced in traditional batches (such as producing 1000 A's, then 750 B's, followed by 500 C's), one or more batches may well be depleted before the other batches are finished. This then necessitates putting a "rush" order through the plant (in order not to lose a customer for the models that are out of stock), disrupting ongoing work, and adding to the cost of all products—not to mention the frustration involved.

Minimizing Lead Times

In the traditional firm, long lead times are often thought to allow more time to make decisions and get work performed. But in the JIT firm, short lead times mean easier, more accurate forecasting and planning. Moreover, a way to capitalize on the increasing strategic importance of fast response to the customer is to minimize all the lead times. If lead times are reduced, there is less time for things to go awry, to get lost, or to be changed. For example, it is not at all uncommon for an order placed two months ago to be changed every three weeks until it is delivered: leave a bracket off, produce 10 more than requested, and so on. However, if the delivery time is one week, the customers get exactly what they need and can delay ordering until the week before they need it (when they know best what they will actually need).

Sometimes this concept of short lead times and fast responsiveness is captured by the phrase, "Don't let the parts touch the floor." In order not to touch the floor, the parts have to be kept on the machines and thus be worked on until completed. A way to help keep the parts off the floor and cut lead times is to move workstations closer together. This facilitates passing the parts from station to station and making small amounts of each part.

Smaller batches result in shorter lead times and less inventory, at the same time. With smaller batches, engineering changes get to the customer sooner, problems with quality are corrected more quickly, rework is reduced, there is less obsolete inventory, and new products get to market more promptly. Thus, although reduced inventory is an important benefit of short lead times and small batches, other benefits are equally valuable, if not more so.

The approach used by Gateway 2000 and Dell Computer to assemble personal computers illustrates the benefits of shorter lead times (Burrows 1995). Specifically, both Gateway and Dell build computers to order rather than producing large inventories of finished computers. Building to order allows these companies to substantially reduce their inventory level—Dell carries 35 days of inventory, compared with Compaq, which carries a 110-day supply. Maintaining less inventory enhances Gateway's and Dell's ability to respond rapidly to changes in technology, such as advances in microprocessors or storage devices. For instance, because Gateway and Dell had substantially less inventory, both companies were able to introduce higher-margin computers featuring the Pentium chip earlier than their competition. In early January 1995, approximately 50 percent of Gateway's computers had the Pentium chip, compared with less than 10 percent for Compaq and IBM. Furthermore, having less inventory better positioned Gateway and Dell to respond effectively to the flaw in the Pentium chip by being among the first in the industry to announce the shipment of computers with replacement chips. Finally, because Gateway and Dell sell directly to the customer, both companies are able to reduce operating costs—Gateway's operating costs are 5.4 percent of revenues compared with Compaq's 13 percent—as well as to reduce the selling price.

Using Kanban

As opposed to the MRP approach of "pushing" materials through a plant, there are **pull systems** based on signals indicating need. Push systems are planning-based systems that determine when workstations will probably need parts if everything goes according to plan. However, operations rarely go according to plan, and as a result, materials may be either too late or too early. To safeguard against being too late and to make sure that people always have enough work to keep busy, safety stocks are used, even with MRP; these may not even be needed, but they further increase the stocks of materials in the plant. Thus, in a push system we see workers always busy making items and lots of material in the plant.

In comparison, a pull system is a control-based system that signals the requirement for parts as they are needed in reality. The result is that workers may occasionally (and sometimes frequently) be idle because more materials are not needed. This keeps material from being produced when it is not needed (waste). The appearance of a plant using a pull system is quiet and slow, with not much material around.

To further contrast the differences between push and pull systems, consider the production system shown in Figure 9.5. The system consists of one machine of type A and one machine of type B. Machine A has the capacity to produce 75 units per day, and machine B has the capacity to produce 50 units per day. All products are first produced on machine A and then processed on machine B. Daily demand for the organization is 50 units.

In a push system each work center would work as fast as it could and *push* the product on to work centers downstream, regardless of whether they needed additional materials. In Figure 9.5, after the first day of operation, machine A would produce 75 units, machine B would process 50 of the 75 units it received from machine A, and 25 units would be added to work-in-process inventory. Each day the system operates in this fashion, 25 more units will be added to the work-in-process

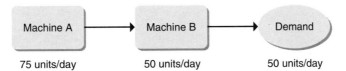

Figure 9.5 Sequential production system with two machines.

inventory in front of machine B. This might seem irrational to you, but the only way for inventory not to be built up is for machine A to produce less than it is capable of producing. In this example, we could idle machine A 33 percent of the day and produce and transport only 50 units to machine B. However, if you were the plant manager and you noticed that the worker assigned to machine A was working only 67 percent of the time, what would you think? You might think the worker was goofing off and order him or her to run the machine. Of course, doing this only increases the amount of money tied up in inventory and does nothing to increase the amount of product completed and shipped to the customer.

In a pull system, the worker at machine A would produce only in response to requests for more materials made by the worker at machine B. Furthermore, the worker at machine B is authorized to make additional product only to replenish product that is used to meet actual customer demand. If there is no customer demand, machine B will sit idle. And if machine B sits idle, machine A will be idle. In this way, the production of the entire operation is matched to actual demand.

The signals used in a pull system to authorize production may be of various kinds. Dover Corporation's OPW Division makes gasoline nozzles for gas pumps and uses wire bins as signals. Each bin holds 500 nozzles, and two are used at any time. Raw material is taken out of one bin until it is empty, and then material is drawn from the second bin. A bin collector constantly scouts the plant, looking for empty bins, and returns them to the stockroom where they are refilled and returned to the workstations. In this manner, no more than two bins' worth of material (1000 units) is ever in process.

Hewlett-Packard uses yellow tape to make squares about 1 foot on a side as the signals for its assembly lines. One square lies between every two workers. When workers finish an item, they draw the next unit to work on from the square between them and the previous worker. When the square is empty, this is the signal that another item is needed from the previous worker. Thus there are never more than two items in process per worker.

These two examples are actually modifications of Toyota's original JIT system. Toyota's materials management system is known as ***kanban***, which means "card" in Japanese. The idea behind this system is to authorize materials for production only if there is a need for them. Through the use of kanban authorization cards, production is "pulled" through the system, instead of pushed out before it is needed and then stored. Thus, the MPS authorizes final assembly, which in turn authorizes subassembly production, which in its turn authorizes parts assembly, and so on. If production stops at some point in the system, immediately all downstream production also stops, and soon thereafter all upstream production as well.

Typically, two cards are used—a withdrawal kanban and a production kanban. The cards are very simple, showing only the part number and name, the work centers involved, a storage location, and the container capacity. The approach is illustrated in Figure 9.6.

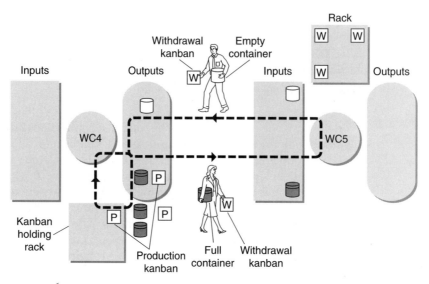

Figure 9.6   Kanban process.

Assume that work flows from work center (WC) 4 to WC5, and containers are used to transport the output from WC4 to WC5, where they are used as inputs. When WC5 sees that it will be needing more input parts, it takes an empty container and a withdrawal kanban back to WC4. There it leaves the empty container and locates a full one, which has a production kanban with it. WC5 replaces the production kanban with its withdrawal kanban, which authorizes it to remove the full container and the withdrawal kanban. It puts the production kanban in a rack at WC4, thereby authorizing the production of another container of parts. Back at WC5, the withdrawal kanban is placed back in its rack. WC4 cannot initiate production and fill an empty container until it has a production kanban authorizing additional production. Thus, withdrawal kanbans authorize the acquisition of additional materials from a supplying work center and production kanbans authorize a work center to make additional product.

The advantage of such a system is its simplicity. Being entirely visual in nature, it facilitates smooth production flow, quality inspection, minimization of inventory, and clear control of the production system.

Layout

The traditional method of layout follows the job-shop approach of using widely spread-out equipment with space for stockrooms, tool cribs, and work-in-process inventories between the equipment. To handle and move all this inventory, automated or semiautomated equipment such as conveyors, carousels, and forklifts is also required, which takes even more space.

With JIT, equipment is moved as close together as possible so that parts can be actually handed from one worker or machine to the next. The use of cells and flow lines dictates small lots of parts with minimal work-in-process and material-moving equipment. The cells are often U-shaped so that one worker can easily access all the machines without moving very far, and finished products will exit at the same point where raw materials enter the cell.

It is not unusual for the work flows in a traditional job shop to look like a plate of spaghetti when traced on a diagram of the shop. With JIT, however, the work flows are short and direct, with only a few major flow streams, because each part family has the same flows.

Work Force

One of the key elements of JIT is the role of the work force as a means of uncovering and solving problems. Rather than considering the workers as the traditional cogs in the great plant machine, each with its own tasks, skills, and narrow responsibilities, JIT strives for a broadly skilled, flexible worker who will look for and solve production problems wherever they appear.

A means to help achieve this with JIT is the use of work teams, whereby each team has the entire responsibility for a set of parts or products. Moreover, to keep JIT working properly, the workers must coordinate themselves, filling in for each other and solving each problem as it arises, since there is no inventory to use as a cover. Broadly skilled, flexible workers who do their own quality inspections and maintain their own equipment also facilitate this goal.

In the traditional approach, a competitive attitude is assumed, not only among workers but also between workers and managers. The manager has the authority and responsibility for the workers' performance. Changes are made according to managerial planning and decisions, with the worker adapting as needed. In JIT systems, everyone in the firm assumes a cooperative attitude, and plans and decisions are made by consensus.

In the traditional shop, much of the employees' time is nonworking time: looking for parts, moving materials, setting up machines, getting instructions, and so on. Thus, when actually working, the employees tend to work fast, producing parts at a rapid pace whether or not the parts are needed. (This, of course, results in errors, scrap, and machine breakdowns, which again provide a reason to stop working.) The outcome is a stop-and-go situation that, overall, results in a relatively inefficient, ineffective pace for most workers.

Conversely, with JIT, the workers produce only when the next worker is ready. The pace is steady and fast, although never frantic. In spite of the built-in rule that workers should be idle if work is not needed, the focus on smooth flows, short setups, and other such simplifications means that workers are rarely idle. (Of course, if they *are* idle, that is an immediate signal to the system designers that work is not progressing smoothly through the plant and adjustments need to be made.) The result is that with JIT the pace is considerably harder, though smoother and less frenetic.

Managerial treatment is different under JIT as well. In the traditional shop, managers are distinguished with a variety of symbols and privileges, most significant of which may be much higher pay rates, which at times approach the ridiculous. The special parking spaces, suits and ties, bonuses, freedom from time clocks, executive cafeterias, and other trappings of status tend to alienate the workers and produce a competitive rather than a cooperative attitude.

In the JIT shop, the managers, who earn higher salaries, share the same facilities as the workers and are expected to work longer hours. There are no particular status differentials. If a pay cut comes, it is taken out of the managers' salaries first and the workers' last. Everyone pitches in to do extra work when hard times roll around, but the managers are expected to do more than the floor workers.

Scheduling

We have already contrasted the traditional scheduling, with its long setups and long runs, and the JIT approach: mixed models and smooth flows. However, it might be of interest to present a more specific contrast of JIT and MRP in terms of their characteristics. For example, JIT is clearly much simpler, more transparent in its operation, and less data- (and computer-) intensive. Major differences regarding inventory have also been noted and will be detailed in the next subsection.

But is there no way to combine the advantages of JIT and MRP? Yes, there is a way. It consists of using MRP to pull the long-lead-time items and purchases *into* the shop, and it then employs JIT once the parts and raw materials have entered the shop. Dover's OPW Division uses this approach, for example. It employs MRP's explosion and lead-time offsetting to identify and order the external parts and raw materials and uses JIT's procedures to run a smooth, efficient plant once the parts and materials arrive. In other cases MRP is used as a planning tool for order releases and final assembly schedules, while JIT is used to execute and implement the plan.

We have not yet focused on how JIT reduces setup times so that mixed-model production and smooth work flows are possible. In the traditional plant, machine setups take a long time, and this has resulted in long runs of items that are subsequently made. It is easy to understand why workers get upset if a five-hour setup has to be "broken" and set up again for a special customer's rush order.

But if small lots of every product must be produced at least once each day, five-hour setups must be reduced. In fact, such setups usually can be reduced fairly easily, because so little attention has been paid to reducing setup time in the past. It is common for firms to reduce setups from n hours to n minutes—for example, reducing a setup that took all day (eight hours) to just eight minutes.

As was discussed in Chapter 5, one approach to reducing setup times is to adopt cellular manufacturing. Another approach, if the equipment is available and utilization rates are not a problem, is to use multiple machines that have already been set up for the new task. Alternatively, some of the more advanced and automated equipment will automatically reset itself. In the remaining cases, the setup task can be made much more efficient through a number of techniques that have been largely identified and catalogued by the Japanese. Some of these are described next.

The Japanese distinguish between internal setup time, which requires that the machine be turned off, and external setup time, which can be conducted while the machine is still working on the previous part. First, a major effort is directed toward converting internal to external setup time, which is easier to reduce. This is largely done by identifying all the previously internal setup tasks that can either be conducted just as easily as external setup work or, with some changes in the operation, be done externally. Then, the external task times are reduced by such techniques as staging dies, using duplicate fixtures, employing shuttles, and installing roller supports. Last, internal time is reduced by such creative approaches as using hinged bolts, folding brackets, guide pins, or lazy Susans.

Once the setup times are reduced to reasonable periods, the firm gains not only in smoother work flows and shorter lead times but also in flexibility to any changes in production schedules stemming from accidents, unexpected breakages, customers' problems, and so on. Clearly, this flexibility is immensely valuable.

Inventories

In Chapter 8, the economic order quantity was presented as the optimal order quantity, given the trade-off between inventory carrying cost and setup or ordering cost. The model also demonstrates the relationship between setup cost and average inventory levels: order quantities, and consequently average inventory levels, increase as setup time and cost increase. Knowing that the EOQ minimized total costs, managers in the United States simply plugged values into the EOQ formula to determine optimal order quantities. However, use of the EOQ model assumes that its inputs are fixed. In contrast to their American counterparts, managers in Japan did not assume that these inputs were fixed. In fact, they invested significant amounts of time and other resources in finding ways to reduce equipment setup times. These efforts led to substantial reductions in setup times and therefore in setup costs, and ultimately to much smaller batch sizes, which became the basis of the JIT system.

In Japan, inventory is seen as an evil in itself. It is a resource sitting idle, wasting money. But, more important, inventory tends to hide problems. In the traditional plant, inventories are used to buffer operations so that problems at one stage don't affect the next stage. However, inventories also hide problems, such as defective parts, until the inventory is needed and then is found to be defective. For example, in a plant with lots of work-in-process inventory, a worker who discovers a batch of defective parts can simply put them aside and work on something else. By the time the worker returns to the defective batch, if ever, so much time has elapsed since the batch was processed upstream that the cause of the problem is unlikely to be discovered and corrected to prevent a recurrence. In contrast, in an environment where there is little or no buffer inventory, a worker who discovers a defective batch has no choice but to work on the batch. Furthermore, the worker is in a good position to notify upstream operations of the problem so that they can correct it and ensure that it does not occur in the future.

The Japanese liken inventory, and the money it represents, to the water in a lake. They see problems as boulders and obstacles under the water, as shown in Figure 9.7. To expose the problems, they reduce the inventories, as shown in Figure 9.7, and then solve the problems. Then they lower the inventory some more, exposing more problems, and solve those, too. They continue this until all the problems are solved and the inventory investment is practically gone. The result is a greatly improved and smoother production system.

In the traditional plant, almost the opposite happens. Because managers know that their plant produces, say, 15 percent defective products, they produce 15 percent

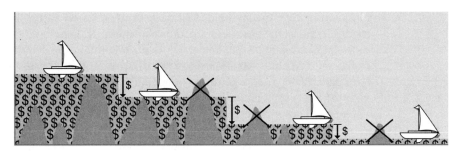

Figure 9.7 Lowering inventory investment to expose problems.

extra, which goes into inventory. That's the wrong way to handle the problem—they should fix the problem in the first place, not cover it up with expensive inventory.

All types of inventories are considered liabilities: work-in-process, raw materials, finished goods, component parts, and so on. By eliminating storage space, not only do we save space, but we also disallow inventories where defectives can be hidden until no one knows who made them. And by eliminating queues of work waiting for machines, we facilitate automatic inspection by workers of hand-passed parts, thereby identifying problems when they begin rather than after 1000 units have been made incorrectly.

If the space saved when operations are moved closer to each other—frequently 33 percent of the original space—is immediately used for something else, then inventory can't be dumped there. This facilitates reducing the lead time, smoothing the workload, and reducing the inventory, all at the same time.

Last, with minimal or no inventory, control of materials is much easier and less expensive. Parts don't get lost, don't have to be moved, don't have to be labeled, and don't have to be held in computer memory or inventory records. Basically, discipline and quality are much improved and cost is reduced, simultaneously.

Supplying in a JIT Environment

Traditional practice has been to treat suppliers as adversaries and play them off against each other. Multiple sourcing purportedly keeps prices down and ensures a wide supply of parts. However, multiple sourcing also means that no supplier is getting an important fraction of the order; thus, there is no incentive to work with the firm to meet specifications for quality and delivery.

With JIT and the desire for frequent, smooth deliveries of small lots, the supplier must be considered part of the team. As part of the team, the supplier is even expected to help plan and design the purchased parts to be supplied. Schedules must be closely coordinated, and many small deliveries are expected every day. Thus, it is in the supplier's interest to locate a plant or warehouse close to the customer. Clearly, then, the supplier must have a large enough order to make this trouble worthwhile; thus, *single-sourcing* for 100 percent of the requirements is common. But with such large orders, the customer can expect the supplier to become more efficient in producing the larger quantities of items, so quantity discounts become available. Moreover, having just one source is also more convenient for a firm that must interact and coordinate closely with the supplier. Companies that develop single-sourcing relationships recognize the mutual dependency of the supplier–customer relationship. Specifically, for the customer to prosper in the marketplace, the supplier must supply high-quality items in the right quantities on time. On the other hand, the more successful the customer, the more business is generated for the supplier.

Perhaps equally significant, there is no incoming inspection of the materials to check their quality—all parts must be of specified quality and guaranteed by the supplier. Again, this requires a cooperative rather than an adversarial approach, with the supplier working with the team. Many JIT firms are now establishing a list of "certified" suppliers that they can count on to deliver perfect quality and thus become members of their production teams. In fact, many organizations implementing such programs will purchase products only from suppliers that pass their certification criteria. Often companies that set up certification programs work with their suppliers to help them become certified.

Single-sourcing also has some disadvantages, however. The largest, of course, is the risk of being totally dependent on one supplier. If the supplier, perhaps through no fault on its part, cannot deliver as needed, the firm is stuck. With the minimal buffers typical of JIT, this could mean expensive idled production and large shortages. There is also some question about the supplier's incentive to become more creative in terms of producing higher quality or less expensive parts, since it already has the single-source contract. Yet the Japanese constantly pressure their suppliers to continue reducing prices, expecting that, at the least, the effect of increased learning with higher volumes will result in lower prices.

In many early and unsuccessful applications of JIT in the automobile industry, rather than change their internal procedures, firms simply required their suppliers to stock finished goods for quick, small deliveries to the firm. However, this added significant costs to the suppliers' operations, and the approach failed. The JIT firm must work with its suppliers and teach them the JIT procedures it is itself employing internally that will reduce costs and increase quality, thereby allowing suppliers also to deliver small lots more frequently.

With the adoption of JIT, the role and importance of purchasing are increasing significantly, while the size of the function is decreasing, owing to a reduced supplier base. Given the opportunities, many of the best managers are now moving into this area. Tremendous cost savings are possible with JIT, and this translates into larger profits and improved competitiveness for the firm.

Planning and Control

In the traditional firm, planning is the focus, and it is typically complex and computerized. MRP is a good example of the level of planning and analysis that goes into the traditional production system. Unfortunately, plans often go astray, but since the firm is focused on planning rather than control, the result is to try to improve planning the next time, and this, in turn, results in ever more complex plans. Thus, these firms spend most of their time planning and replanning and very little time actually executing the plans.

In the JIT approach, the focus is on control. Thus, procedures are kept simple and visual. Rather than planning and forecasting for an uncertain future, the firm attempts to respond to what actually happens in real time with flexible, quick operations. Some planning is certainly conducted, but to be even more effective and efficient in responding to actual events, the planning is directed to simple expectations and improvements in the control system.

Quality

The traditional approach to quality is to inspect the goods at critical points in the production system to weed out bad items and correct the system. At the least, final inspection on a sample should be conducted before a lot is sent to a customer. If too many defectives are found, the entire lot is inspected and the bad items are replaced with good ones. Scrap rates are tracked so that the firm knows how many to initiate through the production system in order to yield the number of good items desired by the customer.

With JIT, the goal is zero defects and perfect quality. A number of approaches are used for this purpose, as described in Chapter 3. But the most important elements are the workers themselves—who check the parts as they hand them to the next worker—and the small lot sizes produced, as described earlier. If a part is bad, it is caught at the time of production, and the error in the production system is corrected immediately.

Maintenance

In the traditional approach to production, maintenance has been what is termed **corrective maintenance**, although **preventive maintenance** is also common. Corrective maintenance is repairing a machine when it breaks down, whereas preventive maintenance is conducting maintenance before the machine is expected to fail, or at regular intervals. Corrective maintenance is more acceptable in the traditional firm, because there are queues of material sitting in front of the machines to be worked on so that production can continue undisturbed, at least until the queues are gone.

But in the JIT shop, if a machine breaks down it will eventually stop all the following *downstream* equipment for lack of work. (It will almost immediately stop all *upstream* equipment as well, through the pull system.) Thus, the JIT shop tends to use preventive maintenance extensively so that stoppages do not occur. JIT firms operate in other ways to minimize the chance of stoppages; for example, they run the equipment at much slower and steadier rates to prevent overloads that lead to failures. (Recall the frenetic pace of traditional shops when they were in a work mode.) Running the machines slowly, at less than their rated capacity, and steadily, throughout 24 hours a day, minimizes their chance of breakdown while maximizing their output.

But a more significant difference between the traditional firm and the JIT firm lies in their approach to maintenance and repair. The traditional shop uses a "crew" of experts who do nothing but repair broken equipment, whereas the JIT shop relies much more heavily on the operator for most maintenance tasks, especially simple preventive maintenance.

$\mathcal{J}$IT: BENEFITS, PROBLEMS, AND APPLICATIONS

In this section we discuss JIT in terms of both its potential benefits and it problems. Full implementation of JIT is not required to obtain some of the benefits; partial implementation can also provide many benefits. We then address the issue of services and how JIT might be applied in this sector of the economy.

Typical Benefits of JIT

As we have seen, JIT offers a variety of possible benefits: reduced inventories and space, faster response to customers due to shorter lead times, less scrap, higher quality, increased communication and teamwork, and greater emphasis on identifying and solving problems. In general, there are five primary types of benefits: (1) cost savings, (2) revenue increases, (3) investment savings, (4) work-force improvements, and (5) uncovering problems.

1. *Cost savings:* Costs are saved a number of ways: inventory reductions, reduced scrap, fewer defects, fewer changes due to both customers and engineering, less space, decreased labor hours, less rework, reduced overhead, and other such effects. Total savings range in the neighborhood of 20 to 25 percent, with significantly higher savings on individual categories such as inventory and defects.

2. *Revenue increases:* Revenues are increased primarily through better service and quality to the customer. Short lead times and faster response to customers' needs result in better margins and higher sales. In addition, revenues will be coming in faster on newer products and services.

3. *Investment savings:* Investment is saved through three primary effects. First, less space (about a third) is needed for the same capacity. Second, inventory is reduced to the point that turns run about 50 to 100 a year (compared with 3 or 4 in U.S. industry). Third, the volume of work produced in the same facility is significantly increased, frequently by as much as 100 percent.

4. *Work-force improvements:* The employees of JIT firms are much more satisfied with their work. They prefer the teamwork it demands, and they like the fact that fewer problems arise. They are also better trained for the flexibility and skills needed with JIT (inspection, maintenance), and they enjoy the growth they experience in their jobs. All this translates into better, more productive work.

5. *Uncovering problems:* One of the unexpected benefits is the greater visibility to problems that JIT allows, if management is willing to capitalize on the opportunity to fix these problems. In trying to speed up a process, all types of difficulties are uncovered and most of them are various forms of waste so not only is response time improved but cost is usually also.

Figure 9.8 illustrates how these benefits are derived from JIT and which elements interact and support other elements. The synergies throughout the JIT system are clear. For example, reduced scrap and better quality lead to faster feedback on remaining scrap and defects, leading, in turn, to better awareness of these problems in the team and a focus on ideas for further reducing scrap and defects. Similarly, smaller lot sizes lead to better quality, which leads to a focus on remaining defects, which in turn leads to ideas for further cuts in lot sizes. All the synergistic aspects of JIT eventually result in lower costs, higher productivity, and better customer response (higher revenues and market shares).

Smart Practice provides an example of how JIT was used to improve customer service (Smart Practice 1997). Smart Practice is a national direct marketer to dentists. Its catalogs list a variety of products, but one of its lines—personalized printed materials—was creating a larger-than-normal number of complaints from customers, resulting in an increasing number of calls, up to 26,000, to the customer service department. Analysis of the calls indicated that two questions accounted for 64 percent of all the calls: "What is this charge on my statement?" and "Where is my order?"

Investigation of the order process for these materials indicated that the long lead times to order (4 to 6 days), produce (7 days), and deliver (up to 10 days) the

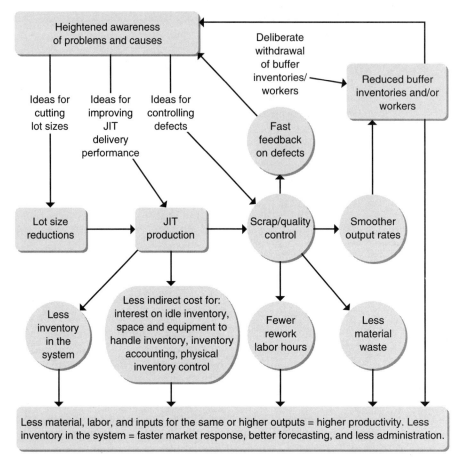

Figure 9.8 Interaction of elements of JIT. *Source*: R. J. Schonberger, "Japanese Manufacturing Techniques," *Operations Management Review* (Spring 1983).

products resulted in charges on the customer's account statement for orders invoiced but not yet received. It was concluded that the problem could be solved by turning to the concepts of JIT to reduce the lead time for these materials.

One major problem was that the orders were "batched" by day as they progressed through the process. Frequent inspections, verifications, new account setup, invoicing, order printing, proofreading, and other activities were all slowed by the need to handle the orders in these batch sizes. To address this problem, the orders are now "batched" every 15 minutes so there is a continuous work flow. At the same time, the process itself was analyzed and improved by eliminating unnecessary or redundant steps, integrating multiple steps into single steps, and generally improving the efficiency of the overall process.

The result of the JIT project was to reduce the average time from order taking to typesetting from 4 days to 1 to 2 hours. Delivering the orders to typesetting in smaller batches has helped reduce the backlog in typesetting and printing and has also improved the productivity and lead times in these areas. Eighty percent of orders are now being processed, printed, and shipped the same day, with the customers receiving the order within 4 business days. After the first month of using the JIT system, service calls relating to the two problem categories fell by 20 percent.

Potential Problems in Implementing JIT

Nevertheless, the use of JIT involves some difficulties and potential problems that should be noted. First, JIT is applicable primarily to repetitive production situations involving relatively standard products—rather than to custom, continuous flow, or project situations. It also means moving toward identical daily mixed-model schedules rather than long runs, so if setups take a long time, JIT will not work. Not only are there frequent setups, but there are also frequent shipments and receipts, so the firm must be prepared for this as well.

JIT also demands discipline. If products don't arrive on time, or if defects occur, production will stop. Again, there are no buffers of inventory or time to absorb mistakes, sloppy work, or bad management. The production system must operate correctly and employees must do their job right, or else JIT will fail.

Moreover, JIT is based on cooperation and trust between people: workers, managers, suppliers, customers, and so on. If the current environment is one of suspicion, distrust, and competition, JIT will not operate. Trust and cooperation must extend outside the plant to suppliers and customers as well. With suppliers, this means moving to risky, single-source contracts and bringing an outsider into the project team, where there may be proprietary secrets.

Paul Zipkin, a researcher at Columbia University, identified a number of other problems with JIT (Zipkin 1991). To begin, Zipkin notes that there is a great deal of ambiguity associated with the term JIT. The term means different things to different managers. Zipkin further points out that while the JIT concept may be easy to understand, implementing JIT is anything but simple. Indeed, it took Toyota 20 years to fully develop JIT. In addition, implementing JIT is often very expensive when the training costs, preventive maintenance costs, and consulting costs are factored in. Third, Zipkin points out that many organizations equate JIT with cutting inventory and in this vein, cut inventory to the point that it causes more harm than good. Finally, Zipkin notes that JIT environments often place additional stresses on the shop workers.

The major reason for not implementing JIT has little to do with these problems, however. Instead, the primary difficulty seems to involve philosophy, or a worldview, as evidenced through the measures used to assess the organization. Most frequently, managers cannot bring themselves to let utilization levels of either capital assets (equipment and machines) or people fall—that is, to let these resources sit idle. They see this low utilization as increasing unit costs, and they are too frequently reinforced in this belief by accounting reports that value inventories as assets rather than liabilities. If this basic mind-set cannot be changed, it may be best not to attempt JIT in the first place.

JIT in Services

Of course many services, and especially pure services, have no choice but to provide their service exactly when it is demanded. For example, a hair stylist cannot build up inventories of haircuts before the actual customers arrive. Now JIT is being adopted in other services that use materials rather extensively, as was illustrated by Smart Practice. The JIT philosophy applies primarily to repetitive operations where the same activities are continually being done, or services, where the same materials are being produced. The volume need not be high, however. In cases where the end products vary, there may still be significant repeatability among the components further down the parts ladder. In addition, the output mix must remain relatively stable, within a month's time, for example. JIT will not work in an environment where the schedule keeps changing.

In summary, it appears that JIT is not one of the annual fads of American management but, rather, a philosophy for efficiently using the resources industry already has at its disposal. As such, it will not soon disappear from the scene, though the name may fade as its tenets are embraced by a wider following in both manufacturing and service firms. Not to adopt JIT will probably mean failure in the marketplace for the majority of U.S. firms.

EXPAND YOUR UNDERSTANDING _____

1. Why is supply chain management such a topic of interest lately, especially multifacility distribution? Why wasn't it previously?

2. Might global information systems be considered a new mode of "transportation," especially for service firms?

3. What appears to be the primary "secret" of successful supply chain management?

4. Which of the three tenets of JIT do you imagine the Japanese consider to be the most important? Which have Americans adopted? Which would Europeans consider most important? Which would apply best to services?

5. Describe how trying to please every customer turns into a "trap" for traditional production. Aren't customization and multiple options the way of the future, particularly for differing national tastes and preferences?

6. The Japanese say that "a defect is a treasure." What way do they mean, and how does this relate to JIT?

7. How smooth is a production flow where every item requires a setup? Wouldn't flows be smoother with long runs where no setups were required for days?

8. American managers hate to see high-paid workers sitting idle, even maintenance employees. What is the alternative, according to JIT?

9. One JIT consultant suggests that managers implement JIT by just removing inventories from the floor. What is likely to happen if they do this? What would the Japanese do?

10. With single-sourcing, how does the firm protect itself from price gouging? From strikes or interruptions to supply?

11. How might JIT apply to a service like a hospital? A department store? A university?

APPLY YOUR UNDERSTANDING _____

J. Galt Lock Company

The J. Galt Lock Company produces a line of door locksets and hardware for the residential, light commercial, and retail markets. The company's single plant, located in a small southern town, is just over 200,000 square feet and is organized into the following functional departments: screw machines, presses, machining, maintenance, tool and dies, latches, plating, buffing, subassembly, and final assembly. The company is not unionized and employs approximately 375 people, 290 of whom are hourly workers. The largest category of employees—assemblers—accounts for two-thirds of the workforce.

The company uses a proprietary planning and scheduling system that uses both an

AS/400 minicomputer and spreadsheet analysis performed on a microcomputer to determine production and purchasing requirements. At any given time there are 1500 to 3000 open work orders on the shop floor. The average lot size is 50,000 parts, but for some products the size is as high as 250,000 parts.

The planning system creates work orders for each part number in the bills of materials, which are delivered to the various departments. Department supervisors determine the order in which to process the jobs, since the system does not prioritize the work orders. A variety of scheduling methods are used throughout the plant, including kanbans, work orders, and expediters; however, the use of these different methods often creates problems. For example, one production manager commented that although a "kanban pull scheduling system is being used between subassembly and final assembly, frequently the right card is not used at the right time, the correct quantity is not always produced, and there are no predetermined schedules and paths for the pickup and delivery of parts." In fact, it was discovered that work orders were often being superseded by expediters and supervisors, that large lag times existed between the decision to produce a batch and the start of actual production, and that suppliers were not being included in the "information pipeline." One production supervisor commented:

> We routinely abort the plans generated by our formal planning system because we figure out other ways of pushing product. Although we use Kanban systems in two areas of the plant, in reality everything here is a push system. Everything is based on inventory levels and/or incoming customer orders. We push not just the customer order but all the raw materials and everything that is associated with the product being assembled.

In an effort to improve its operations, J. Galt Lock hired a consulting company. The consultant determined that 36 percent of the floor space was being used to hold inventory, 25 percent was for work centers, 14 percent for aisles, 7 percent for offices, and 18 percent for nonvalue-adding activities. The production manager commented:

> We have an entire department that is dedicated to inventory storage consisting of 10 to 11 aisles of parts. What is bad is that we have all these parts, and none of them are the right ones. Lots of parts, and we still can't build.

The consultants also determined that supplying work centers were often far from the downstream work center, material flows were discontinuous as the parts were picked up and set down numerous times, and workers and supervisors often spent a considerable amount of time hunting for parts. The production manager commented:

> Work-in-process is everywhere. You can find work-in-process at every one of the stations on the shop floor. It is extremely difficult to find materials on the shop floor because of the tremendous amount of inventory on the shop floor. It is also very difficult to tell at what state a customer order is in or the material necessary to make that customer order, because we have such long runs of components and subassemblies.

The plant manager commented:

> My biggest concern is consistent delivery to customers. We just started monitoring on-time delivery performance, and it was the first time that measurement had ever been used at this operation. We found out actually how poorly we are doing. It is a matter of routinely trying to chase things down in the factory that will complete customer orders. The challenge of more consistent delivery is compounded by the fact that we have to respond much faster. Our customers used to give us three to six weeks of lead time, but now the big retailers we are starting to deal with give us only two or three days. And if we don't get it out in that small period of time, we lose the customer.

Questions

1. Evaluate and critique the existing operation and the J. Galt Lock Company.

2. How applicable is JIT to a situation like this? Would converting from a functional layout to a cellular layout facilitate the implementation of JIT?

3. What problems would JIT alleviate at the J. Galt Lock Company?

BIBLIOGRAPHY

Ansari, A., and B. Modarress. "The Potential Benefits of Just-in-Time Purchasing for U.S. Manufacturing." *Production and Inventory Management*, vol. 28, no. 2 (Second Quarter 1987): 30–35.

Auguston, K. "How We Produce Printers on a JIT Basis." *Modern Materials Handling* (January 1995): 47–49.

Bowersox, D. J. and D. J. Closs. *Logistical Management: The Integrated Supply Chain Process*. New York: McGraw-Hill, 1996.

Burrows, P. "The Computer Is in the Mail (Really)." *Business Week* (January 23, 1995): 76–77.

Ellram, L. "A Managerial Guideline for the Development and Implementation of Purchasing Partnerships." *International Journal of Purchasing* (Summer 1991): 2–8.

Esparrago, R. A., Jr. "Kanban." *Production and Inventory Management*, vol. 29, no. 1 (1988): 6–10.

Fisher, M. L. "Making Supply Meet Demand." *Harvard Business Review* (May–June 1994): 83–93.

Fisher, M. L. "What Is the Right Supply Chain for Your Product?" *Harvard Business Review* (March–April 1997): 105–116.

Gould, L. "Staging Fills in Honda JIT Orders in 2 Hours." *Modern Materials Handling* (July 1994): 44–45.

Handfield, R. B. and E. L. Nichols, Jr. *Introduction to Supply Chain Management*. Upper Saddle River, NJ: Prentice-Hall, 1999.

Hay, H. J. *The Just-in-Time Breakthrough: Implementing the New Manufacturing Basics*. New York: Wiley, 1989.

Heinritz, S. F., P. V. Farrell, and C. L. Smith. *Purchasing: Principles and Applications*, 7th ed. Englewood Cliffs, N.J.: Prentice-Hall, 1986.

Johnson, J. C., and D. F. Wood. *Contemporary Physical Distribution and Logistics*, 3rd ed. New York: Macmillan, 1986.

Lee, H. L. and C. Billington. "The Evolution of Supply-Chain-Management Models and Practice at Hewlett-Packard." *Interfaces*, vol. 25, no. 5 (Sept.–Oct. 1995): 42–63.

Levis, personal communication, 1997.

Lewis, J. D. *The Connected Corporations: How Leading Companies Win Through Customer-Supplier Alliances*. New York: Free Press, 1996.

Poirier, C. C. and S. E. Reiter. *Supply Chain Optimization: Building the Strongest Total Business Network*. San Francisco: Berrett-Koehler Publishers, 1996.

Richman, T. "Logistics Management: How 20 Best-Practice Companies Do It." *Harvard Business Review* (Sept.–Oct. 1995): 11.

Schonberger, R. J. "Some Observations on the Advantages and Implementation Issues of Just-in-Time Production Systems." *Journal of Operations Management*, vol. 2, no. 1 (November 1982): 1–12.

Schonberger, R. J. *World Class Manufacturing: The Lessons of Simplicity Applied*. New York: Free Press, 1986.

Spekman, R. E. "Strategic Supplier Selection: Understanding Long-Term Buyer Relationships" *Business Horizons* (July–Aug. 1988): 80–81.

Tully, S. "Purchasing's New Muscle." *Fortune* (February 20, 1995): 75–83.

Verity, J. W. "Invoice? What's an Invoice?" *Business Week* (June 10, 1996): 110–112.

Zipkin, P. H., "Does Manufacturing Need a JIT Revolution?" *Harvard Business Review* (January–February 1991): 4–11.

Project Management

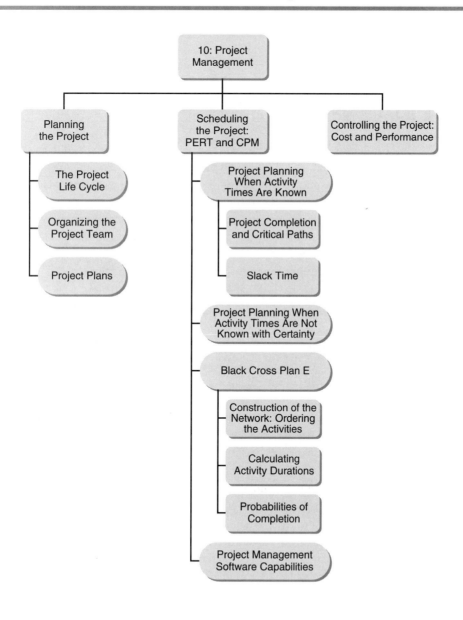

In this chapter we continue our discussion of scheduling from Chapter 7 but shift our attention to the scheduling of projects. Projects are actually processes that are performed infrequently or ad hoc. The chapter begins with a discussion of the crucial topic of project planning and organizing the project team. We then move on to an expla-nation of some project-scheduling techniques for situations where activity times are known and not known with certainty. Some typical project man-agement software printouts are illustrated. The chapter concludes with a discussion of controlling project cost and performance.

INTRODUCTION

- Numerous examples of projects have already been discussed in this book. For example, Chapter 1 described a project for transporting the Olympic Flame to Atlanta. You may recall that two years of planning went into this project and completing it required coordinating 10,000 runners who carried the Olympic Torch 15,000 miles in 84 days. In Chapter 4, a product development project was discussed: Thermos's revolutionary electric grill. In another example from the automobile industry, Mercedes-Benz formed a project team to find a location for its new manufacturing facility, as was described in Chapter 6.

- At a more detailed level, consider that the team formed to develop the Chrysler Viper had only 3 years to complete the development project from concept to roadster. This included developing an entirely new 8.0-liter V-10 aluminum engine and a high-performance six-speed transmission. Typically, such development projects required 5 years at Chrysler. Thus, from the very beginning of the project, managers at Chrysler recognized the importance of consistent end-to-end project management.

  Team members for the project were hand-picked, and a project management system called Artemis Prestige was selected as a tool to help manage the project. According to managers at Chrysler, the project management system required the ability to track multiple projects concurrently, allow users to use it interactively, provide project personnel with a broad picture of the entire project, and help identify the impact of each activity on the ultimate completion of the project. These capabilities could then be used to perform "what if" analyses to assess the effect of changes in resource allocations and other engineering changes. With these capabilities, personnel could determine the effect of a proposed change before making a commitment to the change. In general, the Artemis software package provided a vital communications network and helped ensure that critical links between different parts of the project were completed according to the plan.

By most accounts, the Viper project was an overwhelming success and yielded several significant innovations. For example, the first test engine required less than a year to develop. This was particularly important because several other major components including the transmission depended on the engine. The transmission was developed in 1½ years, down from the usual 5 to 6 years. Additionally, many important innovations in the frame, body, and brakes were incorporated into the Viper (O'Keeffe 1994).

● Zeneca Pharmaceuticals U.S. is a unit of the research-intensive pharmaceutical business of Zeneca Group PLC, headquartered in the U.K. The Zeneca Pharmaceuticals mission is to develop new drugs for the medical community. The development of a new drug is a complex project requiring extensive management and guidance over a long duration, typically 10 years. Basically, drug development is the process by which a new chemical entity is synthesized, found to have therapeutic pharmacologic "activity" in living animals, tested in more animals and in humans, and approved by the Food and Drug Administration (FDA) as a "new drug." After approval, the drug is sold to patients, usually by prescription. Unfortunately, in the process that begins with research and ends with approval for market, only about 1 drug in 10,000 meets with success, due to the many hurdles that must be overcome.

The major steps that the project manager must follow in the development process are as follows. (1) *Preclinical testing* is done in the lab and with animals to determine if the compound is biologically active and safe. (2) Before tests with human subjects can be conducted, an *investigational new drug* (IND) application, giving the test results and describing how the drug is made, must be filed. (3) *Human clinical testing* is conducted—Phase I: Pharmacological profile of a drug's actions; safe dosages; patterns of absorption, distribution, metabolism, and excretion; duration of action from tests on a small sample of healthy subjects. Phase II: Pilot efficacy studies in 200 to 300 volunteer patients to assess effectiveness, which may last two years. Phase III: Extensive clinical trials (in 1000 to 3000 patients) to confirm efficacy and identify low-incidence adverse reactions; this phase may last three years. (4) *New drug application* (NDA): The results of the previous testing must be reported, typically in thousands of pages, in an NDA filed with the FDA. Additional information includes the structure of the drug, its scientific rationale, details of its formulation and production, and the proposed labeling. (5) Following *approval* of the NDA, the company must submit periodic reports to FDA concerning adverse reactions and production, quality control, and distribution data.

There are some major differences between project management of pharmaceutical R&D and that in other industries. For one thing, the final result here is not so much the physical product, but rather information—reams of paper giving proof that the drug is safe and efficacious. Because of the abstract nature of this "proof," the result may be sufficient at one point in time, or for one drug, but not at another time or for another drug. In addition, the long duration, extreme costs (averaging $250 million per drug), and high chances for failure anywhere along the route to development are generally rare in other projects. Moreover, failure can come from diverse causes, including the success of competing drugs, adverse patient reactions, escalating costs, or insufficient efficacy. The extensive and sophisticated use of project management techniques is the main tool that pharmaceutical R&D firms like Zeneca Pharmaceuticals can use to improve their chances of success.

Project management is concerned with managing organizational activities. As these examples illustrate, many organizations use project management techniques to integrate and coordinate diverse activities. For example, in the traditional functional organization, a product development team with representatives from production, finance, marketing, and engineering can be assembled to ensure that new product designs simultaneously meet the requirements of each area. Ensuring that each area's requirements are being met as the new design is developed reduces the likelihood that costly changes will have to be made later in the process. The result is that new products can be developed faster and less expensively, thereby enhancing the firm's overall responsiveness. Perhaps a better product is developed as well, owing to the synergy of including a variety of different perspectives earlier in the design process.

Up to this point, you might not have realized that projects are actually a special type of process. As described in Chapter 5, the term *process* refers to a set of activities that, taken together, create something of value to customers. Typically, the term process is used to refer to a set of activities that are routinely repeated, such as processing insurance forms, handling customers' complaints, and assembling a VCR. The term *project* also refers to a set of activities that, taken together, produce a valued output. However, unlike a typical process, each project is unique and has a clear beginning and end. Therefore, projects are processes that are performed infrequently and ad hoc.

In Chapter 5, the project form of the transformation process was briefly described. The choice of the project form usually indicates the importance of the project objective to the organization. Thus, top-grade resources, including staff, are often made available for project operations. As a result, project organizations become very professionalized and are often managed on that basis. That is, minimal supervision is exercised, administrative routine is minimized, and the professional is given the problem and the required results (cost, performance, deadline). The individual is then given the privacy and freedom to decide *how* to solve his or her portion of the problem.

A great many projects require varying emphases during their life cycle. For example, technical performance may be crucial at the beginning, cost overruns in the middle, and on-time completion at the end. The flexibility of making spur-of-the-moment changes in emphasis by trading off one criterion for another is basic to the project design form. This ability results from the close contact of the project manager with the technical staff—there are few, if any, "middle managers."

Following are some examples of projects:

- Constructing highways, bridges, tunnels, and dams
- Building ships, planes, and rockets
- Erecting skyscrapers, steel mills, homes, and processing plants

- Locating and laying out amusement parks, camping grounds, and refuges
- Organizing conferences, banquets, and conventions
- Managing R&D projects such as the Manhattan Project (which developed the atomic bomb)
- Running political campaigns, war operations, advertising campaigns, or firefighting operations
- Chairing ad hoc task forces, overseeing planning for government agencies, or conducting corporate audits
- Converting from one computer system to another

As may be noticed in this list, the number of project operations is growing in our economy, probably at about the same rate as services (which many of them are). Some of the reasons for this growth in project operations are as follows:

1. *More sophisticated technology.* An outgrowth of our space age, and its technology, has been increased public awareness of project operations (e.g., Project Apollo) and interest in using the project form to achieve society's goals (Project Head Start).
2. *Better-educated citizens.* People are more aware of the world around them, and of techniques (such as project management) for achieving their objectives.
3. *More leisure time.* People have the time available to follow, and even participate in, projects.
4. *Increased accountability.* Society as a whole has increased its emphasis on the attainment of objectives (affirmative action, environmental protection, better fuel economy) and the evaluation of activities leading toward those objectives.
5. *Higher productivity.* People and organizations are involved in more activities, and are more productive in those activities, than ever before.
6. *Faster response to customers.* Today's intense competition has escalated the importance of quick response to customers' needs, and projects are many times more responsive and flexible than bureaucracies or functionally organized firms.
7. *Greater customization for customers.* Intense competition has also increased the importance of better meeting the customer's unique needs in terms of both the service and the facilitating good. Again, as long as a major technical breakthrough isn't required, the project form of organizing is much more likely to meet this need.

In physical project operations, such as bridge construction, most of the *production* per se is completed elsewhere and brought to the project area at the proper time. As a result, a great many project activities are *assembly* operations. The project design form concentrates resources on the achievement of specific objectives primarily through proper *scheduling* and *control* of activities, many of which are simultaneous. Some of the scheduling considerations in project management are

DILBERT ©United Feature Syndicate. Reprinted with permission.

knowing what activities must be completed and in what order, how long they will take, when to increase and decrease the labor force, and when to order materials so that they will not arrive too early (thus requiring storage and being in the way) or too late (thus delaying the project). The control activities include anticipating what can and might go wrong, knowing what resources can be shifted among activities to keep the project on schedule, and so forth.

PLANNING THE PROJECT

In this section we focus in some detail on the planning of projects. In the area of project management, planning is probably the single most important element in the success of the project, and considerable research has been done on the topic.

The Project Life Cycle

It has been found, for example, that progress in a project is not at all uniform, but instead follows one of two common forms, as shown in Figure 10.1. In the stretched-S life cycle form, illustrated in Figure 10.1*a*, when the project is initiated, progress is slow as responsibilities are assigned and organization takes place. But the project gathers speed during the implementation stage, and much progress is made. As the end of the project draws near, the more difficult tasks that were postponed earlier must now be completed, yet people are being drawn off the project and activity is "winding down," so the end keeps slipping out of reach.

In the exponential form, illustrated in Figure 10.1*b*, after the project is initiated there is continuous activity on numerous aspects of the project, but until all the elemental parts come together at the end, there is no final output. This is typical of projects that require final assembly of components to produce the whole (like a car), or goods (like a cake, which is only glop until it is baked in the oven). It is especially typical of office and other such service work where the final output is a life insurance policy, or ad piece, or perhaps even an MBA degree. Without that last signature, or piece of paper, or earned credit, there is virtually no product.

The reason it is important to contrast these two forms, besides pointing out their difference in managerial needs, is that during the budgeting stage, if there is a flat across-the-board budget cut of, say, 10 percent and the project is of the stretched-S form, then not being able to spend that last 10 percent of the budget is of no urgent

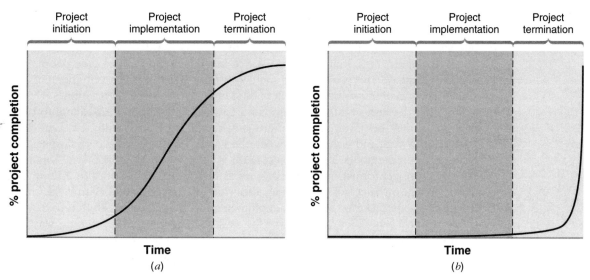

Figure 10.1 Two project life cycles. (*a*) Stretched-S. (*b*) Exponential

matter, since probably 97 percent of the benefits will be achieved anyway. However, if the project is of the exponential form, then missing the last 10 percent is catastrophic because this is where all the value is attained. Another perspective on the same issue is the effect of early termination of the project. Terminating the stretched-S form early will have negligible impact, but terminating the exponential form will be a complete disaster. It is imperative the project manager and top management know which type of project they are working with before taking such actions.

Organizing the Project Team

Projects can be organized in any of a number of ways. There is the ad hoc project form in a functional organization that reports to a senior executive. And there are projects that are just another activity in a project organization that is completely organized in terms of projects. Management consulting firms typify project organizations. There are matrix organizations where projects have both a functional and a program superior. Combinations of these forms are also common, such as the "weak" or functional matrix, and the "strong" or project matrix. Each of these has its own advantages and disadvantages and what works the best depends largely on the circumstances of the organization and the reason it started a project.

Regardless of the form of the project, a team will be required to run the project. Some members of the team may be directly assigned to the project manager for the duration, while others may have only partial responsibilities for the project and still report to their functional superior. There are three types of team members who should report directly to the project manager (PM), however:

- Those who will be having a long-term relationship with the project
- Those with whom the PM will need to communicate with closely or continuously
- Those with rare skills necessary to project success

Yet, even if these people report to the PM, it is still not common for the PM to have the authority to reward these people with pay bonuses, extra vacation, or other such personnel matters—that authority normally still resides with the functional manager. Thus, there are not a lot of incentives the PM can give people for working hard on the project. The main ones are the fun and excitement of the challenge, and doing something that will be important to the organization.

With the pressures that tend to gravitate toward such important and high-profile projects, it may be assumed that there is also a lot of opportunity for conflict to arise. This is true, and not only between the PM and other organizational units, but even between members of the project team. According to Thamhain and Wilemon (1975), at project formation the main sources of conflict were priorities and procedures. As the project got under way, priorities and schedules became the main points of conflict. During the main implementation stage, conflict shifted to technical issues and schedules. But toward the end of the project when timing was becoming crucial, only schedules were the source of conflict. Knowing when to expect trouble, and what kinds, throughout the project can help the PM keep peace within the project team and facilitate smooth project progress.

Project Plans

One of the project manager's major responsibilities during the initiation stage is to define all the tasks in as much detail as possible so that they can be scheduled and costed out, and responsibility can be assigned. This set of task descriptions is called the **work breakdown structure (WBS)**, and it provides the basis for the project master schedule.

A typical WBS and master schedule are illustrated in Figures 10.2 and 10.3 for a project installing assembly-line robots. Milestone, commitment, and completion points are shown, and actual progress is graphed. The last status update shows that the project is a month behind schedule.

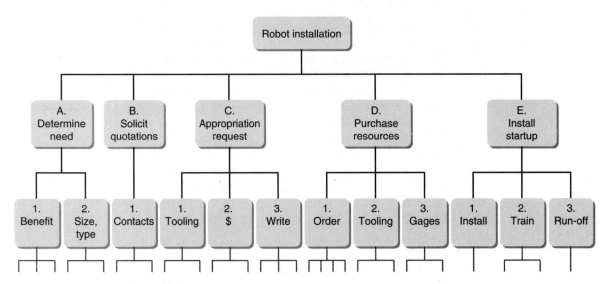

Figure 10.2   Work breakdown structure.

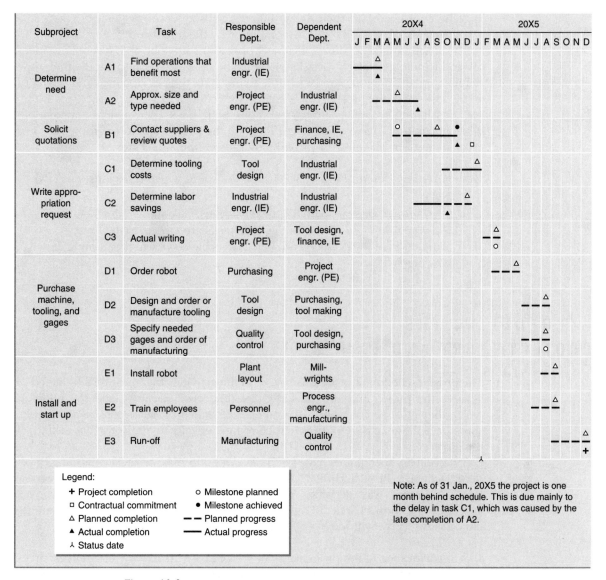

Figure 10.3 Project master schedule. Reprinted from J. Meredith and S. J. Mantel, Jr., *Project Management: A Managerial Approach*, 3rd ed. New York: Wiley, 1995. Used with permission.

The scheduling of project activities is highly complex because of (1) the number of activities required, (2) the precedence relationships among the activities, and (3) the limited time of the project. Project scheduling is similar to the scheduling discussed earlier in some ways but still differs significantly. For example, the basic network approaches—***program evaluation and review technique (PERT)*** and ***critical path method (CPM)***—are based on variations of the Gantt chart. Figure 10.3 is, in a sense, a type of Gantt chart but is inadequate for scheduling the multitude of subtasks that compose, for example, task A1. That is, a project schedule has to handle an enormous number of different operations and materials, which must be coordinated in such a way that the subsequent activities can take place and the entire project (job) can be completed by the due date.

The scheduling procedure for project operations must be able not only to identify and handle the variety of tasks that must be done, but also to handle their time sequencing. In addition, it must be able to integrate the performance and timing of all the tasks with the project as a whole so that control can be exercised, for example, by shifting resources from operations with slack (permissible slippage) to other operations whose delay might threaten the project's timely completion. The tasks involved in planning and scheduling project operations are:

- *Planning:* Determining what must be done and which tasks must *precede* others
- *Scheduling:* Determining *when* the tasks must be completed; when they *can* and when they *must* be started; which tasks are *critical* to the timely completion of the project; and which tasks have *slack* in their timing and how much

*S*CHEDULING THE PROJECT: PERT AND CPM

The project scheduling process is based on the activities that must be conducted to achieve the project's goals, the length of time each requires, and the order in which they must be completed. If a number of similar projects must be conducted, sometimes these activities can be structured generically to apply equally well to all the projects.

Two primary techniques have been developed to plan projects consisting of ordered activities: PERT and CPM. Although PERT and CPM originally had some differences in the way activities were determined and laid out, many current approaches to project scheduling minimize these differences and present an integrated view, as we will see here. It will be helpful to define some terms first.

- *Activity:* One of the project operations, or tasks; an activity requires resources and takes some amount of time to complete
- *Event:* Completion of an activity, or series of activities, at a particular point in time
- *Network:* Set of all project activities graphically interrelated through precedence relationships. In this text, network lines (or *arcs*) represent activities, connections between the lines (called *nodes*) represent events, and arrows on the arcs represent precedence. (This is typical of the PERT approach; in CPM the nodes represent activities.)
- *Path:* Series of connected activities from the start to the finish of the project
- *Critical path:* Any path that if delayed will delay the completion of the entire project
- *Critical activities:* Activities on the critical path or paths

Project Planning When Activity Times Are Known

The primary inputs to project planning are a list of the activities that must be completed, the *activity completion times* (also called *activity durations*), and precedence relationships among the activities (i.e., what activities must be completed before another activity can be started). In this section we assume that activity completion times are known with certainty. Later, we relax this assumption and consider situations in which activity completion times are not known with certainty.

Important outputs of project planning include:

- Graphical representation of the entire project, showing all precedence relationships among the activities
- Time it will take to complete the project
- Identification of critical path or paths
- Identification of critical activities
- Slack times for all activities and paths
- Earliest and latest time each activity can be started
- Earliest and latest time each activity can be completed

Project Completion and Critical Paths

Table 10.1 shows the activity times and precedence for seven activities that must all be finished to complete a project. According to the table, activities A and B can be started at any time. Activities C and D can be started once activity A is completed. Activity E cannot be started until both activities B and C are finished, and so on. The network diagram for this project is shown in Figure 10.4, in which nodes (circles) represent events (i.e., the start or completion of an activity) and arcs (lines) correspond to activities. Each arc is labeled with a letter to identify the corresponding activity. Activity durations are shown in parentheses next to the activity labels. Finally, arrows are used to show precedence relationships among activities.

From Figure 10.4, it can be seen that there are three paths from node 1 to node 6: A–D–F (or 1–2–4–6), A–C–E–G (or 1–2–3–5–6), and B–E–G (or 1–3–5–6). Summing the activity times on a particular path provides the path completion time. For example, the time to complete path A–D–F is 35 (10 + 13 + 12).

TABLE 10.1 • Data for a Seven-Activity Project

Activity	Time (days)	Preceded By
A	10	—
B	7	—
C	5	A
D	13	A
E	4	B, C
F	12	D
G	14	E

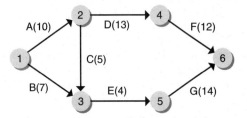

Figure 10.4   Network diagram for project.

To determine the expected completion time of the entire project, *early start times* T_{ES} and *early finish times* T_{EF} can be calculated for each activity, as shown in Figure 10.5. The values of T_{ES} and T_{EF} are calculated moving left to right through the network. Thus, we begin with the leftmost node (node 1) and work our way to the rightmost node (node 6). To illustrate, if the project is started at time zero, then activities A and B can be started as early as time zero, since neither of them is preceded by another activity. Since activity A requires 10 days, if it is started as early as time zero, it can be completed on day 10. Likewise, if activity B is started at time zero, it can be completed as early as day 7. Continuing on, since activity A can be finished as early as day 10, activity C can start as early as day 10 and finish as early as day 15. Now consider activity E. Activity E cannot be started until activities B and C are *both* completed. Since activity B can be finished as early as day 7 and C can be finished as early as day 15, activity E can be started only as early as day 15 (remember E cannot start until both activities B and C are completed). If activity E is started as early as day 15, it can finish as early as day 19. The remaining earliest start and finish times are calculated in a similar fashion. After T_{ES} and T_{EF} are calculated for all the activities, we can determine the earliest time that the project can be completed. Since this project cannot be completed until all paths are completed, the earliest it could be completed is day 35.

Once T_{ES} and T_{EF} have been calculated for each activity, the latest times each activity can be started and finished without delaying the completion of the project can be determined. In contrast to T_{ES} and T_{EF}, *latest start time* (T_{LS}) and *latest finish time* (T_{LF}) are calculated by moving backward through the network, from right to left. Times T_{LS} and T_{LF} for this example are shown in Figure 10.6.

In calculating T_{ES} and T_{EF}, we determined that the project could be completed by day 35. If the project is to be completed by day 35, then activities F and G can be completed as late as day 35 without delaying completion of the project. Thus, the latest finish time for activities F and G is 35. Since activity F requires 12 days, it can

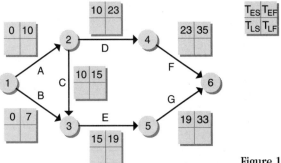

Figure 10.5   Early start and finish times.

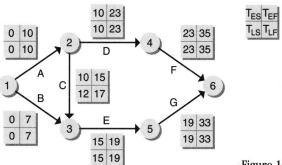

Figure 10.6 Latest start and finish times.

start as late as 23 (35 − 12) and still finish by day 35. Likewise, activity G can start as late as 21 (35 − 14) and still finish by day 35. Continuing on, since activity F can start as late as day 23, activity D can finish as late as day 23. Since activity D requires 13 days, it can start as late as day 10 (23 − 13) without delaying the entire project. Activity E must finish by 21 so as not to delay activity G and thus can start as late as day 17. To permit activity E to start by day 17, activities B and C must finish by day 17. Activity C can start as late as day 12 and still finish by day 17. Activity A precedes both C and D. Activity C can start as late as day 12 and D as late as day 10. Since activity A must be finished before either of these activities is started, A must be finished by day 10. (If A finished later than day 10, then activity D would start later than its latest start time and the entire project would be delayed.)

Slack Time

Times T_{ES}, T_{EF}, T_{LS}, and T_{LF} can be used by the project manager to help plan and develop schedules for the project. For example, if an activity requires a key resource or individual, its earliest and latest start times provide a window during which that resource can be acquired or assigned to the project. Alternatively, if an activity falls behind schedule, the latest completion time provides an indication of whether the slippage will delay the entire project or can simply be absorbed.

Notice in Figure 10.6 that for some activities T_{ES} is equal to T_{LS} and T_{EF} is equal to T_{LF}. For these activities, there is no flexibility in terms of when they can be started and completed. In other cases, an activity's T_{ES} is less than its T_{LS} and its T_{EF} is less than its T_{LF}. In these cases the project manager can exercise some discretion in terms of when the activity is started and when it is completed. The amount of flexibility the project manager has in terms of starting and completing an activity is referred to as its **slack** (or **float**) and is calculated as:

$$\text{Activity slack} = T_{LS} - T_{ES} = T_{LF} - T_{EF}$$

All activities on the critical path have zero slack—that is, there is no room for delay in any activity on the critical path without delaying the entire project. Activities off the critical path may delay up to a point where further delay would delay the entire project. Table 10.2 shows T_{ES}, T_{EF}, T_{LS}, T_{LF}, and slack for our seven-activity project shown earlier in Figure 10.6.

In addition to calculating slack times for individual activities, slack times can be calculated for entire paths. Since all paths must be finished to complete the project,

$\mathcal{T}$ABLE 10.2 • Activity Early and Late Times

Activity	T_{ES}	T_{EF}	T_{LS}	T_{LF}	Slack
A	0	10	0	10	0
B	0	7	10	17	10
C	10	15	12	17	2
D	10	23	10	23	0
E	15	19	17	21	2
F	23	35	23	35	0
G	19	33	21	35	2

the time to complete the project is the time to complete the path with the longest duration. Thus, the path with the longest duration is critical in the sense that any delay in completing it will delay the completion of the entire project. Path slacks are calculated as:

$$\text{Path slack} = \text{duration of critical path} - \text{path duration}$$

Table 10.3 contains the slack times for the three paths in our example project. Path A–D–F has the longest duration, and therefore its completion determines when the project is completed. The other paths require less than 35 days and therefore have slack. For example, path B–E–G has a slack of 10 days, implying that its completion can be delayed by 10 days without delaying the completion of the entire project.

Before leaving the topic of slack, it is important to point out that the slack times computed for individual activities are not additive. To illustrate, when the slack times were calculated for the individual activities, slack times of 10, 2, and 2 were computed for activities B, E, and G, respectively (see Table 10.2). If these slack times were additive, then path B–E–G would have a slack of 14 days. However, from Table 10.3 we observe that the slack for path B–E–G is only 10 days. The point is that slack times for individual activities are computed on the assumption that only one particular activity is delayed. As an example, activity B's slack of 10 days means that it can be delayed by up to 10 days without delaying the entire project, as long as the other activities on the path (activities E and G) are not delayed. However if activity B is delayed by 10 days and either activity E or G is delayed by even 1 day the entire project will be delayed.

Project Planning When Activity Times Are Not Known with Certainty

The previous section discussed project planning in situations where the activity completion times were known with certainty before the project was actually started.

$\mathcal{T}$ABLE 10.3 • Calculation of Path Slacks

Path	Duration	Slack	Critical?
A–D–F	35	0 (35–35)	Yes
A–C–E–G	33	2 (35–33)	No
B–E–G	25	10 (35–25)	No

In reality, however, project activity times are frequently not known with certainty beforehand. In these cases project managers often develop three estimates for each activity: an optimistic time t_o, a pessimistic time t_p, and a most likely time t_m. The *optimistic time* is the amount of time the project manager estimates it will take to complete the activity under ideal conditions. The *pessimistic time* refers to how long the activity will take to complete under the worst-case scenario. The *most likely time* is the project manager's best estimate of how long the activity will take to complete. In addition to these three time estimates, the precedence relationships among the activities are also needed as inputs to the project planning process.

The primary outputs of project planning when activity times are not known with certainty include:

- Graphical representation of the entire project, showing all precedence relationships among the activities
- Expected activity and path completion times
- Variance of activity and path completion times
- Probability that the project will be completed by a specified time

We now illustrate project planning in a situation where activity durations are not known with certainty before the project starts.

Black Cross Plan E

Black Cross is a volunteer service organization recently formed in California to prepare for and respond to "the big one," a major earthquake that has been expected for a decade. Black Cross has developed a single, efficient, uniform response plan (plan E) consisting of 10 major activities for all cities where the earthquake causes major damage. Clearly, completing the project activities as quickly as possible is crucial to saving lives and property and aiding victims in distress. The staff of Black Cross has determined not only the most likely times for each activity but also the fastest time in which each could probably be done (i.e., the *optimistic time*), as well as the slowest time (i.e., *pessimistic time*) that might be encountered by a project team out in the field (if everything went wrong). The project operations and the optimistic, most likely, and pessimistic times, in hours, are listed in Table 10.4, along with the activities that must precede them.

Construction of the Network: Ordering the Activities

The project network illustrating the activities and their interdependence is constructed by first examining Table 10.4 for those activities that have no activities preceding them. These activities—a, b, and c—are all drawn out of a starting node, which, for convenience in Figure 10.7, we have labeled 1.

Next, the activity list is scanned for activities that require only that activities a, b, or c be completed. Thus, activities d through h can be drawn in the network next. Activity d can be drawn directly out of node 2, and activity h can be drawn out of node 4. But if node 3 indicates the completion of activity b, how can activities e, f, and g be drawn, since they also depend on the completion of activity c? This is accomplished by the use of a **dummy activity** from node 4 to node 3, which indicates that event 3 depends on the accomplishment of activity c (event 4) as well as

$\mathscr{T}$ABLE 10.4 • Plan E Activity Times (Hours)

Project Activity	Optimistic Time t_o	Most Likely Time t_m	Pessimistic Time t_p	Required Preceding Activities
a	5	11	11	none
b	10	10	10	none
c	2	5	8	none
d	1	7	13	a
e	4	4	10	b, c
f	4	7	10	b, c
g	2	2	2	b, c
h	0	6	6	c
i	2	8	14	g, h
j	1	4	7	d, e

activity b. The dummy activity, shown as a dashed line in Figure 10.7, requires no time to accomplish, but the link is necessary, so that activities e, f, and g cannot start before both activities b and c are completed.

What if activity e did not require that activity c be completed, whereas f and g did? If this was the case, the diagram would be drawn as shown in Figure 10.8. Care must be taken to ensure that the proper precedence relations are drawn; otherwise, the project might be unnecessarily delayed.

The remainder of the diagram is drawn in the same manner. Activity i, which depends on activities g and h, comes out of node 5, which represents the completion of g and h. A similar situation occurs with activity j. All of the remaining activities without completion nodes (f, i, and j) are then directed to the project completion node 7.

Calculating Activity Durations

We have now completed a graphic network representation of the information about precedence shown in Table 10.4. Next we can place the expected activity times on

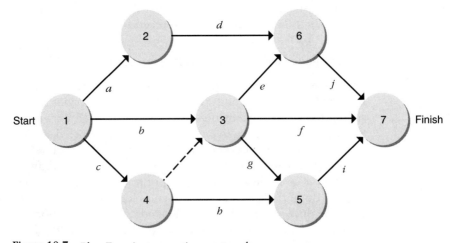

Figure 10.7   Plan E project operations network.

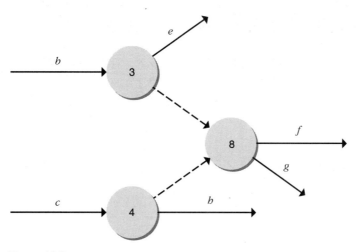

Figure 10.8 Proper use of dummy activities.

the network to get an indication of which activities should be scheduled first and when they should be completed, in order for the project not to be delayed.

The estimation of the three activity times in Table 10.4 is based on the assumption that the activities are independent of one another. Therefore, an activity that goes wrong will not necessarily affect the other activities, which can still go right. Additionally, it is assumed that the difference between t_o and t_m need *not* be the same as the difference between t_p and t_m. For example, a critical piece of equipment may be wearing out. If it is working well, this equipment can do a task in 2 hours that normally takes 3 hours; but if the equipment is performing poorly, the task may require 10 hours. Thus, we may see nonsymmetrical optimistic and pessimistic task times for project activities, as for activities e and h in Table 10.4. Note also that for some activities, such as b, the durations are known with certainty.

The general form of nonsymmetrical or skewed distribution used in approximating PERT activity times is called the beta distribution and has a mean (expected completion time t_e) and a variance, or uncertainty in this time, σ^2, as given below. The results of these calculations are listed in Table 10.5 and are indicated on the network in Figure 10.9 in parentheses.

$$t_e = \frac{t_o + 4t_m + t_p}{6}$$

$$\sigma^2 = \left(\frac{t_p - t_o}{6}\right)^2$$

The discussion of project management with known activity times included critical paths, critical activities, and slack. These concepts are not particularly useful in situations where activity times are not known with certainty. To demonstrate this we will use Table 10.6, where the paths and their expected completion times, earliest completion times, and latest completion times are listed for the network diagram shown in Figure 10.7. To calculate a path's expected completion time, the activity expected times t_e were summed up for all activities on the path. Similarly, times t_o and t_p were summed up for all activities on a given path to determine the path's earliest completion time and latest completion time, respectively.

$\mathcal{T}_{ABLE}$ 10.5 • Expected Times and Variances of Activities

Activity	Expected Time, t_e	Variance, σ^2
a	10	1
b	10	0
c	5	1
d	7	4
e	5	1
f	7	1
g	2	0
h	5	1
i	8	4
j	4	1

Referring to Table 10.6, path a–d–j is most likely to take the longest (i.e., 21 hours). However, to see why this path is not considered the critical path, observe that if all the activities go exceptionally well on this path it can be completed in as few as 7 hours. Referring to the last column in Table 10.6, we can see that it is possible for any of the other paths to take longer than 7 hours. Therefore, without knowing the activity times with certainty we see that any of the paths has the potential to be the longest path. Furthermore, we will not know which of the paths will take longest to complete until the project is actually completed. And since we cannot determine before the start of the project which path will be critical, we cannot determine how much slack the other paths have.

Probabilities of Completion

When activity times are not known with certainty, we cannot determine how long it will actually take to complete the project. However, using the variance of each

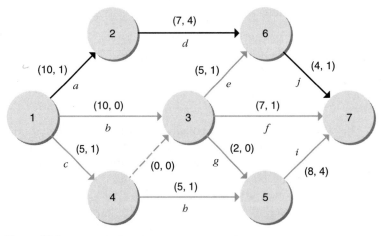

Figure 10.9   Expected times and variances of activities.

$\mathscr{T}$ABLE 10.6 • Expected, Earliest, and Latest Completion Times of Paths

Path	Most Likely Completion Time (hours)	Earliest Completion Time (hours)	Latest Completion Time (hours)
a–d–j	21	7	31
b–e–j	19	15	27
b–f	17	14	20
b–g–i	20	14	26
c–e–j	14	7	25
c–f	12	6	18
c–g–i	15	6	24
c–h–i	18	4	28

activity (the variances in Table 10.5), we can compute the likelihood or probability of completing the project in a given time period, assuming that the activity durations are independent of each other. The distribution of a path's completion time will be approximately normally distributed if the path has a large number of activities on it. For example, the mean time along path a–d–j was found to be 21 hours. The variance is found by summing the variances of each of the activities on the path. In our example, this would be

$$V_{\text{path a–d–j}} = \sigma_a^2 + \sigma_d^2 + \sigma_j^2$$
$$= 1 + 4 + 1$$
$$= 6$$

The probability of completing this path in, say, 23 hours is then found by calculating the standard normal deviate of the desired completion time less the expected completion time, and using the table of the standard normal probability distribution (Appendix A) to find the corresponding probability:

$$Z = \frac{\text{desired completion time} - \text{expected completion time}}{\sqrt{V}}$$
$$= \frac{23 - 21}{\sqrt{6}}$$
$$= 0.818$$

which results in a probability (see Figure 10.10) of 79 percent.

So far, we have determined only that there is a 79 percent chance that path a–d–j will be completed in 23 hours or less. If we were interested in calculating the probability that the entire project will be completed in 23 hours, we would need to calculate the probability that all paths will be finished within 23 hours. To calculate the probability that all paths will be finished in 23 hours or less, we first calculate the probability that each path will be finished in 23 hours or less, as we just did for path a–d–j. Then we multiply these probabilities together to determine the probability that all paths will be completed by the specified time. The reason we multiply these probabilities together is that we are assuming that path completion times are independent of one another. Of course, if the paths

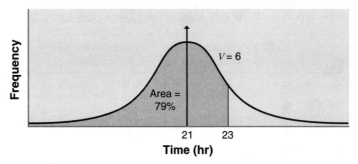

Figure 10.10   Probability distribution of path completion time.

have activities in common, they are not truly independent of one another and a more complex analysis or simulation, illustrated next, is necessary. However, if a project has a sufficiently large number of activities, the assumption of path independence is acceptable.

To simplify the number of calculations required to compute the probability that a project will be completed by some specified time, for practical purposes it is reasonable to include only those paths whose expected time plus 2.33 standard deviations is more than the specified time. The reason for doing this is that if the sum of a path's expected time and 2.33 of its standard deviations is less than the specified time, then the probability that this path will take longer than the specified time is very small (i.e., less than 1 percent), and therefore we assume that the probability that it will be completed by the specified time is 100 percent. Finally, note that to calculate the probability that a project will take longer than some specified time, we first calculate the probability that it will take less than the specified time and then subtract this value from 1.

Spreadsheet Analysis: Simulating Project Completion Times

When activity times are uncertain, it is usually not possible to know which path will be the critical path before the project is actually completed. In these situations, simulation analysis can provide some insights into the range and distribution of project completion times. To illustrate this, we use the following network diagram consisting of six activities labeled **A** through **F**.

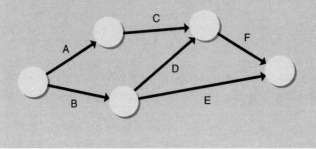

Based on historical data it has been determined that all the activity times are approximately normally distributed with the means and standard deviations given in the following table.

Activity	Mean (days)	Standard Deviation
A	32.1	1.2
B	24.6	3.1
C	22.2	2.2
D	26.1	5.2
E	34.4	6.2
F	34.5	4.1

Inspection of the network diagram reveals three paths: A–C–F, B–D–F, and B–E.

To simulate the completion of this project, the following spreadsheet was developed. In the spreadsheet, completing the project is simulated by generating random numbers for the six activities and then adding up the activity times that make up each path to determine how long the paths take to complete. The longest path determines the project completion time. The spreadsheet was created to simulate 25 replications of the project (rows 3 to 27).

Activity A	Activity B	Activity C	Activity D	Activity E	Activity F	Path 1 (A–C–F)	Path 2 (B–D–F)	Path 3 (B–E)	Project Finish Time
					0.00	0.00	0.00	0.00	
					0.00	0.00	0.00	0.00	
					0.00	0.00	0.00	0.00	
					0.00	0.00	0.00	0.00	
					0.00	0.00	0.00	0.00	
					0.00	0.00	0.00	0.00	
					0.00	0.00	0.00	0.00	
					0.00	0.00	0.00	0.00	
					0.00	0.00	0.00	0.00	
					0.00	0.00	0.00	0.00	
					0.00	0.00	0.00	0.00	
					0.00	0.00	0.00	0.00	
					0.00	0.00	0.00	0.00	
					0.00	0.00	0.00	0.00	
					0.00	0.00	0.00	0.00	
					0.00	0.00	0.00	0.00	
					0.00	0.00	0.00	0.00	
					0.00	0.00	0.00	0.00	
					0.00	0.00	0.00	0.00	
					0.00	0.00	0.00	0.00	
					0.00	0.00	0.00	0.00	
					0.00	0.00	0.00	0.00	
					0.00	0.00	0.00	0.00	
					0.00	0.00	0.00	0.00	
					0.00	0.00	0.00	0.00	
				Minimum	0.00	0.00	0.00	0.00	
				Minimum	0.00	0.00	0.00	0.00	

In the spreadsheet, columns A–F are used to store the randomly generated activity times for activities A–F, respectively. In column G the time to complete path A–C–F is calculated based on the activity times generated in columns A–F. For example, in cell G3, the formula = A3 + C3 + F3 was entered. In a similar fashion, columns H and I are used to calculate the time to complete paths B–D–F and B–E, respectively. Thus, the formula = B3 + D3 + F3 was entered in cell H3, and = B3 + E3 was entered in cell I3. The formulas entered in cells G3:I3 were then copied to cells G4:I27.

Column J keeps track of when the project is actually completed on a given replication. Since the longest path determines the time when the project is completed, = MAX(G3:I3) was entered in cell J3 and then copied to cells J4:J27.

Finally, in rows 28 and 29 (columns G–J) the minimum and maximum path and project completion times are calculated. For example, in cell G28, = MIN(G3:G27) was entered and in cell G29, = MAX(G3:G27) was entered. The formulas in cells G28:G29 were then copied to H28:J29.

To generate the random numbers for activities A–F, first select *Tools* from Excel's menu bar. Next, select *D*ata Analysis and then select Random Number Generation in the Data Analysis dialog box, as follows.

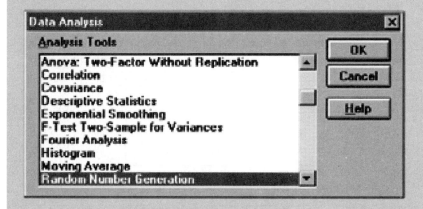

After selecting Random Number Generation, the Random Number Generation dialog box is displayed. First, we will generate 25 random numbers for activity A (cells A3:A27). Recall that activity A is approximately normally distributed with a mean of 32.1 and a standard deviation of 1.2.

To generate 25 random numbers for activity A, specify 1 for the Number of *V*ariables and 25 for the Number of Random Num*b*ers. Next, specify that the random numbers should be generated from a normal distribution. Finally, to place the random numbers in cells A3:A27, specify this range in the *O*utput Range box. After entering this information, the Random Number Generation dialog box appears as follows:

After selecting OK in the Random Number Generation dialog box, 25 random numbers from a normal distribution with a mean of 32.1 and a standard deviation of 1.2 are entered in cells A3:A27, as shown on the following spreadsheet.

Activity A	Activity B	Activity C	Activity D	Activity E	Activity F	Path 1 (A–C–F)	Path 2 (B–D–F)	Path 3 (B–E)	Project Finish Time
30.80						30.80	0.00	0.00	30.80
31.91						31.91	0.00	0.00	31.91
32.21						32.21	0.00	0.00	32.21
32.65						32.65	0.00	0.00	32.65
31.91						31.91	0.00	0.00	31.91
34.78						34.78	0.00	0.00	34.78
32.07						32.07	0.00	0.00	32.07
29.27						29.27	0.00	0.00	29.27
30.26						30.26	0.00	0.00	30.26
30.55						30.55	0.00	0.00	30.55
32.17						32.17	0.00	0.00	32.17
31.74						31.74	0.00	0.00	31.74
32.15						32.15	0.00	0.00	32.15
33.23						33.23	0.00	0.00	33.23
31.05						31.05	0.00	0.00	31.05
34.07						34.07	0.00	0.00	34.07
32.81						32.81	0.00	0.00	32.81
30.39						30.39	0.00	0.00	30.39
33.99						33.99	0.00	0.00	33.99
31.18						31.18	0.00	0.00	31.18
32.17						32.17	0.00	0.00	32.17
32.94						32.94	0.00	0.00	32.94
30.94						30.94	0.00	0.00	30.94
31.15						31.15	0.00	0.00	31.15
32.25						32.25	0.00	0.00	32.25
				Minimum	29.27	0.00	0.00	29.27	
				Maximum	34.78	0.00	0.00	34.78	

This procedure is repeated to generate activity times for activities B–F. For example, to generate activity times for activity B, change the mean to 24.6, the standard deviation to 3.1, and the output range to B3:B27 in the Random Number Generation dialog box. After random numbers have been generated for all six activities, the spreadsheet appears as follows:

Activity	Activity	Activity	Activity	Activity	Activity	Path 1	Path 2	Path 3	Project
A	B	C	D	E	F	(A–C–F)	(B–D–F)	(B–E)	Finish Time
30.80	18.57	23.00	30.58	39.13	28.68	82.48	77.83	57.70	82.48
31.91	26.65	25.00	26.64	39.65	35.16	92.06	87.45	65.30	92.06
32.21	23.30	20.97	33.93	29.43	34.91	88.09	92.14	52.73	92.14
32.65	19.35	16.53	31.36	24.52	35.08	84.26	85.79	43.87	85.79
31.91	20.69	23.51	27.48	28.52	29.13	84.55	77.30	49.21	84.55
34.78	21.48	20.99	24.39	38.38	33.23	89.00	79.10	59.86	89.00
32.07	28.65	20.76	30.02	35.64	34.28	87.11	92.95	64.29	92.95
29.27	27.70	20.83	21.12	42.70	40.94	91.15	89.75	70.40	91.15
30.26	19.01	25.00	19.11	44.07	33.54	88.80	71.66	63.09	88.80
30.55	22.83	18.65	11.08	33.58	30.46	79.66	64.36	56.40	79.66
32.17	21.70	24.19	21.25	35.78	34.60	90.96	77.55	57.47	90.96
31.74	19.48	22.75	28.11	28.60	28.96	83.45	76.56	48.08	83.45
32.15	26.80	20.63	19.65	37.05	35.27	88.06	81.72	63.85	88.06
33.23	21.96	22.69	17.70	50.66	26.21	82.13	65.86	72.62	82.13
31.05	23.12	21.86	31.91	32.60	32.37	85.29	87.40	55.72	87.40
34.07	28.74	20.97	25.75	38.23	31.79	86.82	86.28	66.97	86.82
32.81	26.78	20.64	24.36	31.34	41.62	95.07	92.76	58.12	95.07
30.39	25.52	21.09	28.20	40.22	39.79	91.28	93.51	65.74	93.51
33.99	23.37	21.29	30.02	30.31	38.59	93.87	91.98	53.68	93.87
31.18	23.37	21.19	23.66	30.58	45.35	97.72	92.39	53.95	97.72
32.17	16.62	22.20	25.22	35.10	32.37	86.74	74.21	51.72	86.74
32.94	24.57	20.54	26.38	14.15	34.34	87.82	85.29	38.72	87.82
30.94	23.71	26.54	22.24	35.23	32.73	90.20	78.68	58.94	90.20
31.15	28.24	22.96	33.34	37.54	30.14	84.25	91.71	65.78	91.71
32.25	28.28	24.06	29.06	31.22	31.98	88.29	89.32	59.50	89.32
				Minimum	79.66	64.36	38.72	79.66	
				Maximum	97.72	93.51	72.62	97.72	

Several interesting insights emerge as a result of this simulation analysis. First, in the 25 replications of the project shown, the fastest project completion time was 79.66 days and the longest was 97.72 days. Furthermore, 72 percent (18/25) of the time path A–C–F was the critical path, while 28 percent (7/25) of the time path B–D–F was the critical path. Of course, the more times the project is replicated, the more confidence we have in the results.

Project Management Software Capabilities

There has been explosive growth in project management software packages and their capabilities. The competition is fierce, and there is a wide range of packages available, depending on the project need and the funds available. The main aspects to consider when selecting a package are the capabilities required and the time and money available to invest in a package. If the project is a very large, complex one, or one that interacts with a number of other projects that must also be managed with the software, then some of the more sophisticated packages are appropriate. Not only do these cost more, however; they also take longer to learn and greater computer power to run. On the other hand, if the project is simpler, a less elaborate package that is easier to learn and use may be the best choice.

A yearly survey and analysis of such packages is conducted by *PM Network*, one of the many publications of the Project Management Institute. These surveys give details on the friendliness of each package, their capabilities (schedules, calendars, budgets, resource diagrams and tables, graphics, their migration capabilities, report generation, tracking capability, etc.), their computer requirements, and their cost.

Probably the most commonly used package these days is Microsoft's Project. This package is fairly sophisticated for the cost and is extremely easy to learn and use. Examples of some of its report capabilities are given in Figures 10.11, 10.12, and 10.13.

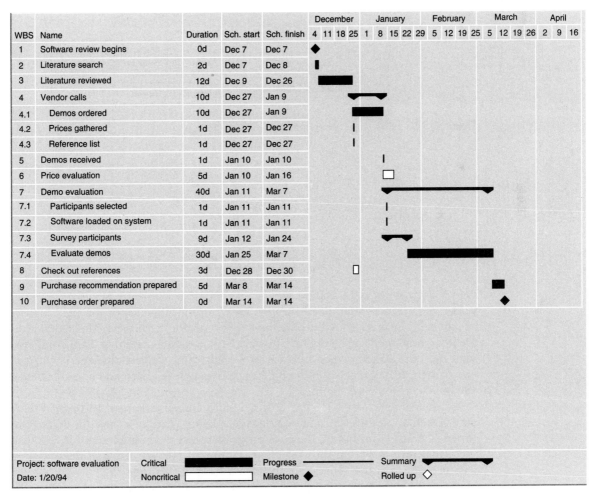

Figure 10.11   Microsoft Project's Gantt chart.

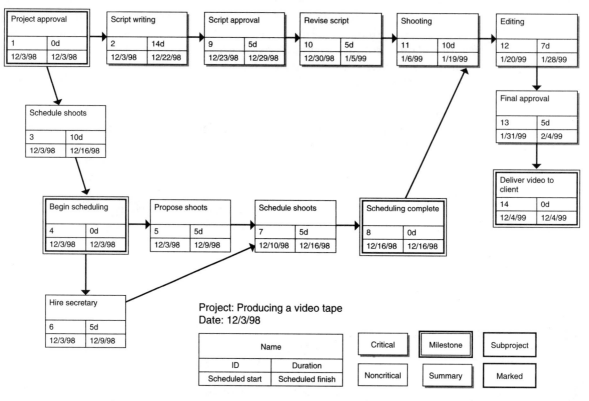

Figure 10.12   PERT chart generated by Microsoft Project.

CONTROLLING THE PROJECT: COST AND PERFORMANCE

One of the control systems most widely used in projects is the cost variance report. Cost standards are determined through engineering estimates or through analysis of past performance. They become the target costs for the project. The actual costs are then monitored by the organization's cost-accounting system and are compared with the cost standard. Feedback is provided to the project manager, who can exert any necessary control if the difference between standard and actual (called a variance) is considered significant.

As an example, consider the cost-schedule charts in Figure 10.14. In Figure 10.14*a*, actual progress is plotted alongside planned progress, and the "effective" progress time (TE) is noted. Because progress is less than planned, TE is less than the actual time (TA). On the cost chart (Figure 10.14*b*) we see that the apparent variance between the scheduled and actual cost at this time (SC − AC) is quite small, despite the lack of progress (earned value, EV). But this is misleading; the variance should be much more given the lack of progress.

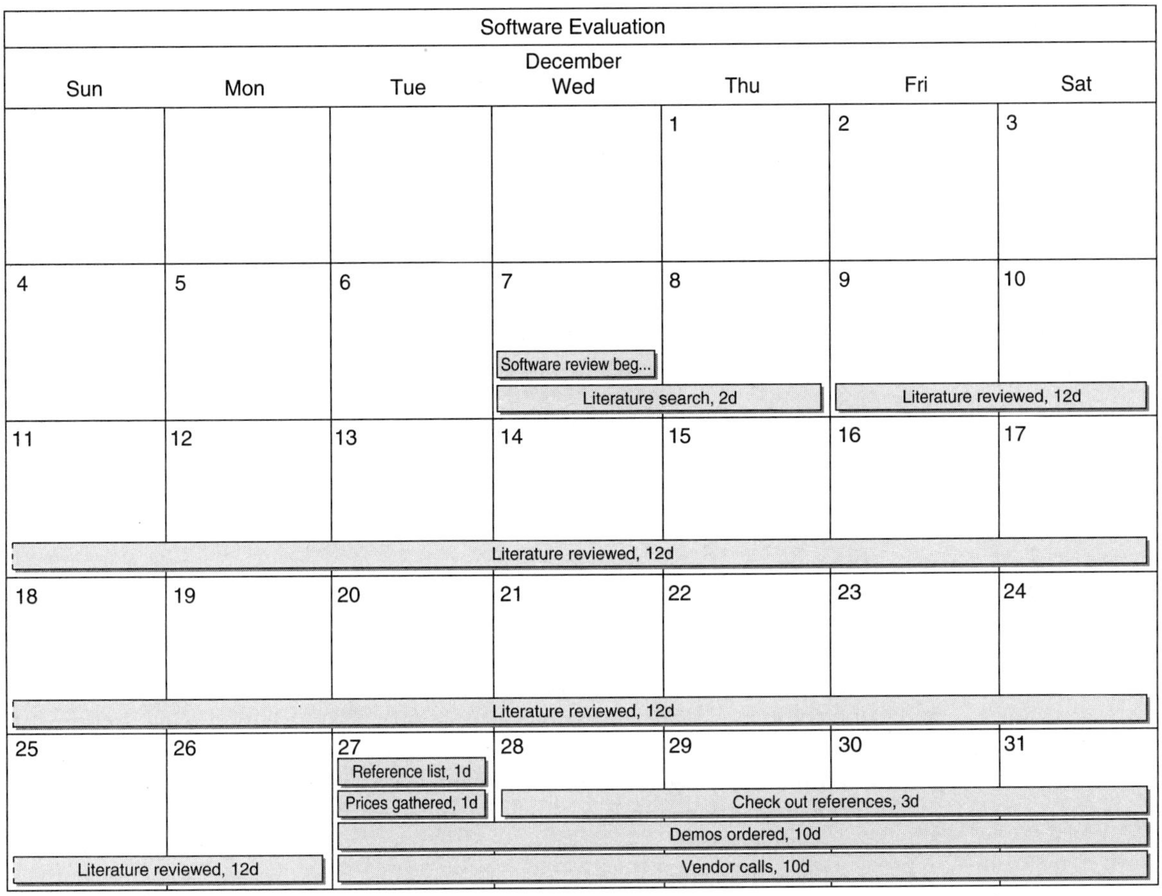

			Software Evaluation			
			December			
Sun	Mon	Tue	Wed	Thu	Fri	Sat
			1	2	3	
4	5	6	7 Software review beg... Literature search, 2d	8	9 Literature reviewed, 12d	10
11	12	13	14	15	16	17
			Literature reviewed, 12d			
18	19	20	21	22	23	24
			Literature reviewed, 12d			
25	26	27 Reference list, 1d Prices gathered, 1d	28	29	30	31
	Literature reviewed, 12d		Check out references, 3d			
			Demos ordered, 10d			
			Vendor calls, 10d			

Figure 10.13   Calendar of activities created by Microsoft Project.

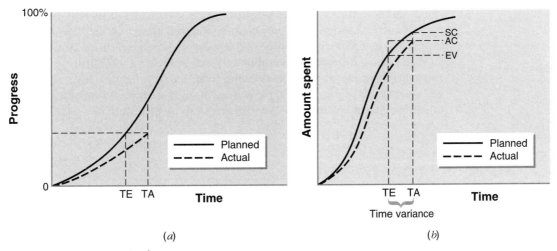

Figure 10.14   Cost-schedule reconciliation charts.

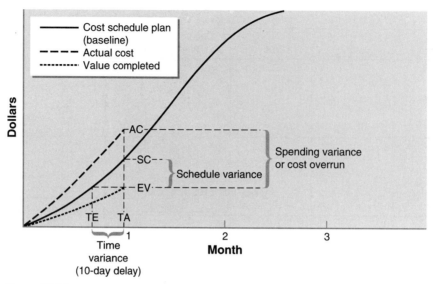

Figure 10.15 Earned value chart.

These two graphs are combined for project managers into an ***earned value*** chart—Figure 10.15—where the planned (scheduled) cost (SC), actual cost (AC), and value completed (actual earned dollars of progress, EV) are plotted. In this situation (which is different from that in Figure 10.14), the actual cost is greater than the plan, even though progress lags behind the plan (thus, the huge spending variance). Plotted in this manner, one chart will serve to monitor both progress and cost. We can then define three variances: (1) a *spending variance* equal to the value completed less the actual cost (EV − AC), where a cost overrun is negative; (2) a *schedule variance* equal to the effective cost or value completed less the scheduled cost (EV − SC), where "behind" is negative; and (3) a *time variance* equal to the effective time less the actual time (TE − TA), where a delay is negative.

When these variances are significant, the project manager must identify (or at least attempt to identify) an *assignable cause* for the variance. That is, he or she must study the project to determine why the variance occurred. This is so that the proper remedy can be used to keep the variance from recurring. A corrective action is called for if some inefficiency or change in the prescribed process caused the variance.

Variances can be both favorable and unfavorable. A significant *favorable variance* (for example, a variance resulting from a large quantity discount on material) will usually not require corrective action, though investigation is still worthwhile so that this better-than-expected performance can be repeated.

EXPAND YOUR UNDERSTANDING

1. Frequently, the project's tasks are not well defined, and there is an urge to "get on with the work," since time is critical. How serious is it to minimize the planning effort and get on with the project?

2. Contrast the cost-schedule reconciliation charts with the earned value chart. Which one would a project manager prefer?

3. How would a manager calculate the value completed for an earned value chart?

4. Do you think people's estimates are more accurate for optimistic or pessimistic activity times?

5. Of the reasons discussed for the growth in project operations, which do you think are contributing most?

6. Why doesn't it make sense to think in terms of a critical path when activity times are not known with certainty?

7. In calculating the probability that a project will be finished by some specified time, the probabilities of each path are multiplied together, on the assumption that the paths are independent of one another. How reasonable is this assumption?

8. Is the stretched-S life cycle project form more common or the exponential form? What other aspects of managing a project are affected by the nature of the project form besides budgeting and early termination?

9. What do you think are the reasons for the topics of conflict among the project team in each of the stages of the project?

10. Given the powerful nature of project management software packages today, why should a project manager have to know how to construct a PERT chart or work breakdown structure?

APPLY YOUR UNDERSTANDING

Nutri-Sam

Nutri-Sam produces a line of vitamins and nutritional supplements. It recently introduced its Nutri-Sports Energy Bar, which is based on new scientific findings about the proper balance of macronutrients. The energy bar has become extremely popular among elite athletes and other people who follow the diet. One distinguishing feature of the Nutri-Sports Energy Bar is that each bar contains 50 milligrams of eicosapentaenoic acid (EPA), a substance strongly linked to reducing the risk of cancer but found in only a few foods, such as salmon. Nutri-Sam was able to include EPA in its sports bars because it had previously developed and patented a process to refine EPA for its line of fish-oil capsules.

Because of the success of the Nutri-Sports Energy Bar in the United States, Nutri-Sam is considering offering it in Latin America. With its domestic facility currently operating at capacity, the president of Nutri-Sam has decided to investigate the option of adding approximately 10,000 square feet of production space to its facility in Latin America at a cost of $5 million.

The project to expand the Latin American facility involves four major phases: (1) concept development, (2) definition of the plan, (3) design and construction, and (4) start-up and turnover. During the concept development phase, a program manager is chosen who will oversee all four phases of the project and the manager is given a budget to develop a plan. The outcome of the concept development phase is a rough plan, feasibility estimates for the project, and a rough schedule. Also, a justification for the project and a budget for the next phase are developed.

In the plan definition phase, the program manager selects a project manager to oversee the activities associated with this phase. Plan definition consists of four major activities that are completed more or less concurrently: defining the project scope, developing a broad schedule of activities, developing detailed cost estimates, and developing a plan for staffing. The output of this phase is a detailed plan and proposal for management specifying how much the project will cost, how long it will take, and what the deliverables are.

If the project gets management's approval and management provides the appropriations, the project progresses to the third phase, design and construction. This phase consists of four major activities: detailed engineering, mobilization of the construction employees, procurement of production equipment, and construction of the facility. Typically, the detailed engineering and the mobilization of the construction employees are done concurrently. Once these activities are completed, construction of the facility and procurement of the production equipment are done concurrently. The outcome of this phase is the physical construction of the facility.

The final phase, start-up and turnover, consists of four major activities: pre-start-up inspection of the facility, recruiting and training the workforce, solving start-up problems, and determining optimal operating parameters (called centerlining). Once the pre-start-up inspection is completed, the workforce is recruited and trained at the same time that start-up problems are solved. Centerlining is initiated upon the completion of these activities. The desired outcome of this phase is a facility operating at design requirements.

The table below provides optimistic, most likely, and pessimistic time estimates for the major activities.

Activity	Optimistic Time (months)	Most Likely Time (months)	Pessimistic Time (months)
Concept Development	3	12	24
Plan Definition			
Define project scope	1	2	12
Develop broad schedule	0.25	0.5	1
Detailed cost estimates	0.2	0.3	0.5
Develop staffing plan	0.2	0.3	0.6
Design and Construction			
Detailed engineering	2	3	6
Facility construction	8	12	24
Mobilization of employees	0.5	2	4
Procurement of equipment	1	3	12
Start-up and Turnover			
Pre-start-up inspection	0.25	0.5	1
Recruiting and training	0.25	0.5	1
Solving start-up problems	0	1	2
Centerlining	0	1	4

Questions

1. Draw a network diagram for this project. Identify all the paths through the network diagram.

2. Simulate the completion of this project 100 times assuming that activity times follow a normal distribution. Estimate the mean and standard deviation of the project completion time.

3. Develop a histogram to summarize the results of your simulation.

4. Calculate the probability that the project can be completed within 30 months. What is the probability that the project will take longer than 40 months? What is the probability that the project will take between 30 and 40 months?

EXERCISES

1. The following PERT chart was prepared at the beginning of a small construction project.

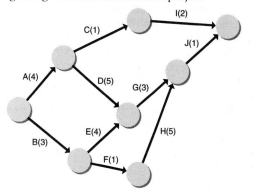

The duration, in days, follows the letter of each activity. What is the critical path? Which activities should be monitored most closely?

At the end of the first week of construction, it was noted that activity A was completed in 2.5 days, but activity B required 4.5 days. What impact does this have on the project? Are the same activities critical?

2. Refer to Exercise 1. Compute the earliest start and finish times, the latest start and finish times, and the slack times for each activity. Also, calculate the slack for each path.

3. Consider Exercise 1 again. Suppose that the duration of both activity A and activity D can be

reduced to 1 day, at a cost of $15 per day of reduction. Also, activities E, G, and H can be reduced in duration by 1 day at a cost of $25 per day of reduction. What is the least-cost approach to shorten the project 2 days? What is the shortest duration, the new critical path, and the cost?

4. Given the following project, find the probability of completion by 17 weeks; by 24 weeks.

		Times (Weeks)	
Activity	Optimistic	Most Likely	Pessimistic
1–2	5	11	11
1–3	10	10	10
1–4	2	5	8
2–6	1	7	13
3–6	4	4	10
3–7	4	7	10
3–5	2	2	2
4–5	0	6	6
5–7	2	8	14
6–7	1	4	7

If the firm can complete the project within 18 weeks, it will receive a bonus of $10,000. But if the project is delayed beyond 22 weeks, it must pay a penalty of $5000. If the firm can choose whether or not to bid on this project, what should its decision be if this is normally only a breakeven project?

5. Construct a network for the project below and find its expected completion time.

Activity	t_e (Weeks)	Preceding Activities
a	3	None
b	5	a
c	3	a
d	1	c
e	3	b
f	4	b, d
g	2	c
h	3	g, f
i	1	e, h

6. Given the estimated activity times and the network below:

Activity	t_o	t_m	t_p
A	6	7	14
B	8	10	12
C	2	3	4
D	6	7	8
E	5	5.5	9
F	5	7	9
G	4	6	8
H	2.5	3	3.5

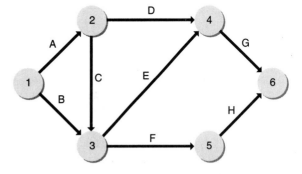

What is the probability that the project will be completed within:

a. 21 days? b. 22 days? c. 25 days?

7. Denver Iron and Steel Company is expanding its operations to include a new drive-in weigh station. The weigh station will be a heated, air-conditioned building with a large floor and a small office. The large room will have the scales, a 15-foot counter, and several display cases for its equipment.

Before erection of the building, the project manager evaluated the project using PERT/CPM analysis. The following activities with their corresponding times were recorded:

		Times		
# Activity	Optimistic	Most Likely	Pessimistic	Preceding Tasks
1 Lay foundation	8	10	13	—
2 Dig hole for scale	5	6	8	—
3 Insert scale bases	13	15	21	2
4 Erect frame	10	12	14	1, 3
5 Complete building	11	20	30	4
6 Insert scales	4	5	8	5
7 Insert display cases	2	3	4	5
8 Put in office equipment	4	6	10	7
9 Give finishing touches	2	3	4	8, 6

Using PERT/CPM analysis, find the expected completion time.

8. As in the situation illustrated in Figure 10.11, a project at day 70 exhibits only 35 percent progress when 40 percent was planned, for an effective date of 55. Planned cost was $17,000 at day 55 and $24,000 at day 70, and actual cost was $20,000 at day 55 and $30,000 at day 70. Find time variance, spending cost variance, and schedule variance.

9. As in the situation shown in Figure 10.12, a project at month 2 exhibited an actual cost of $78,000, a scheduled (planned) cost of $84,000, and a value completed of $81,000. Find the spending and schedule variances. Estimate time variance.

10. A project at month 5 had an actual cost of $34,000, a planned cost of $42,000, and a value completed of $39,000. Find the spending and schedule variances.

BIBLIOGRAPHY

Cleland, D. I., and W. R. King. *Project Management Handbook,* 2nd ed. New York: Van Nostrand Reinhold, 1988.

Gobeli, D. H., and E. W. Larson. "Relative Effectiveness of Different Project Structures." *Project Management Journal,* vol. 18, no. 2 (June 1987): 81–85.

Kerzner, H. *Project Management: A Systems Approach to Planning, Scheduling, and Controlling,* 6th ed. New York: Van Nostrand Reinhold, 1998.

Knutson, J. *How to Be a Successful Project Manager.* Saranac Lake, N.Y.: American Management Association, 1989.

Martin, P. K. *Leading Project Management into the 21st Century.* Flemington, N.J.: Renaissance Education Services, 1996.

Meredith, J. R., and S. J. Mantel, Jr. *Project Management: A Managerial Approach,* 2nd ed. New York: Wiley, 1989.

O'Keeffe, S. W. T. "Chrysler and Artemis: Striking Back with the Viper." *Industrial Engineering* (December 1994): 15–17.

Posner, B. Z. "What It Takes to Be a Good Project Manager." *Project Management Journal,* vol. 18, no. 1 (March 1987): 51–54.

Thamhaim, H. J. and D. L. Wilemon. "Conflict Management in Project Life Cycles." *Sloan Management Review* (Summer 1975).

Area Under the Normal Distribution

Example: the area to the left of $Z = 1.34$ is found by following the left Z column down to 1.3 and moving right to the 0.04 column. At the intersection read 0.9099. The area to the right $Z = 1.34$ is $1 - 0.9099 = 0.0901$. The area between the mean (dashed line) and $Z = 1.34 = 0.9099 - 0.5 = 0.4099$.

Z	0.00	0.01	0.02	0.03	0.04	0.05	0.06	0.07	0.08	0.09
0.0	0.5000	0.5040	0.5080	0.5120	0.5160	0.5199	0.5239	0.5279	0.5319	0.5359
0.1	0.5398	0.5438	0.5478	0.5517	0.5557	0.5596	0.5636	0.5675	0.5714	0.5753
0.2	0.5793	0.5832	0.5871	0.5910	0.5948	0.5987	0.6026	0.6064	0.6103	0.6141
0.3	0.6179	0.6217	0.6255	0.6293	0.6331	0.6368	0.6406	0.6443	0.6480	0.6517
0.4	0.6554	0.6591	0.6628	0.6664	0.6700	0.6736	0.6772	0.6808	0.6844	0.6879
0.5	0.6915	0.6950	0.6985	0.7019	0.7054	0.7088	0.7123	0.7157	0.7190	0.7224
0.6	0.7257	0.7291	0.7324	0.7357	0.7389	0.7422	0.7454	0.7486	0.7517	0.7549
0.7	0.7580	0.7611	0.7642	0.7673	0.7704	0.7734	0.7764	0.7794	0.7823	0.7852
0.8	0.7881	0.7910	0.7939	0.7967	0.7995	0.8023	0.8051	0.8078	0.8106	0.8133
0.9	0.8159	0.8186	0.8212	0.8238	0.8264	0.8289	0.8315	0.8340	0.8365	0.8389
1.0	0.8413	0.8438	0.8461	0.8485	0.8508	0.8531	0.8554	0.8577	0.8599	0.8621
1.1	0.8643	0.8665	0.8686	0.8708	0.8729	0.8749	0.8770	0.8790	0.8810	0.8830
1.2	0.8849	0.8869	0.8888	0.8907	0.8925	0.8944	0.8962	0.8980	0.8997	0.9015
1.3	0.9032	0.9049	0.9066	0.9082	0.9099	0.9115	0.9131	0.9147	0.9162	0.9177
1.4	0.9192	0.9207	0.9222	0.9236	0.9251	0.9265	0.9279	0.9292	0.9306	0.9319
1.5	0.9332	0.9345	0.9357	0.9370	0.9382	0.9394	0.9406	0.9418	0.9329	0.9441
1.6	0.9452	0.9463	0.9474	0.9484	0.9495	0.9505	0.9515	0.9525	0.9535	0.9549
1.7	0.9554	0.9564	0.9573	0.9582	0.9591	0.9599	0.9608	0.9616	0.9625	0.9633
1.8	0.9641	0.9649	0.9656	0.9664	0.9671	0.9678	0.9686	0.9693	0.9696	0.9706
1.9	0.9713	0.9719	0.9726	0.9732	0.9738	0.9744	0.9750	0.9756	0.9761	0.9767
2.0	0.9772	0.9778	0.9783	0.9788	0.9793	0.9798	0.9803	0.9808	0.9812	0.9817
2.1	0.9821	0.9826	0.9830	0.9834	0.9838	0.9842	0.9846	0.9850	0.9854	0.9857
2.2	0.9861	0.9864	0.9868	0.9871	0.9875	0.9878	0.9881	0.9884	0.9887	0.9890
2.3	0.9893	0.9896	0.9898	0.9901	0.9904	0.9906	0.9909	0.9911	0.9913	0.9916
2.4	0.9918	0.9920	0.9922	0.9925	0.9927	0.9929	0.9931	0.9932	0.9934	0.9936
2.5	0.9938	0.9940	0.9941	0.9943	0.9945	0.9946	0.9948	0.9949	0.9951	0.9952
2.6	0.9953	0.9955	0.9956	0.9957	0.9959	0.9960	0.9961	0.9962	0.9963	0.9964
2.7	0.9965	0.9966	0.9967	0.9968	0.9969	0.9970	0.9971	0.9972	0.9973	0.9974

(continued)

Z	0.00	0.01	0.02	0.03	0.04	0.05	0.06	0.07	0.08	0.09
2.8	0.9974	0.9975	0.9976	0.9977	0.9977	0.9978	0.9979	0.9979	0.9980	0.9981
2.9	0.9981	0.9982	0.9982	0.9983	0.9984	0.9984	0.9985	0.9985	0.9986	0.9986
3.0	0.9987	0.9987	0.9987	0.9988	0.9988	0.9989	0.9989	0.9989	0.9990	0.9990
3.1	0.9990	0.9991	0.9991	0.9991	0.9992	0.9992	0.9992	0.9992	0.9993	0.9993
3.2	0.9993	0.9993	0.9994	0.9994	0.9994	0.9994	0.9994	0.9995	0.9995	0.9995
3.3	0.9995	0.9995	0.9995	0.9996	0.9996	0.9996	0.9996	0.9996	0.9996	0.9997
3.4	0.9997	0.9997	0.9997	0.9997	0.9997	0.9997	0.9997	0.9997	0.9997	0.9998

Index